THE LIFE AND DEATH OF
ANDY WARHOL

THE LIFE AND DEATH OF
ANDY WARHOL

by

VICTOR BOCKRIS

Bantam Books

New York   Toronto   London   Sydney   Auckland

THE LIFE AND DEATH OF ANDY WARHOL
A Bantam Book/October 1989

Lyrics from "Heroin" by Lou Reed printed with
permission, copyright © 1967
Oakfield Avenue Music Ltd.

Photo Research: Gerard Malanga

Library of Congress Cataloging-in-Publication Data
Bockris, Victor, 1949–
The life and death of Andy Warhol/by Victor Bockris.
    p.   cm.
Bibliography: p.
Includes index.
ISBN 0-553-05708-1 $19.95 ($24.95 Can.)
1. Warhol, Andy, 1928–1987. 2. Artists—United States—Biography.
I. Title.
N6537.W28B63   1989
700'.92—dc20
[B]   89-6856
                                                              CIP

Bantam Books are published by Bantam Books, a division of Bantam
Doubleday Dell Publishing Group, Inc. Its trademark, consisting of the
words "Bantam Books" and the portrayal of a rooster, is Registered in
U.S. Patent and Trademark Office and in other countries. Marca
Registrada, Bantam Books, 666 Fifth Avenue, New York, New York 10103

PRINTED IN THE UNITED STATES OF AMERICA

0 9 8 7 6 5 4 3 2 1

This book is dedicated to
Andrew Wylie and Bobbie Bristol

Acknowledgments

For inspiration, support, ideas, and belief in this book, I want to thank, above all, Andrew Wylie, Jeff Goldberg, Bobbie Bristol, Miles, Gerard Malanga, Stellan Holm, Steve Mass, John Lindsay, Ingrid von Essen, and Elvira Peake.

For sharing their experiences with me, I want to thank all the people interviewed in the book who gave so generously of their time, particularly Paul Warhola, George Warhola, James Warhola, Ann Warhola, John Warhola, Margaret Warhola, Billy Linich, Ondine, John Giorno, Nathan Gluck, and Ronald Tavel.

For emotional support, lodging, and aid through the nearly six years it took to complete the book, I want to thank Price Abbott, Susan Aaron, Terry Binns, Legs McNeil, Rick Blume, Jeffrey Vogel, Otis Brown, Joe Fiedler, Kym Garfunkel, Gisela Freisinger, Debbie Harry, Chris Stein, Duncan Hannah, Beauregard Houston-Montgomery, Karen Mandelbaum, Rosemary Bailey, Laura Cavestani, Stewart Meyer, Christopher Whent, Claude Pelieu, Mary Beach, David Rattray, David Rosenbaum, Terry Sellers, Terry Spero, Miriam Udovitch, Maryann Erdos, Suzanne Cooper, Liddy Lindsay, Liza Stelle, Helen Mitsios, and Lisa Rosset.

For advice, I wish to thank William Burroughs, Dr. James Fingerhut, Vincent Fremont, Allen Ginsberg, Lou Reed, Raymond Foye, Albert Goldman, and Paul Sidey.

Jeff Goldberg played a major role in organizing and editing the manuscript during its fourth year. My brilliant editor at Bantam Books, Charles Michener, was vital in bringing the book to its final shape. Heartfelt thanks to both of them.

Prologue

THE FIRST THING the appraisers saw when they opened the doors of Andy Warhol's New York townhouse at 57 East Sixty-sixth Street was a larger-than-life bust of Napoleon, staring at them from an antique table in the center of the soaring entrance hall. Looking to their left, they paused to take in superb busts of the Marquis de Lafayette and Benjamin Franklin, standing amidst bronze statues of horses, hounds, boxers, and dancers. Beyond them was a fine Chippendale sofa, and opposite that a George I wing armchair. On the cream and gold walls, above boxes of tulips, hung an impressive assortment of American ancestral portraits. A life-size oil of a male nude, signed "George Bellows, 1906," leaned against the far wall. Moving across the dark, polished floorboards, they passed a small elevator and came to a set of doors. Opening them, they stopped—dumbfounded.

There, in the spacious dining room, was a handsome Federal dining table, surrounded by a dozen Art Deco chairs. Underneath lay a luxurious carpet—obviously an Aubusson. The paintings, hanging or leaning against the walls, most of them American primitives, and a small woodcut by the Norwegian master Edvard Munch, were all of the first order. But their entrance to the room was blocked. Occupying every inch of floor, table, and sideboard space were so many boxes, shopping bags, and wrapped packages—so much sheer *stuff*—that they could not penetrate farther. This was not a room where anyone had dined, at least not in years. It wasn't even the room of a collector who liked to gaze on his treasures with the eye of a connoisseur. It was, instead, the room of a shopper, an accumulator, a pack rat with all the money in the world. "I was flabbergasted," recalled Barbara Deisroth, Sotheby's curator for Art Deco. "Most of what Andy Warhol bought never saw the light of day."

Their wonder deepened as they proceeded upstairs. On the second floor, they entered a sitting room of almost severe formality. Here, the furniture was largely French Art Nouveau and Art Deco of the very highest quality—pieces, Deisroth estimated, that might fetch as much as sixty thousand dollars. The art on the walls was a jarring flash-forward: major works by such Warhol contemporaries as Jasper Johns, Claes Oldenburg, Roy Lichtenstein, James Rosenquist, and Cy Twombly, many in the bright, bold hues of pop art. They would be worth, Sotheby's curator of contemporary art noted at a glance, several million dollars.

Beyond double doors, they found themselves in the back parlor— and another century. Here, the look was neoclassical and neo-Egyptian, the Empire-style taste of a nineteenth-century robber baron: elaborately carved and gilded mahogany furniture and massive marble-topped sideboards; bronzes of mythological creatures; florid urns and candelabras; gold-framed nineteenth-century American and French academic paintings; another bust of Napoleon.

Opulent as these rooms were, they seemed dead: They had the air of a never-visited but exceedingly well kept provincial museum. Deisroth thought: "There was no life, no laughter."

Upstairs in the elegant sleeping quarters, the appraisers found objects that did seem to reveal something more personal about the man who had lived there: the green boxes of wigs stacked next to the television set; an antique crucifix on a side table next to the Federal four-poster bed; an American primitive painting of two little girls in red dresses and white pantaloons that clearly occupied pride of place over a mantelpiece, directly facing the bed; and in the sparkling white bathroom, a cabinet overflowing with skin creams, makeup tubes and jars, bottles of perfume.

What they soon realized was that they were seeing only the tip of an astonishing iceberg. In the folds of the four-poster's canopy they found women's jewels squirreled away. In every closet and cupboard, in the guest bedrooms on the third and fourth floors, in the basement kitchen, they found more of what they had seen in the dining room—unopened shopping bags and boxes, crates and packages, stuff and more stuff. Every drawer was crammed with jewels, watches, cigarette cases, gadgets, gewgaws, and bric-a-brac. Masterpieces rubbed shoulders with junk. What remained wrapped often had as much value as what had been unwrapped.

Two months later, when the appraisers finished their inventory of this Xanadu, they had catalogued on computers more than ten thousand items to be put on the auction block, ranging from Picassos to Bakelite bracelets, rare silver tea services to Fiestaware, museum-quality American Indian art to cigar-store Indians, Austrian Secessionist furniture to vending machines, rare books to cookie jars—forty-seven lots of them. Conspicuously absent, apart from one small painting of Chairman Mao in a guest bedroom, was anything by the owner himself, the man who may have been the most prolific American artist of the twentieth century.

It should have surprised nobody. Had there ever been a more "public" artist than Andy Warhol? Had there ever been an artist more eager to send his art out, to cover the globe with it, to make it as recognizable as one of his favorite images, a Coca-Cola bottle? Andy Warhol had not made art in a studio; he had turned it out with assembly-line regularity in a populous workshop he called the Factory. And he had been, without question, the most publicized artist of his time, a social butterfly who had once cracked that he would even attend the "opening of a toilet seat," an artist whose most famous work of art was himself.

At the same time he had been, as his strange hoard suggested, the most "unwrapped" of public figures, as elusive as he was ubiquitous, a man of whom it could be said that he used the limelight in order to hide in it. From the early sixties, when he seemed to turn "high art" on its head with his paintings of subjects as lowly as Campbell's soup cans, the debate over whether he was "important" or "worthless" had never ceased to rage.

Who *was* Andy Warhol? Was he, as *Time* magazine had persisted in vilifying him, the supreme "huckster of hype"? Or was he, as his legions of collectors and followers insisted, a seer whose vision captured the true, ephemeral fragmentation of our time? And the man: Was he, as many claimed, a modern Mephistopheles, coldly indifferent to the self-destructiveness that overtook so many who had pledged allegiance to him, including one deranged groupie who had tried to assassinate him? Or was he, as others said, something of a "saint"?

On April Fools' Day 1987, a little more than two months after Andy Warhol's death, the critic John Richardson came down on the latter side in his eulogy of the artist at a memorial service before two thousand mourners in Saint Patrick's Cathedral in New York. Citing the deceased's little-known practice of going to Catholic mass "more often than is obligatory," Richardson went on to say: "Never take Andy at face value. The callous observer was in fact a recording angel. And Andy's detachment—the distance he established between the world and himself—was above all a matter of innocence and of art. Isn't an artist usually obliged to step back from things? In his impregnable innocence and humility Andy always struck me as a *yurodstvo*—one of those saintly simpletons who haunt Russian fiction and Slavic villages."

So, perhaps, had he struck the six thousand people who turned up at Sotheby's auction house in New York on Saturday, April 23, more than a year later, hoping to buy one of the *yurodstvo's* relics. More than five thousand of them were turned away: The bidding room could hold only a thousand, all of whom had to produce evidence of their seriousness as buyers.

The outcome far exceeded anyone's imagination. In the course of ten days of bidding for a piece of Andy, nearly every item went for many times the price that had been hoped for: Andy's Rolls-Royce, estimated at $15,000, went for $77,000; a ring, estimated at $2,000, fetched $28,000; a Cy Twombly painting racked up a record price for the artist of $990,000. And the cookie jars? During his lifetime they had cost Warhol perhaps as much as $2,000. When the gavel came down on the last one, the total for the batch had reached $247,830. Sotheby's appraisers had anticipated that the Warhol collection would bring in as much as $15 million. What it yielded was $25.3 million.

To be sure, there must have been not a few who, upon returning to the cold light of day, felt disillusioned by their purchases, even swindled: When all is said and done, even an Andy Warhol cookie jar is still only a cookie jar. Such feelings had always accompanied the adulation of Andy. Indeed, it was one of his most remarkable qualities that he had never done anything to discourage them. And this, of course, had only added to his great, confounding mystery.

In the deluge of comment that descended on Sotheby's disposition of Andy Warhol's earthly possessions, perhaps the only unarguable point was made by Fran Lebowitz, the humorist, who had written a column for the artist's *Interview* magazine. Asked how *he* might be feeling about the event, she said: "Andy must be so furious that he is dead."

1

HIS MOTHER WAS the first great nonstop talker in his life. He would always be mesmerized by such women. Gathering her three sons around the kitchen table in their dark, dank apartment in what her youngest son, Andy, would later describe as "the worst place I have ever been in my life," Julia Warhola would weave and reweave the story of her coming to America, to the city of Pittsburgh.

Her legend began in the last century, in Mikova, a medievally snug village in the Carpathian Mountains in what is today the northeastern corner of Czechoslovakia. Back then it was a volatile border outpost of the Austro-Hungarian empire: To the east, less than an hour's walk, was Russia; to the north, a bit farther away, was Poland. The people of Mikova were principally Ruthenians or Rusyans— "little Russians"—whose only larger identity lay in their allegiance as Byzantine Catholics to the Russian Orthodox church in Kiev, across the border in the Ukraine. In *Dracula,* it is the Ruthenians who are identified as the Count's God-fearing, God-loving peasants. And indeed, the world conjured up by Julia Warhola, in her wire-rimmed glasses and long peasant dress, scarcely differed from that of Bram Stoker's novel: pretty women with fine skin and high cheekbones, wearing vibrant babushkas; handsome men with flowing mustaches, their baggy white trousers tucked into high boots.

One of the handsomest, as she would tell it, was their father, Andrei Warhola, now the bald, burly man with the bulging belly and massive upper arms, pudgy nose, and bristling sideburns, taciturn as always behind an American newspaper. Andrei and Julia had been the typical village lad and lass. He, born in 1889, was three years older than she and from a very different family: pious, nose-to-the-grindstone, and decidedly stingy, in contrast to her own, the laughing, music-loving, and marginally better off Zavackys. Not that anyone in Mikova in those days was free from torturous struggles. (Like all the Zavackys, Julia cherished life's tragedies, elevating her own to biblical proportions.) Andrei had grown up working the fields with the diminishing hope that he could sustain much of a livelihood. At seventeen, he had joined the wave of eastern Europeans seeking a future in the industrial heart of America—the promised land of Pittsburgh. There he had worked for two years in the coal mines before returning to Mikova to, as Julia put it, "recruit a bride."

Julia always claimed that her mother, Josephine Zavacky, had had fifteen children. If so, six must have died in early childhood, for by the time Julia was of "recruiting" age, there were only nine. Two of her brothers, John and Andrew, had already emigrated to Lyndora, Pennsylvania. Two others, Steve and Yurko, as well as her sisters, Mary, Anna, Ella, and Eva, remained with her in Mikova. Theirs, she would say, getting a dreamy look in her eyes and a faraway tone in her voice, was an idyllic existence. Nothing, certainly, was "so good" in America as the Mikovan water, the Mikovan soil, the Mikovan potatoes; no feeling so free as that of herding the goats or walking barefoot in the snow. There was always singing, laughing, talking. She and Mary had wanted to be famous singers and, for a season, had toured around Mikova, performing in a caravan of gypsies, with one of whose men—she slyly implied—she had had a romance. But then, she would point out, chuckling, "My body like a magnet. Only attract good men." Indeed, she had grown into not only the most beautiful and exuberant of the Zavacky daughters but the artistic one as well. Their house was decorated with her small sculptures; their simplest utensils were embellished with her painted designs.

In 1909, when she was sixteen, her father could not support her any longer: It was time to get married. Andrei Warhola had been her brother John's best man at his wedding that year in Lyndora, and after his return to the village Andrei—clean-shaven, with a head of curly blond hair, and with a reputation for being hard-working, devout, and kind—was the talk of Mikova. "Every girl want him," Julia would say. "Fathers would offer him lots of money, lots of land to marry daughter. He no want. He want me. I knew nothing. He wants me, but I no want him. I no think of no man. My mother and father say, 'Like him, like him.' I scared." When she refused to marry Andrei, her father beat her. When she still refused, he called on the village priest. "The priest—oh, a nice priest—come. 'This Andy,' he says, 'a very nice boy. Marry him.' I cry. I no know. Andy visits again. He brings candy, wonderful candy. And for this candy, I marry him."

They spent the next three years in Mikova, living with his family and working in the fields. To avoid conscription in Emperor Francis Joseph's army—which would have obliged him to fight in the Balkan conflict against his own people on the Russian side of the border—Andrei decided to return to Pittsburgh. Julia, who was pregnant, stayed behind. Of her immediate family, only her mother and two younger sisters remained in Mikova; her father had died, her beloved brother Yurko had been drafted; her other siblings had gone to America. Andrei promised to send for her as soon as he had saved enough to make it possible. Their separation would last nine years.

Life with the Warholas had never been easy for Julia. Now, with Andrei gone, "everything bad." The Warholas resented having to support Julia; to pay for her upkeep she was obliged to work twelve hours a day. In the winter of 1914 she gave birth to a daughter, Justina. It was bitter cold, and the baby contracted influenza. There was no doctor in the area. The Warholas insisted that Julia leave the sick child during the day and work in the fields. One day she returned to the house to find the six-week-old baby dead. In a fit of weeping she would reenact many times later, she flung open the window and screamed into the night: "My baby dies! My little girl!"

Soon after, Julia went to the authorities to find out where Yurko was stationed; she was told that he had been killed. The news broke the spirit of her mother, who died a month later, leaving Julia responsible for her sisters Ella and Eva, then six and nine. The tale darkened further: That spring, the harvest failed and the people of Mikova faced starvation. Julia, Ella, and Eva subsisted on potatoes and bread for months. Then, in the fall, the clouds parted: A letter arrived from Yurko. His death had been reported because he had switched uniforms with a dead soldier, leaving his identification papers in the pocket of the discarded clothes. On the heels of that news came the First World War. Hostilities were especially fierce in the Carpathians. Longstanding class and religious hatreds erupted violently, and the area around Mikova was devastated. Julia's house was burned down and she lost all her possessions—most grievously her wedding album. In a neighboring village the men of thirty-six families were rounded up and shot. As far as Julia was concerned, everyone was the enemy—the Russians, the Germans, the Poles.

That she and her sisters survived the war was due to her knowledge of the countryside. From 1914 to the cessation of fighting in 1918, she and her sisters would pile into a horse-drawn cart at the first warning of approaching soldiers and hide in the forests for days at a time. Andrei and America now seemed an impossibly distant dream. He would later insist that five times he had sent her money for the journey, but no money or letter ever reached her.

The war was followed by the worst flu epidemic Europe had ever seen. It took an especially heavy toll in the Carpathians. Shortly before the United States imposed an embargo on immigration from eastern Europe, Julia Warhola borrowed $160 from a village priest and made her way by horse cart, train, and ship to find her husband in America. It was 1921.

Throughout his adult life Andy Warhol shrouded his childhood in exaggerations, half-truths, and outright lies. Reared on his mother's constant feeding of her own historical legend—equal parts horror and nostalgia—he early on set about creating his own, and with the same punch line: He had survived the most appalling odds. It was a picture painted in heavy chiaroscuro: rock-bottom poverty; a coal-miner father who was never home and who died when he was young; bullying brothers; a mother who was always sick; a life of social ostracism, no fun, no friends. Not to mention the humiliation of his albino-like pigmentation. He was blithely contradictory about the place and year of his birth. For some reason he would often say that he came from McKeesport, a community of immigrant workers south of Pittsburgh. At other times he would say Philadelphia, and once in a while Hawaii. Sometimes he made himself out to be three years older than he actually was, saying that he had been born in 1925; sometimes the year was 1931. Most telling, perhaps, was the staging of his birth in David Bailey's 1971 film portrait *Andy Warhol*, in which Andy had the actress playing his mother claim to have given birth to him alone at midnight in the midst of a fire. The actress was made to recall his very first words as: "Look at the sunlight!"

If true, it was a most unusual day, for as the steel and coal capital of America, Pittsburgh seemed hell-bent on keeping out as much sunlight as possible. During its boom years in the 1920s, the sprawling city at the confluence of three rivers was ringed by fire twenty-four hours a day. Huge balls of flame shot out of the maws of the steel mills, turning the night sky bizarre shades of fuchsia and chartreuse and occasionally sparking conflagrations in the poorer neighborhoods that gave Andy a fear of fire he never lost. In the hills flanking the rivers, coke fires glowed like red animal eyes, and by day pollution hung everywhere in an inky pall. (Pittsburgh, indeed, was where the word *smog* was coined.) Cars kept their headlights on during the day; street lamps would stay lit from morning to night. Society ladies sometimes wore gas masks to go shopping downtown.

A disproportionate number of America's superrich—with names such as Carnegie, Frick, Mellon, and Westinghouse—had made huge fortunes out of this industrial frenzy and built mansions in the Shadyside section of town to match and outmatch one another. But the neighborhoods of the vast immigrant work force—the Warholas' neighborhood—were something else. "Here," wrote H. L. Mencken, in one of his most savage condemnations of an American place, "was wealth beyond computation, almost beyond imagination—and here were human habitations so abominable that they would have disgraced a race of alley cats. I am not speaking of mere filth. One expects steel towns to be dirty. What I allude to is the unbroken and agonizing ugliness, the sheer revolting monstrousness, of every home in sight."

"This is hell if there is a hell anywhere," one Pittsburgh miner was quoted as saying. "No work, starving, afraid of being shot, it is a shame for a man to tell such bad truth." During Prohibition the police turned a blind eye to liquor barons who rode in flashy cars up and down Sixth Street, otherwise known as "The Great Wet Way," where cabarets like the White Cat, the Devil's Cave, and Little Harlem played to full houses. Nor did the police bother to patrol the slums of the Hill district, where roving gangs of juveniles terrorized the tenants. For many of the immigrant workers, the only escape was playing the numbers racket, frequenting prostitutes, or taking to the bottle.

Few of the rickety wooden houses in the Hill had proper sewage systems; most of them depended on outside toilets without drainage. When it rained, the excrement ran down the hills to join the piles of irregularly collected rubbish on which spindly, pale children played. In the Pittsburgh of the 1930s, the sociologist Philip Klein wrote in *A Social Study of Pittsburgh,* published toward the end of the decade, "the traditional optimism of the American people yielded to dismal pessimism." For some it gave grounds for questioning the basis of American capitalism. When the Populist presidential candidate Father Cox marched his exhausted jobless army of fifteen thousand men back to Pittsburgh from their futile protest march on Washington, D.C., for immediate relief, his warning that "something must be done to avert violence" was taken seriously enough for the private police force of Pittsburgh's leading citizen, Andrew Mellon, to be issued with machine guns.

Here, for a sensitive, highly intelligent child like Andy Warhol, was a cartoon of all the dark forces of twentieth-century America writ large: driving confidence and ambition, greed and power, corruption and violence, entropy, chaos, madness, and death—all the themes that would later inform his work.

His view was from the bottom up, for as immigrants from eastern Europe with a funny-sounding name, the Warholas were "Hunkies"—people stereotyped as brutish, untrustworthy, and fit only for low pay and hard labor. As Ruthenians, dispossessed people without any claim to a country of their own, they were at the bottom of the Hunkie heap. Looked down upon by their old and present neighbors, the Ukrainians, Hungarians, Rumanians, Moldavians, and Slovaks, they kept to their own kind and language—*po nasemu* (which translates as "in our own manner")—the mongrelization of Hungarian and Ukrainian that Julia, Andrei, and their boys spoke at home.

Baby Andy was born on August 6, 1928, in his parents' bedroom at 73 Orr Street in the immigrant ghetto of Soho. It was a year before the stock market crash, and nowhere did the depression hit harder than in Pittsburgh. His father (called "Nonya" by his three sons) had a good steady job with the Eichleay Corporation, laying roads and moving houses from place to place, a common practice during Pittsburgh's construction boom. A hard worker who, unlike many fellow Ruthenians, neither gambled nor drank, he managed to put away several thousand dollars in postal savings bonds and move his family to a larger house on Beelan Street in 1930. But a year later he lost his job, and the Warholas were forced to move to a tiny two-room apartment on Moultrie Street that rented for six dollars a week. Andrei was reduced to taking odd jobs. Julia helped out by doing part-time housecleaning for two dollars a day and making flowers planted in tin cans, which she would sell door-to-door for twenty-five to fifty cents. (Andy recalled her "flower sculptures" fifty years later: "The tin flowers she made out of those fruit tins, that's the reason why I did my first tin-can paintings. . . . My mother always had lots of cans around, including the soup cans. She was . . . a real good and correct artist, like the primitives.")

The Warholas' new home was minimal. "The building had two stories," said Andy's brother John. "We lived on the first floor in two rooms, a kitchen, and a bathroom. The bathtub was just a steel tub, and we heated the water on the stove. The three of us kids slept in one bed."

Family tensions ran high in those conditions. Order was kept only because of the three boys' fear of their father. "Sometimes he'd yell at us if we were slapping at one another at the table or fighting in bed," remembered Andy's oldest brother, Paul. "Dad didn't like us starting a commotion because he was so exhausted and he would get emotionally upset. Usually all he had to do was look at you. That was enough."

"He'd warn us once," recalled John Warhola, "and then if we did it again he would pull off his belt, but we ran and hid under the bed. He never hit us but the threat was the same. Dad was so strict that when you were a kid you'd think he was a mean father, starting from, like, we didn't have no dessert. Like if I asked for cake he would get angry: 'If you're still hungry,' he'd say, 'rye bread with butter is better for you.' We never had any pop. I drank just water and coffee. But he made sure we had enough to eat and that it was good. It wasn't junk food."

Throughout his life, Andy's closeness to his warm-hearted, garrulous, wise mother was well-known. But the controlling, patriarchal distance—as well as his appetite for relentless work—that he would later exhibit toward his assistants came, undoubtedly, from his father.

Andrei Warhola was particularly strict in matters of religion. Pittsburgh in the early 1930s was the scene of the country's most violent workers' demonstrations for jobs and food, protests brutally put down by the Mellons' private police force, but Andrei turned his back on political action. His expressions of hope for better times were rooted in the ancient place, the ancient way: prayers before every meal and devotions on Sunday in the somber, majestic Byzantine Catholic service of his childhood, transplanted to the tiny wooden church of St. John Chrysostom on Saline Street, a six-mile walk away. Every Sunday he would march his family to mass, which lasted an hour and a half. Afterward, he insisted that Sunday be absolutely a day of rest.

"You weren't even allowed to pick up a pair of scissors on Sunday," said Paul Warhola. "It was going to church and then taking off your church clothes and then no playing around or nothing. My dad was very strict on that."

John recalled it differently: "It was a joyous occasion—people really visited with each other. My mother taught you she liked going to church better than material things. She never believed in being wealthy—she believed just being a real good person made you happy. We were brought up never to hurt anybody, to believe you're just here for a short time and you're going to leave the material things behind."

In the absence of a radio, the chief diversion on those long shut-in days was listening to Julia Warhola tell the old stories in *po nasemu*. For although her husband could speak English passably and even read the American newspapers, Julia stubbornly resisted mastering the strange language. And her inability to converse with anyone but her own kind made her that much more voluble at home. Closest to her when she told those stories about the war, the old church in Mikova, the ghost of their sister Justina, was the baby of the family, little "Andek," as she called him. He was a pale, chubby boy, and precocious from the start ("aggressive" and "pushy" was how Andy remembered himself). "You could see he was picking up things much better than we had," said Paul. "But he was really mischieful between three and six. Andy picked up some bad language when he was about three. He'd heard some kids swear. Swearing wasn't allowed in our house—you couldn't even say 'hell!' We'd go to a relative's place and Andy'd say some of these things and it wasn't nice. I'd sometimes smack him in the face. And the more you smacked him, the more he said it—the worse he got. He was real bad: Just because we *didn't* want him to say it, he said it." "Being born," Andy later wrote, "is like being kidnapped. And then sold into slavery."

When Andy was four, his father got his old job back at the Eichleay Corporation, which frequently took him away from his home for weeks at a time. With "Nonya gon na contry," Paul, now ten, became the man of the household. Already contributing to the family till by selling newspapers on trolley cars and hawking peanuts at the baseball park, Paul was having problems at school. He had never overcome his embarrassment at not being able to speak English when he entered first grade, and having to speak up in class still terrified him. He began cutting school, and he developed a speech impediment. He was too frightened to tell his father about his problems, and his mother would not have understood. Perhaps to vent his frustration, he became an archdisciplinarian of wayward Andy. Although the normal age for entering first grade was six, Paul took it upon himself to force Andy into school at four. Remembering his own difficulties in his first years at Soho Elementary, he was convinced that Andy would be effectively tamed. "At first he didn't want to go, but I forced him," Paul recalled. "They didn't ask for no records. The guy in the principal's office just took him right by the hand and I says, 'He's starting.' "

When Paul came to collect Andy at the end of the day, he found him in tears. Andy continued to cry all the way home, where he announced he was not going back. As Paul described the scene:

"Some little black girl had slapped him, so my mother said, 'Well, you stay home then.'" Paul protested, but Andy clung to his mother's skirts, begging her to keep him at home. "So Mother says, 'Don't push him, he's just too young yet.'"

For the next two years, Andy spent most of his time at home with his mother. Julia was a wonderful companion ("She could really make you laugh," recalled John), and she liked to draw. "I drew pictures, so Andy made pictures when he was a little boy," she would recall. "He liked to do that, sure, he made very nice pictures. We made pictures together. I like to draw cats. I'm really a cat woman."

Visitors to the Warhola home always found Andek glued to his mother's side. He kept his head down, and when he did look up it was furtively, as if he were afraid of being hit. If Julia could not see him when she came into the room she would always ask, *"Deya Andek?"* "Where is Andek?"

In early 1934 the Warholas moved from Moultrie Street to 3252 Dawson Street in the better working-class neighborhood of Oakland. The schools—Holmes Elementary and Schenley High—were safer, and the house was a vast improvement over anything the Warholas had lived in before. A semidetached two-story brick affair, it had a front porch, a real living room with a fireplace, a small dining room and kitchen, and, on the second floor, two bedrooms, one for John and Andy in the back, one for their parents in the front. Paul converted the attic into a third bedroom. Best of all was the coal-burning furnace in the basement. "It was," said John, "just like going into a different world." Nonya immediately began trying to improve the house by digging out the cellar in the evening after work. Julia started a vegetable garden in the back, which Andy helped her turn over.

Oakland was a large neighborhood divided into two sections by the city's major artery, Fifth Avenue. To its north were the massive institutional buildings erected as symbols of their empire by the Pittsburgh millionaires: the Soldiers and Sailors Memorial Hall, the Syrian Temple, and the forty-two-story Cathedral of Learning at the University of Pittsburgh. On a rising slope to its south stretched row upon row of tightly packed workers' houses, culminating at the top of the rise in Dawson Street, which ran parallel to Fifth. Beyond Dawson the ground fell away into the beautiful green bowl of Schenley Park and Panther Hollow. Julia Warhola soon became something of a legend for her hospitality. Friends and relatives were always greeted with a hug and a bowl of chicken soup. Her quirky humor, love of conversation, and constant dispensing of advice made her a neighborhood focal point. An Italian neighbor painted a vivid picture of the community during Andy's childhood: "It was fairly safe in those days. The children played together and they more or less brought the parents together. There were maybe about forty, fifty young guys down there. We were tight. Maybe 7:30, 8:00 in the morning pitchin' horseshoes. Then when enough guys came, we'd start playing softball or baseball. Around 12:30, 1:00, we'd go out swimming in Schenley Park. And then we'd play craps behind the Board of Education. But Andy was so intelligent, he was more or less in a world all his own. He kept to himself like a loner."

From an early age Andy chose girls for his friends. His best friend at Holmes was a little Ukrainian girl, a Byzantine Catholic like him, named Margie Girman. Margie was a year younger, but they were almost the same size and build. When Andy wasn't at home he could usually be found playing in the street with Margie or sitting with her on her stoop. Margie's best friend, Mina Serbin, who also attended Holmes, recalled that "Margie was very bright and she never stopped talking, and she stimulated Andy to do well in school. She always talked about how hard she was going to study for a test. Andy liked that, and he did everything she did." The extent to which Andy modeled himself after Margie is evident in a photograph of them together when they were seven: His expression and stance are identical to hers, suggesting that their personalities have almost merged. Andy's adoration of Margie Girman set up a pattern for his later relationships with women: Part of him wanted to be her.

Andy and Margie began going to the movies together on Saturday mornings. For eleven cents each child had an ice cream bar, saw a double feature, and on the way out got an eight-by-ten-inch glossy signed by the star. Andy soon had a boxful of publicity stills, the beginning of his collector's mania. They were the same sort of photos he would use twenty years later in his silk-screen portraits of movie stars. His favorite film, he always said, was *Alice in Wonderland*.

With other boys, Andy was more elusive. "We'd play softball," remembered John Warhola, "and when Andy was out in the field, by the time you hit the ball he wasn't there. So when I came home he was there drawing on the porch. He did that a lot as a kid. The kids would say, 'Now, don't run home, Andy!' He just loved to draw with crayons."

Two of Julia's brothers and one of her sisters had settled with their families in the farming community of Lyndora, and every month or so she and her three sons would make the fifty-five-mile train trip to visit the boisterous Zavacky clan. In Lyndora, Andy had another best friend in his cousin Lillian ("Kiki") Lanchester, a prankish, musical little girl with whom he would immediately run to the corner candy store, then disappear into the countryside to talk and giggle for hours. She recalled: "He was particularly neat and very clean, all the time. With me he talked a lot, but he was very shy with other people. When a picture was taken of him he would have his head down and he would look up at you as though he was afraid he didn't trust you."

Every other Sunday, Julia and the boys would visit her sister Mary Preksta on Pittsburgh's Northside. At Aunt Mary's, Andy's friend was his cousin Justina. "Tinka," four years older than he, remembered these visits as intensely sentimental ones for her mother and Aunt Julia. "While we played outside, they would read their letters from Europe. It was always so sad, because they didn't have the money to send to their sisters Ella and Eva, who were still in Mikova. They would talk about Europe and cry." Julia sometimes came down with migraine, and Mary would put her to bed, heat some salt in a bag, and put it on her head. At other times the sisters would sing the old songs, harmonizing beautifully as they had in Mikova.

It was during a visit to Aunt Mary's that Andy had what he later described as his introduction to sex: "The first time I ever knew about sex was in Northside, under the stairs, and they made this funny kid suck this boy off. I never understood what it meant. I was just sitting there watching." (A friend in the art world would describe him with less ingenuousness: "Andy was the greatest voyeur I ever met. He was really interested in who did what to whom.")

Andy, remembered Margie, Kiki, and Tinka, was a wonderful playmate, charming, sweet, and kind. As for his evincing any particular artistic interests, Tinka recalled: "Well, he used to go to town with his mother and help pick her hats out. I remember her buying a black felt hat that he painted gold around the edges. He was very young when he did that. Even then, he was sort of an artist, I guess.

He also liked to pick out his mother's clothes. He was a mother's boy."

His new school, Holmes, was a success. Because his single day at Soho Elementary had been recorded as a full year, he went straight into the second grade at age six. "He was very quiet, not at all outgoing, and he was real good in drawing," his teacher, Catherine Metz, recalled fifty years later. With his vacant stare—he seemed to want to pass through the halls as though he were invisible—and his Botticelli choir boy appearance, he was an obvious target for the gangs of boys who loafed on the corner outside the candy store opposite the school. But, according to John Warhola, "He was happy-go-lucky and well-liked, and I never saw him get angry." In any case, he always came straight home after school, and was diligent about his homework, after which he would draw pictures. (The only "entertainment" in the house, said Paul, "was drawing pictures.") He seemed to have passed through his rebellious phase. Now, according to John, "he was so religious I thought he would become a priest." Still, he often asked his mother for things the family could scarcely afford. When he was seven, he wanted a cartoon projector. It seemed the most outlandish idea anyone had ever heard of, but Julia took a job doing housework for a dollar a day until she had earned the twenty dollars to buy one. "We didn't have money to buy a screen—he'd show the pictures on the wall," said John. "Andy would watch Mickey Mouse or Little Orphan Annie and get ideas for his drawings."

"I had three nervous breakdowns when I was a child," Andy wrote in *The Philosophy of Andy Warhol (from A to B and Back Again)*. This was probably another exaggeration. Whatever "breakdowns" he had were certainly not perceived as such. But his was, in any event, a childhood scarred by illness. When he was two, his eyes had swollen up so badly that his mother had to apply boric acid daily. At four he had fallen on streetcar tracks and broken his right arm. Despite his complaints of pain, nothing was done until several months later, when a neighbor noticed an odd bend to the arm—which then had to be rebroken and set. At six he had come down with scarlet fever. And in the autumn of 1936, when he was eight, he contracted an illness that had a major effect on his development. Before the discovery of penicillin, rheumatic fever was common among children who lived in unsanitary proximity in poor neighborhoods. A small percentage of the victims died. About ten percent of the cases developed into chorea, popularly called St. Vitus' dance (after a third-century Christian child martyr), which is a disorder of the central nervous system. In the worst cases the victim loses coordination of the limbs and has a series of what appear to be spastic seizures.

By the time Andy got sick he had become the perennial teacher's pet at Holmes; but now when he tried to write or draw on the blackboard his hand would shake, and the other boys laughed at him. Sensing his fear, they started pushing him around and punching him. Andy had no idea what was happening to him, and he became, once again, terrified of going to school. He grew increasingly disoriented, was easily provoked to tears, and found the simplest tasks, like tying his shoes or writing his name, difficult to coordinate.

At first nobody at home took any notice of these symptoms, perhaps because Andy had a reputation as a crybaby. But the symptoms worsened. He started slurring his speech, touching things nervously with shaking hands, fumbling, and finding it hard to sit still. A physician, Dr. Zeedick, was called. He diagnosed a mild case of St. Vitus' dance and ordered Andy to stay in bed for a month. Julia moved him into the dimly lit dining room next to the kitchen and devoted herself to nursing him back to health. Her greatest concern was that he would go into convulsions and die, as had her baby daughter, Justina, because she had been unable to move her bowels. In times of sickness, Julia always believed in giving her boys enemas, and Andy was no exception. (At the height of his career as a filmmaker, Andy insisted on shooting a number of his performers being given enemas. The footage was never used in a movie.)

This was a golden time in Andy's childhood. For a month he was able to detach himself from the world. Julia made sure that he was constantly entertained with a stream of movie magazines, comic books, cut-out paper dolls, and coloring books. "I buy him comic books," Julia later recalled. "Cut, cut, cut nice. Cut out pictures. Oh, he liked pictures from comic books." She also moved the family radio, which Andrei had recently bought in a rare moment of indulgence, from the living room to the dining room. As soon as Andy's hands stopped shaking, he colored book after book, cut up and pasted magazine illustrations to make collages, and played with his paper dolls. He got Paul to send away for movie stills of the stars he was daydreaming about, and it was Paul who gave him his first lesson in a process that would become crucial to his mature art—the transfer of an image from one sheet of paper to another. "I showed him how to put wax on the surface of a comic strip, turn it over on white paper, take a spoon and rub it in, and trace it right on." As further incentive, Andy later wrote in his *Philosophy,* Julia would "give me a Hershey bar every time I finished a page in my coloring book."

In the movie magazines Andy discovered the world of celebrity and glamour, his dream cities of Hollywood and New York. Julia was his studio assistant, patron, and audience of one. She marveled at his drawings and collages, laughed along at the radio shows. She made sure he was comfortable night and day, sleeping in the same bed, sometimes sitting up all night to watch him sleep.

According to his brothers, Andy greatly exaggerated his bouts of St. Vitus' dance: He came down with it seriously only once, and was really too young to have been worried about it. According to John, "It was like having chicken pox or a sore throat." Yet the emphasis Andy gave his illness in later life indicates how important the experience was to him.

After he had been in bed for a month, the Warholas decided it was time for Andy to go back to school. On the appointed morning he balked. Standing on the front porch with Julia, he held onto her skirts and started crying. Andrei was away, and Julia was uncertain what to do. Paul came out on the porch and found Andy throwing a tantrum, just as he had after the incident at Soho Elementary four years earlier. "He's gotta go back to school," Paul declared. He assumed that Andy was afraid of being beaten up by the kids who had laughed at him for being a mama's boy, but he did not consider that a good enough reason for him to stay home.

Andy started screaming. Hearing the commotion, the next-door neighbor, Pete Elachko, an undertaker's apprentice, came out on the porch. He was used to playing surrogate father to the Warhola boys when Andrei was away. He immediately assessed the situation: Andy was just a crybaby who was afraid of everything and didn't want to go to school. Stepping over the wall that divided the front porches, he grabbed Andy by the shoulder and shouted, "You're going to school!"

Andy's knees buckled, as often happens with chorea victims, and he fell down and refused to move. Grabbing the terrified child by the shoulders, Elachko dragged him down the front steps.

As Paul recalled: "Andy tried to kick him, and then the neighbor grabbed him. He just held his arms and legs and forced him to school. Now that was the worst thing to do. After that Andy developed a nervous twitch."

"We didn't know he wasn't completely cured," said John. "Pete thought he was doing us a favor when he carried him there."

Andy immediately had a relapse and had to be returned to bed for four more weeks. But the incident bred in him a lifelong abhorrence of violence and a strong desire to detach himself from any kind of force. One way to unleash his rage in later life would be to try physically to make him do something.

Andy's second period in bed was much like his first. Once again he was allowed to spend long, uninterrupted hours dreaming about being a movie star in Hollywood. But this time, when he emerged from his sickroom, his position in the family had changed. Julia had been warned by Dr. Zeedick that a relapse was likely. The illness had also left Andy with a skin condition that would plague him for the rest of his life. He had suddenly developed large reddish-brown blotches on his face, back, chest, arms, and hands. He appeared more frail and became like a clinging vine, rarely leaving Julia's side. She, for her part, became more protective of him than ever and was determined that nobody would lay a hand on him again. Andy was now accorded the position of an eccentric invalid who must be treated with special care and understanding, and his brothers began to watch out for him at school. "What I didn't understand," said John Warhola, "was when he went back to school after a couple of months, even though he had lost so much time, they put him ahead."

In perhaps the most revealing comment he ever made about his childhood, Andy wrote in POPism: The Warhol '60s, "I learned when I was little that whenever I got aggressive and tried to tell someone what to do, nothing happened—I just couldn't carry it off. I learned that you actually have more power when you shut up, because at least some people will start to maybe doubt themselves." Now, the fantasy life he was developing at age eight seemed to give him an inner focus. His two-sided character began to emerge. While continuing to be as sweet and humble as ever with his girlfriends, he started to act the arrogant little prince at home. If Freud is right in saying that subconsciously we remain the same age throughout our life, then Andy would always remain the two-sided eight-year-old who emerged from the cocoon of his illness.

This was a new, eager, impatient, and sometimes aggressive Andy, who would constantly challenge Paul, saying, "Well, whaddya do now?" and who would run off to the movie house every Saturday morning. The movies became his passion, a necessity, an escape. It was not always easy to get the eleven-cent entrance fee, but Andy pursued it with great determination. Often he would help Paul or John sell peanuts at ballgames, earning a penny a bag. And it was at this time that he began his lifelong practice of writing to movie stars, asking for their pictures and autographs. Just as he identified with girls rather than boys in his friendships, he chose a female rather than a male star to idolize. In 1936, the year of *Poor Little Rich Girl,* Shirley Temple became Andy's idol. In the film, eight-year-old Shirley escapes by chance from the shelter of her father's wealth and ends up working with a vaudeville team. Her attitude toward life is that it's a game. Here was the philosophy that would guide Andy: work all the time, but make it into a game.

Andy mailed off a dime to her fan club and received a photograph with "To Andy Warhola from Shirley Temple" written on it. It became his most cherished possession and the centerpiece of his collection. He also sent away a cereal-box top and got a blue glass with his idol's face imprinted on it. Just as he had imitated Margie Girman so assiduously, he now tried to emulate Shirley Temple. For the rest of his life he would imitate her stock gestures, folding his hands as if in prayer and placing them next to his cheek, or twisting them together and holding them out to the right just below his waist. He dreamed about learning to tap-dance. The only thing he didn't like about Shirley Temple films, he told a friend, was the inevitable appearance of her father to take her home at the end. "It ruined everything," he said. "She had been having such a good time, tap-dancing with the local Kiwanis Club or the newspapermen in the city room. I don't want to know who the father is."

By the end of the 1930s the balance of power in the Warhola household had shifted. For some time now Andrei's health had been slowly failing. Always the disciplinarian, he could still freeze his sons with a glance and the threat of his hand moving to his belt. But Paul, who was now seventeen and working in a steel mill, was reasonably independent, and Andrei was usually so tired when he came home from work that it was all he could do to stand in the backyard, silently hosing the tiny garden.

Julia begged Andrei to slow down. He had accumulated nearly fifteen thousand dollars in postal bonds and a savings account, a fortune for a man of his background. Paul was bringing a salary into the house, enough to buy his mother dining-room furniture and a refrigerator. It was no longer necessary for Andrei to take every job he was offered, to keep up the backbreaking pace of twelve hours a day, six days a week; but he was a workaholic, and Julia's pleas fell on deaf ears. Paul remembered the time Andrei left the house on what would turn out to be his last job, in Wheeling, West Virginia: "He had been sick with yellow jaundice for a couple of years earlier on, after he was operated on to have his gallbladder removed, and then for so many years it was okay. And then all at once he was getting yellow. Apparently his liver was failing him. Mother says, 'Don't go on a trip, you don't have to go away.' She'd say, 'Andrei, you have money, why go? *Please* don't go!' But my dad, he wanted to push himself."

At the Wheeling job site a number of the men, including Andrei, had drunk some contaminated water, and when he returned to Dawson Street, he came down with hepatitis and was confined to bed. The effect on the close-knit family was severe.

In order to make up for the lost income the Warholas took in boarders, but this only aggravated the situation. Paul and John started spending more and more time away from home. For Julia, these years were especially hard. America's entry into the Second World War after the attack on Pearl Harbor revived terrifying memories for her. Many boys in the neighborhood were going off to war. Paul's turn would come soon.

As the family bonds unraveled, old dissensions between the brothers hardened. The combination of Andrei's distant severity and Julia's embracing softness had pitched them into fierce, unspoken conflict with one another for their parents' attention. Cleaving to his mother and detaching himself from his father, Andy was less affected than John and Paul, who now found themselves in the terrifying position of receiving the final judgment of their dying patriarch.

Andrei's greatest concern was over what would happen to his hard-won savings after he died. He knew that Julia had no head for figures and that anything could happen if she were left in control. He was tormented by visions of the precious college fund he had been putting aside for Andy being dispersed among the hungry Zavackys in Lyndora or floating off to Mikova. He was equally uncertain of Paul's ability to manage money. No sooner did Paul make a buck than he spent it, and he had already developed a habit that Andrei abhorred—gambling. Paul, his eldest and heir, had further disappointed Andrei by dropping out of high school without consulting him. Andrei's silent displeasure rested heavily on his son, who, for all his brusque hustle and energy, took after his mother and was a soft, warm soul inside.

That left John to take responsibility for the Warhola household. Sixteen in 1942 and taking courses at Conlee Trade School, Johnny had pleased his father with his diligence and steadiness. In his last months at Dawson Street Andrei began telling the relatives who mattered—his brother Joseph, Julia's sister Mary, and of course Julia herself—to listen to John when it came to matters of finance. The choice to promote John over Paul as head of the family created a rift between the brothers that never healed, setting them in interminable competition with each other for their mother's affection. "Mother always tried to say, 'All my sons mean the same to me,'" Paul would claim years later, "but I can just feel that I was her favorite."

The use Andy made later on in life of the same devices his mother and father employed to keep their children in constant, edgy competition for their attention indicates that he was intuitively aware of the family dramas surrounding his father's death.

One day before Andrei went into Montefiore Hospital for a series of tests, he called John out onto the back porch. John recalled: "He says to look after Mother and Andy because Paul is going to get married soon. 'You're going to be real proud of Andy,' he says. 'He's going to be highly educated, he's going to college.' He told me he had enough postal bonds saved up to pay for Andy's first two years in college, and he said, 'Make sure the money isn't spent in any other way. Make sure the bills are paid and we don't lose the house.'"

Remembering the day Andrei Warhola died, John continued: "Andy came down to breakfast and asked Mother, 'How come you tickled my nose with a feather?' And she says, 'I wasn't even in the

24

room.' And Andy says, 'Well, somebody tickled my nose and I woke up and saw a body going out the door into the hall.' About eight hours later my dad passed away, and my mother said, 'That must have been an angel or God letting you know.' "

"Andy sure had an emotional reaction to his father's death," recalled Ann Warhola, who married Paul the following year. "As was traditional, his dad was laid out in the house for three days with somebody sitting up with him through the night, and his mother always told me Andy refused to go down and see him when he was laid out."

Paul remembered: "When they brought the body into the house, Andy was so scared he ran and hid under the bed. He just didn't wanna see Dad. He started crying. He begged Mother to let him stay with Tinka at Aunt Mary's or to have Tinka come over and keep him company. Mother was always fearful that his nervous condition might come back, and agreed."

His father's funeral may have been the only one Andy ever went to. Throughout his life he would always react to death with a show of utter indifference. On that occasion, at thirteen, he betrayed no emotion; his feelings appeared completely submerged as his father's coffin was lowered into the ground in St. John Divine Byzantine Catholic Cemetery in suburban Bethel Park. In photographs taken outside the family house after the funeral, Andy seems to be bursting as if relieved of some inner burden and fueled by new energy. Years later John Warhola said: "If there was any outstanding thing that affected Andy during his childhood more than anything else, I think it was when my dad passed away."

Now Julia began to cling to Andy the way he had clung to her throughout his vulnerable childhood. They became equals in a pact of mutual support. She later told John that she would not have made it through this hard time without Andy. Their bond was strengthened by family squabbles. Uncle Joseph's wife, Strina, who had been Andrei's most outspoken critic during his lifetime for being tightfisted, announced that she thought her family should inherit a portion of his savings. Julia refused. "My husband was a good man," she said. "Not a drunk man. I had eleven thousand dollars in the bank. I just pay taxes. I raise my children."

Then there was Paul's marriage. In April 1943 he asked his

mother how she felt about his getting married: "I says, 'Is this gonna maybe change the situation?' She says, 'I'm not gonna stand in your way. If you want to get married, that's fine.' I says, 'Well, we'll live here. We'll rent the second floor and I can pay you so much a month.' "

The arrangement was doomed from the start. Ann Warhola struck Paul's family as overbearing. She was apparently given to religious soul-searching and believed that everybody must find his "inner truth" and declare it openly. Nothing could have been less natural for the Warholas, whose intricate family ties were based on not expressing their true feelings. Ann seemed to dislike Andy in particular, perhaps because of his effeminacy, and Andy was tormented by her presence. Paul was caught in the middle. He began staying out late. Ann would fly into rages, turning the house into a war zone. The situation deteriorated further when Ann announced that she was pregnant and that Paul, who had been called up to join the navy, would shortly be leaving her in Julia's care.

By the time the baby, Paul Warhola, Jr., was born in early 1944, it was evident that the arrangement could not continue. This was brought to a head by Julia's ill health. For some time she had been suffering from hemorrhoids. Now she found herself physically incapable of caring for a recuperating, difficult new mother and a baby. To everyone's relief Ann moved back into her parents' house to await Paul's return from the war.

Their relief was short-lived. Julia's hemorrhoids started bleeding so badly that she was forced to call in her doctor, who prescribed a series of tests and diagnosed colon cancer. Her chances of survival were at best fifty-fifty, he informed both Julia and John, and that chance depended entirely on her agreeing to an operation—a colostomy—which was at the time still experimental. Since Julia was incapable of making the decision, Paul was rushed home from training camp to give the doctors permission to cut out Julia's bowel system and replace it with a bag against her stomach. The boys and Julia seem not to have been completely aware of what was involved. They were simply told that the operation was essential and must be done at once. For the rest of her life Julia remained convinced that she had never had cancer, that the whole terrible ordeal had been unnecessary. True or not, when Andy later tried to persuade her to have another operation to replace the colostomy bag with tubes, Julia flatly refused because the first operation had been so painful.

For Andy, his mother's ordeal was terribly traumatic: Her experience, coming after the harsh medical treatment his father had received, bred in him a fear of hospitals and surgery that may have contributed to his own premature death. It also seems to have stimulated a lifelong reliance on prayer. "I'll never forget the day Andy came down to the hospital after Mother was operated on," recalled John Warhola. "The first thing he asked me, he says, 'Did Mumma die?' We visited her in the hospital every day, and we just prayed. We prayed a lot, and I think that had a bearing with me and Andy getting real close. We were brought up to believe that prayers are the only thing that are going to help you, and when Andy had nowhere else to turn, he got closer to God. I think prayer really helped him through a tough life."

As if his mother's condition were not trouble enough, adolescence now struck Andy with a fury. When Julia was released from the hospital after three weeks' confinement, her youngest son's angelic looks had vanished. His nose had become a great bulbous cherry; his skin had broken out again. "He didn't feel much like eating," John recalled. "He says, 'Open a can of soup,' and the quickest thing I grabbed was tomato soup."

2

PITTSBURGH IN THE 1930s and 1940s was an excellent place to study art. The Carnegies, Mellons, and Fricks were among the leading collectors in the world, and they sponsored competitions, art centers, and free Saturday morning art classes at the Carnegie Museum for talented children from all over the city. Pittsburgh boasted at least two outstanding local artists during Andy Warhol's childhood—the folk artist John Kane, who had received a great deal of publicity when it was revealed that he painted over photographs, and the academic painter Sam Rosenberg, whose street scenes of Oakland and Greenfield emphasized the hot pinks and reds of the city and the Old World "nobility" of its immigrants.

The city's public schools put a premium on the teaching of art, employing a number of innovative instructors who gave Andy not only a solid technical grounding but the inspiration to see art as a way of life. Chief among them was Joseph Fitzpatrick, who taught the Saturday-morning classes at the Carnegie Museum. His prize pupil was nine-year-old Andy Warhola, who had been recommended by Annie Vickerman, his art teacher at Holmes.

The Carnegie Museum classes were split into two groups: the Tam O'Shanters, named for Scottish-born Andrew Carnegie, comprised the fifth to seventh grades, and the Palettes were the older students, in grades eight to ten. The Tam O'Shanters' class was held on the first floor of the museum in the ornate Music Hall, where three hundred or so students would assemble on Saturday mornings. Their teacher, the tall, flamboyant Fitzpatrick, was a Pittsburgh character of some renown. Teaching for him was a performance. "Look, to See, to Remember, to Enjoy!" he would bellow from the stage at the children, who listened in rapt silence. "Art," he would say, "is not just a subject. It's a way of life. It's the only subject you use from the time you open your eyes in the morning until you close them at night. Everything you look at has art or the lack of art." What, for example, had their bus driver looked like that morning?

Fitzpatrick taught them to draw with authority, starting with an understanding of the fundamentals of drawing and painting, then encouraged them to manipulate the basic forms. Of his work with his most famous pupil he said: "What I taught him may not have helped with the kind of thing he did later on, but it acquainted him with different styles."

The children sat in rows and worked in crayon on Masonite boards. Each student would describe what he had observed during the week that had helped him improve on the previous week's drawing and would then do a new drawing based on this knowledge. The subjects were simple—a coffee pot, a table. Local artists sometimes came to talk about their work and techniques. The students visited the museum's galleries to relate what they had learned to what they could see. For Andy, these classes opened his eyes in other crucial ways. As Ultra Violet, one of his "superstars," later wrote in her memoir *Famous for Fifteen Minutes*: "They gave him his first chance to meet children from neighborhoods beyond his ethnic ghetto and to observe how the well-to-do dress and speak. Several times he mentioned two youngsters who arrived in limousines, one in a long maroon Packard and the other in a Pierce-Arrow. He remembered the mother who wore expensively tailored clothes and sumptuous furs. In the 1930s, before television and with no glossy magazines for poor families like Andy's . . . the art classes opened a peephole for Andy to the world of the rich and successful."

According to Fitzpatrick, Andy was an original even then: "A more talented person than Andy Warhol I never knew. I encouraged him to do whatever he wanted to do because he was so individualistic. Personally he was not attractive. He had no consideration for other people. He lacked all the amenities. But he did seem to have a goal from the very start. You weren't exactly conscious of what it was, but he stayed right with it. And knew exactly what to do to get the attention he outwardly seemed to avoid."

In September 1941, Andy entered Schenley High School. With a mix of black, Jewish, Greek, Polish, and Czechoslovakian students, Schenley was a lower-middle-class school with mediocre academic standards. Nonetheless, the art department was quite good, and Andy made the most of it.

Determined to fulfill his father's prediction and go to college, Andy had become highly disciplined in his work. As Ann Warhola observed of the time before she moved out of Dawson Street, "When Andy came home from school he would go straight to his room and work. Dinner would be ready and you could hear his mother yelling for him to come down and eat. Sometimes she would take food up to him. When he did come down and sit with us he never had much to say, and when he did talk it was always about his work and nobody paid too much attention."

Andy's talent was gaining him approval from both teachers and students. He drew compulsively and amazingly well. Drawings piled up in stacks all over his room. "In Miss McKibbin's art class he went straight to his desk, got out his materials, and drew and drew," recalled Lee Karageorge, a classmate. "But socially he was sort of left out. He wasn't even in the art club because his talent was so superior to the rest of us."

Small and beset with an acne so pronounced that his family dubbed him "Andy the Red-Nosed Warhola," he was nonetheless not picked on by other boys at school. His brother John recalled "a fellow there that really protected him, an Irish kid, Jimmy Newell, who later on became a policeman. He was a friend of mine and I asked him to look out for Andy. He was the toughest kid in the neighborhood." He was further protected by his art. Anywhere—in home room, at Yohe's drugstore, during breaks—he could be found with a sketchbook. Boys would huddle around his desk and hold up drawings of his, exclaiming: "Look at this, guys!" He even made a sketching friend, a boy named Nick Kish, who lived down the block on Dawson. "We weren't twenty-four-hour bosom buddies," remembered Kish, "but on Saturday mornings we'd go to the park and sketch. Andy would say, 'Hold your hand out. I want to draw it.' I painted Andy, he painted me."

Years later Andy commented, "I wasn't amazingly popular, although I guess I wanted to be, because when I would see the kids telling one another their problems, I felt left out. No one confided in me." Nevertheless, he didn't seem that strange, according to several old classmates. "He was oddball-looking but not oddball as a person," one Schenley graduate said. "He didn't dress outlandishly. He often wore a favorite sweater-vest with the sleeves of his shirt rolled up, and, like almost everyone else, he wore saddle shoes. But he had that white hair which he wore down in bangs or swept back. Most of the other boys wore crewcuts, and sometimes they made fun of him. They called him 'the albino.' He was more serious than most of us were, but that doesn't mean he didn't have fun."

As at Holmes, his friends were mostly girls. With one, Ellie Simon, he maintained a close friendship throughout college and into his early years in New York. Another friend recalled: "Ellie had a thing about helping other people, particularly if they had emotional or physical problems." By now Andy had a lot of problems, and Ellie was a font of sympathy. Although there was no romance involved, they spent so much time together that Julia became jealous and warned Andy that they would not be able to marry because Ellie was Jewish.

He remained close to Margie Girman and her friend Mina Serbin, who was, like him, a member of the school safety patrol. Every afternoon after school, Andy and Mina would patrol the street crossings until the students had all withdrawn from the area. Then he would accompany her to Yohe's drugstore and join the other kids eating ice cream, playing the jukebox, and fooling around. Andy always had a sketchbook and would draw while the others talked, joining in only during their more serious discussions about who was going to college and how many neighborhood boys had been killed in the war. Says Mina Serbin: "Andy was always complimenting me. I was captain of the cheerleaders and I was popular, but I wasn't that pretty. He would always say how beautiful my hair was or what nice colors I was wearing. We didn't really have dates in those days. Who could afford it? But we went bowling in Oakland together, and we went ice-skating, and we'd walk to the movies holding hands. One time, when I was about fourteen, a man sat next to me at the movies and put his hand on my knee and offered me candy. I was very upset, and I told Andy. I remember he went off looking for the man like he was going to do something to him. Andy was going to protect me."

During his junior year a student canteen called the High Spot opened where, for twenty-five cents, the students could drink Cokes and dance to a jukebox. Andy was a member of the board of the High Spot, and could usually be found there on Friday nights. "I didn't think Andy was the greatest jitterbugger," Mina recalled, "but he did slow-dance very nicely."

He was successful enough with girls to stir jealousy. Seeing him walking Mina or Ellie home, the other boys would wonder how Warhola, with his pimply face and high-pitched voice, was able to talk so easily to the creatures who made them tongue-tied.

For at least one old classmate, Andy provoked confused feelings. Back then, he said, he was emotionally insecure because his parents were getting a divorce, and he attracted a lot of derision because he was one of the smallest boys in the class. At first, Andy befriended him. But the friendship turned sour when Andy started taunting him. It began in the showers during the compulsory nude swimming period: "Everybody hated to go into the pool, so for most of the hour everybody would just stand in the shower. Andy was always in that shower. He used to twit me because I was on the lower end of the scale, as was he, in terms of being the shortest-hung studs in the shower. The short-hung guys would face the shower and the other guys would turn around. I very distinctly remember he always stayed in the back of the shower and never went in the swimming pool. Andy had an ugly body. He had a little dick and a kind of hunched back. He wore his hair straight back and had this bulbous nose. I did not suspect him of being gay. It wasn't the sort of thing one thought about at that time."

Andy's taunting got worse. In the school corridors he would point at the younger boy's crotch and go "euuugh . . . euuugh." "He used to ridicule others, too," his victim recalled. The old classmate, who is Jewish, had the distinct impression that some of this was inspired by the anti-Semitism that was common among boys of Andy's background. But the sudden turnabout in their budding friendship may have been caused by deeper confusions in Andy's always complicated feelings about intimacy.

"I tried and tried when I was young to learn something about love and since it wasn't taught in school I turned to the movies for some ideas about what love is and what to do about it," Andy wrote years later in his *Philosophy.* "In those days you did learn something about some kind of love from the movies, but it was nothing you could apply with any reasonable results."

This may have been less disingenuous than it sounds, for as a teenager he was the quintessential movie junkie. His special favorites were the films from Warner Brothers, the studio that owned the only two movie houses in Oakland, and one whose products—films noir starring the likes of Humphrey Bogart and James Cagney, and slapstick cartoons with Bugs Bunny, Tom and Jerry, and so on—were perfect nourishment for the two sides of his imagination, the dark and the goofy. (Significantly, he would later claim that Warner Brothers' heroic yokel Popeye the Sailor was his favorite childhood hero.)

The radio had become the family hearth, particularly with the war bulletins and voices of Hitler, Churchill, and Edward R. Murrow coming every night from Europe. According to Mina Serbin, Andy's favorite subject of conversation was the war's death toll, and his favorite radio character was the Shadow, with the show's signature statement "Who knows what evil lurks in the hearts of men? The Shadow knows."

Serbin further recalled that Andy's preoccupation with death extended to his fascination with homegrown disasters. Railroad accidents, hotel and circus fires, earthquakes, hurricanes, epidemics, plane crashes, bizarre suicides: The newspapers and magazines were full of "on-the-spot" photographs of such events, the grislier the better. And since Andy never left Pittsburgh, it was the movies and the news that provided him with the "scenes of his childhood" that he would use and reuse throughout his life. As he later wrote, "You live in your dream America that you've custom-made from art and schmaltz . . . just as much as you live in your real one."

By his senior year at Schenley, Andy had developed a special relationship with his art teacher, Joseph Fitzpatrick. Mina Serbin vividly remembered the mentor and his protégé "bending over Andy's drawings, scrutinizing them together. It was a very warm relationship. Joe would make him sit and do things that Andy didn't think he could do. He brought all of that out of him."

But it wasn't a matter of imposing a vision—which would, in any case, have been impossible. With uncanny aptness, the inscription next to Andy's high school yearbook photograph reads: "As genuine as a fingerprint."

During his senior year at Schenley, Andy was accepted at both the University of Pittsburgh and the Carnegie Institute of Technology. He chose the latter because it had the stronger art department. Things had improved at home. Julia Warhola had survived the shock of her colostomy and was devoting all her energies to supporting Andy's ambitions. She moved out of the front bedroom so that he could have the best room in the house to work in, and she paid his first year's college tuition out of the postal savings bonds left by Andrei. With Paul away from home, John was the man of the house, and he took care of the monthly bills by working as a Good Humor ice-cream vendor. Still, enrolling Andy at Carnegie Tech was fraught with problems.

First, it turned out that Andy had no birth certificate, because Julia had failed to register the event. Although this problem was remedied with a signed affidavit, John recalled, "they weren't going to accept him because he was going to just go in the evenings to save money, but my mother told him to go back and tell them that he'll go in the daytime and she gave him the money. I think it was two hundred dollars a semester. I remember before he went to talk to the people at the office he had to kneel down and say some special prayers with my mother."

Carnegie Tech, on its beautifully landscaped campus in Oakland, near the rows of mansions where the Pittsburgh elite lived, was a zone of culture distinctly separate from the workaday life of the city. The university's academic standards were high, the courses competitive, and hard work was stressed. *Laborare est orare*, "To labor is to pray," was the school motto. Warhol's freshman courses were Drawing 1, Pictorial and Decorative Design, Color, Hygiene, and Thought and Expression. In one way or another he had trouble with all of them, but his most serious problem came in Thought and Expression.

The course was taught by Gladys Schmidt, a stern woman who ran the only artistic salon in Pittsburgh. One of the course's requirements was attending plays staged by the drama department and writing interpretive essays about them. Andy, with his immigrant accent and vocabulary—he would say "ats" for "that is," "Jeetjet" for "Did you eat yet?" and "yunz" for "all of you"—and his inability to write grammatically, was in trouble from the start. "It was said that his mutilations of the English language were the despair of Gladys Schmidt," one of the other teachers recalled. "Andy was never very strong in his academics, but that had nothing to do with his intelligence. There was a language problem at home, and it was also difficult for Andy to follow directions in the beginning, because he had already developed enough to be very self-directed."

Warhola never spoke in Gladys Schmidt's class and was incapable of forming his thoughts coherently in writing, often relying on the help of two classmates: his old friend Ellie Simon and Gretchen Schmertz, a slender, talkative young woman whose father was a professor in the architecture department. Gretchen Schmertz remembered Andy's appearance at the time as "thin, soft-spoken, and very pale, as if he never came out in the sun. He appeared to be frail, but I don't think he really was because he always produced a lot of work, most of it at night." Working at night was a habit Andy had developed in high school because he was afraid of the dark, and it was the only time he could be completely uninterrupted. Now that he had his own room, he could work as late as he liked.

The two girls helped him write his papers. They would get together after class and ask him what he thought about the book or play in question. Gretchen would put his ideas into proper English, then the three of them would go over the paper to make sure it sounded as if he had written it. This ploy, however, could not cover up Andy's difficulties when he was called upon to speak or write exam papers.

At the same time, he was having trouble with his art teachers. The faculty was led by a group of older academicians, including the department director, Wilfrid Readio, and the anatomy teacher Russell ("Papa") Hyde. Neither knew what to make of the strange young man. Often his work seemed completely slapdash. He would, for example, tape a piece of torn construction paper over the gaps between one figure and another in a drawing, or leave the paw prints of the family cat on his work as a sign of creativity. On occasion he would bring in something completely different from what the class had been told to do, as if he had simply ignored the assignment.

Robert Lepper, who was a younger, broader-minded teacher than some of his colleagues, recalled Andy as "a timid little boy who was often in academic difficulty. At that time the work of the students was graded by a jury system. The majority prevailed. At first, Andy was regularly proposed for 'drop' from the institution for failure to maintain standards. It is to the credit of the faculty, some ten or twelve, that the proposal to 'drop' failed by at least one vote, and that Andy was permitted to continue his studies. He regularly split the faculty down the middle. Some of them thought he couldn't draw at all. Others recognized his talent immediately. Andy was the baby of the class; the other students all looked after him. Still, if anyone had asked me at the time who was the least likely to succeed, I would have said Andy Warhola."

He had found a mother figure in the art department chairman's secretary, Lorene Twiggs. Most people who met Andy during his first year at Tech say that he was so shy he could hardly speak. Soon, however, he was pouring his heart out daily to Mrs. Twiggs. Conjuring up a tale of abject woe, he told her how ill his mother was, in clinical detail. He emphasized how poor they were and how difficult it was for him to get any work done at home. His brothers, he claimed, made fun of him for wanting to be an artist and let their children stomp all over his work. To illustrate his predicament, he always wore the same pair of baggy jeans, a turtleneck, a frayed workshirt, and a pair of sneakers that looked as if they had been found in a Goodwill box.

Gretchen Schmertz believed that "the main threat to him was poverty. We were concerned that he was warm enough in the wintertime. Nobody did the Joe College dressing at the time—the girls wore blue jeans—but it was a case of: Does he have gloves for his hands and a decent coat or sweater? I never visited his house; it was off-limits." The truth was that his mother served Andy delicious, piping hot meals whenever he would eat them, and chased him around the living room every morning trying to force a woolen hat onto his head because he caught cold so easily. Andy evaded these attempts but finally agreed to take a pair of earmuffs, which he rarely wore.

In the economic recession following the war, jobs were scarce, and many returning soldiers began to take advantage of the opportunity of going to college on the GI Bill. Since the art department could accommodate a maximum of a hundred students, it was announced that thirty to forty members of Andy's class would be dropped at the end of the first year to make room for the veterans. In fact, only fifteen of the forty-eight in Andy's class would survive. Despite the help of his friends, Andy failed Thought and Expression, and his other grades were also poor. At the end of his freshman year Andy was dropped from Carnegie Tech. On hearing the news, he burst into tears. (Throughout his life, rejection was one of the few things that could reduce him to tears.) This rejection so scarred Andy that later on, he would deny ever having attended college.

"When Andy came home that day," said John Warhola, "he was very upset and very determined, alternating between crying and saying that if they threw him out he would go to art college in New York. I wondered how he would be able to do that, but Andy just said he would. Then Mother said, 'We'll say some prayers and everything will be all right.' "

A few teachers and Mrs. Twiggs put up a fight for him, and finally the faculty offered him the option of going to summer school and producing work in order to be considered for readmission in the fall. There was less pressure at summer school, and Andy, accompanied by the ever-faithful Ellie Simon, thrived on it. He made up Thought and Expression, and took "Papa" Hyde's course in anatomy.

Russell Hyde was in his seventies. Over six feet tall with a big head of neatly swept-back silver hair, he was as formal in his appearance, always wearing three-piece suits, as he was keen on Nicoleydes' "natural" approach to drawing. "I think Andy's relationship with Papa Hyde that summer was extremely important," recalled one of Andy's classmates. "In my opinion, it was the metamorphosis of Andy Warhol. He gave Andy a lecture one day, saying, 'Andy, damn it, you just must stop drawing in a manner where you try to please me.

You do it the way you see it. I don't care how good it looks, how bad it looks. You've got to do it to please yourself. And if you don't do it, you'll never amount to a damn.' "

In the meantime, Paul Warhola had started a new business. He had bought a flatbed huckster's truck and was selling fruit and vegetables door to door. He gave Andy a job for the summer, helping him three or four mornings a week for three dollars a day. They would load the truck early in the morning at the produce market and follow a regular route. Andy would run from door to door yelling, "Fresh strawberries! Fresh corn!" and delivering orders as Paul drove the truck down the street.

Soon Andy started to carry a sketchbook on the truck. He sketched everything he saw around him at the produce yard and in the streets, using a "speed-sketching" technique he had learned at school. He would put the pencil on the paper and draw a figure in ten seconds without taking the pencil off the paper. He drew people standing in doorways or gathered around the truck. "It was a very uninhibited style," one witness recalled. "He drew what he saw. You could see the nude bodies of the women through their tattered clothes, babies hanging on their mothers' necks. In a very simple manner he really got the essence of this depressed side of life."

Andy presented a notebook full of these drawings to the art department and was reinstated at Tech. In fact, the first thing his classmates saw when they came back for the fall semester of 1948 was Andy's huckster drawings hanging in a group, accompanied by a striking self-portrait. This display was Andy's first show, and it made him into something of a figure in the department and on campus, especially when the school paper announced that he was to be honored for the best summer work done by a sophomore. The forty-dollar Leisser Prize was the first money Andy ever received for his art.

"I think Andy was a natural ground-breaker," recalled Betty Ash, one of the few black students in the department. "Like Courbet, who came from peasant stock and was on the upwardly mobile road via art, Andy wore his peasant heritage like a badge of honor. His use of the working-class vernacular was part of it."

The brightest students in the department formed a group led by Philip Pearlstein, a twenty-four-year-old intellectual from a middle-class Jewish family. Like Andy, Pearlstein had been taught by Fitzpatrick as a child, and he had made a splash by having two of his paintings reproduced in *Life* magazine when he was fifteen. He would become Andy's closest friend at Tech. Other members of the circle were Leonard Kessler, Arthur Elias, Jack Regan, George Klauber, Pearlstein's girlfriend Dorothy Kantor, Regan's girlfriend Grace Hirt, Ellie Simon, and Gretchen Schmertz. They were a noisy, argumentative, high-spirited bunch, and their seriousness about what they were doing, shaped by the war years, was unprecedented even by the already high Tech standards. Shortly after he won the Leisser Prize, they all began to notice Andy. As Leonard Kessler remembered it: "Here was this cherubic little guy drawing these beautiful, graceful pictures of cherubs, and we started to talk to him. He was never argumentative, never put anybody down. He was a gentle and very kind person, and he had a whimsical smile and a wide eye, as if he was always ready to make some outlandish remark. Once we were sitting on the grass and he was looking up at the sky and he said, 'Maybe there are giants out there in the universe and we're like the ants on the ground.' "

"Here was this kid who just drew like an angel," said Gretchen Schmertz. "He had his own quality of line, this wonderful shaggy, jagged line." Jack Wilson, another student, recalled that "Andy was the damndest mixture of a six-year-old child and a well-trained artist. He put them both together totally without inhibition." And Philip Pearlstein said: "It was very apparent to all of the students that Andy was extraordinarily talented. It was not apparent to the faculty. But there was this marvelous quality. Andy was a very young person. He liked to laugh. He was very naive and left himself open in a way. He was like an angel in the sky at the beginning of his college times. But only for then. That's what college gets rid of." Jack Wilson saw a darker side: "He was very naive and left himself open, but I can't remember Andy laughing. He always had a kind of sad face."

Andy blossomed with their association. He was able to play up the bad-little-boy side of his personality, delighting in trying to shock the not-easily-shocked veterans by drawing pictures of little boys masturbating and urinating. They, in turn, delighted in his naiveté and talent. The women in the group all mothered him. Soon he had them all thinking of him as the class baby. Without being the leader of the group, he was always at its center, protected and nurtured.

Many of Andy's professors in the art department were commercial and industrial designers. The teachings of the Bauhaus, the German-based movement led by Walter Gropius and Laszlo Moholy-Nagy to bring about the marriage of art and technology, was particularly emphasized. The Painting and Design faculty believed that fine art and commercial art were essentially the same thing, and their avowed aim was to break down the barriers between them. The P&Ds, as their students were called, were taught that the most important thing to learn was good design. Moholy-Nagy's *Vision and Design* and Paul Klee's *Pedagogical Sketchbook* were two of their principal texts. Moreover, the Bauhaus emphasis on art as business, as an organization of people, was something that Andy would not forget when it came to building his New York studio, the Factory.

By his second year Andy was thriving in this environment and casting off some of the shyness of his freshman year, although he still needed a lot of help with his written work. He joined a student film club, the Outlines, that screened films from the Museum of Modern Art in New York. The club hired guest speakers, and Andy heard lectures by the avant-garde filmmaker Maya Deren and the composer John Cage. Pittsburgh had a fine symphony orchestra, and he started going to concerts. He also became interested in ballet and modern dance. José Limon was a particular hero, and Andy and Philip Pearlstein saw him every time he came to town. Martha Graham arrived for a series of performances and made a tremendous impact on the group. Andy was particularly moved by her performance of *Appalachian Spring,* and he and his friends posed for photographs parodying her style.

Indeed, Andy was so interested in dance that he began going to modern dance classes with Kessler's sister, Corkie Kaufman. He had little natural rhythm and found it agonizing to do his pliés, but twice a week he would change into a leotard and join the girls to explore rhythm, space, and movement for an hour. He also joined the modern dance class at Tech, in which he was the only male student, and posed somewhat defiantly with the girls for their yearbook picture. Asked many years later if she recalled him, his teacher Dorothy Kanrich snorted, "He was a nut!"

His greatest pleasure was the parties. In the living room of Gretchen Schmertz's house or at the Kesslers', Andy would sit at the tables with his fingers covering his mouth in a characteristic gesture he had copied from his mother as he listened to the conversation swirling around him. "He enjoyed parties immensely," said Kessler. "He glowed. You could see the little cherubic face lighting up."

Andy never spoke about homosexuality and never made any sexual advances, but it was evident from his mannerisms and the way he dressed that he was probably gay. He used to wear a corduroy jacket with the collar turned up, which he would hold closed across his throat with one delicate hand. Walking with a dance step, he whispered "Hi!" to everyone he met, in a surprised, breathless voice. When he was sitting down, his hands were always artfully placed or suspended from his wrists. Betty Ash said, "People tended to shield him from others who said unkind things about him. I remember admiring one of Andy's drawings in an exhibition, and there was this one guy who liked to tell dirty jokes and make fun of any fella he thought less than fully masculine. I remember him making a comment about how he didn't understand why everybody was always celebrating the work of this fruitcake." But according to Perry Davis, the teacher who was closest to Andy, "Homosexuality was pretty well accepted in art school. No one really thought much about Andy and sex because he left a very sexless impression."

In the summer of 1947, Pearlstein, Elias, Jack Regan, Dorothy Kantor, and Andy rented a studio—a landmark event. The biographer Albert Goldman, a student in Tech's drama department at the time, recalled the significance of such an act: "Art was something that went on in a *studio.* That was a very important word—a bohemian ideal. And you always wore [as Andy did throughout his life] turtlenecks—a very vital element of being an *artist.*" The Barn, as Andy and his friends called their bohemian ideal, was the carriage house of a Victorian mansion across from the Carnegie Tech campus. It cost ten dollars for two and a half months. They all had their own space to work in. To inaugurate it they threw a bohemian party with a chamber orchestra, then settled down to a spell of serious work. "That was the summer we all decided to dedicate ourselves to painting," recalled Art Elias. Andy did a series of paintings of children on swings and little boys picking their noses. Even this early on he was drawn to serial imagery and intent upon reviewing periods of his childhood. "Andy was very influenced by Ben Shahn and Paul Klee," recalled Elias, "but he and the rest of us didn't really know what painting was. We were all rather nonverbal, but we all bent over backward to help Andy, possibly because he was so passive. One day we were walking over the Schenley Bridge together, and he said, 'Entertain me.'"

While Andy was at Carnegie Tech, he discovered the blotted-line drawing technique that was to be the mainstay of his commercial art career in New York during the 1950s. Just how he came upon it is unclear. Wilfrid Readio taught blotting in his technical-resources course, but Andy always maintained that he discovered the technique when he accidentally spilled some ink on a piece of paper. What seems most likely is that he copied it from the well-known artist Ben Shahn.

For these drawings Andy would take two pieces of paper, lay them next to each other, and attach them by a piece of tape that would act as a hinge. He would then draw on the right-hand sheet. Before the ink could dry, he would lift that sheet and press it down on the left-hand sheet. The "blotted" line was a smudged mirror image of the original line drawing. Not only did Andy like the look, but he also liked the implication that, since his hand had not actually drawn the line on the paper that would hold the final image, he had removed himself one step from the result.

From early childhood Andy had been using elements from magazines in his pictures. At Tech he was always ripping pages out of *Life* and using parts of them in his blotted-line drawings. If he were doing a drawing with a chair in it, he might trace a chair from a photograph. If he traced another object from a photograph onto a drawing via the blotted line, he was distancing himself two steps from the final result. What Andy did by combining the blotted-line technique and tracing details from photographs was directly influenced by the Bauhaus approach to art: "personal comment" was removed from the work in favor of clear, strong design; the traditional boundary between commercial and fine art was blurred.

Some of his teachers later agreed that Andy had come to Tech with a style and developed it on his own, that what he got from the institution was what he took, not what he was given. Many of Andy's friends insist, however, that Robert Lepper's course, Painting and Design, was a crucial influence, although Lepper himself was modest about his role, saying only that Andy did very good work in his class. Lepper taught a psychological approach to art: It was necessary to know how a person in a drawing felt before you drew him. Lepper assigned his students modern novels and short stories to read and illustrate. Andy excelled at the task. He began a series of large blotted-line drawings that showed a keen understanding of what the books were about and an acute ability to choose an image that captured their essence. One memorable example, now in the Carnegie Museum Library, was a large blotted-line drawing illustrating the fictionalized character of Huey Long giving a Nazi-style salute in Robert Penn Warren's *All the King's Men*.

Among the other faculty members, perhaps the most influential on all the aspiring young painters was Balcomb Greene, who seemed to exemplify best what being an artist was all about. Tall, with a deep disembodied voice, Greene looked like John Carradine and was the heartthrob of many of the women students. The fact that he was an abstract painter and painted at night—and in the nude—added to his legend. His wife, "Peter," a constructivist sculptor, spent most of the winter in her studio in New York, making him even more of a target for the mad crushes of the female students. Greene, like Perry Davis, Robert Lepper, and a few others on the Tech faculty, maintained a high-minded attitude toward art, and their example encouraged Andy to think of himself as "an artist," to see art as a possible profession.

In the spring of 1948, with one more year of college to go, Andy was given a job in the display department of Pittsburgh's premier department store, Joseph Horne's, painting backdrops for windows. He thought the store a wonderful, bizarre paradise, and he dressed accordingly, painting his shoes and fingernails a different color every day. Once again he charmed people before they could object. Larry Vollmer, his boss and the only person in Pittsburgh Andy ever openly acknowledged as an "idol," was a suave businessman, a display director who had worked in New York with topflight artists.

Vollmer once told Andy how he and Salvador Dalí had installed a fur-lined bathtub in the window of Bonwit Teller. There was a dispute between the great surrealist and Vollmer, and when Dalí attempted to remove the tub, it went crashing through the plate-glass window onto Fifth Avenue. In the ensuing uproar, Dalí spent a brief time in jail, and as a result of the publicity his show sold out. Here was a lesson in public relations that Andy would not forget; nor was it lost on him that an artist as famous as Dalí would agree to do commercial installations for a department store.

Vollmer was as impressed with Andy as was Andy with him. Andy's commercial work was eclectic and varied. His only fault was that he worked too slowly. The most important thing he learned at Horne's was that to make it as a commercial artist, he would have to work at top speed.

At the store he was also exposed to a group of unabashed homosexuals. According to Perry Davis, "There were a number of flaming queens in the display department, and he was fascinated with them and the talk of their costume parties. The students always talked about Andy's being innocent and naive, but I felt that wasn't quite it. He just hadn't had the exposure. And then I think he still was so loyal to Mama that he had to go home at night, even though he might have wanted to do something else."

This was the first time Andy was making any money to speak of. He bought himself an elegant cream-colored corduroy suit that became known to his friends as his "dream suit." Although it was not the most practical outfit, it defined his emerging self-image as an artist and dandy. It also signaled what his relationship with money would come to be: He would splurge on impractical extravagances, but he would also plough his money back into his work. He spent the rest of his summer earnings on his first trip to New York to scout out job possibilities and to visit galleries and the Museum of Modern Art.

At the beginning of September 1948, Andy Warhola put his portfolio of paintings and drawings in a brown paper bag and, with Philip Pearlstein and Art Elias, boarded an eastbound Greyhound bus. He first boldly visited the two worlds that were foremost in his mind. In the offices of *Glamour* magazine he received a sympathetic reception from the art director, Tina Fredericks. She was impressed by Andy's portfolio and promised him freelance work after he graduated. At the Museum of Modern Art he saw for the first time original work by Picasso, Klee, Shahn, and Matisse.

The group clowned for snapshots outside the museum and roamed the city. Joan Kramer, a former Tech student, had invited them to stay at her apartment in Greenwich Village. George Klauber, who had graduated from Tech the previous year and was already working as the assistant art director at *Fortune* magazine, had asked them to dinner at his parents' house in Brooklyn. George spent the evening talking about his success, about how exciting the magazine world was. He offered his contacts should any of his friends move to the city. It seemed to Andy that George knew everybody.

Before Andy left New York, he visited the offices of *Theater Arts* magazine, where he fell instantly in love with a blow up of the sexually provocative photograph that appeared on the back of Truman Capote's novel, *Other Voices, Other Rooms,* which had just been published. He must have turned on all his charm, because he left the office with the photograph of Capote.

The twenty-three-year-old Capote was everything the twenty-year-old Andy wanted to be and was not. He lived in New York and was said to give dinner parties for Greta Garbo and Cecil Beaton in his boyfriend's apartment. He was young, attractive, talented, glamorous, rich, and suddenly spectacularly famous. Moreover, Andy felt that Truman's description of himself at thirteen in the opening chapter of *Other Voices, Other Rooms* could just as well have been a description of himself: "He was too pretty, too delicate and fair-skinned; each of his features was shaped with a sensitive accuracy, and a girlish tenderness softened his eyes, which were brown and very large. . . . A kind of tired, imploring expression masked his thin face, and there was an unyouthful sag about his shoulders."

Truman Capote now became Andy's idol, superceding Shirley Temple. As soon as he got back to Pittsburgh, Andy began to write Capote fan letters, but he got no response. He began a series of sensitive blotted-line watercolors to illustrate Capote's novel. And he worked to refine his mystique of the sensitive working-class aesthete.

Most often he could be found in the coffee shop at the campus Beanery dressed in baggy blue jeans, open-necked work shirt or T-shirt, and heavy work shoes—a precursor of James Dean, Allen Ginsberg, and Jack Kerouac. People began telling each other "Andy stories," imitating him, and speculating about what he would have thought or done in such-and-such a situation. He had become the object of a little cult, complete with his first worshipful (and self-destructive) fan, an underclass art student who tried to commit suicide and eventually had to leave school.

At the art department parties Andy always kept slightly apart. "We would get costumed and do song and dance," said Betty Ash. "One time Andy arrived with chartreuse-green hair combed forward. I think he was trying to look like a woman in a painting by Matisse." (It is more likely that Andy was imitating the role Dean Stockwell played in the 1948 film *The Boy with Green Hair,* about a young waif who is shunned by society when his hair mysteriously turns green.) "Andy," she continued, "would always wind up isolating himself. One evening I had gone out to the hall, and I could see a figure in the shadows on one of the little narrow stairways that led up to the studios. Andy was sitting in a characteristic pose. He had his hands clasped, his fingers entwined between his knees, and he was sitting on the steps with his head leaning against the wall. When the party got to the stage where everyone thought, 'Well, now we're really partying,' he would tend to fade away. In fact, all the conversations I had with him would be marked by a certain reticence. He would say a few words and pause, reflecting on what he was saying. But he seemed to be able to see things on a couple of levels simultaneously—always with a wry quality, seriousness mixed with humor."

His work was now beginning to cause a stir. Balcomb Greene acquired a Russian wolfhound, and this inspired Andy to do a series of dog paintings. In one work a woman was shown nursing her "baby," a little dog. Andy confided to Perry Davis that as a child he had always felt like a puppy, and the creature in the picture may have been inspired by a mutt—half dalmation, half chow—the Warholas had acquired when he was nine. (According to Harold Greenberger, who lived down the block, he and John and Paul used to play roughly with the dog. When the animal got bigger, it became so vicious that nobody in the family could go near it except Julia.)

Andy's dog painting was hung in a small exhibition but was removed on the orders of Wilfrid Readio, who thought it was disreputable. On another occasion Andy asked the most conservative students from the engineering and women's colleges to stick out their tongues so he could draw them. He was so unthreatening that many complied. When Professor Lepper assigned him to build a model of an Egyptian room for his final project, Andy presented him with the candy-coated model of a nightclub.

His greatest cause célèbre was a painting he called "Nosepicker." Every year the Pittsburgh Associated Artists held an exhibition of local work. Andy had shown two paintings the previous year, and for their March 1949 exhibition he submitted an autobiographical painting, somewhat in the manner of George Grosz, of a little boy with one finger thrust defiantly up his nose. The painting (officially titled *The Broad Gave Me My Face, but I Can Pick My Own Nose*) created a sensation among the jury, which included Grosz himself, as well as several regional academic painters. Just as Andy had polarized the faculty at Carnegie Tech, he now polarized the jurors. Half of them thought it was a terrible insult; the other half, championed by Grosz, thought it was an important work. In the end the painting was rejected, which only got it more attention. It was Andy's first succès de scandale.

Among the multifarious projects he took on during his final, triumphant year at Tech were several collaborations with Philip Pearlstein. These two artists, who in their maturity would become leaders of major schools of painting, were complementary opposites, Pearlstein being heavyset, intellectual, bourgeois, and heterosexual. Pearlstein clarified points over which Andy was confused and introduced him to classical music and intellectual conversation.

Andy "used" Pearlstein, as he used everything, to the hilt. He was always receptive to people who could teach him. In return, Andy's energy and lightness of vision helped keep Pearlstein afloat with his own ideas. They designed the set for a student play, using a large collage of newspapers and signs. They wrote and illustrated a children's book about a Mexican jumping bean called Leroy. When Andy wrote out the title, he misspelled it "Leory." This accident seemed perfect to both of them, so they left it that way. Pearlstein later observed: "I would say if there's any relationship between Andy Warhol's work and my own, it would be a kind of cold looking at something, not worrying about what meaning it had, but just that it is interesting as an object."

Several of his friends noted that Andy adopted an unusually businesslike attitude toward his work. At the end of each semester, when most of the students gave away or discarded their pieces, Andy would sell what he did not need for his portfolio to other students. He drew portraits of people at the Pittsburgh Arts and Crafts Center for five dollars each, but when he was offered seventy-five dollars for a painting on show in the Pittsburgh Associated Artists annual exhibition, which he had listed at one hundred dollars, he refused to lower the price, and the painting did not sell. This showed a remarkably uncompromising attitude toward business, for seventy-five dollars was a lot of money in 1949.

During his four years at Carnegie Tech, Andy took several steps toward becoming Andy Warhol. He began to experiment with changing his name. As art director of the university's literary magazine, *The Cano,* he was Andrew Warhola. On the Christmas card he designed, reproduced, and sent to all his friends he signed himself André, an affectation he had picked up from George Klauber, who had spent time in Paris after the war. On the painting in the Associated Artists exhibition he was credited as Andrew Warhol. To his friends he was Andy.

As graduation approached, he was becoming increasingly concerned about what to do. He faced a real dilemma. On the one hand, he was worried about leaving his mother—and, for her part, Julia could not imagine living without Andy. But, on the other hand, what was he going to do in Pittsburgh? For a while he seriously considered becoming a high school art teacher. Mina Serbin remembered asking Andy what his post-Tech plans were at a graduation party in the Schenley Hotel: "He said he was going to go into teaching. I think he felt that Mr. Fitzpatrick was the kind of teacher he would like to be, and I think he contemplated being a teacher because he didn't feel he was good enough to make it in New York." According to John Warhola, Andy had sent his portfolio to an art school in Indiana to get a teaching post: "He was really disappointed when they sent everything back and says they can't use him. That's when he said, 'Well, I'm going to New York.' "

Julia warned him that if he went to New York, he would end up dead in the gutter without a penny in his pocket, like "Bogdansky," a

Ruthenian artist whom his father had once tried to help. But his friends urged him to go. They knew Andy could make it. What gave him the final push was Pearlstein's decision to move to New York: Why not do it together? he suggested. Balcomb Greene gave them his blessing and offered to arrange a cheap summer sublet. Once he had made up his mind to go, Andy was enormously excited, and Julia, despite her invocations of Bogdansky's ghost, did not stand in his way.

Just before graduation Andy performed in a show put on by the art department's Take It Easel Club, in which several students put on skits satirizing their professors. While one of them imitated a teacher lecturing on the importance of the T-square, Andy suddenly burst on stage waving a large piece of colored paper in each hand, singing a song written by Leonard Kessler: "Oh, you can't scare me, I'm sticking to emotion. It's my devotion. Oh, you can't scare me, I'm sticking to emotion . . ."

3

I N June 1949, Andy and Philip Pearlstein moved into an apartment on St. Mark's Place in the heart of the Lower East Side overlooking Tompkins Square Park. It was a sweltering, cockroach-infested, sixth-floor cold-water walk-up, with a bathtub in the kitchen and a toilet in the closet, conditions as squalid as any Andy had known in Pittsburgh. Provided he could keep his personal expenses to a bare minimum, the two hundred dollars he had saved would suffice to see him through the summer. Beyond that, he was counting on his portfolio of drawings to get him work. Pearlstein recalled: "He had familiarized himself with all the elegant fashion magazines of the period. His portfolio was simply dazzling."

Pearlstein was also hoping to be able to make enough from commercial art to support his larger endeavors. His inclination toward realism and portraiture was already apparent, if pointedly out of sync with the direction being taken by the action painters—Jackson Pollock, Willem de Kooning, and Franz Kline—who were beginning to be recognized as artists of heroic stature. Critics had lumped together Pollock's "all over" paintings with their lyrical riot of pigment, de Kooning's fierce "Women," and Kline's huge black-and-white canvases with the work of "cooler" nonfigurative artists such as

Mark Rothko and Barnett Newman into a movement, abstract expressionism, although there was little agreement among the artists themselves as to what that meant.

The Cedar Bar on MacDougal Street was where they all hung out, and it was already a subterranean legend for their occasionally violent, chair-smashing arguments. The Cedar was a short walk from Andy and Philip's apartment, but it was hardly welcoming to the two arrivistes. Whereas Pearlstein might identify with the abstract painters' love of intellectual justification of their work, it was unlikely that he was going to follow in their footsteps. For Warhol, the influence of the abstract expressionists would be of critical importance to his art and pop art in general, but the two-fisted world of the Cedar Bar was not for him. He was far more taken with the plays of Tennessee Williams and the heavily homosexual theatrical world than he was with Jackson Pollock's anguished drips, which he did not understand.

In any case, as Pearlstein recalled, "the chances of making it as a fine artist in those days were nil," the growing recognition of the abstract expressionists notwithstanding. But the opportunities in commercial art seemed unlimited. America was fast becoming the most productive nation in the world: In the early 1950s, the nation's spending on advertising rose to nearly $9 billion—fifty-three dollars for every man, woman, and child in the country—and the need for images that would "persuade" was inexhaustible. At the same time, owing largely to increased advertising revenues, magazines were proliferating. "The [commercial art] crowd was the smuggest, meanest, drunkest bunch of people you ever saw," one fashion veteran would recall. But George Klauber, Andy's old friend, had already demonstrated that the prospects were good for someone with flair and hustle.

On his second day in New York, Andy went to see Tina Fredericks at *Glamour* magazine in the Condé Nast building in the heart of Madison Avenue's "ad alley." Fredericks, who remembered him from his visit the previous year, was as intrigued by Andy's manner—his loose way of standing, his breathless whisper—as she was by the way his drawings blended commercial and fine art. She even bought a small drawing of an orchestra for herself for ten dollars. Then she said: "I need some drawings of shoes, Mr. Warhola. I need them tomorrow morning at ten o'clock. Can you do them?" (A friend later commented: "Little did she know the wellspring she stirred. Andy not only loved shoes. He loved feet.")

Andy said he could draw anything, and the next morning he was back in her office at ten: To Fredericks' surprise he had drawn the shoes with a lived-in, rumpled look that had a slightly suggestive sexual edge to it. "They were terrific, but they wouldn't sell shoes," she recalled. She explained that *Glamour* needed something with cleaner, harder lines; the shoes must look new. That night, with a little help from Pearlstein, Andy completed a new set of drawings. This time Fredericks bought them for the magazine and gave him a second assignment—more footwear. Andy had found his calling card as a commercial artist: shoes.

He quickly set about making himself unforgettable. "Brush your hair! Put on a suit!" Pearlstein would say as they set out to launch their assault on Madison Avenue, heading forth every day with their portfolios to meet the art directors of agencies and magazines whose names Klauber had supplied. But Andy paid no attention. Inspired by the publicity surrounding Marlon Brando's Stanley Kowalski in *A Streetcar Named Desire*, his uniform was chinos, T-shirts, and worn sneakers, and he carried his drawings in a brown paper bag. To confuse matters, he spoke in a fey whisper, sounding, one friend remembered, "as if he had written his own part in a play by Truman Capote." His friends nicknamed him "Raggedy Andy," and his image of traumatized naiveté and hipster innocence gained the sympathy of art directors, particularly women. Sometimes he would give a cheap bouquet of flowers to each of the receptionists he saw. Asked by one embarrassed recipient, "Have I done something special?" Andy replied, "No, you're just a nice lady." Other times, while waiting for hours on the off chance of getting to see a busy art director, he would serve as a gofer, fetching coffee and doughnuts and ingratiating himself with everyone he could at any level of the business.

These were the golden years of the fashion magazines, which had attracted the most innovative graphic-design talent in the field, much of it European-born and Bauhaus-influenced. In this milieu, Andy's drawing ability was immediately recognized and his eccentricities regarded as a plus. Art directors were also struck by how much fun he seemed to have doing the work. Unlike most commercial artists, who felt that they were prostituting themselves, he made each job a special celebration. "The impression he left," recalled George Klauber, who had become his most valuable New York contact (Andy later said Klauber "invented" him), "was of this eager, interested person, who drew beautifully." Within days of Andy's arrival in the city, Klauber's boss, Will Burton, whose prestigious clients included Upjohn Pharmaceuticals, had assigned him to design a cover for one of the drug company's pamphlets. More work quickly followed from *Charm* and *Seventeen* magazines, as well as from Columbia Records for a series of album covers.

Andy would later insist, "I never wanted anything. Even when I was twenty and hoped that maybe one day I would be a success and very famous, I didn't think about it." But Pearlstein recalled him as "a workaholic who sat at a table and worked all day and often late at night. He would do several versions of each assignment, showing all of them to art directors, who loved him for that."

Whereas Andy's portfolio fit perfectly into the magazine world, Philip's was more political, and it was almost immediately apparent that he was going to get nowhere as a freelance illustrator. Soon he settled into a full-time job with the graphic designer Ladislav Sutner, doing layouts and mechanicals for plumbing and ventilator catalogues during the day and working on his own paintings in the evenings, while Andy labored over his commercial art assignments in the hot, dingy kitchen. Despite Pearlstein's presence, Andy would recall that summer as lonely: "I used to come home and be so glad to find a little roach to talk to. It was so great to have at least someone there to greet you, and then just go away." One of the climactic moments in the "Raggedy Andy" saga occurred when he presented his drawings to the grande dame of the fashion magazines, Carmel Snow of *Harper's Bazaar*, and a cockroach crawled out of the pictures. "She felt so sorry for me," he told everyone, "that she gave me a job."

Although Andy gave art directors the impression that he thoroughly enjoyed his work, his Tech classmate Jack Regan had a different sense of him. Dining with Philip and Andy on St. Mark's Place, Regan and his wife, Gail, got the impression that Andy was struggling with old feelings of inferiority. Throughout dinner he complained of being rejected because of his Pittsburgh accent and ungrammatical speech patterns. Indeed, he was still very much a Pittsburgh boy. Every day he wrote his mother a postcard, saying, "I am fine and I will write again tomorrow." Two or three times a week he would pop into a church to pray. Julia wrote back regularly, enclosing a one- or a five-dollar bill when she could.

Near the end of the summer, shortly after he turned twenty-one, he was published in *Glamour* with an illustration for an article entitled "Success Is a Job in New York," showing a career girl climbing a ladder. The credit listed his name as Andy Warhol, a misspelling he adopted from then on. With their sublet running out, Philip and Andy answered an ad in the *New York Times* and found themselves a single large room at one end of a loft over a truck garage at 323 West Twenty-first Street. The loft's principal tenant, Francesca Boas, was a dance therapist working with disturbed children, and she had fixed it up like a theater: toward the back was a proscenium arch behind which she lived with a huge dog named Name. Andy and Philip took up residence in the front of the loft. Klauber visited them there and was not favorably impressed. If anything, he thought, the place was an even worse dump than their apartment on St. Mark's Place.

"Francesca took an interest in us," Pearlstein said. "I guess we were both odd enough, but Andy especially intrigued her. During the course of that winter, she actively encouraged him to 'open himself up,' and he slowly metamorphosed from Andy Warhola into Andy Warhol."

He was still painfully insecure. One day a friend from Tech, Joseph Groell, overheard him telephoning around to various magazines. He introduced himself by saying, "Hello. This is Andy Warhol. I planted some bird seeds in the park today. Would you like to order a bird?" Then, in a whimsical, whining voice, he declared that it was raining, that he had "a hole in my shoe and do you have any work for me?" When whoever he was talking to said no, Andy replied, "Well, I'm not coming out today." Hanging up after one of these calls, he turned to Groell and said in his normal voice, "Isn't this ridiculous? I don't want to behave like this."

Days on Twenty-first Street quickly settled into a routine. Philip would go to his job, while Andy hustled up new assignments. Recalled Pearlstein: "He would study the printed results carefully for the effectiveness of his work and apply the results of these self-critiques to his next assignment. At the other end of the room, I worked at painting after the day's work at Sutner's office. I had some records that I played—Bartók, Stravinsky, Mahler, and Walton's *Façade,* with Edith Sitwell reciting her poetry. That was Andy's favorite, but he hated Mahler."

Together they battled the cockroaches, which went after the black paint they used for lettering. Andy would leave an empty soda-pop bottle out after lunch; by night it would be full of them. Some evenings, if they had money to spare, they would buy standing-room tickets for Broadway shows such as *Death of a Salesman* and *Member of the Wedding* or would go to the movies, mostly second runs on Forty-second Street. There was little intellectual exchange between them, according to Pearlstein, but he did recall a telling moment after the movies one night when Andy complained that the film had been terrible, and he replied that nothing could be so bad that there was not *something* interesting in it. At the time, Andy made no comment. But it was a line he would use about his own films many years later.

By the fall of 1949 the rest of their group from Tech—the Kesslers, Leila Davies, and Ellie Simon—had all moved to New York, and they picked up where they had left off. None of them seemed sure of what they were going to do. Kessler was making a little headway as a children's book illustrator, and Leila was working in a jewelry shop in Greenwich Village. While their education had given them skills in design, it had also confused them about what art meant beyond being a possible livelihood. Andy saw little difference between his commercial and fine-art drawings, but the others said he shouldn't waste his time and talent, he should be painting more. These criticisms floated back to friends in Pittsburgh. Betty Ash commented, "Part of the disappointment was, well, if Andy's got a job as an ordinary commercial artist, does that mean he's sold out, that he's just like the rest of us?"

In March 1950, Andy, Philip, and Francesca were evicted from the West Twenty-first Street loft. With Philip about to marry his college sweetheart, the painter Dorothy Kantor, he and Andy now parted company. Andy always found it hard to maintain close relationships with friends after they got married, for he needed their undivided attention. But Dorothy was also a friend from Tech. He attended their wedding and remained close to the Pearlsteins for a few more years.

Through Leila Davies, Andy arranged to move uptown into a

two-bedroom basement apartment at 74 West 103rd Street, off Manhattan Avenue near Central Park. The place was officially rented by a dancer with the Ballet Theater, Victor Reilly, and inhabited by a changing roster of as many as six tenants at a time. Word passed among his bemused, protective Pittsburgh friends that Andy had "moved in with a bunch of dancers." It was a transition period, introducing him to the bohemian world of dance and theater—people with whom he felt a greater affinity than with intellectuals like the Pearlsteins.

Sharing the girls' bedroom at one end of the corridor were Margery Beddows and Elaine Baumann, both dancers, and Leila Davies. Andy, Victor, and another Ballet Theater dancer, Jack Beaber, shared the boys' room, where Andy arranged a small drafting table with neatly aligned pens, inks, and brushes under a bright light next to their three permanently unmade mattresses. He thrived on working in the crowded apartment. "It was an impossible scene," recalled Lois Elias, Art's wife, who visited that summer. "All I remember is Andy sitting there drawing, surrounded by this complete chaos and people doing things that would seem to be disruptive of any concentration. The food was mixed in with the clothes."

The kids were playful and friendly, leading the kind of existence portrayed in a favorite play of theirs, *My Sister Eileen*, about immigrants from the midwest to New York. They shared spaghetti suppers, went to Judy Garland, Fred Astaire, and Gene Kelly movies, and sang along to Carol Bruce's rendition of their anthem, "Bewitched, Bothered, and Bewildered." They can be seen in a series of photos Leila Davies kept, munching ice-cream cones and camping it up outside the apartment under a banner reading, "WE LOVE OUR MOTHERS, EVERYONE." Leila and Elaine were in charge of taking care of Andy and making sure he ate; he called Leila "Mother" and Elaine "Little One." Since he was doing a lot of his assignments at night, he began the habit of sleeping well into the day, often not sitting down to breakfast until the afternoon. He was usually so noncommittal about what he wanted to eat that Elaine once became frustrated enough to throw an egg at him.

Despite the appearance of camaraderie, Andy would write twenty-five years later: "I kept living with roommates, thinking we could become good friends and share problems, but I'd always find out that they were just interested in another person sharing the rent.

At one point I lived with seventeen different people in a basement apartment on 103rd and Manhattan Avenue, and not one person out of the seventeen ever shared a problem with me. I worked very long hours in those days, so I guess I wouldn't have had time to listen to any of their problems even if they had told me any, but I still felt left out and hurt." Reading this came as a surprise to many of his roommates, who recalled cooking for him, mending his clothes, taking him to parties, movies, and dance recitals, listening to his problems about his work and his mother, and posing for him. "We certainly cried on each other's shoulders enough," says Leila Davies. "He used to get discouraged a lot, but he kept going. I don't think there was anything more important than his work."

By now Andy had fulfilled one of his early ambitions, turning out a series of powerful blotted-line illustrations for plays by Giraudoux and William Inge and an article on García Lorca for *Theater Arts* magazine, drawings that captured the ambiguous sexual nature of the characters with a highly sophisticated, ethereal touch.

He was spending very long hours working and experimenting, and his eyes were beginning to weaken under the strain. At Tina Fredericks' urging, he went to an optometrist and got himself a pair of glasses with very thick lenses, which he wore conscientiously. Now he was filling his sketchbooks with drawings of his roommates and the apartment cat. He also did a number of large paintings on canvas, which have since been destroyed. One of them prefigured his later celebrated "death-and-disaster" paintings. Based on an old *Life* magazine photograph by H. S. Wong of a screaming baby who had been abandoned in the ruins of Shanghai after a 1937 Japanese bombing attack, the painting was horrific yet surprisingly decorative, executed with the blotted-line technique and pastel colors. The *Life* caption stating that up to 136 million people had seen the photograph reproduced in various media had undoubtedly caught Andy's attention as much as the shocking image itself. Nonetheless, it may have touched a nerve he did not want to expose, expressing too much his own feelings of vulnerability, for he quickly abandoned the subject in favor of more decorative images such as chubby cherubs and butterflies. With images of acrobats and trapeze artists he filled a ten-foot mural on the walls of Elaine Baumann's bedroom in her parents' apartment (later painted over).

With the building on Manhattan Avenue slated for demolition in the fall of 1950, the group broke up. Andy moved in with another former Tech classmate, the painter Joseph Groell, who had an apartment on East Twenty-fourth Street. When Groell returned to Pittsburgh for several months that winter, Andy found himself living alone for the first time in his life.

By the beginning of 1951, he had added to his credits a series of book-jacket illustrations for the publishing firm New Directions. And he had made his first television "appearances": *Art Director and Studio News*, in a showcase article entitled "Andy: Upcoming Artist," reported that his right hand was being shown on NBC's morning news programs, drawing the weather map.

He had also produced a provocative drawing of a young sailor on his knees injecting heroin into his arm, which was published as a full-page advertisement in the *New York Times* on September 13, 1951, for a radio program about crime called "The Nation's Nightmare." This ad, for which he earned more than he had ever been paid before, gained him a great deal of attention. It was reproduced as an album cover for a recording of the program and eventually, in 1953, won him his first Art Directors' Club gold medal, the Oscar of the advertising industry. The "Nation's Nightmare" drawing, though atypical for him, was in keeping with the sensationalism of much illustration in the early 1950s. As Vance Packard had noted in his best-seller *The Hidden Persuaders*, advertising had begun to play on the darker side of human psychology, combining sex with violence, status-seeking with loneliness. Such influences would not fully come to light until Warhol completed his best-known pop paintings in the sixties.

Andy's next major assignment was to illustrate Amy Vanderbilt's *Complete Book of Etiquette*. He was making enough money now to afford a new Brooks Brothers suit and trenchcoat, which he wore to go out in the evenings, while assiduously maintaining his poor-boy image for art directors. According to several of Andy's old Pittsburgh friends, who were becoming increasingly critical of him as he became successful, he would sometimes charge ridiculously low prices for his drawings if a magazine would, in exchange, include a brief biographical sketch of him.

He was also beginning to experience what he would refer to for the rest of his life as "boy problems." Although he seems never to have spoken very directly about the subject of homosexuality with any of his friends—it was always characteristic of him to draw out the details of their personal lives rather than confiding anything about his own—his difficulty in getting romantically involved was obvious to friends like Klauber, who were relatively open about their gayness. For all Klauber's bravado, being gay in America in the 1950s was not only illegal but dangerous. It was the heyday of Joseph McCarthy, whose Senate subcommittee had named as "national security threats" not only suspected communists but "homosexuals and other sex perverts," and the threat of being beaten up on the street or shaken down by the police was felt by the entire gay community.

Soon Andy was frequenting New York's "lavender" social world, which could only flourish underground. Again, George Klauber was his guide. Klauber was familiar not only with the distinctly homosexual enclaves, stylish bars like Regents Row, but also, and more important, with the salons of interior decorators and set designers at which Andy, having persistently begged Klauber to take him along, was a frequent guest. According to one veteran of that milieu: "There was still all this hate and fear of the underground, but being underground wasn't tense or fearful, it was quite relaxed. There were a lot of people in that scene and there were lots and lots of parties. It was extremely outgoing and, as long as you didn't disturb the straight world, completely nice."

From all accounts, the glamour of this secret world was of far greater appeal to Warhol than any opportunity it provided for sexual liaisons. In this respect he was still extremely tentative. Like many gay men of the time, Andy feared that he was sick, emotionally stunted—that, after all, was what the psychiatrists said—and he imagined that "normal," heterosexual people were "happier" than he. Moreover, he was acutely sensitive about his physical appearance. His hair was thinning rapidly, his skin would still erupt in blotches when he was nervous, and his new thick-lensed glasses, with only a tiny area to focus through, made him feel even odder than before.

Not that everyone shared this view of him. One friend recalled, "I always thought of him as a rather good-looking chap and I don't know why people made fun of the way he looked." George Klauber found him attractive enough to fantasize having an affair. Andy did not reciprocate his advances, and Klauber "got the feeling he was inaccessible, untouchable." ("Kiss me with your eyes" was one of his pet expressions.) It seemed to Klauber that Andy limited his romantic life to crushes on attractive but unavailable young men. One friend of the time observed: "He more or less expected to be rejected by the beautiful boys he was always falling for. His attitude was, 'Aren't they beautiful creatures?' He just wanted to look at them, to be around them, to admire them. It wasn't that he wanted to get into bed with them. He was much too self-conscious for that. He was watching a beauty pageant."

Still at the top of Andy's list of beauties was Truman Capote. During his first year in New York, he had written Capote fan letters almost daily, announcing that he was in town and asking if he might draw Truman's portrait.

Capote later told Jean Stein, the author of *Edie: An American Biography*, "I never answer fan letters. But not answering these Warhol letters didn't seem to faze him at all. I became Andy's Shirley Temple. After a while I began getting letters from him every day! Until I became terrifically conscious of this person. Also he began sending along these drawings. They certainly weren't like his later things. They were rather literal illustrations from stories of mine . . . at least, that's what they were *supposed* to be. Not only that, but apparently Andy Warhol used to stand outside the building where I lived and hang around waiting to see me come in or go out of the building."

Months later Andy screwed up his nerve and called Capote about the drawings. He got Nina Capote, the author's mother, on the line, and she invited him up to her Park Avenue apartment. Andy quickly realized that Mrs. Capote was more interested in acquiring a drinking companion than in looking at his work. They repaired to the Blarney Stone, a bar on Third Avenue, where they drank boilermakers and Nina talked at length about Truman's problems and what a disappointment he had been to her. By the time they returned to her apartment, Nina Capote was drunk and listening intently to all of Andy's problems. This is how Truman found them when he entered the apartment later that afternoon. Not wishing to be unkind, he sat down and listened to Andy's story, which he found woeful. "He seemed one of those hopeless people that you just know *nothing's* ever going to happen to," Capote recalled in *Edie*. "Just a hopeless, born loser, the loneliest, most friendless person I'd ever seen in my life." Yet, after the visit, when Andy telephoned daily, Truman took the calls, which would center on Andy's activities. This relationship soon ended when Capote's mother answered the phone and told him, "Stop bothering Truman!"

"Like all alcoholics, she had Jekyll-and-Hyde qualities," Capote said, "and although she was basically a sympathetic person and thought he was very sweet, she lit into him." Surprised and upset, but long accustomed to obeying his own mother's instructions, Andy stopped writing and calling.

Warhol would speak animatedly to friends about other, equally unattainable mad crushes—on the dancers John Butler and Jacques D'Amboise, the photographer Bob Allyson, and a succession of anonymous beauties. He claimed, to the disbelief of his listeners, that someone had given him a "sore bum" by "fucking the ass off" him the previous night. Even in the Manhattan Avenue apartment, his strange private life had been characterized by a detached, voyeuristic interest in sex, and he began painting nude figures of men and coy, stylized drawings of genitalia, which he said he was assembling into a "*Cock Book.*" Sometimes he asked if he could draw his friends' feet. Andy was a classic foot fetishist and had what many of his friends found to be a creepily erotic relationship with his own shoes, which he would always wear scrunched down at the back and falling apart, with holes in the soles and his toes sometimes sticking out at the front. Later, when he did begin to have sexual relations, he found the ritual of kissing his lover's shoes particularly erotic. A surprisingly large number of people are said to have acquiesced to his requests, and he did hundreds of cock and foot drawings, the latter to be included in a "*Foot Book.*"

One of those who posed for him regularly was Robert Fleischer. Fleischer, who, with his bushy red mustache, struck an elegant figure, was a stationery buyer at Bergdorf Goodman and a part-time model. He had first been introduced to Warhol by Elaine Baumann at the Manhattan Avenue apartment. Later, Fleischer had commissioned Andy to do a stationery design, a job that had proven frustrating since Andy seemed incapable of accurately aligning the acetate sheets that separated each color. This later became a Warhol trademark, but then it was an annoyance that had to be corrected at the printer's. Nevertheless, the two men had become friends.

At first Fleischer, like so many others who knew Andy, felt "a tremendous sense of protecting this poor innocent waif who was going to get strangled in the big city." But soon he came to believe that Andy was using his "helplessness" to manipulate people, particularly after Andy began drawing a series of increasingly explicit portraits of Fleischer and his lover, which seemed to be testing what he could get away with as well as the limits of their friendship. "Andy sketched us screwing a couple of times," Fleischer told the art historian Patrick Smith. "Andy would get very excited. He wouldn't quite join in, but he loved watching. He would very often like to draw me nude and see me with an erection, but he never actually touched me, and I think that I never really put myself in a position of letting him, or leading him to think that I was interested physically, because I wasn't. At one time he said that he got so hot when he saw men with erections that he couldn't have an orgasm himself. But he started to strip that day. Wasn't it all right if he sketched in his jockey shorts? And he did."

In his own way Andy was opening up. While part of his image at Tech had been his delight in shocking classmates, it was nothing compared to the behavior he displayed at a party back in Pittsburgh at Balcomb Greene's. "There were a bunch of students there," Perry Davis recalled, "and he came in and said, 'Okay, everybody take off their clothes, I brought my sketchbook.'" Robert Fleischer told Patrick Smith that when the Manhattan Avenue apartment had been breaking up, Elaine Baumann's parents gave a Halloween party, which Andy was expected to attend with several other roommates. "It got later and later and all of a sudden at midnight—they had obviously done this on purpose to make an entrance—they rang the bell, and in they walked, hand in hand, and around each of their necks was a big cut-out daisy, and they were carrying garlands, as they do in high school graduations. They came in as a daisy chain, and that's what they used to call orgies in those days. The whole place fell apart hysterical." To Fleischer, however, their laughter was humiliating. It may have been Andy's idea of a joke, but he felt exposed.

It was while he was living alone that Andy developed his lifelong dependency on the telephone, which he would later call his best friend. It became not only his lifeline to art directors and money but a magical machine that enabled him to have more intimate conversations than he could manage in person. Since he was frightened of going to sleep alone but was not able to sleep with anyone else, it was also the perfect companion for him in bed. Klauber, who was "going madly crazy" for a young man that winter, grew to expect the regular late-night phone call from Andy to ask about the evening's activities. "This was Andy's big vicarious connection. The kid would leave about two o'clock in the morning, at which point I'd speak to Andy about what happened. He had to know all the details, and, naturally, I told him. Hearing stories is what made him happy: 'Tell me more, tell me more.' Then I introduced him to my second great love, Ralph Thomas [Corkie] Ward, and I think Andy fell in love with Corkie."

A tall, freewheeling poet and artist with curly brown hair, Ward was something of a romantic ideal to his friends, but it wasn't until Christmas of 1951 that Klauber noticed Andy's interest in him. On Christmas Eve the three of them, along with a young man named Charles, had gone to see a French film. Afterwards they had picked up a Christmas tree and taken it back to Klauber's apartment, where they celebrated the season by dancing around the living room. Klauber recalled the scene vividly: "I had taken my trousers off, and Ralph and I were waltzing wildly around and crashed into a table, and when I got up I had this big gash in my side. So we called for an ambulance, which meant the police would come too. Andy got quite sick with apprehension and flew the scene. He was really terrified. Of course to the cops it was apparently a gay party, and they thought somebody had stabbed me."

Whereas he had previously been content to indulge himself in voyeuristic games, Andy became more forward with Ward. In the weeks that followed he wrote him a number of love letters, but his overtures were rejected. A close enough friendship did develop, however, to make others wonder if they were lovers, even though they were not. It was Klauber who now felt left out.

Early in the spring of 1952, Ward and Warhol began collaborating on a series of privately printed books. It was the first of many times he would keep a romance going by collaborating on some work. The first, *A Is an Alphabet*, consisted of twenty-six Warhol drawings, outlines of heads and bodies with doggerel captions by Corkie. *Love Is a Pink Cake* was a bit more interesting, consisting of twelve Warhol illustrations of famous love stories with accompanying verses by Ward, such as, "The moor of Venice pulled a boner, when he throttled Desdemona." The third book, *there was snow in the street*, with blotted-line drawings mostly of children, remained unprinted for years. The underlying whimsy of these books was delightful, and they made excellent promotional gimmicks to send to art directors and Andy's other clients. "The nature of Andy's promotion was so personal that it really had an influence in making him known," Klauber recalled. "People began collecting [the books]. If you went into an ad agency you would often see an Andy Warhol thing on display."

Whatever intimacy existed between Andy and Ward ceased during the following year. As Ward discovered, maintaining a close friendship with Andy was difficult because he was so easily hurt. Moreover, Ralph also tended to look down on Andy's devotion to work—and reward—which was all-consuming. "Andy," said Ward, "did everything for money."

4

THE RELATIONSHIP WITH Corkie Ward coincided with Andy's move in the fall of 1952 into his own apartment, a dirty, mouse- and louse-ridden cold-water basement flat in a building under the tracks of the since-demolished Third Avenue elevated train on East Seventy-fifth Street. Soon his mother and brother Paul arrived for a visit. After cleaning the apartment and cooking a big meal, Julia did Andy's laundry and questioned him about his finances. He had never had to fend for himself before, and she was understandably worried that he wouldn't be able to take care of himself. She found all his clothes dirty and in need of mending, and realized that he was subsisting largely on candy and cake. During the fourteen-hour drive back to Pittsburgh, Julia recited her litany of fears and prayers for her youngest son.

In Pittsburgh, Paul was just beginning to be successful in the scrap-metal business, and Julia was considering moving with John to a house in the suburb of Clairton, where Paul lived. Paul recalled: "We bought her a house out there. Then my brother John decided that he was getting married. So Mother felt that there was no need for her to come out to a big house. She says, 'Well, the only thing that I can see, I guess, is I'd like to be with Andy in New York.'"

In the early spring of 1952, Julia rode to New York with her son John in his ice-cream van. "Andy had a hole in the sole of his shoe as big as a silver dollar," recalled John, "so I left him my best pair of shoes."

The Dawson Street house was put up for sale and was sold a few months later for $6,800. Julia put the money in the bank (and held on to it until her death). John took his father's memorabilia, and Andy's schoolbooks and student artworks were carted out to Paul's. "I asked what I was supposed to do with these things," Paul recalled. "Andy told me, 'Just discard 'em. Just pitch 'em.'" On further consideration, Paul decided not to throw away ten paintings done on Masonite board. "I stuck 'em in the rafters and never figured much on 'em." His children would later use them as dart boards. (Like his father, Paul believed that his younger brother would be famous one day and the paintings would be worth a lot of money. At the same time, he viewed Andy's work with some indifference. Never once, for example, did he attend one of his shows.)

In early summer Paul again drove his mother to New York, this time to stay. He was not happy about leaving Julia to live in Andy's "terrible place," but he could see that they needed each other. The first months on East Seventy-fifth Street were hard. Andy's income was still irregular, and he invested as little as possible in his living quarters. Like his father, he was intent on saving money, and he was not going to squander any of it on what most people considered basic necessities. On his last visit John had accompanied Andy to a printer to pick up one of his promotional books and was struck by Andy's similarity to their father: "He told the printer, 'This isn't what I told you to do.' And the printer says, 'Well, I thought you wanted it this way.' Andy says, 'Well, no, you didn't listen to me.' The way Andy stood up to him just reminded me of my father. So when we left I told Andy, 'Well, aren't you going to pay him?' 'No,' he says. 'He didn't do what I wanted.' My father was that way. Even though he wasn't built like Dad, Andy was tough."

Mother and son shared the bedroom, sleeping on mattresses on the floor, while Andy used the kitchen table as a studio. The bathtub was usually full of paper he was marbling, leading friends to believe that he rarely used the tub for bathing. He had bought a Siamese cat to keep the mice at bay, and a second Siamese was soon adopted. Before long the two, Hester and Sam, began multiplying.

Andy was clearly concerned about his mother's presence in New York just as he was starting to enjoy success, although George Klauber remembered that he was "very gentle with her, very nice about it." At first he did not think she would stay long, certain that she would miss her large, loving family and her church and priest in Pittsburgh. It soon became clear, however, that she wanted to dedicate her life to supporting his efforts.

Most of Andy's friends were kept at a distance from Seventy-fifth Street. A part of him was ashamed of his mother in her peasant dress and babushka, her persistence in speaking *po nasemu,* her nagging him for not dressing properly and not getting married. A steady refrain was that she was only there until he found a "nice girl and settled down." Nonetheless, it became increasingly clear to Andy's friends that the two of them were made for each other. "Julia was the source of the tenacity and gentleness and down-to-earth resilience, which were at the core of Andy's character," commented the art historian John Richardson. "Narrow and uneducated she may have been, but Julia struck those who met her as humorous, mischievous, and shrewd—like him." Underneath her naive peasant exterior Julia was the only person in Andy's life as manipulative and powerful as he. Indeed, by the end of the decade their personalities would become so intertwined that Julia would claim, in more than one bitter tirade, that *she* was Andy Warhol.

Still, for the time being Julia's arrival on the scene was more positive than negative. She was good company and she knew how to make Andy laugh. With his mother to take care of him and run the household, Andy was free to focus completely on his work. Furthermore, ever canny in the development of his legend, Andy promoted her presence as much as he kept her hidden. When the fashion crowd heard that the strange, fey, talented boy lived with his mother, they became even more amused and fascinated.

In March 1952, Andy achieved another of his goals: to publish in *Park East,* a magazine about the rich and celebrated denizens of the Upper East Side of Manhattan. Moreover, he had taken his first tentative steps toward acceptance as a fine artist when he showed his illustrations of Truman Capote's writings to Alexandre Iolas, a dealer in surrealist art, at his Hugo Gallery. David Mann, Iolas' assistant and part of George Klauber's smart set, recalled that Iolas' initial response was uncharacteristically enthusiastic: "Andy came in looking like a poor boy with a pimply face and very ordinary clothes. It was the end of the season—it was almost June—but Iolas said to me, 'Look at this man's work!' We both thought it was amazing, and he said, 'Well, we have nothing else to do. Why don't we just take on another show in June?' " Unfortunately, Iolas himself was in Europe along with almost everyone else of importance in the art world when Andy Warhol's first gallery opening took place on the afternoon of June 16, 1952.

Of Andy's close friends, only Klauber came. All evening long, Andy paced the gallery nervously, upset that Truman Capote had yet to arrive. Julia came to the opening and hovered in the background in her coat and babushka, making Andy even more nervous—the first and last time she appeared at one of his public events. Among the other visitors to the gallery that day was a young commercial artist named Nathan Gluck, who, a few years later, would become Andy's assistant. Days later, just before the show closed, Truman and Nina Capote did come to see it. According to David Mann, Mrs. Capote was particularly enthusiastic about the drawings, and Andy was thrilled.

Art Digest gave these drawings of boys, butterflies, and cupids a brief review: "For various reasons one thinks of Beardsley, Lautrec, Demuth, Balthus, and Cocteau. The work has an air of precocity, of carefully studied perversity." But for the most part, *15 Drawings Based on the Writings of Truman Capote* was not taken seriously, except by Andy's friends and those few others who admired his talents as a draftsman. Nor did any of the pieces, priced around three hundred dollars, sell. Nonetheless, Andy had made an invaluable connection in David Mann, his first champion in the world of serious art.

Andy's commercial career turned a corner in the spring of 1953. Wearing his scrunched-down shoes, his chinos, and a paint-spattered T-shirt under a sloppy jacket, he was visiting the office of Klauber's boss, Will Burton, to give the art director a hand-painted Easter egg, when Burton introduced him to an energetic, intelligent woman named Fritzie Miller, who had just become an agent for commercial artists. "Andy," Burton said, "meet Fritzie. You need her."

"Fritzie Miller's help in getting Andy's work into *McCall's* and the *Ladies' Home Journal* and later into *Vogue* and *Harper's Bazaar* was key in establishing Warhol as the most sought-after illustrator of women's accessories in New York," wrote Calvin Tomkins in a 1970 profile of Warhol. "It was amazing, Fritzie thought, how someone with Andy's background could hit the right note so unerringly. The childish hearts and flowers and the androgynous pink cherubs he used were not quite what they seemed to be—there was a slight suggestiveness about them that people in the business recognized and approved. He could kid the product so subtly that he made the client feel witty." In the next six months his earnings from illustration work would nearly double his income that year to over twenty-five thousand dollars. Warhol, at twenty-five, despite all outward appearances, was doing well enough to have confounded the early expectations of his friends. The driving ambition behind his hapless "Raggedy Andy" facade was now fully apparent.

As soon as he began to make money, it became clear that he was to have what one friend described as an "unhealthy" relationship with it: He either wildly overspent or underspent. He seemed oblivious to his need for new clothes and furnishings for the apartment. Yet he would go regularly to the Plaza Hotel for breakfast (afterwards sitting outside the Palm Court, hoping to be mistaken for Truman Capote). He'd become a regular at the Café Nicholson, an expensive restaurant celebrated in *Park East* as a gathering place for young writers, dancers, and designers. Andy was a favored customer because he always tipped lavishly and left the waiters a cluster of Hershey's chocolate kisses. A daily excursion was a visit to the most expensive pastry shops, where he might buy a whole birthday cake for himself, to be devoured the moment he got home. Such expenditures were a great annoyance to Julia, who began to treat him as she had her husband, nagging him to contribute some of his earnings to their family in Pittsburgh.

These extravagances were in marked contrast to the marginal life Andy and Julia were living beneath the rumbling El. Whether because he was momentarily short of cash or embarrassed to be seen with her anywhere else, he took Julia to a Woolworth's lunch counter for their first Thanksgiving dinner in New York. ("It would make him incredibly sad," recalled Pat Hackett, Andy's secretary in the 1970s and 1980s, to dredge up this memory from the winter of 1952.) For all the strength she brought him, Julia's presence was also a constant reminder of Andy's less than affluent childhood.

In the summer of 1953 Andy sublet a fourth-floor walk-up at 242 Lexington Avenue, near the corner of Twenty-fourth Street, from his Tech classmate Leonard Kessler, with the proviso that for several months Kessler be allowed to keep one of the smaller rooms as a studio for his work as a children's book illustrator. George Klauber, who had a car, was recruited to help Andy move. He arrived to find Andy sitting helplessly at East Seventy-fifth Street, totally unprepared. It was left to George, as he recalls it, to "help him pack all his boxes, *and* carry them out to the car."

The new apartment was larger than its predecessor. The door opened into a big kitchen that Andy furnished with a table and a set of straight-backed chairs and decorated with a picture of Jesus pointing to his Sacred Heart. There was a large room in front overlooking the busy street and a smaller one off to the side. In the back was one big room and a small bedroom. While Kessler kept the small front room as his studio, Andy and Julia shared the little back bedroom, still sleeping on mattresses on the floor. The rest of the place quickly filled with stacks of paper, magazines, photographs, and art supplies until every surface was covered, and Andy was confined to doing his work at a portable desk on his lap. The shoes, gloves, scarves, hats, handbags, belts, and jewelry he was assigned to draw added to the clutter. One day when Kessler was helping to shift some piles around, he turned up a check for seven hundred dollars that someone had sent Andy months earlier but which had got overlooked.

The cat population, meanwhile, multiplied to anywhere from eight to twenty, depending on how quickly Andy could give them away. Most of his friends received at least one Warhol kitten, a number of which turned out to be unusually skittish and vicious. One day, one of the cats bit Julia's hand so badly that she had to go to the hospital. The cats roamed through the paper jungle, clawing and urinating on Andy's materials, storming through the unruly heaps of artwork in fits of feline mania. Julia was forever cleaning up after them with a bucket and mop. The television set was on continually, as often as not accompanied by Broadway show tunes on the record player. One friend noted that being in the apartment without knocking anything over or tripping was like walking on a tightrope. Other friends described the place as a "bat cave." To Klauber the cats appeared to be Andy's "surrogate children." They became part of his legend: Andy was living in a mad studio with his mother and twenty-one cats. The smell, people added, was indescribable.

The apartment was situated over a night club, Shirley's Pin-Up Bar, and the booming beat of "You're So Adorable" floated up through the front windows, along with the thunder of the Lexington Avenue subway. For the first time in his life Andy, who could now think of himself as a New Yorker, was in his element.

That summer both of Andy's brothers visited him, now that there was enough room for them and their children to camp out in the apartment. His mother always enjoyed their visits, and the children seemed to have fun playing with Uncle Andy, who supplied them with crayons so they wouldn't bother him and always gave each of them a present when they arrived.

Visitors generally became more frequent, although they could seldom find a place to sit among the piles of paper and the cats. Regardless of who was there, Andy would continue working on the next day's assignments. The only time he wasn't working, apparently, was when, on impulse, he would go to the Café Nicholson or the theater, paying for dinners and tickets with crumpled bills extracted from various pockets and even out of his shoes. He'd suddenly get a whim to see the most successful show on Broadway, often ending up with a friend in the most expensive seats in the front row. He also revived his interest in dance, now that he could afford tickets to see Paul Taylor, John Butler, and Martha Graham.

Julia, with her folksy manner, muddled English, and ready laughter, became a favorite among his friends as she sewed, cooked, and, on occasion, colored in Andy's drawings. "I got to know Julia quite well," Leonard Kessler recalled. "She used to make kapushta, which is cabbage with short ribs of beef. It's marvelous if you live in Alaska or the Yukon. On the hottest day of the summer she'd say, 'Kapushta will keep you warm.' 'Mrs. Warhola,' I'd say, 'I am warm.' 'You can be warmer,' she would reply."

George Klauber was a regular guest for kapushta. "Dinner was just an eating thing," he said. "Andy was always impatient to be going somewhere afterward. His mother was not much interested in conversation. She was lonely. The thing is, he didn't know what to do with her."

Other friends who visited the Lexington Avenue apartment were fascinated by the relationship between the two of them, particularly by their antagonistic moments, during which Julia would "sit on" her eccentric son. One constant subject of contention was Andy's way of dressing. He was beginning to "dress up," but in his own way. "He often bought expensive shoes," one visitor recalled, "but before wearing them, he would spill paint on them, soak them in water, let the cats pee on them. When the patina was just right, he'd wear them. He wanted to appear shabby, like a prince who could afford expensive shoes but couldn't care less and treated them as worthless." Often he would leave his shoes untied. Nor did he seem to know how to knot a tie: "When he couldn't make the ends match up," a friend recalled, "he just cut them off. Eventually he had a whole box of tie ends. This drove his mother crazy. As he was going out of the house, she'd be going after him about why he didn't meet a nice girl and get married, etc. She herself hardly ever went out except to go to the A&P."

For his part, Andy would cringe with embarrassment and whine, "Oh, Ma! Leave me alone, Ma!"

Overall, however, it was apparent that Julia was overjoyed to be with her son. "I like New York," she would bubble. "People nice. I have my church, nice big church on Fifteenth Street and Second Avenue. And the air . . . air better than in Pennsylvania."

Andy's life had taken on a fairly regular pattern. He would get up around nine, and his mother would make him breakfast. Then he would work briefly, put on his "Raggedy Andy" costume, and leave the house by taxi, heading for a magazine or ad agency. He would later write: "It was like being a laboratory rat and they put you through all these tests and you get rewarded when you do it right, and when you do it wrong you're kicked back. Somebody would give me an appointment at ten o'clock, so I'd beat my brains out to get there at exactly ten, and I would get there and they wouldn't see me until five minutes to one. So when you go through this a hundred times and you hear, 'Ten o'clock?' you say, 'Weeeellll, that sounds funny, I think I'll show up at five minutes to one.' So I used to show up at five minutes to one and it always worked."

After seeing the art director, he might have a business lunch at an expensive East Side restaurant. After lunch he would go to another office to pick up materials for an assignment. Late in the afternoon he usually dropped by a new favorite hot spot, Serendipity, for coffee and pastries. Situated in a basement on East Fifty-eighth Street, Serendipity dispensed ice cream, cakes, and coffee, along with fashionable knickknacks, in a tasteful, all-white setting. It was a mecca for celebrities such as Gloria Vanderbilt and Truman Capote. The proprietors, Steven Bruce, Calvin Holt, and Patch Harrington, formed an impression of Andy as somebody special and spirited with the sad, forlorn manner of a poor relative visiting from out of town. Before leaving, he would usually buy pastries to take home, stopping on the way to buy a book, a record, or magazines.

During the evening he was frequently invited out to parties or would go to the opera, ballet, or theater with friends. After the evening's entertainment, he would usually work for a few hours before going to bed around three or four in the morning. Into this setting he brought a new friend who would briefly become his first real lover.

Alfred Carlton Willers met Andy in 1953 in the photo collection of the New York Public Library, where Warhol frequently went to look for source material for his illustrations. Andy would take home a number of photographs at a time. He would trace a face from one, part of a chair from another, the head of a cat from a third, then apply the blotted-line technique to the composition, and presto! an original drawing whose sources were unrecognizable. (The most important thing, he liked to say, was what he left out.) To make sure no one could detect his sources, he would hold on to the photographs long after they were overdue, paying large fines rather than returning them. This way he soon built up a sizable resource bank of photographs. Willers, who had learned typing and shorthand in the air force, was working as a secretary to the collection's curator while waiting to begin an art history course at Columbia University.

Carl, as he called himself (Andy teased him by calling him Alfred), was twenty years old, a native of Iowa, whose boyish good looks were accentuated by a thatch of blond hair so long some friends jokingly nicknamed him "Palm Tree." It was his first year in New York, and he was, perhaps, more innocent than he cared to admit.

That fall he became a frequent visitor to the Lexington Avenue apartment and one of Andy's companions for dinners at the Nicholson and for spur-of-the-moment theater outings. Julia appeared to be delighted that Andy had found a close friend and treated him as if he were another son. Carl was amazed by the Warhol household: Andy, Julia, and the cats, who all seemed to have emerged from a European folk tale, were a distinctly different reality from the impression Willers had initially formed of his new friend. Typically, Andy had tried at first to obscure the details of his private life by telling "Alfred" that he came from Hawaii. (Marlon Brando reportedly did the same thing, making up different stories about his background. One need often look no further than Hollywood stars for clues to Andy's conduct, since he was constantly appropriating aspects of their behavior.)

In the evenings Carl began helping Andy color in drawings; often he served as a hand or foot model. Frequently they went out. Willers recalled: "In the fifties, there just seemed to be a party every night. He had many friends who had plenty of money and who would give these wonderful parties. I think Andy liked parties because he didn't have to be trapped. If he wanted to leave, he could. If he really didn't want to go somewhere, which happened often, he could be very adamant about it. When someone else came up with an idea—'Andy, let's suddenly go here!'—he would say, 'No, no, no, no,' often because he was afraid he would be shy in a strange place." Sometimes, if it got late, Carl would stay over, sleeping on a couch in the front room while Andy worked through the night.

The Andy Warhol Willers knew "used his shyness like a little boy, but it was a really playful thing, it was very obvious. He really felt people should be playing, but he wasn't at all boisterous. He was in fact rather quiet." At the Nicholson, their dinner conversations were superficial, never emotional or intellectual. Andy was amused by any tidbit of gossip, and he would laugh about something he'd seen on television while blissfully devouring his third chocolate soufflé, after which he would become remorseful. "He had a great deal of guilt about all this eating of sweet things," said Willers, "because he thought that was making him fat and causing these skin eruptions.

He thought he was totally unattractive—too short, too pudgy. He thought he was grotesque."

Andy's increasing baldness was also a source of particular distress. At the time Willers met him, Andy had little hair on top of his head and had begun wearing a cap with a snap-down brim even to dinner parties, a practice Willers considered uncouth. "Andy, this is insane," he would tell him. "People think it's either phony or rude. Why don't you buy a wig?" Finally, Andy bought a light-brown toupee, the first of several hundred hairpieces he would accumulate—brown, blond, white, silver, gray. Years later in his *Philosophy* Andy explained, somewhat satirically, his decision to "go gray":

> I decided to go gray so nobody would know how old I was and I would look younger to them than how old they thought I was. I would gain a lot by going gray: (1) I would have old problems, which were easier to take than young problems, (2) everyone would be impressed by how young I looked, and (3) I would be relieved of the responsibility of acting young—I could occasionally lapse into eccentricity or senility and no one would think anything of it because of my gray hair. When you've got gray hair, every move you make seems "young" and "spry," instead of just being normally active. It's like you're getting a new talent.

It was apparent to Willers that Andy was attracted to him but found it very difficult to act on his feelings, especially around Julia. Even when Andy thought he had locked her in her bedroom for the night, she would suddenly emerge, grinning and laughing, with a bucket and mop. Sometimes she would stagger, appearing to be slightly drunk and giggling over some private thought. At other times she would curl up under a pile of drawings on a chair and fall asleep, only to spring out from underneath them in the middle of the night and lurch into the bedroom. In her loneliness she was beginning to develop the same kind of drinking problem her sister Mary had, and which had gotten her sister Anna labeled the black sheep of the family. Perhaps a part of Andy delighted in this. He seems to have been what is called in Alcoholics Anonymous a "para-alcoholic," a person who thrives on relationships with alcoholics, enjoying their behavior while acting as if he were trying to get them to stop drinking.

Although Carl was sure that Julia thought that he was only helping her son and suspected nothing more between them, she was also
an inhibiting force. One night, as Carl casually bent over to kiss him
good night, Andy brushed him away and silently motioned for Carl
to follow him to the other room. He was concerned that his mother
might emerge from the bedroom and catch them in an embrace.
Safe from her eyes, Andy was finally able to kiss him good night. On
another occasion, when one of Andy's friends asked Julia if she had
slept well the night before, she replied, quite seriously, "Oh, no! I
stayed up all night watching Andy sleep." (Ten years later Andy
would make a film called *Sleep* about staying up all night to watch his
boyfriend sleep.)

It was in his art that his intimacy with Willers was best expressed.
He began a series of portraits of Carl, at one point impressing him
with the seriousness of his intentions by stopping work on his illustrations for several days and clearing a space in the apartment to
concentrate on five large canvases of Willers posing naked. He drew
him lying on his back and leaning on his side facing forward. One
finished canvas depicted not one man but two men as lovers.

Around this time Andy and Carl consummated a brief, nervous
affair. "I think Andy's sex life is a truly complex subject," Willers
remarked years later. "When I knew him, he was already celibate,
for all intents and purposes, except that if somebody pushed him a
little bit, or said, 'Come on, Andy, let's get in the sack,' he would,
maybe . . . *maybe*. But if he could barely get into bed with someone
like me, whom he knew probably as well as he did anyone at that
particular point, I can't imagine who else he could ever have
managed with. He was so incredibly self-conscious, he really had
such a low opinion of his own looks." (In this area of her son's
development, Julia was no help. Whenever she was threatened by
his interest in somebody else, she would fix him with a hard look and
tell him, so there could be no mistaking the message, the story of a
Ruthenian peasant whose beautiful wife only married him for his
money.)

Andy's sole comment on the affair with Carl came years later
when he said that he was twenty-five when he had his first sexual
experience and twenty-six when he stopped.

Like Corkie Ward, Willers came to the conclusion that for Andy,
work was more important than sex, and that he was not interested in

getting physically involved with anyone. They would remain close friends for the next ten years, although unbeknownst to Carl, Andy destroyed all the portraits he had made of him.

In the fall of 1953, George Klauber recruited Warhol, along with three other Tech classmates, Art and Lois Elias and Imelda Vaughn, to join a play-reading group in an apartment on West Twelfth Street. Andy's first appearance with the Theater 12 Group is remembered vividly by the apartment's tenant, Bert Greene: "The first play we worked on was Congreve's *The Way of the World,* and Andy couldn't even read the words. He was really having difficulty. Finally, we stopped and I said, 'Andy, do you want to read the scene over?' And he said, 'No, no, I'll stumble through.' I thought he'd never come back, because it was a big public embarrassment to not be able to read in front of all these other people, but he wasn't abashed at all."

For the next six months Andy attended rehearsals and designed programs and sets. Often he came with Imelda Vaughn, a charmingly eccentric woman who had been a friend of his at Tech. "She seemed to be Andy's lodestone when he started becoming a little off the wall," recalled Greene.

Warhol was an anomaly in the group, looking like a slightly gaga preppie, with his granny glasses, his weirdly knotted ties, and the ballet slippers he now wore. "When he liked people's performances," said Greene, "he would give them presents. Once he gave someone a walnut with a tiny doll inside. Or he would give you little drawings with messages on them like, 'I'm happy to be here tonight.' His spelling was atrocious, but it was endearing and he was ingenious. He was a great admirer of physical beauty and was never abashed about it. When there was a handsome man, or even a beautiful woman, in the group, Andy would be riveted to them and instantly make them gifts."

Greene could also see that Andy was soaking up as much culture as he could. He was introduced to the idea of Bertolt Brecht by another member of the group, Harold Fine, whose explication of the German playwright's "alienation effects" undoubtedly influenced Andy's "passive" aesthetic. In time, Andy's thespian skills also improved considerably. Greene was impressed by his portrayal of the old servant, Firs, in Chekhov's play *The Cherry Orchard.* As Andy read the line "Life has passed me by as though I had never lived," Greene felt that he was expressing what was perhaps a real inner melancholy. Andy was, he thought, still trying to learn "how to live."

By now the old Tech group was breaking up. Leonard Kessler had decided to move to Long Island, leaving the Lexington Avenue apartment to Andy. Leila Davies was giving up her jewelry business and returning to Cleveland. With others from his old crowd, she shared a sense of pleasure at how far Andy had come. (Elias was struggling, and Pearlstein, who had yet to make his mark, had begun supplementing his income as a magazine paste-up man by giving private painting lessons.) But they all worried that Andy was making a mistake by neglecting his talent as a fine artist.

Strong currents were pulling Andy in conflicting directions. As the art critic Hilton Als wrote in an analysis of Warhol's career in the 1950s, by juxtaposing fragility of line with a strong sexual subtext (mostly in his images of boys), Andy was satirizing the common ad-world concept of the "weird" boy window dresser or illustrator, producing the images they would expect from such a creature but also getting away with more than they realized. "Not only were his various assignments pleasing to the eye and therefore bought, but he made a style out of his sissy preoccupations with butterflies and ladies' shoes and boys," Als wrote. "The style was made powerful through its reproduction in magazines and in books. It became a taste. That was Warhol's difference." And in that difference there was a trap.

In 1954 Andy showed three times at the Loft Gallery on East Forty-fifth Street, which was run by the well-known graphic artist Jack Wolfgang Beck and his assistant Vito Giallo. Andy, who had been introduced to Beck and Giallo by Nathan Gluck, was included in the group show in April. The painter and influential critic Fairfield Porter came to the opening and later wrote a scathing put-down, saying that they were all commercial artists trying to be fine artists and branding the Loft a commercial-art gallery.

Andy appeared unwilling to engage in the conflict between commercial and fine art, acting as if he thought the whole subject beyond him. His first one-man show at the Loft Gallery consisted of a series of marbled-paper sculptures with small figures drawn on them. Art Elias thought: "This was really a genius show, because it was anti-art, the death knell of abstract expressionism."

Andy's second show, which was devoted to drawings of the dancer John Butler, received a brief review in *Art News* by Barbara Guest, who wrote: "Andy Warhol has developed an original style of line drawing and a willingness to obligate himself to that narrow horizon on which appear attractive and demanding young men involved in the business of being as much like Truman Capote or his heroes as possible. His technique has the effect of the reverse side of a negative."

If the work attracted little serious attention in the fine art world, Andy had by now emerged as a star of commercial art. All the art directors of the major agencies flocked to the opening. Vito Giallo recalled: "Even though he was shy and withdrawn at times, they all wanted to talk to him. And he would just listen. He was always like that; he wouldn't make any comments, never had much to offer, but everybody liked him. He had tons and tons of friends, because he was different. He would never swear, for instance. He used things like 'Holy cow' and 'Wow' and 'Gee whiz,' and people just thought that was so cute and different and funny. He had this childlike quality that people were fascinated by. They just had to know this person and what made him tick. I could never figure out why, because he just stood there and said 'yes' or 'no.' "

Shortly after meeting Giallo, Andy hired him as his first assistant. Of his year with Warhol, Giallo says: "I got there [the Lexington Avenue apartment] around ten or eleven o'clock and I'd work into the early afternoon. Andy was probably the busiest commercial artist at that point, making a tremendous top-notch salary, thirty to fifty thousand dollars a year. His mother liked me, and that meant a lot to him, that someone could talk to her and get along with her very well. She was constantly offering us sandwiches all day, and would never understand what we were talking about. I don't think he respected her very much. One time I said to Andy, 'You know your mother has to go down these five flights to go to the A&P and come up the steps all by herself with all these shopping bags. Don't you think that's too much for her?' He said, 'Oh no, she loves it.' She'd be floating in and out of the rooms, cooking, cleaning, picking up. He depended on her completely, which always kind of shocked me, but I think she really enjoyed it.

"Andy liked gossip. I like gossip. We always had that wonderful rapport of, What's happening? What's going on? We would never talk about art. It was always about people and parties—who's going with whom. He would want to know everything about me. What do you do? Who do you see? But he would never give any information about himself. He would like to talk about guys—who was hot, who was sexy. He would like to know if I had seen this guy or what he was like—how he was built. I think Andy did get an actual sexual excitement out of talking about it.

"He had a friend named Valerie who had a boyfriend who was a sailor. On certain nights of the week he would go for lessons—they gave him sex lessons. I think he was there just to observe and take notes—I thought that was kind of cute.

"And what was so refreshing about him was that he never complained, never talked about anything that was a problem. I never saw him upset—never, never. Everything was always 'wonderful.'"

5

I N THE FALL of 1954, Andy fell in love with the most exciting person he had ever had such feelings for. Charles Lisanby, who designed sets for the immensely popular *Garry Moore Show* on television, was good-looking, tall, elegant, and well connected. If some people thought he was a trifle snobbish, that was fine with Andy, for Lisanby moved in exactly the world Andy wanted to be part of: He was an escort of the actress Carol Burnett; he knew James Dean; he had worked with the photographer Cecil Beaton. Lisanby, for his part, was intrigued—and disturbed—by Warhol: "Inside he was a very beautiful person. That's what I really liked about him. But he had an enormous inferiority complex. He told me he was from another planet. He said he didn't know how he got here. Andy wanted so much to be beautiful, but he wore that terrible wig which didn't fit and only looked awful."

The two friends went everywhere. "I would circulate, and Andy would sit in a corner without saying a word," recalled Lisanby. "People thought he was dumb, but he was anything but dumb—he was more brilliant than even he knew." Charles thought Andy "the most interesting person I ever met, the strangest little guy with an original and unique approach to everything."

Lisanby's effect was enormous. Immediately, Andy decided to improve his appearance. Seymour Berlin, the printer who did his promotional books, was enlisted to put him through a workout at the McBurney YMCA three nights a week. "When he got there," Berlin recalled, "he could not do a push-up, but he worked out very good because I saw a big change in strength." Berlin saw Andy at his most relaxed: He would talk about his adventures in the world of New York celebrities; about how he would buy five-hundred-dollar suits and cut them with razor blades and spatter them with paint to draw attention to himself; about sending Truman Capote and Cecil Beaton presents in the hope that they would want to meet him. Berlin was all ears, but he thought there was something seriously unbalanced about Andy's need to be with famous people. "The wrong things were always important to Andy," he concluded. "He would get very upset if these people did not respond to his gifts and letters. He'd complain that *they* were taking advantage of *him*!"

In 1955, Andy's career took a big leap forward when he got his biggest account of the fifties—a weekly ad in the society pages of the Sunday *New York Times* for the fashionable Manhattan shoe store I. Miller. The store's vice president, Geraldine Stutz, and the art director, Peter Palazzo, who had known Andy since his arrival in New York, decided that he was the perfect choice to launch a campaign to revive the store's sagging image. Stutz was thrilled by what he brought in: "The strength and spareness of Andy's work took people's breath away. Andy always prided himself on doing exactly what he wanted, but the reality was that we presented Andy with an idea in simple form; he took it away and came back, having transformed this idea into something that was universal yet special. The effect was a sensational resuscitation of the I. Miller name."

Shortly before getting the I. Miller account, Andy's relationship with his assistant, Vito Giallo, had broken down. As Giallo remembered it, "Andy had a way of dropping people. He would constantly call me and say, 'Oh, let's go to a party tonight.' But he really expected you never to refuse. One night when he wanted me to go and see Valerie and her boyfriend perform and I couldn't, he was peeved. I didn't hear from him for a long time after that."

That autumn Nathan Gluck, who had originally introduced Vito to Andy, took Giallo's place. When he was excited or upset he would exclaim, "Oh, Jesus Christ!" and Andy had to tell him, "My mother would like it if you wouldn't say that." Nathan soon developed an easy relationship with Julia, who regaled him with retellings of biblical tales, in one of which "Moses was born in the bull." Over the next nine years Gluck's ideas would have such an influence on Warhol that many of their friends came to feel that he was being shamefully exploited. Gluck calmly denied this: In his view, he was nothing more than Andy's assistant.

One of his important early contributions was to get Andy assignments to decorate windows for Gene Moore at Bonwit Teller. Moore was highly impressed by Warhol and his work: "On the surface he always seemed so nice and uncomplicated. He had a sweet, fey, little-boy quality, which he used, but it was pleasant even so—and that was the quality of his work, too. It was light, it had great charm, yet there was always a real beauty of line and composition. There was nobody else around then who worked quite that way."

As the I. Miller ads began to make an impact with their freshness and startling use of white space, Andy jumped at the chance to develop his reputation as the man who drew shoes. Steven Bruce, one of the owners of Serendipity, remembered Warhol coming into the restaurant with a huge portfolio of rejected I. Miller drawings and saying, "What do I do with these?" Bruce suggested that Andy frame them and sell them in the shop for fifteen to twenty-five dollars. The next thing he knew, Andy had brought in a whole portfolio of watercolored shoe drawings called "A la Recherche du Shoe Perdu" to be sold as well. Serendipity was one of Warhol's first "factories"; he would make drawings at tables in exchange for his meals. "At first I thought Andy never changed his shirt," recalled Bruce. "I said, 'I see you day after day in the same shirt.' He said, 'Oh no, I bought a hundred of them, I wear a new one every day.' "

But selling drawings in a coffee shop was not going to win Andy acceptance as an artist. Labels were everything, and if someone was known as a commercial artist, no serious gallery was going to be interested. It was especially galling that, while Andy was at the peak of his commercial career, his old roommate Philip Pearlstein was being accepted at the prestigious Tanager Gallery. Pearlstein's struggles had been a subject of some derision among Andy and his gay friends, who felt that they had a more discerning sense of the zeitgeist than the intellectuals. Andy responded to his old friend's good fortune with the subtle aggression that would later become typical of him. The Tanager was a co-op gallery, which meant that the artists decided whose work was to be shown. Andy asked Pearlstein to submit some of his paintings of nude men on his behalf. Nudes were a perfectly acceptable subject, but these were so overtly homoerotic that Philip felt he would have been insulting his high-minded colleagues by presenting them. When he tried to explain that the paintings should be done more objectively, Andy cut him off, pretending not to understand what he meant. Pearlstein got the impression that Andy "felt I had let him down." After that, he recalled, "we were seldom in touch." But Andy would not compromise himself. He showed a portfolio to David Mann, "Drawings for a Boy Book," consisting mostly of penises decorated with bows, kisses, and faces of beautiful young men. Mann, who now had his own Bodley Gallery next to Serendipity, liked the work and decided to give Andy a show.

Charles Lisanby helped hang the show, which opened on Valentine's Day 1956. Champagne and martinis were served, and Andy was dressed in an elegant custom-tailored suit. Although the gallery was packed with friends, mostly good-looking young men, he seemed ill at ease. Although the drawings were priced at only fifty to sixty dollars, just two or three sold. Moreover, the reviews were lukewarm. Critics could not be expected to take drawings of narcissistic boys by a homosexual display artist seriously, even if they were in the style of Cocteau and Matisse. Nonetheless, with the help of Mann, a few of the less overtly sexual drawings were included several months later in the *Recent Drawings* show at the Museum of Modern Art. The "window decorator" had crossed over.

Julia Warhola never openly acknowledged that her son was gay. All through the 1950s she more or less ignored the situation by accepting the objects of his adoration as adopted sons. Charles Lisanby had been coming to dinner at Lexington Avenue regularly and got along very well with her. For Andy, however, the relationship was deeply troubling. He was in love, but that love was unrequited; he and

Charles had never even kissed. Charles was certainly aware of what Andy wanted, but he preferred to remain strictly friends. Nonetheless, Andy's hopes for real intimacy soared when Charles mentioned that he was planning a trip to the Far East in the summer of 1956 to look at Oriental art and asked if Andy wanted to come. Andy said yes as casually as possible, and by the time they left on June 19, the trip had developed into a journey around the world.

Andy's hopes were dashed almost immediately. He had carefully suggested that they take separate rooms in San Francisco, their first stop, but when they got to Honolulu on the second night, Charles said, "This is ridiculous," and got them a double room with twin beds, overlooking the beach. It was the middle of the afternoon, and Charles wanted to check out the beach. Andy, pleading jet lag, stayed behind.

As soon as Charles got to the beach he ran into a young man whom he persuaded to come to his room "to take some pictures." When they reached the room, Charles discovered he'd forgotten his key. He knocked, and after a long pause Andy peeked out: "Who's tha—— what are you *doing*?" Then, as Lisanby remembered, he went berserk, screaming, "How dare you bring someone back here?"

"Andy, stop it!" Charles cried, and grabbed hold of his wrists.

Andy screamed, "How dare you? Get out of here and don't come back!" He slammed the door. Lisanby then took the young man to another hotel and bought him exotic drinks for the balance of the afternoon.

He returned to Andy at seven. "I still didn't have my key and he wouldn't open the door," he recalled. "I shouted, 'Andy, I know you're in there and you might as well open up because I can go and get another key!' Finally he did, then slouched on the bed and said, 'I want to go home. There's no use in going on.' He was very aloof, trying to shake the whole thing off. I was feeling very guilty. I wanted very much to stay his friend. I didn't want to lose him. I said, 'Yes, we are going on. You've come this far and I won't let you go back.'

"I realized he wanted to be persuaded to go on, that he wanted me to give in. I remember the windows and the ocean outside. It was close to sunset. I sat down beside him and I put my arms around him, trying to calm him down, and he totally broke down crying. It got worse. He couldn't stop. He couldn't stop sobbing hysterically. It was that he didn't want to be alone. Andy always wanted to be in his own center, but he wanted somebody to share it with.

"I knew that he loved me, but he said, in a soft, trembling voice, 'I love you.' I said, 'Andy, I know, and I love you too.' And he said, 'It's not the same thing.' And I said, 'I know it's not the same thing, you just have to understand that, but I do love you.'"

They stayed in that night. Lisanby ordered dinner. Andy did not eat anything. The next morning he acted as if nothing had happened. In the afternoon he took some photographs of Charles in a swimsuit on the beach in front of the hotel. Before they left that evening for Tokyo, Charles made it clear that there were to be no more such confrontations on the trip.

As far as Lisanby could tell, Andy had got over the incident completely once they'd left Hawaii. They had a wonderful time in the Far East, traveling through Japan, Indonesia, Hong Kong, the Philippines, and ending up in Bali. Andy proved to be the more courageous traveler, refusing to leave a restaurant during a small earthquake because the locals didn't, riding over a deep gorge on a narrow bridge without fear whereas Lisanby was terrified, wanting to try the most authentic food. At the same time he was utterly impractical, refusing to take any responsibility for the practicalities of traveling.

In some places they were quite an exotic couple. Visiting a gay bar in Japan, they were surrounded by fawning teenage boys. Deep in the jungle of Bali in the middle of the night, at a traditional dance by teenage girls, they found themselves the only white men. Andy appeared to be enjoying himself but would hold back from getting involved. He preferred, it seemed, to experience things vicariously through Charles, who danced with the boys and girls.

Somewhere along the way Lisanby got food poisoning, and he was terribly sick by the time they arrived in Calcutta. A doctor recommended several weeks in bed. Charles declared that he did not want to die in Calcutta, and they flew to Rome via Cairo. From here on the trip took on a new madness. When the plane landed in Cairo they were astonished to see the airport surrounded by soldiers and tanks—a prelude to the Suez crisis. All passports were confiscated, and the passengers were herded across the runway while fighter jets screamed overhead. In a Quonset hut they were forced to watch a propaganda film, then were marched back onto the plane. Andy, according to Lisanby, walked through the scene like a zombie, oblivious to the danger to their passports, luggage, and lives. They went on to Rome the next morning, and at the Grand Hotel, Charles collapsed and summoned an Italian doctor.

For the next two weeks he was confined to bed. To his dismay Andy decided to stay right there too. Rather than see Rome, he preferred to draw Charles, asleep and awake. After a while, Charles found it hard to have Andy constantly in the room, depleting what little energy he had. He begged Andy at least to go and see the pope, and Andy made a few excursions, returning forlornly with some scarves he had picked up. When Charles recovered, they went up to Florence, but Andy seemed barely interested in the art, mumbling "Wow" or "Gee" at a Titian or Botticelli, seemingly disconsolate that the object of his desire was back on his feet. Their final stop, Amsterdam, was, according to Lisanby, a success. With the prospect of going home, Andy seemed to have cheered up enormously.

The moment he got through customs at the airport in New York, Andy took off without so much as a good-bye, leaving Lisanby, with all his bags and packages, to get into a cab alone. Lisanby was shocked: "I had never imagined Andy could be that decisive. It was as if the whole trip had been an act, and he had really meant everything he'd said in Honolulu and was just waiting to get home. I was very angry."

So, apparently, was Andy. To a friend he complained that he had "gone around the world with a boy and not even received one kiss."

After waiting several days for Andy to phone, Lisanby finally called him: "I said, 'Why did you do that?' And he said, innocently: 'I thought I was supposed to go home alone.' Over the next eight years they saw a lot of each other, but it was never the same. In his *Philosophy* years later Andy (perhaps) explained his behavior:

> I was walking in Bali, and saw a bunch of people in a clearing having a ball because somebody they really liked had just died, and I realized that everything was just how you decided to think about it. Sometimes people let the same problems make them miserable for years when they should just say, So what. That's one of my favorite things to say. So what.
>
> My mother didn't love me. So what.

My husband won't ball me. So what.

I don't know how I made it through all the years before I learned how to do that trick. It took a long time for me to learn it, but once you do you never forget.

Lisanby's rejection had been a terrible blow, but there were distractions. Andy's friends at Serendipity had persuaded him to rent the second-floor apartment at 242 Lexington, which one of them, Calvin Holt, was vacating; let Julia keep the fourth floor, they argued; he should be leading his own glamorous life. They offered to decorate the place for him, and when they finished, they had created a look that would be widely imitated: in the living room, a long white wicker sofa, at either end of which were placed white columns with globe lights on top; behind the sofa, an imposing potted palm; nearby, a couple of rockers made out of twigs and branches. In the front room, they put a round oak table and bentwood chairs under an enormous Tiffany glass shade. White curtains covered the windows; the kitchen cabinets were filled with white china. In the bedroom was a Louis XIV-style gilded four-poster bed and a tiger-skin rug à la Eartha Kitt. A stereo phonograph had been rigged up to be heard throughout. It was all vaguely reminiscent of a Tennessee Williams play.

Andy now had his own stage set, and he started giving parties. They were, by all reports, great fun: Broadway show tunes on the stereo, hordes of the eccentric girls Andy was always trying to promote, and the most beautiful boys, everyone in the bloom of youth.

Influenced by Nathan Gluck, whose own apartment was like a museum, Warhol had begun collecting art. He bought watercolors by Magritte and Tchelitchev, a drawing by Steinberg, an early Klee, a colored aquatint by Braque, a Miró, lithographs by Picasso, and a sand sculpture by Constantino Nivola (which Julia tied to the bookcase with a rope when she discovered how much it had cost). Nathan was disturbed by the cavalier attitude with which Andy handled his acquisitions. Most of them were left leaning against the wall or were tacked up without frames.

On the spur of the moment his brothers in Pittsburgh, Paul or John, would decide, "Hey, let's go to New York and see Bubba [Julia]!" and descend on Andy's apartment with their kids. Andy appeared to enjoy their visits almost as much as Julia did. George

Warhola, his nephew, recalled: "He had bunk beds set up for us. Bubba used to go to the market and buy vegetables and cook on a big stove. Andy would buy us presents. Once it was a real nice camera. You took the picture and a mouse shot out."

Socially and artistically Andy's next show at the Bodley Gallery in December 1956 was a breakthrough. These were large blotted-line drawings of shoes painted gold, or decorated with gold metal and foil, like the lacquer furniture he had seen in Bangkok. The "distanced," iconographic golden slippers were a distinct contrast to the voyeuristic male portraits he had shown at the beginning of the year and—perhaps consequently—more successful. He gave each shoe a name: among others, "Elvis Presley," "James Dean," "Mae West," "Truman Capote," and "Julie Andrews,"—who arrived at the opening with her husband, the designer Tony Walton.

The show was followed by a two-page color spread in *Life* magazine. Andy had been so worried that his work was going to be rejected that he had taken David Mann to *Life*'s offices with him. According to Mann, "Andy kept saying, 'Oh God! They're not going to like these, this is going to be absolutely terrible, they're going to tear me down.' "

With Mann's help Andy was beginning to get some footing in the gay-fashion-celebrity world. The socialite Jerome Zipkin commissioned a shoe portrait. Patrick Higgins, aide to cosmetics tycoon Helena Rubinstein, came to the gallery: "Madame," said Mann, "had seen the show, and would Andy consider doing a portrait of her? Andy did it. Then I got this call from Patrick. 'About that portrait,' he said, 'Madame likes it very much but do you think you could better the price?' It was $125 and I said, 'Well, you know, it's only $125 and it was commissioned.' I could hear her going on in the background, 'Tell him $100!' and he said, 'She suggests $100.' I said, 'Well, no, I don't think so,' and so he said, 'Well, all right, she'll buy it anyhow.' Andy got so upset. He said, 'Oh God! What does she think of me?' "

The socialite D. D. Ryan bought the gold shoe Andy had dedicated to Truman Capote, and sent it to Truman as a Christmas present with an accompanying note describing Warhol: "He's becoming very well known. Very on-coming." "Even then I never had the idea he wanted to be a painter or an artist," Capote recalled. "I thought he was one of those people who are 'interested in the arts.' As far as I knew he was a window decorator. . . . Let's say a window-decorator type."

Capote's bitchy response was, unfortunately for Warhol, on target. And if Warhol had any illusion that his shoes were going to put him in a class with Jackson Pollock, all he had to do was read the caption for the spread in *Life*. It described him as a "commercial artist" who sketched "imaginary footwear ornamented with candy-box decorations as a hobby."

In the fall of 1956, Andy—who, after two years of going to the gym, could now do fifty push-ups—made another determined effort to change his appearance, this time by having his nose scraped. If not, his doctor had said, he would end up looking like W. C. Fields. Andy had the operation done in St. Luke's Hospital, but after waiting two weeks for the scars to heal, he felt he only looked worse. "He thought the operation would change his life," said Charles Lisanby. "He thought that I and other people would suddenly think that he was as physically attractive as the people he admired because of their attractiveness. When that didn't happen, he became rather angry."

As David Mann remembered: "Andy had a bad complexion, bad hair, no shoulders. I mean, he was a mess! But he was always falling in love with these beautiful boys. Even when they became friends and went to his parties, the last thing in the world they were interested in was going to bed with him. That wasn't a very happy thing for him."

Indeed, friends began noticing a pronounced change in the "sweet" Andy to whom everything had been "wonderful." When an old friend of Corkie Ward's died, Andy presented no condolences but only asked if his Tchelitchev paintings were for sale. And when the fashion photographer Dick Rutledge remarked, "I can't stand this fucking fashion world any more. I'm going to kill myself!" Andy said, "Oh, can I have your watch?" It was a very expensive watch, and Rutledge took it off and threw it at him. Andy kept the watch for the rest of his life.

Worries about his appearance did not seem to dampen Andy's ardor for the next object of his desire, a good-looking young photographer named Ed Wallowitch. Wallowitch shared a basement apartment with his brother John, a pianist, on Barrow Street in Greenwich Village. It was a salon for the downtown gay scene—lots of red wine and old movie posters—and Andy began spending a good deal of time there. At first, John was happy about Andy's passion for his brother: "Ed couldn't keep his hands off Andy, and Andy was all over Ed. Andy was very sweet in those days. Adorable. *Artistique*. Once we all went up to his apartment to see Mrs. Warhol and he showed us two refrigerators. He kept one filled with champagne, which he said was for her."

The writer Robert Heidie, who would work with Warhol on several films in the 1960s, saw the relationship from another angle: "Ed and John were heavy into the martinis, but Andy wasn't drinking. He was more like the little boy." Andy had started wearing dark glasses, and Heidie felt that "on some level he was always acting— the real person was submerged and there was definitely a pre-Oedipal thing about him. His mother was a very important, almost spooky presence—'My Andy can do no wrong. He's a good boy'— and Andy would retreat into that four- or five-year old."

The affair with Ed was the most sexually active one Andy had ever had: He let Ed take photographs of him in bed, in which he looks extraordinarily at peace.

By 1957 Andy was doing so well financially that on the advice of an accountant he established Andy Warhol Enterprises. He also began investing a good deal in the stock market as well as broadening the area of his collecting. Through a new friend, Ted Carey, he had developed a particular interest in American folk art.

The year ended with another successful show at the Bodley Gallery. Although they did not receive as much publicity as the "Golden Slippers," his "Gold Pictures"—black line drawings of street kids and handsome young men done on gold paper—sold well. Moreover, the *Gold Book*, which Andy sent out as a promotional gift that Christmas, was widely appreciated. Only John Wallowitch began to feel a little uncomfortable when he realized that Andy had traced all of the book's drawings from Ed's photographs without giving him any credit.

There was at least one contemporary of Andy's who was so far ahead of him on the path he wanted to follow that it made his head swim with envy. This was Jasper Johns, at twenty-seven just two years older than Andy, whose first one-man show at the Leo Castelli Gallery, *Flags, Targets, and Numbers,* had opened four weeks after the closing of Andy's show at the Bodley. It had caused a sensation. The Museum of Modern Art had bought four of the paintings—unprecedented for such a young artist.

Johns had done what Andy had dreamed of. He had appeared, seemingly from nowhere, with an exhibition so controversial and powerful (and featuring Warhol's favorite subject, the penis) that the worst his critics could do was to call him unpatriotic because he had painted the American flag. Each work was a kind of compressed historical essay about the boundaries of art, in both the choice of subject matter and the application of paint; each asked bold questions about people's expectations of art—about what, when all was said and done, "art" really *was.* Overnight Johns had created an earthquake in the New York art world, separating "old" modern art from something radically new.

In fact, profound change, as always in the art world, had been occurring without anyone quite realizing it. The pop art movement that had begun in England in 1956 had spread to France and was beginning to find followers in America among such young artists as George Segal, Roy Lichtenstein, and Claes Oldenburg. The New York scene still centered on the abstract expressionists, but they were not moving with the same velocity as they had in the early- and mid-fifties. De Kooning, for example, had spent all of 1957 on one canvas, painting it over and over again because he didn't think it was working. "It was an insane time," recalled the photographer and filmmaker Robert Frank. The majority of the painters were, in the words of one such artist, "a scruffy, excitable lot. It was us against the world." "Everybody was in everybody else's pocket," recalled another. "There was rivalry—egos were gargantuan—and there was a lot of competition, but at least the struggle was private and not corrupted by the media."

It was a scene from which Andy Warhol was still excluded because of his success as a commercial artist and his open homosexuality, and this made the success of Jasper Johns all the more rankling. For Johns, too, had been a commercial artist (and for the same man, Gene Moore, at Bonwit Teller). Two months later, when Johns's close friend Robert Rauschenberg, whose roots were also in commercial art, had an almost equally dramatic success at Castelli, Andy was more determined than ever to make a real mark. He began haunting the Castelli Gallery at 3 East Seventy-seventh Street with a vengeance.

Gaining acceptance was another matter. In the 1950s the public revelation that two men were "a couple" would have destroyed their careers. Now, when Warhol approached Johns and Rauschenberg at openings, they cut him dead. "He was unpopular with the people he wanted to be popular with and very unhappy about it," said David Mann.

It was at this time that Andy, through Tina Fredericks, met Emile de Antonio. The eloquent and stylish artists' agent had already been a catalyst in many careers of the period. His circle of friends included not only Johns and Rauschenberg but the composer John Cage and the choreographer Merce Cunningham. "Andy was fascinated by the collaborative nature of their friendship," recalled de Antonio. "But they were not interested in knowing him. The mystique of the great artist was already on them, and Andy was too 'commercial.' He was also, frankly, too swish. A number of times I said to them, 'Why don't we invite Andy to dinner?' and they said no."

"De," as de Antonio was called, was also struck by another characteristic: Andy seemed to be "engrossed" by the idea of evil. "That used to be one of his favorite subjects. He'd ask, 'Isn't that evil?' or exclaim, 'Oh, De, that's absolutely evil.' I sensed that what he meant was someone dominating another person."

Meanwhile, his affair with Ed Wallowitch was beginning to go badly. Ed had finally moved into his own place. When Ed's sister, Anna May, decided to get married, he felt abandoned and began drinking heavily. After a while Andy began seeing less of him. Ed suffered a psychological collapse and had to move back into his brother's apartment, where he stayed, while taking Thorazine, for six weeks. John Wallowitch remembered: "The analyst thought it would be better for Edward to go to a place out on Long Island that could handle this kind of thing. But it cost $250 a week. At the time, I was making three dollars an hour and there was no money coming in from Ed, or our parents. I called Andy up and asked him for $600 to help Ed out. He said, 'Oh, I'm sorry. My business manager won't let me do it.' It would be nice if Andy had come to see him or called, but no, there was nothing. I loved Andy, but there was something malevolent and evil about the way he sucked off Ed's energy."

Emboldened by the example of Johns and Rauschenberg, Andy in 1959 was steadily progressing toward the pop art that would make him, a few years later, an art world sensation in his own right. Now he was using repeated images more and more. Like everything he would do from this point on, Warhol's repetition was double-edged: on the one hand, it seemed to celebrate St. Francis' assertion that "there are thousands of flowers, thousands of people, thousands of animals, and each one is different, each one unique." On the other, in Warhol's hands, repetition underscored the banality of existence. Perhaps by this time he had come to believe that people never really change, that his problems would repeat themselves over and over.

The show he was working on for David Mann, *Wild Raspberries*, prefigured his brand of pop art in its imagery of fanciful food—hot dogs and desserts—although it was still a bit precious, not fully "cool." Andy's collaborator on the work was an important new friend, Suzi Frankfurt, who was helping him devise fantasy recipes to be handwritten by Julia under each drawing. Suzi took a dislike to Mrs. Warhola: "She was talented in some mad way, but she was so manipulative. Andy had to chain her to the light box to get all the calligraphy done. She said she'd copy it over and she didn't. He gave her too much bloody credit—he adored her too much. She was too weird for me—too much the Czechoslovakian peasant."

Wild Raspberries opened on December 1, 1959. "Clever frivolity *in excelsis*," the *New York Times* judged the work, effectively putting the lid on Andy's serious aspirations. No publisher wanted a book of the recipes and drawings, so he and Suzi published it themselves. "We went around with shopping bags full of books," she recalled, "but nobody wanted them." Nor was the rest of Andy's life going well. He had bought a townhouse at 1342 Lexington Avenue between East Eighty-ninth and Ninetieth streets for $67,000 but had lost his I. Miller account and was scrambling to keep his income up to his needs. Now he had to do more commercial art than ever to pay his expenses, and most of the joy had gone out of the work. The break-up with Ed had persuaded him to stay celibate for a while, but he was leveling a new round of "bottomless" demands at Charles

Lisanby, with whom he was still in love. "I was very concerned about him," said Lisanby, "but I did not want to go and live with him. I felt trapped. Perhaps [the relationship] became so intense because it was never consummated. I always knew he never forgave me for not being his lover."

Worst of all was the crisis with Julia. Now, in the big new house, she was relegated to the basement. Julia had become increasingly lonely in New York. She returned to Pittsburgh twice a year, and John and Paul visited New York with their growing families, but her only regular social life was provided by her weekly visits to church and daily outings to the supermarket. Living in such isolation, she had begun to drink heavily—Scotch whisky much of the day. Andy, according to most visitors, continued to behave as sweetly as ever with her, but there were growing signs of conflict. Ted Carey, one of Andy's assistants and closest friends, said: "She was very lonely. Whenever I was there she'd come upstairs and talk. Andy didn't like me talking to her because I wouldn't work fast enough to suit him, and he'd come in and yell at her, 'You've been talking to Ted!' And she'd go downstairs. But the moment he left, she'd come back and talk. She loved television—programs like 'I Love Lucy.' "

Julia, for her part, was always nagging Andy about money. "Built into Andy," observed de Antonio, "was the fear that there was never going to be enough money, there was never going to be enough of anything; things were always going to turn out badly. That seemed to me his mother's voice."

Whenever he went out, Andy carried wads of money, and he kept piles of it around the house. Andy's friends thought him unbelievably generous to his family. According to Suzi Frankfurt, "He used to feel guilty about his brothers. He said, 'I made more in two minutes than they make in a year.' He loved them." Indeed, both John and Paul recalled that not only did Julia send regular care packages, but Andy paid all their expenses when they visited, and he helped them out with loans and gifts. Nonetheless, at this time Julia appears to have felt that he was not contributing enough. And so she packed her bag one day and declared that she was moving back to Pittsburgh.

She stayed away for some time. According to Suzi Frankfurt, "the house became a nightmare—a disgusting mess." Joseph Giordano, a painter and art director who knew Andy and Julia well, told the art historian Patrick Smith years later: "He just couldn't function. I think he expected me to get in there and function, but it was just too much of a household to run. So he finally called her back. She insisted I be there that night, and when she came in, she slammed her suitcase on the floor, looked at him, and said, 'I'm Andy Warhol.' And there was a big discussion about why she was Andy Warhol. . . . The crux of Andy Warhol is that he felt so unloved, so unloved. I know it came from his mother. . . . She made him feel insignificant. She made him feel that he was the ugliest creature God ever put on this earth."

In 1959 and through half of 1960, Andy had what he called a nervous breakdown. Later he made light of the situation in *The Philosophy of Andy Warhol,* blaming his troubles on "picking up problems from the people I knew. I had never felt that I had problems, because I had never specifically defined any, but now I felt that these problems of friends were spreading themselves onto me like germs."

He went to a psychiatrist, but the visits were not successful and he soon stopped going. (About psychiatry he once remarked: "It could help you if you don't know anything about anything.") How near Andy actually was to a breakdown is a matter of conjecture. Nathan Gluck, who was with him five days a week, noticed no sign of anything wrong at all. Seymour Berlin, his body-building friend, said: "I wouldn't say that he was a manic-depressive, but at times he was very elated and then somehow, if something didn't go the way he wanted, very depressed." Suzi Frankfurt recalled this period as "the only time in his life when if you said, 'Oh, Andy, that's terrible. That's ugly!' he'd get very hurt."

Emile de Antonio probably got to the heart of the matter: "He was so jealous and envious then of Johns and Rauschenberg. Andy never expressed anger. He was always cool and understated, but in maybe two hours of conversation, in his silent, withdrawn way, he'd say, 'Why don't they like me? Why can't I see them? Why do they say no when you ask if you can invite me to dinner? Why can't I be a painter?' That tension was underlying his entire existence in New York because that was why he came here—to be a painter."

6

I N 1960 LEONARD KESSLER ran into Warhol coming out of an art-
supply store carrying paint and canvas. "Andy! What are you
doing?" he greeted him. Andy said, without skipping a beat,
"I'm starting pop art."

"Why?" Kessler asked. And Andy said "Because I hate abstract
expressionism. I hate it!"

A few weeks later, when Ted Carey admired a Rauschenberg
collage at the Museum of Modern Art, Andy snapped, "That's nothing. That's a piece of shit!"

Carey said, "Well, if you really think it's all promotion and anyone
can do it, why don't *you* do it?" He answered, "Well, I've got to think
of something different."

In "starting" pop art (the term had actually been around since
1958) Warhol called upon everything he had learned from advertising and television, where the dollar sign and the gun were predomi-
nant symbols, where the subliminal message was sexual desire
without gratification, and where the immediate aim was to shock. He
decided to paint a series of big black-and-white pictures of what
"artists" were supposed to hate most: advertisements. He took from
the backs of magazines the simplest, crummiest, cheapest ads—for

wigs, nose jobs, television sets, canned food—made them into slides, and projected them onto blank canvas. Then he "copied" an enlarged, fractured section of the ad in black paint, letting drips and splashes accidentally splatter. The paintings were ugly and banal, but they reverberated with anger and contempt. The art dealer Ivan Karp noted: "Basically it was an act of compulsion; he had to do it. As a person working in commercial art, which was essentially towering blandness, Andy had to apologize in his mind for being involved. To make an art of it seemed a way of getting the anxiety out, which is what much art is about: You need to confront the images which cause you distress in order to relieve the distress."

A second series depicted some of Andy's childhood cartoon favorites: Dick Tracy, Popeye, Little Nancy. He painted large pictures of cartoon frames using bright colors but obliterating most of the words with messy hash marks and drips (fearing that the work would not be taken seriously without such "abstract expressionist" references). De Antonio was coming around regularly to encourage him, but Andy was frustrated. One day he urinated on some canvas to see what it would look like but, unsatisfied with the results, rolled it up and put it away. Another day he put a piece of canvas outside the front door to see what kind of picture people's footprints would make.

The summer of 1960 brought a breakthrough. De Antonio was present: "One night I went over and had a bunch of drinks and he put two large paintings next to each other against the wall. Usually he showed me the work more casually, so I realized this was a presentation. He had painted two pictures of Coke bottles about six feet tall. One was just a pristine black-and-white Coke bottle. The other had a lot of abstract expressionist marks on it. I said, 'Come on, Andy, the abstract one is a piece of shit, the other one is remarkable. It's our society, it's who we are, it's absolutely beautiful and naked, and you ought to destroy the first one and show the other.' "

With his interest in American folk art, Andy wanted to paint twentieth-century "folk" objects like Coke bottles just the way they looked, but he had feared that people would dismiss this as the work of a commercial artist. Hearing de Antonio's response, he was excited. He called up other people in the art world. The first was Leo Castelli's assistant, Ivan Karp, whom he invited to look at the paintings. Karp was a classic early sixties character who wore dark Brooks Brothers suits like the Kennedys', sported sunglasses, smoked big cigars, and called people "baby." He was a highly articulate man who had a feeling that something big was about to happen in the art world and that it was going to happen in America. When he knocked on the door of 1342 Lexington Avenue he knew nothing about Andy Warhol other than that he was enthusiastic enough about the new art to have spent $475 on a Jasper Johns drawing he had bought from Castelli.

Karp encountered Andy just as he was taking steps to change his image. The new Andy had decided to draw attention to his physical oddness: He had, for example, begun wearing a silver-blond wig, which he wore uncombed and just slightly askew. He had also started to change the way he spoke, mumbling monosyllabic, often incoherent replies to any questions. And he exaggerated everything else in his repertoire, like his slightly effeminate dancer's walk and his limp wrists—a bizarre takeoff of Marlon Brando and Marilyn Monroe. "He made a virtue of his vulnerability, and forestalled or neutralized any possible taunts," the critic John Richardson would later write. "Nobody could ever 'send him up.' He had already done so himself."

Once Karp had stepped into Andy's domain, negotiating his way around a sculpture of a wrecked car by John Chamberlain that partially blocked the entrance, he followed the artist down a dimly lit corridor lined with ghostly figures—a wooden statue of Punch, a life-size Mr. Peanut, a cigar-store Indian. The stereo was blaring rock music in the living room/studio. Andy positioned himself silently in a corner, did not turn down the sound, and Karp was left to take in a somber, surreal Victorian setting. The room had previously been a psychiatrist's office, and the windows were boarded over to keep out light and noise. There were several works by modern masters on the walls—Karp noticed a large Toulouse-Lautrec print of a man on a bicycle—and a long Empire sofa against one wall. Warhol's own paintings were neatly stacked against another wall. What made the biggest impression on Karp was the record playing over and over. (Andy, who was drawn to falsetto renditions of songs about broken hearts, later explained that he was in the habit of playing one song a day at least a hundred times until he "understood what it meant.")

As Karp remembered it, he started dancing around the room, shouting out comments. "I was being quite arrogant. I told him that the only works I thought of any consequence were the cold, straightforward ones like the Coca-Cola bottle." He thought that the same people who were interested in the new painter Castelli was looking at—Roy Lichtenstein—might also be interested in Warhol, and as he left, he agreed to show Castelli several slides of Andy's work. Andy was so excited that he immediately sent Karp a Little Nancy painting he had admired, tied up with a red ribbon and with a note signed "Love from Andy."

During the next few weeks, Ivan brought several collectors to Andy's house. They were at first dumbfounded when Andy answered the door wearing an eighteenth-century mask festooned with jewels and feathers (Karp was under the impression he wore it to conceal the blotches on his face), and offered similar masks to each of them. They were further taken aback when the masked artist stood mutely in the corner while the day's rock single blared from the phonograph. Nonetheless, each collector bought one or two paintings for a few hundred dollars each—much less than Andy was used to earning for a single commercial drawing. But Andy was enormously grateful to Ivan and insisted he take a commission.

Although Andy continued to work with Nathan Gluck every day, his commercial art friends were gradually excluded from his new world. Karp accidentally discovered that Warhol was well known in the advertising community while walking with him one day on Madison Avenue. "He knew every fifth person. I said, 'My God, Andy, I thought you were a secret soul!' He said, 'Oh, I know them . . . I just know them casually.' "

In July, Karp brought Henry Geldzahler, the new young assistant curator for twentieth-century American art at the Metropolitan Museum, to Warhol's studio. While they talked, Andy kept painting on the floor, surrounded by a television set, radio, and phonograph all playing at the same time, stacks of teen, movie, and fashion magazines, and a telephone. He explained that he was trying to make his mind as empty and blank as possible so no thought or emotion could go into the work.

"I had heard all my life that Stuart Davis played jazz records when he was painting," said Geldzahler, "so I knew I was *somewhere*. Once I had gotten used to the flickering of the television set, the first thing I noticed was a pair of Carmen Miranda's platform shoes far higher than they were wide. Their placement on a shelf in his wood-paneled living room made a smile-provoking introduction to a camp sensibility."

As the new boy at the Metropolitan, Geldzahler was supposed to discover what was going on in contemporary American art. He and Ivan had been running around town introducing each other to a string of emerging artists who were as yet largely unaware of each other—James Rosenquist, Claes Oldenburg, Tom Wesselmann, Roy Lichtenstein, Frank Stella. When Andy took up his invitation to stop by the Met to look at Florine Stettheimer's paintings the following day, Geldzahler felt as if he had known Andy all his life, that he was in the presence of "someone who epitomized the age in a very special way." He agreed to take Warhol's work around to the galleries.

It was a period of opulence, and Henry and Andy were soon having a wonderful time going to dinners and parties and gossiping about the art world. According to a friend: "There was a phenomenon that came out of the fifties: Everyone was a prince. Andy was a prince. Henry Geldzahler was a prince. They operated on a broad, extravagant level of endless expense, privilege, and freedom. There was infinite money. Everyone was really smart and naive and sweet and grasping and powerful and brilliant."

As their acquaintance grew into what would become a lifelong friendship, Henry enjoyed playing "humanist scholar" to Andy's "Renaissance painter."

"Oh, you know so much," Andy would say. "Teach me a fact a day and then I'll be as smart as you."

"Cairo is the capital of Egypt," said Henry.

"Cairo is the capital of Egypt," repeated Andy.

Although they were never lovers, the relationship became intimate. Andy spoke to Henry on the phone every night before he went to sleep and every morning as soon as he woke up. "He was very much a night creature and literally afraid to go to sleep at night," recalled Geldzahler. "He wouldn't fall asleep until dawn cracked because sleep equals death and night is fearsome, and if you fall asleep at night, you're not quite sure about waking up again. But if you fall asleep in the daylight, it's kind of a comfort knowing that the sun is out there. It's very primitive, it's a kind of inverted sun worship, because Andy actually detested the real sunlight."

By the fall of 1960, the Castelli, Green, Judson, Tanager, Martha Jackson, Stable, and Hansa galleries were putting on or planning shows by Johns, Rauschenberg, Oldenburg, Wesselmann, Lichtenstein, Rosenquist, Segal, Indiana, Stella, Red Grooms, Jim Dine, Lucas Samaras, Robert Whitman, and others in the new American wave. As his allies stepped up their campaign to get his work shown, Andy was only too aware that "the new movement" had arrived and that until he got a gallery to represent him, he could not be a "new person." Unfortunately, both his cartoon and advertising series fell short when compared with much of the other new work, especially the paintings of Roy Lichtenstein.

Lichtenstein was also appropriating cartoons and advertisements, but he had taken the bolder step of copying the images as precisely as possible—with no "comments" by brushstrokes and drips—then "blowing them up." Rosenquist was also using cartoon images, with strong results. Next to their work Warhol's looked uncertain, and the reaction to it was largely negative, even from his early supporter David Mann: "Whenever he had come to me before, I had been very enthusiastic and said, 'Oh, great, let's do a show.' Now when he came to me with his early pop paintings, I wasn't for them. The break was not unpleasant. He said, 'If you don't think they're good and if you're not interested in them, I'll take them elsewhere.' "

Other prominent dealers, including Sidney Janis, Richard Bellamy, and Robert Elkron, agreed with Mann. Martha Jackson offered Andy a show, then canceled it out of fear for her reputation as a "serious" dealer. Despite the enthusiasm of Karp and Geldzahler, much of the art world considered the work ridiculous. In time, many people said, Andy Warhol would return to commercial art, which was right where he belonged.

Typical of the way Andy was generally regarded in the New York art world at the beginning of the 1960s was the reaction of the socialite Frederick Eberstadt: "You couldn't miss him, a skinny creep with his silver wig . . . . To put it mildly, I was not impressed. Andy asked me if I ever thought about being famous. Andy would start off conversations like that . . . . He said he wanted to be as famous as the Queen of England. Here was this weird coolie little faggot with his impossible wig and his jeans and his sneakers and he was sitting there telling me that he wanted to be as famous as the Queen of England! It was embarrassing. . . . In fact he was about the most colossal creep I had ever seen in my life. I thought that Andy was lucky that anybody would talk to him."

In the face of such disgust not even Karp's considerable salesmanship could make much headway on behalf of his discovery. "I had a little network of friends in the art business," he recalled, "and when I said, 'Look at Warhol's work, it's terrific, it's going to be a revelation,' they said, 'You're nuts. It's nothing at all. It's empty stuff, shabby, squalid, horrible.' "

"If you think he's so great," other gallery owners would tell Karp, "why don't you take him yourself?" And that, of course, was the question. In January 1961, Karp finally steered his boss, Leo Castelli, to Andy's house. Castelli remembered Warhol's pale, mottled face from numerous visits to the gallery, but they had never spoken, and Karp was concerned about the impression Andy's bizarre environment would make on the fastidiously civilized Italian. On the way he assured Castelli that the eccentric young artist was actually a "fine and sensitive gentleman who is a serious artist but has a curious way of being."

This was certainly evident as soon as Andy opened the door, wearing one of his eighteenth-century masks and offering two others. A nonplussed Leo received "a very curious impression" from the dark, cluttered house and the blasting rock music. Karp's hopes sank: "The exoticness presented as a bohemianism Leo wasn't interested in. He was as warm and sociable as he could be, but I saw him troubled and anxious during the whole interview."

Castelli left the house without committing himself, saying they would talk in a few days. According to him: "We didn't stay long—not more than half an hour. I just felt the paintings were not interesting. They seemed to be spoofing all kinds of things. You really weren't quite sure what he was going to do."

Moreover, there was the problem of Lichtenstein. According to Karp: "Leo said, if we were interested in Roy, could we really be legitimately interested in Warhol? He thought there might be, in the fragile beginning of an artist's career, a jeopardy to one or to the other, and if we were to commit ourselves to Lichtenstein, it would be a threat to his career to have another artist working like him."

Several days later Andy met Castelli alone in his office. Castelli said he liked what Andy was doing but told him what he had told Karp. Andy appeared dejected but was unusually outspoken. "You're mistaken," he insisted. "What I'm doing will be very different from what anybody else is doing. I really belong in your gallery and you should take me, because I'm very good." When Castelli repeated that it would be impossible for him to represent him, Andy became upset and cried out, "Well, where should I go?" His final words, however, were defiant: "You will take me. I'll be back."

Despite his brave façade, Andy's mood was shaky in the spring and summer of 1961. For one week in April his paintings *Advertisement, Little King, Superman, Before and After,* and *Saturday Popeye* were shown by Gene Moore in a Bonwit Teller window behind five mannequins in spring dresses and hats. Not surprisingly, this display received no attention in the art world.

Andy was working at what was to him great financial risk. Painting was not only expensive but time-consuming, and his income had dropped. He told his brother John that he had made sixty thousand dollars in 1960 and hadn't saved a dime. "What did you spend the money on?" John asked. "That's what I'd like to know," Andy replied.

But he had become an aggressive salesman, as Robert Scull, the New York taxi magnate and collector, discovered when he visited Warhol after the Castelli rejection. Scull, who bypassed the dealers and paid cold cash to artists for their works, was busy acquiring on the cheap a pop art collection that he would sell for millions ten years later. "I want to sell you some paintings," Andy told him. "I don't care how many you take. I just need $1,400. Here's five. Will that do?" When Scull, taken aback, paused, Warhol snapped, "Okay, take six." Andy soon became a regular at Robert and Ethel Scull's parties. Presented with a lavish meal, he would eat nothing, mumbling, "Oh, I only eat candy."

But as he lay awake at night, he would become so terrified that his heart would stop if he fell asleep that he grabbed the bedside phone and called up friends to talk all night until dawn. As Karp was beginning to realize, "Andy was a tender, fragile person. He couldn't stand having anything bad said about him or his work. He took rejection very poorly."

By the end of the year Andy was back where he had started. He had just come out of a "nervous breakdown" and feared he might be slipping into another. After he attended Claes Oldenburg's celebrated Lower East Side exhibition, *The Store,* in early December, with its garishly painted soft sculptures of some of his favorite subjects—underwear, ice cream, and pies—he was so upset that he hadn't had the idea that he told his assistant Ted Carey that he was too depressed to go out to dinner. Later that evening Carey stopped by with an interior designer, Muriel Latow, who was struggling unsuccessfully to support her own gallery. Andy usually rallied around Muriel's forceful personality, but on this evening she and Ted could see he was in a funk.

According to Ted Carey: "Andy said, 'It's too late for the cartoons. I've got to do something that will have a lot of impact, that will be different from Lichtenstein and Rosenquist, that will be very personal, that won't look like I'm doing exactly what they're doing. I don't know what to do! Muriel, you've got fabulous ideas. Can't you give me an idea?' "

Yes, she could, Muriel replied, but it would cost Andy some money.

"How much?" he asked.

"Fifty dollars," she answered.

Andy promptly wrote out a check and said, "Okay, go ahead. Give me a fabulous idea!"

"What do you like most in the whole world?" Muriel asked.

"I don't know. What do I like most in the whole world?"

"Money," she replied. "You should paint pictures of money."

"Oh, gee," Andy gasped, "that really is a great idea!"

In the silence that followed, Muriel elaborated. "You should paint something that everybody sees every day, that everybody recognizes . . . like a can of soup."

For the first time that evening Andy smiled. As he would later tell Robert Heidie: "Many an afternoon at lunchtime Mom would open a can of Campbell's tomato soup for me, because that's all we could afford. I love it to this day."

The next morning Andy sent Julia out to buy one of each of the thirty-two varieties of Campbell's soup at the local A&P, and he started to work. First he did a series of drawings. Then he made color slides of each can, projected them onto a screen, and began experimenting with different dimensions and combinations. Meanwhile, he was doing the same thing with dollar bills, painting them individually, then in rows of two, then in rows of one hundred.

Finally he hit upon his format for the soup cans. Many pop artists were using supermarket food images in their work, but they crammed their pictures with them. Andy invested the same objects with a new seriousness, an iconic dignity, by isolating them: He decided to do one portrait of each of the thirty-two cans as exactly as possible, pristine against a white background.

While the art world would become inflamed over this act of subversion, Andy saw the whole thing much more simply, directly—and deeply. Behind his patented mixture of bravado and self-deflation there is a poignancy about the essential "worthlessness" of all art in a statement he made a few years later to the *New York Herald-Tribune:* "Just ordinary people like my paintings. It took intelligent people years to appreciate the abstract expressionist school and I suppose it's hard for intellectuals to think of me as art. I've never been touched by a painting. I don't want to think. The world outside would be easier to live in if we were all machines. It's nothing in the end anyway. It doesn't matter what anyone does. My work won't last anyway. I was using cheap paint."

7

AS THE TEMPO of Andy's work picked up, his studio became a nightly salon for visitors, among them the proto-pop artist Ray Johnson, who was an important influence on many artists of the period, and the art critic David Bourdon. Bourdon, who had known Andy in the late fifties but had not seen him for several years, called on him as soon as he heard of the new work: "I first visited him in March 1962 to see the soup cans. They had been illustrated in a newsletter. From that moment on we became really fast friends and I was there a couple of evenings a week. It was kind of an informal sitting room. He had a hard, phony, Empire-style sofa, floor lamps, chairs and tables, and some Planter's Peanut ashtrays. He was doing all his painting in that room, and as the months went by the furniture gradually disappeared as the rolled-up canvases took over." While his guests sat drinking Scotch, Andy would drift in and out, taking phone calls from Henry Geldzahler or checking on his mother in the basement.

From 1959 to 1971, Julia Warhola lived alone in the dark, dank subterranean room where she invented a world of her own that could have been in depression Pittsburgh, or for that matter in Mikova. Along the wall under the half-window that faced the street at eye level was a couch covered by a sheet. Against another wall was her bed. In the corner stood her altar with a crucifix. Apart from the simple kitchen table and chairs at the other end of the room next to the stove, that was all her furniture. The rest of the room was cluttered with shopping bags, mail, a talking parrot in a cage, and cat hairs. A multitude of skittish Siamese cats could be seen under the kitchen cabinets between sudden forays to overturn a stack of mail or a bag full of junk.

Julia Warhola was by nature a pack rat, and she never discarded anything no matter how useless. Her long cotton peasant dress and apron were usually covered with buttons, paper money, notes, and other memorabilia affixed with safety pins. Andy spent a modicum of his time in his mother's domain, appearing regularly each morning for breakfast and before going out, when they would recite a brief prayer together and she would caution him to watch himself.

As with everything else about his life, Andy mythologized his mother's exile in the basement, telling friends she was an alcoholic whom he had to keep locked up with a case of Scotch, except at five in the morning, when she would ascend to clean the house. As the years went on, Andy's own quarters upstairs sank beneath his accumulation of junk, and Julia was largely reduced to mopping up after the cats. The Pittsburgh Warholas, who continued to visit as often as they could, noticed that whenever they came, Julia was so lonely that she could not stop talking.

In his own way, however, Andy treated Julia well. He gave her five hundred dollars a week for household expenses, some of which she spent on care packages for Pittsburgh and Mikova or put aside in a large glass jar. (Paul once found six or seven thousand dollars stashed away in a large jar.) Since the house was only eight blocks south of Harlem, she was afraid to go farther afield than the corner supermarket, drugstore, and post office on her daily sorties into the neighborhood. But once, when Andy suggested that she would be better off in a house on Long Island, she balked, claiming that this was the best place she had ever had and she did not want to leave it.

"Uncle Andy" had become something of a hero to his nephews and nieces. "We'd always wait for him to wake up," remembered George Warhola, Paul's third son. "Bubba used to bring his orange juice up every morning and then we'd go up and talk to him. One time we went in and pulled the covers off his head and saw him bald. He yelled, 'Get out of here!' When he was going out we'd be up there watching him shave and get dressed. He was like a movie star to us. He was our idol. And he'd have his Chanel perfume and he'd say, 'Here, you want to try it?' We always wanted to know, 'Well, gee, Uncle Andy, who'd you meet that's famous?' And he'd tell us all about the people he went out to dinner or parties with. Sometimes we'd help him stretch canvases. He'd pay us two dollars an hour and bring us home presents."

In May 1962, Irving Blum, who owned the Ferus Gallery in Los Angeles, paid Andy a visit. He found him kneeling next to the glowing television set with the radio and the record player blasting opera and rock simultaneously, painting his sixteenth portrait of a soup can. "What happened to your cartoons?" asked Blum, who had seen his paintings of Superman a year earlier.

"Oh," replied Andy nonchalantly, "Lichtenstein was doing them better, so I'm not doing them any more. Now I'm doing these." He explained that his intention was to paint all of Campbell's thirty-two varieties. After watching him for an hour, Blum asked if he was going to show them in New York. When Andy said that he didn't have a gallery, Blum offered to show the whole set in L.A. that July. Andy paused. He knew from experience that summer was a bad time to show art in New York, but when Irving assured him it was the best time to be shown in Los Angeles, he whispered, "Oh, I would adore it." They agreed that the paintings would sell for one hundred dollars each (the same price Warhol had charged for a painting his junior year at Carnegie Tech, and a tenth of what he was getting for a commercial drawing). Andy would receive fifty percent.

According to David Bourdon, Andy's ambition bordered on the desperate. "It was very naked, but so was the weak side. Andy wasn't as adept at concealing his vulnerability as he was later. When dealers wouldn't take him on or collectors wouldn't buy, his face would fall and he would whine. Andy's most voluble emotions were always ones of distress and disappointment, a kind of plaintive 'How could they leave me out? How could they do this?' "

As Andy relentlessly hustled the art scene, going to an opening or party every night, keeping his eyes and ears attuned to every development, he began finding some acceptance (although the presence of Jasper Johns at one of these events reportedly would make him so nervous that he would have to keep running to the toilet to urinate). Reaction to the Campbell's soup can paintings began well before they were shown. Andy was featured in the first mass-media article on pop art—in the May 11, 1962, issue of *Time*—in which he was quoted: "I just paint things I always thought were beautiful, things you use every day and never think about. I'm working on soup and I've been doing some paintings of money. I just do it because I like it."

When the Ferus show opened on July 9 (there was no formal opening and Andy did not attend), the public, according to Blum, was "extremely mystified. Artists were provoked, but they tended to shrug, not really condemn. There was a lot of amusement. A gallery dealer up the road bought dozens of Campbell's soup cans, put them in the window, and said, 'Buy them cheaper here—sixty cents for three cans.' *Not* a great deal of serious interest."

But John Coplans, who edited a bright new West Coast art magazine, *Artforum,* saw the show and was impressed. As word spread, people took strongly opposing positions on the work.

The soup cans had grown in Blum's estimation as well: "After about three weeks I rang Andy up and said, 'I'm haunted by these pictures and I want to suggest something. I'm going to attempt to keep these thirty-two paintings together as a set.' Andy said, 'Irving, I'm thrilled, because they were conceived as a series. If you could keep them together it would make me very happy.' I said I had reserved a few of the paintings, but that I could approach the various collectors to get them back. As soon as I hung up, I called the first collector I had promised one of the paintings to—the movie actor Dennis Hopper. I explained what I wanted to do, and he gracefully relinquished the picture to me. I did that six times, and when I had the complete set, I called Andy and asked what price could he make me on the group. Andy offered me all of them for a thousand dollars over the course of a year, and we agreed that I would send him one hundred dollars a month."

The one hundred or so artists, dealers, critics, and collectors who made up the hard core of the pop movement were as diverse and eccentric a group as only New York could put together in one room.

Among them were a number of unusual women, most prominently
Eleanor Ward, who owned the Stable Gallery. She was a legendary
character—"a composite of all the movie stars of the thirties and
forties, Joan Crawford and Bette Davis rolled into one," her assistant Alan Groh said. That same summer, when an autumn show at
her gallery was canceled, Mrs. Ward considered giving Andy his
first one-man pop exhibition in New York.

Although not as businesslike as Castelli's, the Stable Gallery—so
called because it was located in an old stable on West Fifty-eighth
Street—had been instrumental in the careers of two of Andy's favorite painters, Cy Twombly and Rauschenberg. The gallery also
represented the surrealist Joseph Cornell, and had just taken
on Robert Indiana and Marisol. But it was not for everybody.
"Eleanor," said Groh, "was completely unpredictable. You wanted to
embrace her and the next moment she could say something unbelievably devastating." Friends who had warned Andy about her
must have been unaware that she was not unlike the women who
had given him his start in the fashion world. When she called to ask
if she could drive in from the country to look at his work, Andy just
said, "Eleanor Ward! Oh, wow!"

She asked Emile de Antonio to take her over to Andy's house that
night. "Andy," said de Antonio, "was incredibly nervous and agitated from the beginning. Eleanor and I drank ourselves into the
wall for about three hours, and I could see Andy was losing his cool
because he looked as if people were sticking pins into him. Finally, I
said, 'Well, come on, look here, Eleanor, are you giving Andy a show
or not? Because he's very good, and he should have one, and that's
why we're here.'

"She pulled out her lucky two-dollar bill and sort of waved it in his
face and said, 'Andy, it just so happens I have November, which as
you know is the best month to show, and if you do a painting of this
two-dollar bill for me, I'll give you a show.' She was a beastly woman
and she was obscene with that two-dollar bill."

According to Eleanor Ward, all Andy said was "Wow."

The summer of 1962 was enormously productive for Andy. He
finished painting the contents of his mother's kitchen, doing canvases of rows of Martinson's coffee cans, Coca-Cola bottles, S&H

Green Stamps, and a number of large Campbell's soup can portraits, as well as *50 Campbell's Soup Cans, 100 Campbell's Soup Cans,* and some "Glass—Handle with Care" labels. The idea of repeated reproduction was very much in the air. John Cage had declared repetition a fundamental principle of twentieth-century art. In his just-published autobiography *Self-Portrait,* another high priest of the avant-garde, Man Ray, had written that reproduction was the only way anything could survive in a society that destroyed everything it laid eyes on. But Andy's use of it was seen as unusually subversive. After all, many artists painted the same subject over and over from different angles, but to paint and repaint the same subject as identically as possible seemed to undermine art's essential value—the uniqueness of each work—seemed designed, in fact, to render it meaningless. To Andy, who as a youngster had counted the sheets hanging on his neighbors' clotheslines during his walks to school, that repetition was a way of pointing up *distinction*—for wasn't every sheet, after all, different?

In July he discovered a technique that would change his career decisively. He was trying to find a quicker way to paint rows of dollar bills. Nathan Gluck suggested he silk-screen them. Photo silk-screening, which Andy would make his primary medium for the rest of his life, is a sophisticated stencil process in which a photographic image transferred to a porous screen can be quickly duplicated on canvas by laying the screen on the canvas and applying paint or ink over it with a rubber squeegee. With a silk screen, an image can be printed on a canvas in a matter of minutes.

Andy quickly realized that this process was tailor-made for his talents, which were largely as a conceptualist and designer. Still foraging in his childhood for images, he went back to his first collection, the movie-star publicity pictures, and did silk-screen paintings of Elvis Presley, Troy Donahue, Warren Beatty, and Natalie Wood, repeating the same picture over and over again in rows across a large colored field. But he didn't hit full stride with the new technique until Marilyn Monroe committed suicide that summer on August 4, the day his *Soup Can* show closed in Los Angeles.

As soon as he heard the news, Andy decided to paint a portrait series using a black-and-white publicity photograph taken by Gene Korman for the 1953 film *Niagara.* On this occasion he first applied a good deal of paint to the canvas. Outlining the shape of Monroe's head and shoulders, he painted in a background, then painted her eyeshadow, lips, and face before applying the silk-screened image from the movie still. During the late summer and early fall, Warhol did twenty-three Marilyn portraits. They ranged from *Gold Marilyn,* a small single image silk-screened onto an expansive gold field (an updating of the icon paintings of his Byzantine Catholic upbringing), to the famous Marilyn diptych, one hundred repetitions of the same face across twelve feet of canvas. The colors were garish ("overworked Technicolor," one critic would write)—bright yellow for her hair, chartreuse for her eye shadow, her lips a smear of red—and they were frequently out of register with the black-and-white background image. When Nathan Gluck pointed out the flaw, Andy mumbled, "Oh, but I like it like that." The misprints and the occasional clogging of the screen gave each face a slightly different "mask," making the point that although her face had been reproduced endlessly, Marilyn Monroe was more than the plastic consumer product she appeared to have become.

"I just see Monroe as another person," Andy would say later, "I wouldn't have stopped her from killing herself. I think everyone should do whatever they want to do and if that made her happier, then that is what she should have done. As for whether it's symbolic to paint Monroe in such violent colors: It's beauty, and she's beautiful, and if something's beautiful, it's pretty colors, that's all. Or something."

The elusive movie star's mask was reproduced to the point where it was impossible to say where the mask ended and the real woman began—in that sense very much like the man who had created them. The Marilyn paintings were to remain a landmark in Warhol's work. As the critic Peter Schjeldahl wrote: "Visually and physically the Marilyn diptych had majesty reminiscent of Pollock and Newman. The effect was like *Moby Dick* retold, to resounding success, in street slang, with a sexy actress standing in for the fearsome white whale. With his subject matter and technique in place, Warhol suddenly let loose a pent-up profound understanding of New York school painting aesthetics."

And the writer Ron Sukenick:

> Warhol's serial photo silk screens of Marilyn Monroe are about as sentimental as Fords coming off the assembly line, each one a different color, but each one the same as every other. . . . What happens to the idea of originality with the advent of mass production, or to the

idea of the unique artifact? As with the computer, there is only the abstract program and the 'hard' print-outs it can reproduce infinitely. It is perhaps because of such factors that Paul Bianchini insists that Pop Art represented America's first real break with European tradition, and, one might speculate, a final and irreversible one, as opposed to Abstract Expressionism, which can be seen as an extension of European ideas.

As soon as he had finished the Marilyns, Andy silk-screened all the paintings of coffee cans, Coke bottles, dollar bills, and soup cans he had done earlier that summer. Released at last to do exactly what he wanted, he made one hundred pictures in the next three months. His living room looked and smelled as if it had been hit by a paint bomb.

And at last he had a real home away from home—the Stable Gallery. "Look what the cat dragged in," Andy would chortle, turning up that fall with rolls of canvases under his arm, dressed in paint-splattered jeans, his hair askew, sneakers unlaced, chewing candy. Eleanor Ward openly adored him and was convinced that he was a great artist. She was also beginning to sell what he was bringing in, buying several of them for herself at a fifty percent discount. She called him "my Andy Candy."

Moreover, the serious art world was rallying around. By now *Art News* had acknowledged his soup cans for their "quality of lofty elegance," claiming there was, as the critic Gene Swenson wrote, "as much humanity and mystery in them as there is in a good abstract painting."

Old friends saw a distinct change in the Andy they had known. That September he attended a Labor Day weekend party at the Brooklyn Heights home of George Klauber. Bert Greene recalled: "We were all waiting for him to arrive, because he was the one among us who had achieved a certain level of fame. He came with an entourage of very good-looking boys—I don't want to say 'call boys,' but expensive boys and certainly like acquisitions. He had more authority, an air of hauteur. He didn't seem so little-boy fey. A close friend of ours, Aaron Fine, was dying of cancer. He had wanted to come but couldn't, so he'd sent a question in his place. I said, 'Andy, Aaron wants to know why you picked the Campbell's soup can to paint.'

" 'Tell him,' he said, 'I wanted to paint nothing. I was looking for something that was the essence of nothing, and that was it.' "

On October 28 the Cuban missile crisis ended when it was announced that the Soviet premier, Nikita Khrushchev, had backed down to all of President Kennedy's demands for the dismantling of Soviet nuclear missiles in Cuba. New York—and America—breathed a euphoric sigh of relief, and three days later, on Halloween, pop art exploded in the media at a group show at the Sidney Janis Gallery. "Pop," the artist Robert Indiana would proclaim, "was re-enlistment in the world. It was shuck the Bomb! It was the American dream—optimistic, generous, and naive." The curator Walter Hopps said of the opening party: "Jean Tinguely showed an icebox that had been stolen from an alley outside Marcel Duchamp's secret studio. When you opened it, a very noisy siren went off and red lights flashed. It set the noise and tone that was to continue all the way through the sixties."

Andy Warhol had three paintings in the show, including *200 Campbell's Soup Cans*. People pointed at him and whispered his name. He was quoted as saying: "I feel very much a part of my times, of my culture, as much a part of it as rocket ships and television." But to at least one onlooker that night, the writer David Dalton, he seemed more "like a white witch, looking at America from an alien and obtuse angle."

The Janis show marked a changing of the guard. The older abstract painters affiliated with the gallery—Philip Guston, Robert Motherwell, Adolph Gottlieb, and Mark Rothko—held a meeting and resigned in protest. De Kooning, who was also a member of the Janis Gallery, did come to the opening. He paced back and forth in front of the paintings for two hours and left without saying a word. James Rosenquist, one of the artists in the show, said: "After the opening, Burton and Emily Tremaine [well-known collectors] invited me to their house on Park Avenue. I was surprised to find Andy Warhol, Bob Indiana, Roy Lichtenstein, and Tom Wesselmann there. Maids with little white hats were serving drinks, and my painting *Hey! Let's Go for a Ride!* and Warhol's Marilyn diptych were hanging on the wall next to fantastic Picassos and de Koonings. Right in the middle of our party de Kooning came through the door with Larry Rivers. Burton Tremaine stopped them in their tracks and said, 'Oh, so nice to see you. But please, at any other time.' I was very surprised and so was de Kooning. He and the others with him soon left. It was a shock to see de Kooning turned away. At that moment I thought, something in the art world has definitely changed."

Warhol's Stable show, which opened one week later, included his best paintings: the Marilyn diptych, *100 Soup Cans, 100 Coke Bottles, 100 Dollar Bills,* and many others that have since become classics. Eleanor Ward was so nervous she would not come upstairs from her office for the longest time, but Geldzahler, Karp, and de Antonio were there to support Warhol, along with a host of other artists and critics riding the wave of exhilaration—Marisol, Indiana, David Bourdon, Ray Johnson, and Gene Swenson—as well as friends from the 1950s like Charles Lisanby, Suzi Frankfurt, Nathan Gluck, and many others. Mrs. Warhola finally made an entrance and passed out soup can buttons. Sarah Dalton, David Dalton's twin sister, modeled a dress reproducing Warhol's painting *Glass—Handle with Care.* The sharp-eyed Leo Castelli was there too, realizing that he had grossly underestimated Andy Warhol.

Nervous but loving every minute of it and accompanied by a group of good-looking young men, Andy arrived late and hurried into Mrs. Ward's office to learn that a prominent collector, the architect Philip Johnson, had already bought the *Gold Marilyn* for eight hundred dollars. Eleanor Ward remembered: "Andy was thrilled and he was happy and he was gay. His work was accepted instantly with wild enthusiasm." For the rest of the evening, however, Warhol seemed withdrawn, standing in a corner with a blank expression. "His eyes were soft, expressive," recalled a friend. "They were the eyes of a fragile night creature who discovered himself living in the blaze of an alien but fascinating world." Philip Johnson later said that Andy's demeanor was the only thing he really liked about the whole crazy show.

"At a party I gave after the show," recalled Henry Geldzahler, "the art critic Barbara Rose referred to Andy as an 'idiot savant.' I later reported this to Andy, who said, 'What's an idiot *souvent?*' " Contrary to his unlettered image, Andy was an avid reader with a quick, punster's love of language.

The show was a controversial smash. Many of those who saw it joked about how terrible it was, but it almost sold out. Typical was the reaction of William Seitz, who bought a Marilyn for the Museum of Modern Art for $250. When Seitz's colleague Peter Selz called him and said, "Isn't it the most ghastly thing you've ever seen in your life?" Seitz replied, "Yes, isn't it? I bought one."

With his dumb-blond image and, as it seemed to many, his dumb paintings, Andy became the number-one target for anybody who wanted to attack pop art, particularly among the first- and second-generation abstract expressionists and their followers. Reviewers in that camp called Warhol's work, among other things, a "vacuous fraud." According to David Bourdon: "That generation of artists had struggled for so long for the little amount of attention they got, only to be eclipsed by pop art, that they had this tremendous amount of animosity, especially toward Andy."

Among those who thought Andy a fraud who had betrayed his real talent were a number of old friends. Charles Lisanby upset Andy greatly by rejecting the gift of a Marilyn portrait. He pleaded that his apartment was too small, but confessed privately that he "really hated it." According to Lisanby, Andy got quite worked up, his voice cracking as he said, "But it's going to be worth a lot of money one day!" "I kept saying, 'I think it's wonderful what you're doing. Just tell me in your heart of hearts you know it isn't art.' He would never admit it, but I knew he knew it wasn't."

Andy gave Ed Wallowitch a Campbell's soup can painting and was furious when Ed sold it for a few hundred dollars. "You should have held on to it," he fumed. "You would have made a lot of money."

Vito Giallo thought Andy was barking up the wrong tree. "I didn't like that pop art school at all and I said to Nathan, 'I can't believe he's doing this, I just can't see it.' "

The new work also got rough treatment from his family. James Warhola, Andy's nephew, remembered his uncle smarting under the sarcastic dismissal of Marge and Ann Warhola: "They said, 'This isn't art, Andy. When are you going to get rid of this stuff?' " Paul recalled: "Mother used to say when I was going home, 'Take a couple of paintings.' And I'd say, 'Ah, Mom, I don't want to take the paintings.' 'Oh, go ahead,' she'd say. In fact she even gave paintings away. She gave one to her sister. Her sister gave it to her grand-daughter, and when the granddaughter sent it to New York for Andy to autograph it, Andy says, 'Hey! How did this . . . ? I was looking for this. You gave away one of my best paintings, Ma!' Mother also wanted to throw out the sculpture in the vestibule. She says, 'When Andy's gone, take this out and put it in the rubbish.' Andy overheard. He cried, 'Ma! Ma! That's from a famous sculptor. Maaaa!' "

In the autumn of 1962, Andy's arrival at public events began to have an effect: at his entrance the party would, as David Bourdon put it, "snap to." Patti Oldenburg summed up his social appeal: "The minute Andy walked into the room you felt really good. He was always smiling and he always looked shiny, brushed, and scrubbed. He was so open you could imagine anything happening."

Andy would never go anywhere alone, and he made a point of gathering around him the most attractive, sexiest women on the scene. Prominent among them were Marisol and Ruth Kligman.

Marisol was a Venezuelan sculptor who was Andy's Stablemate at Eleanor Ward's gallery, and, like Andy, a new star. She belonged to no "school" but her own—and she was both beautiful and spooky, as silent and distant as Andy. With each other they were, recalled a friend, like "two pussycats rubbing their heads together." (Marisol said she found Andy sexually attractive because he was so strong. On at least one occasion she expressed the desire to go to bed with him, but nothing came of it.)

Ruth Kligman had a beauty that resembled Elizabeth Taylor's, and she had been a close companion of some of the greatest abstract painters—Kline, de Kooning, and Pollock, who was with her the night he killed himself by ramming his car into a tree on Long Island.

"Andy," she recalled, "was fascinated with de Kooning and Pollock, and through me, he wanted to be part of that lineage. And I wanted to be part of him, because I knew that he was this incredible talent and genius. He asked equally about their work and personalities. He felt that I was much too nice to everybody. He used to say, 'Oh, be aloof, be aloof, be aloof.' He was always telling me that I should behave more like Marisol."

Ruth started seeing Andy regularly after his Stable show. "We had a terrific crush on each other, and I think it was sexual. We didn't act it out, but we would hug sometimes. I remember getting a little carried away once and he said, 'Oh, Ruth,' and squirmed out of it. We'd have frivolous conversations about, 'We should get married and, Ooooh, how wonderful it would be,' but then he would talk about not wanting to invest his emotions that much. He was always curious about what other people did sexually, and he would say, 'Oh, you're better off putting all your energy into your work. Sex takes up too much time.' But he was never judgmental of other people's problems. If someone was committing suicide over love, he completely understood it. He gave you the feeling he'd experienced it. To me, his complexity was in his humanism juxtaposed to his desire to be detached and machinelike. He could be very loving, very kind, very generous, and yet cut you off if it wasn't going to be good for his career."

His effect on other friendships could be just as devastating. As a result of their rivalry over Andy, Marisol and Ruth Kligman, who'd been friends for years, stopped speaking. (Ruth found herself abruptly cut off two years later when she told Andy she was getting married. He told her he found it impossible to maintain relationships with married people. He had to come first or not at all.)

Now, the Peter Pan of the commercial art world was, in the serious art world, a threat. His strange, alien appearance—that pale slab of a Slavonic face, inscrutable beneath a blond wig—along with the steady hint of homosexuality was confounding. Stealing the beautiful young darlings of the art establishment was a brilliant move. It partially masked his homosexuality, leaving him less open to homophobia. It associated him with the great painters they had been close to. And it caught the attention of the media, for Andy knew that photographers were more likely to snap away if he were standing next to a beautiful woman.

"He would try to appear artless and naive," said Charles Lisanby. "But he knew exactly what he was doing. He really knew the effect he was having. Always, always."

Still, Andy probably did not calculate the degree of enmity he had stirred up in the abstract expressionist camp, inspired as much by his manner as by the work itself and the methods he used to produce it. For dating Andy, Ruth Kligman was made to feel that she was somehow betraying the old group. "De Kooning," she said, "never liked me to mention Andy. Andy polarized the departure from abstract expressionism to pop art because he *looked* like pop art, and also he was very anti-painting. De Kooning represented a classical approach. Andy was more modern, more 'anti-art.' "

One Sunday in Greenwich Village, Andy and Ruth ran into Mark Rothko. When Ruth said, "Mark, this is Andy Warhol," Rothko turned and walked away without a word. On another occasion, Marisol took Andy and Robert Indiana to a party. When they walked in, the room fell silent. Then Rothko could be heard demanding of his hostess, "How could you let *them* in?"

Andy handled the uproar brilliantly. His strategy was, "Don't *think* about making art, just get it done. Let everyone else decide whether it's good or bad, whether they love it or hate it. While they're deciding, make even more art." Indeed, rather than defend himself, he encouraged the attacks. It was true, he declared, that anybody could do what he did. In fact, he liked that idea. It was true, he said, that his subject was "nothing." And it was true that his paintings would not last. By accepting all the criticism with open arms, he demolished it.

Andy immediately revealed himself to be a master of the interview. One of his famous responses was a direct steal from an old play of Tallulah Bankhead's. The reporter asked, "Do you think pop art is—"

"No," he replied.

"What?"

"No."

"Do you think pop art is—"

"No," he replied. "No, I don't."

Vulgarity—or the charge of vulgarity—has often been the spur to major shifts in the development of Western art. As it was in the sixteenth century with Caravaggio and his use of Roman street people in religious allegories, with Manet and his *Déjeuner sur l'herbe,* which sent French academicians reeling in the nineteenth century, so it was with the pop artists of 1962. As the social critic Tom Wolfe was to observe: "Pop art absolutely rejuvenated the New York art scene. It did for the galleries, the collectors, the gallery goers, the art-minded press, and the artists' incomes about what the Beatles did for the music business at about the same time. Avant-gardism, money, status, Le Chic, and even the 1960s idea of sexiness—it all buzzed around pop art."

Like the other forces that made what was shortly to become "the sixties"—rock music, the Vietnam war, the civil rights struggles, the political assassinations, the moon walk—pop art was a great leveler, scrambler, and disregarder of old boundaries. And at the head of this uprising, for that is what it essentially was, stood the unlikeliest of standard-bearers, an artist who seemed determined to remain as blank a slate as possible. Which meant that commentators could find in the phenomenon of Andy Warhol just about anything they wanted to find.

For many, it was a matter of sexual politics. In the critic Kenneth Silver's view, "Warhol made blue-collar gay American art. His subjects were drawn from both the mass culture in which he grew up and the 'campy' culture which he grew into. Indeed, that second, gay culture is really a gloss on Warhol's first aesthetic experiences, the mass ones in the picture press and on the silver screen, just as his own art was in turn a focused and selective form of both popular and gay culture."

Ron Sukenick observed that Warhol's art was essentially an attack on elitism:

> Warhol deflated the mystifications connected with high culture, but at the same time he devastated the adversary position of avant-garde art in relation to the middle class. . . . Warhol assured [the middle class] that, don't worry, there's nothing about art you don't understand. There is an element of vindictive contempt in Warhol's activities, in view of which it is fascinating to consider [Peter] Schjeldahl's observation that Warhol is one of the few American artists who have ever come out of the lower working class. "Warhol went from the bottom of the heap to the top without ever passing the middle, so it's like he was completely free of the middle-class perspective. [His art had] no anguish, no doubt, no apology, no existentialism, no expressionism, nothing except what it was."

Whatever its ultimate significance, there was no denying its immediate impact. Using Marcel Duchamp's 1912 shocker as a touchstone, Henry Geldzahler best summed up Andy's astonishing ascendancy in 1962: "The *Campbell's Soup Can* was the *Nude Descending a Staircase* of pop art. Here was an image that became the overnight rallying point for the sympathetic and bane of the hostile. Warhol captured the imagination of the media and the public as had no other artist of his generation. Andy was pop and pop was Andy."

8

WARHOL NOW ENTERED his most intense period as a painter. By June 1963, he could no longer work at home. Canvases were spread over the living room; paint and ink from the silk screen had splattered on the floor and furniture. Junk lay everywhere. Andy rented a studio in an abandoned hook-and-ladder firehouse a few blocks away on East Eighty-seventh Street. The annual rent for the second floor of the city-owned building was only one hundred dollars, but he had to hopscotch over the holes in the floor; the roof leaked, sometimes destroying paintings, and there was no heat.

Andy's engagement with his work was demonic. In order to keep up the pace, he decided to hire an assistant to help him with his silk screens the way Nathan Gluck was continuing to help on his commercial art projects. Gerard Malanga got the job.

Malanga looked like Elvis Presley as a fashion model. He came from a poor family in the Bronx, where, like Andy, he lived alone with his mother. He had been rescued from poverty by some admiring poets and groomed in the homosexual literary community that floated around W. H. Auden and Charles Henri Ford. Malanga was only twenty and primed for action when Andy hired him.

Malanga's account of his work (some would say collaboration) with Andy is as good a description of what made Warhol's art as anyone can give: "Andy loved all sorts of machines and gadgets—tape recorders, cassettes, Polaroid, Thermofax. But the focus for all this experimentation was silk-screening for making a painting. Andy's reasoning was that the silk screen would make it as easy as possible to create a painting. When the screens were very large, we worked together; otherwise, I was pretty much left to my own devices. I had a first-hand knowledge of silk-screen technique, having worked for a summer as intern to a textile chemist in the manufacture of men's neckwear, so I knew what I was doing from the start. Andy and I would put the screen down on the canvas, trying to line up the registration with the marks we made where the screen would go. Then oil-based paint was poured into a corner of the frame of the screen, and I would push the paint with a squeegee across the screen. Andy would grab the squeegee still in motion and continue the process of putting pressure on pushing the paint through the screen from his end. We'd lift the screen, and I would swing it away from the painting and start cleaning it with paper towels soaked in a substance called Varnolene. If this was not done immediately, the remaining paint would dry and clog the pores."

Nathan Gluck took an instant dislike to Malanga, and it is easy to see why. With his droopy eyes, his mouth constantly open in a pout, and his insouciant poetic air, Gerard represented the new model of the boy peacock, proud of his beauty, and actively bisexual. Moreover, he was immediately accepted as an equal by Andy and rapidly propelled into his personal life, whereas Nathan had never once been invited by Warhol to a social affair.

Almost immediately Andy asked Gerard back to the house to meet his mother and have lunch—a rare invitation. Malanga still had no idea that his new boss was anything more than a commercial artist, and as he walked into the living room, he was afraid that Andy might make a pass at him. This was something he wouldn't know how to deal with, for Andy looked so fiendish—"real weird, threatening, and overpowering," he recalled.

Warhol left him alone in the room, which reminded Malanga of nothing so much as the seedy archives of a pornographer, while he went to check in with his answering service. Malanga looked around, saw some paintings of Campbell's soup cans, and it dawned on him that Warhol was one of those pop artists he had read about in a magazine. He felt "in awe of the situation," but when Andy returned to the room with Julia carrying a tray of hamburgers and 7-Ups, he began to relax. With his mother in the room, he noticed, Andy became a little boy, which put him on just about the right level for Malanga, who had the innocent and spontaneous intelligence of a somewhat louche eight-year-old. Indeed, Gerard wrote later, they often felt like children together. In one of Andy's favorite fantasies that would have meant feeling like two little girls playing in the street after school.

And yet, during those first few weeks, Malanga had a sense of fear around Andy. "That was the paradox," he said. "The word *alien* is the perfect description of him, because this very sweet presence was coming out of this demonic-looking person." Gerard soon discovered that the two of them had much in common. They were both collectors of movie memorabilia, and they were soon going out to the movies several nights a week, calling each other "Andy Pie" and "Gerry Pie." Gerard was struck by Andy's ability to make people feel like his best friend, even after knowing them for only five minutes: "If you were to meet him for the first time and Andy liked you, he became your instant fan, and this, in turn, would give you a feeling of self-esteem."

In the spring and summer of 1963, Warhol painted a number of outstanding portraits. A series of six-foot-tall silver images of Elvis Presley holding a gun, based on a film still, were among the best. Andy had first brought Elvis into his work in 1956 in the *Crazy Golden Slippers* show at the Bodley Gallery, in which the pop idol was represented by an elaborately festooned boot. Elvis was the only subject Andy took with him from the fifties into the sixties. A multiple *Red Elvis* had appeared in the Stable Gallery show; one of his many experiments with the soup cans was called *Campbell's Elvis* (the singer's face was superimposed over the can's label). Just how conscious Andy was of his long affinity with Elvis is problematic, but in his study *The Iconography of Elvis,* John Carlin noted striking parallels between the two men:

> Both came from humble backgrounds and meteorically captured their respective fields in a way that seemed to break entirely with the past. Each betrayed his initial talent as soon as it became known, and opted for a blank and apparently superficial parody of earlier styles

which surprisingly expanded, rather than alienated, their audience. Both went into film as a means of exploring the mythic dimensions of their celebrity.

On the surface both men shared a scandalous lack of taste. Particularly as both took repetition and superficiality to mask an obscure but vital aspect of their work: the desire for transcendence or annihilation without compromise, setting up a profound ambivalence on the part of both artist and audience as to whether the product was trash or tragedy.

Another notable portrait series from this period was devoted to Robert Rauschenberg (with whom Andy had become friendly) using a sequence of Rauschenberg family snapshots. Another was devoted to the Mona Lisa, the multiple reproductions of which Ivan Karp described as quintessential pop: "cold, mechanical, tough, alien, and bland." That fall the collector Robert Scull gave Andy the opportunity to do something different on a large scale when he commissioned a portrait of his wife.

Ethel Scull was nervous about Andy doing her portrait because "with Andy you never knew what to expect." When he came to pick her up to be photographed for the silk screen, she expected to go to Richard Avedon's studio and was dressed accordingly in a designer outfit. Instead, Warhol took her to a Photo-Matic machine on Forty-second Street. She protested that she would look terrible, but Andy told her not to worry and took out one hundred dollars' worth of coins. "He said," she recalled, " 'I'll push you inside and you watch the little red light.' I froze. He came into the booth and poked me and made me do all kind of things and I finally relaxed. We were running from one booth to another. Pictures were drying all over the place. At the end he said, 'Now, do you want to see them?' They were sensational."

Andy, she recalled, delivered the portrait in pieces, and her husband invited him to complete the work in their apartment. Andy demurred: " 'Oh, no,' he said, 'The man who's up here to put it together [Warhol's assistant]—let him do it any way he wants.'

"Bob said, 'But Andy, this is your portrait.'

"Andy said, 'It doesn't matter.'

"So he sat in the library, and we did it. Then, of course, he did come in and gave it a critical eye. 'Well, I do think this should be here and that should be there.' When it was all finished, he said, 'It really doesn't matter. It's just so marvelous. But you could change it any way you want.' "

"Andy's attitude toward women was very complicated," said Henry Geldzahler. "He admired them. He wanted to be one. He wanted to be involved in their creation. *Ethel Scull Thirty-Six Times* was the most successful portrait of the 1960s. It was a new kind of look at a single human being from thirty-six different points of view, obviously influenced by the cinema and television. He was creating an image of a superstar out of a woman who could have been any one of a series of women."

Andy knew that he needed to come up with a new idea that would shock as much as the soup cans and dollar bills. For a while he played with pornography. As Robert Indiana, who spent a lot of time with Warhol in 1963, recalled: "Everybody who was involved with the art world in New York was convinced that the next concern of young artists after pop was going to be pornography. I remember going around New York visiting studios with Warhol just to see all the really rather raw pornography that was being done. I had the feeling that he was going to go in that direction." Andy did two large paintings called *Bosoms I* and *Bosoms II*, using paint that could be seen only under ultraviolet light, and was enthusiastic enough to tell Gene Swenson, who wrote for *Art News*, "My next series will be pornographic pictures. They will look blank; when you turn on the black lights, then you see them—big breasts. If a cop comes in, you could just flick out the lights, or turn to regular lights—how could you say that was pornography? The thing I like about it is that it makes you forget about style; style isn't really important." But he quickly dropped the idea when he discovered that the breast paintings would be impossible to sell.

It was Henry Geldzahler who steered him in a more productive direction. As early as June 1962, Geldzahler had suggested that Andy start looking at the dark side of American culture. "There's enough affirmation of life," he had said.

"What do you mean?" Andy had asked.

"It's enough affirmation of soup and Coke bottles. Maybe everything isn't always so fabulous in America. It's time for some death. This is what's really happening." He gave Andy a copy of the *New*

York Daily News with the headline "129 DIE IN JET" emblazoned on its front page. From it Andy executed a large, stark black-and-white painting that was much admired in the Stable show.

The death portraits of Marilyn had brushed up against the theme once again. Then, in the spring of 1963, Andy silk-screened a photograph from *Life* of a police dog tearing the trousers off a black man in Alabama onto a seventeen-foot-high yellow canvas and called it *Mustard Race Riot*. Following a suggestion by the painter Wynn Chamberlain, he started doing a series of paintings based on news photos of violence—car crashes, suicides, funerals, the electric chair, and the hydrogen bomb.

"I realized that everything I was doing must have been Death," he told Gene Swenson. "It was Labor Day and every time you turned on the radio they said something like, 'Four million are going to die.' That started it. But when you see a gruesome picture over and over again, it doesn't really have any effect. The death series I did was divided into two parts: the first on famous deaths and the second on people nobody ever heard of and I thought that people should think about some time: the girl who jumped off the Empire State Building or the ladies who ate the poisoned tuna fish and people getting killed in car crashes. It's not that I feel sorry for them, it's just that people go by and it doesn't really matter to them that someone unknown was killed, so I thought it would be nice for these unknown people to be remembered. There was no profound reason for doing a death series, no 'victims of their time'; there was no reason for doing it at all, just a surface reason."

Working with Malanga, Andy painted the series rapidly, silk-screening images onto canvas painted with a single coat of garishly colored paint—lavender, pink, mint green. He reproduced photographs of dead bodies torn limb from limb, wrapped around wrecked, burning cars, sixteen or twenty times on a single canvas. As a result of the silk screen clogging or slipping out of line, some pictures were clear, some were blurred, some were lined up straight, some were crooked. The effect was raw and hard. The paintings were given titles like *Vertical Orange Car Crash, Green Disaster Twice, Purple Jumping Man, Lavender Disaster*.

"Each painting took about four minutes," said Malanga, "and we worked as mechanically as we could, trying to get each image right, but we never got it right. By becoming machines we made the most imperfect works. Andy embraced his mistakes. We never rejected anything. Andy would say, 'It's part of the art.' He possessed an almost Zenlike sensibility, but to the critics Andy became an existentialist because the accidents were interpreted as being intentional statements."

These were Warhol's most political statements to date, although in a conversation with Oldenburg and Lichtenstein on radio station WBAI in New York he rejected such imputations, claiming the disaster pictures were an expression of indifference. "Ask somebody else something else," he told the moderator. "I'm too high right now." On another occasion, he said: "The United States has a habit of making heroes out of anything and anybody, which is so great. You could do anything here. Or do nothing. But I always think you should do something. Fight for it, fight, fight. I feel I represent the United States in my art, but I'm not a social critic: I just paint those objects in my paintings because those are the things I know best. I'm not trying to criticize the United States anyway, not trying to show up ugliness at all: I'm just a pure artist."

But the critics had discovered a new "profundity." In *Pop Art*, John Rublowsky wrote about the "death-and-disaster" paintings: "In his search for artistic truth, Warhol has stripped away the layers of pretenses and repression that obscure dark memories and knowledge all of us share. . . . It takes a special kind of person to venture into an entirely new dimension."

Gerard Malanga was often amused by such effusions: "I was with Andy twenty-four hours a day at that time, and I know he would never choose an image for the reasons critics dug up. He was really on a roll because every one of those images was a hot image. Andy used shocking colors in his paintings; even the silver was hot when he juxtaposed red lips on it. I think Andy put his sexual energy into his work, but he never talked about it. The emphasis was on pretty. That was the word he used. It was never 'beautiful,' it was always 'pretty.' "

"I don't think he was trying to make social statements in these paintings," said Henry Geldzahler. "I think that he's turned on by certain images, and those images that turn him on are loaded, supercharged images. I think the death image, the image of corruption, the image of decay, is really closer to his heart."

Geldzahler wrote: "What held his work together in all media was the absolute control Andy Warhol had over his own sensibility, a sensibility as sweet and tough, as childish and commercial, as innocent and chic as anything in our culture."

The "death-and-disaster" paintings have since become recognized as among Warhol's best work, but at the time, many of his supporters found them unacceptable. Just as Lisanby had rejected a Marilyn, David Dalton refused a gift of a disaster painting, commenting that he didn't want to have to look at dead people on the living-room wall every day. Eleanor Ward flatly refused to show them, and cracks began to appear in Andy's relationship with her. During 1963 he did not have a one-man show in New York. The paintings were soon to make him famous in Europe, however. In Germany, where pop art was already being collected, they were admired, the art critic Heiner Bastian recalled, "as the greatest things we had ever seen."

In January 1964 they were shown at Ileana Sonnabend's gallery in Paris. The focal point of the exhibition was *Blue Electric Chair*, a large painting on two panels, one of which consisted of the same image of a death chamber, with a sign reading "SILENCE" in one corner, repeated twelve times. The other panel was simply an empty blue monochrome, which had been added not only as an ultimate "comment" on death but to double the value of the painting.

The French greeted the work rapturously. "Their subjective quality is neither sadness nor melancholy, nor regret nor even bitterness," the critic Alain Jouffroy wrote. "The traditional feelings attaching to death are banished. In front of these pictures we are cleansed. The paintings become the holy scenes of a godless world."

9

VIRTUALLY EVERYONE WHO claimed to know Andy Warhol during his years of ascendancy thought of him as someone whose only sexual release was his work—which explained, perhaps, the almost fetishistic power of his "scenes of a godless world." In fact, as early as 1961, he had recommenced having sexual relationships. His first affair after his period of celibacy was with a man in the art world who wishes to remain anonymous. A promiscuous man with a reputation as a seducer, he claims to have gone to bed with Warhol many times between 1961 and 1963. In those days a gay man was forced into being either "butch" or "femme"; when he was picked up he would be asked which he was. Andy was definitely "femme." Years later, "Mr. X" said that Andy was extremely good in bed, so "light-fingered" that Andy had brought him to greater heights of pleasure than he had ever known before.

Theirs was a purely sexual relationship with no emotional ties. (On one occasion, "Mr. X" says, when he and the art writer Gene Swenson stopped to pick up Andy at his house before going out, he went upstairs and engineered Andy into bed while Swenson waited unwittingly downstairs.) When the affair began, Andy was not yet a celebrity, but as soon as he became famous he turned cautious and took great pains to cover his tracks, at least as far as his active sex life was concerned. Nonetheless, in public he seemed to become more overtly "gay" than ever. John Giorno, who was a stockbroker on Wall Street by day and a figure in the gay scene by night, recalled: "Andy made a point of his gayness by the way he walked, talked, and gestured as a kind of statement, but the reason it worked is, it was very qualified. He kept it out of his work; he didn't try to put the make on anybody he was involved with professionally."

Giorno was the first in a long line of younger men with whom Andy became infatuated during the sixties. In April 1962 he and Andy started dating. A typical evening would begin with an art opening or dinner, followed by a film screening, and ending with the two of them back at Giorno's apartment. Andy had started taking diet pills—amphetamines—and on many occasions he and Giorno would sit up talking through the night, Giorno drinking, while Andy broke open one capsule after another, licking the tiny pills off his fingers. For Andy the relationship grew increasingly painful: Giorno, who was good-looking as well as promiscuous, refused to go beyond kissing. The idea of going to bed with someone who looked like Andy, recalled Giorno, was "gross and disgusting," and the most intimate he allowed their two-year relationship to become was letting Andy perform fellatio on him several times. On one of those occasions Giorno noticed five or six different colored hairs emerging from under Andy's wig at the nape of his neck. "It looked like a Frank Stella painting," recalled Giorno, "and I said, 'Andy, what in the world . . .?' He explained that he went to a chichi uptown hairdresser once a month to have it dyed."

The turning point came a year later, when Andy took John to the firehouse to look at the Elvis paintings. Standing at the top of the stairs, they started to kiss. John was drunk, and as they headed down the steep flight, still kissing, he slipped and fell, pulling Andy with him. They tumbled to the bottom, body over body, landing in a stunned, silent heap, both miraculously unhurt.

"We coulda been killed!" Andy cried out, meaning—John recalled—"You tried to kill me!"

After that Andy started to look at Giorno in a different way: A month later he would release his pain by transmuting his reluctant lover into an object of art.

By then Andy had already cast Gerard Malanga as John's rival.

Andy soon began using him to make John feel as bad as possible, playing Gerard off against John just as he had played Marisol off against Ruth. And for the first time with a man, it worked. Giorno would have gone to bed with Andy, but it was too late. Now that Andy had subjugated him, he spurned him. It was a pattern that Andy would perfect.

Andy had started taking the diet pills to keep him going through his twelve-hour workdays, followed by rounds of social events that often kept him out till three or four in the morning. Soon, it would be not at all unusual for him on being offered a cocktail or a plate of food to say, "No thanks!" and pop a pill in his mouth instead, chasing it with a glass of soda. In time, he would make not sleeping or eating as much a part of his legend as his silver wigs and beatnik clothing.

Andy knew what he was doing with drugs. He was also very careful to take only what was legal, for as he started to gain notoriety, he knew that he would be a prime target for the police. At the beginning of 1963 he got a prescription for Obetrol, a diet pill that produced a sense of infinitely expanding time without inducing the teeth-grinding verbosity or the awful crash of Dexedrine and many of the other amphetamine pills so easily obtainable in the sixties. Declaring that he had to become pencil thin, Andy started working out at the gym again, going several afternoons a week.

His path was not always as smooth as his "Wow! Gee whiz!" pop persona suggested. Henry Geldzahler once got a frantic call at 1:30 A.M., only an hour after he and Andy had parted. Andy wanted to meet him at The Brasserie in the Seagram Building in half an hour. When Geldzahler protested that he was already in bed, Andy said it was very important: "We have to talk, we have to talk." Imagining that something of creative import was at stake and wanting to be in on its every moment, Geldzahler rushed to the restaurant to find a pale, trembling Andy perched on a banquette.

"Well," Henry said, hurtling into the booth breathlessly, "what is it? What is so important that it can't wait until tomorrow?"

Staring at him with wide-awake blank eyes, Andy replied, "We have to talk, Henry. Say something!"

It was, as Geldzahler heard it, a cry for help from a man who had got stuck in a metaphysical twilight zone where he was too alone with his work.

This was also a period when Andy would go to the movies fanatically. If he wasn't spending an afternoon sitting with Emile de Antonio through one of De's monumental hangovers in a Forty-second Street cinema, watching one of the worst monster and gangster movies ever made, he was squiring Malanga to the glittering premiere of *Dr. No* or to Orson Welles's version of Kafka's *The Trial*. In between he would sit with John Giorno, the poet Charles Henri Ford, and sometimes Malanga, in the Film-Makers' Co-op run by Jonas Mekas and watch hour after gruelling hour of underground art films. "There are so many beautiful things," Andy would whisper to John between reels. "Why doesn't somebody make a beautiful movie?"

In July 1963, Gerard and Charles Henri took him to Peerless Camera, where he spent $1,200 on a Bolex 8-mm camera. He told anybody who would listen that he had no idea how to load or focus the camera, chortling gleefully, "I'm going to make bad films!"

One night that summer, John and Andy spent the weekend together on Eleanor Ward's estate in Old Lyme, Connecticut, sharing a room with twin beds. As usual, John passed out in a drunken stupor around 4:30 in the morning. When he woke up to go to the bathroom several hours later, he discovered Andy lying in bed next to him wide awake and staring. "What're you doing?" Giorno mumbled.

"Watching you," came the mechanical reply.

Several hours later Giorno awoke again: Warhol had switched angles and was on a chair at the foot of the bed, "looking at me," John recalls, "with Bette Davis eyes. I said, 'Andy, what are you doing?' "

"Watching you sleep," he said.

For the longest time Andy had been wanting people to "do things" for him while he watched. Having abandoned the naked-boy drawings and paintings of the 1950s and then turned his attention to media subjects for his art, he began asking friends to undress for his camera. Ruth Kligman had been insulted when he asked her to let him film her while she got up, took a shower, and got dressed. Now Andy was becoming bolder. On the train back to New York that night he told John he wanted to make a movie and asked him if he wanted to be a "star."

"Absolutely!" said Giorno. "What do I have to do?"

"I want to make a movie of you sleeping," Andy replied.

Giorno agreed, and several nights later they took a taxi over to his flat, where Andy set up his equipment. Giorno later wrote: "I was sitting on a seventeenth-century Spanish chair as he checked out where to put his tripod and lights, and suddenly Andy was on the floor with his hands on my feet, and he started kissing and licking my shoes. I had always heard he was a shoe fetishist. 'It's true!' I thought with a rush. 'He's sucking my shoes!' It was hot, and I got some poppers to make it better. I jerked off while he licked my shoes with his little pink tongue and sniffed my crotch. It was great. Although Andy didn't come. When I wanted to finish him off, he said, 'I'll take care of it.' "

For the next two weeks Andy shot four hours of footage per night on several different occasions. When he had the film developed, he discovered he had ruined all of it because he had not rewound the camera properly. Now, he shot the whole film again. While the footage was being developed, Andy decided to visit Hollywood.

Pop art was rapidly taking over the West Coast scene. Irving Blum was planning his second Warhol show of the Elvis Presley and Elizabeth Taylor portraits that September. The Oldenburgs had moved to California, and Claes was having an opening the day after Andy's. Furthermore, Marcel Duchamp, the spiritual godfather of pop art, was having a retrospective the following week. To make the scene even more inviting, Dennis Hopper offered to give Andy a movie-star party, and Hopper's wife, Brooke Hayward, had arranged for him to stay in the suite of her father, the producer Leland Hayward, at the Beverly Hills Hotel. This was an invitation Andy could not refuse. "Being a star was absolutely a dream of his," said Ruth Kligman. "But he didn't want to just be a movie star, he wanted to be the head of a studio."

Dispatching the Elvises in a giant roll of silver canvas and blithely instructing the astonished Blum to cut them up and stretch them any way he liked, as long as the entire wall was covered, Andy announced that he would be arriving the day before the opening and would see Blum at the Hoppers' party that night.

In the course of that summer, Andy's reputation had risen fast on the West Coast. He had been prominent among the artists included in the *Pop Art/USA* show at the Oakland Museum, leading the California painter Larry Bell to write, "It is my opinion that Andy Warhol is an incredibly important artist. He has been able to take painting as we know it and completely change the frame of reference, and do it successfully in his own terms." California was ripe for Andy's arrival. "Vacant, vacuous Hollywood," Warhol wrote, "was everything I ever wanted to mold my life into. Plastic, white on white." And also: "I always wanted Tab Hunter to play me in the story of my life."

After the death of Elizabeth Taylor's husband Mike Todd in a plane crash in 1961, Julia had told Andy, "Too many big shot die in plane." Since then he had acquired a fear of flying that would last the rest of his life. Rather than taking a plane or train to the West Coast like the movie stars of his dreams, Andy made the decision to drive across America, as in Jack Kerouac's beat classic *On the Road*.

As a teenager Andy had been given driving lessons by his brother Paul, and one day in 1952 Paul had tried to give him a lesson in New York. It had ended in a minor accident on Park Avenue, with Andy blaming Paul for not having put on the brakes, even though he had been in the driver's seat. He never attempted to drive again. Now, to make the cross-country trip in four days, he needed two drivers. Characteristically he picked two of the least responsible candidates for the job: Taylor Mead, a clownish star of underground films with a huge appetite for marijuana and Quaaludes, and the painter Wynn Chamberlain, whose beat-up Ford station wagon would furnish their transportation. They planned to make the journey as fast as possible, stopping only to eat and sleep. As Andy's boon companion and glorified valet, Gerard Malanga was persuaded to take a sabbatical from Wagner College, where he was studying poetry.

For their comfort, Chamberlain put down the back seat and placed a mattress in the back. There Warhol and Malanga lolled, listening to hit tunes of the day like "Puff the Magic Dragon," "Dominique," and "If I Had a Hammer." Except for Andy, everyone smoked pot. Their first stop was St. Louis. Andy, who was paying for everything with his Carte Blanche card, treated everyone to a big steak dinner, after which he declined to join the others in hitting the town. When Malanga returned to their motel room several hours later, he was struck by the studied manner in which Andy was sitting there, doing absolutely nothing. He had the impression that Andy regarded the whole trip as a movie in which he was the mysterious star from a script by Samuel Beckett.

The next night they came close to getting killed when Chamberlain raced through a red light at a crossroads in the middle of nowhere and narrowly escaped colliding with a car coming at them broadside. After a brief silence, Andy said in the small, tight voice of a complaining wife, "Wynn, where were *you?*" After that he insisted that the radio be turned on all the time with the volume as high as possible.

On the third day Taylor freaked out and said if they didn't stop for a break he was getting out of the car and hitchhiking. Andy agreed, and they pulled into a truck stop full of teenagers and truckers. "It was like we were from outer space," Mead recalled. Andy commented that these heartland innocents were living in the past while they were living in the future. It was frightening to be homosexual in that context, said Mead, but Andy clearly enjoyed all the attention.

As soon as they got to Hollywood, things started to happen fast. No sooner had Andy checked into his suite at the Beverly Hills Hotel than there was a knock on the door. In walked the underground movie star and filmmaker Naomi Levine, whom Andy had recently met in New York and who had flown out on Film-Makers' Co-op business. From the moment Andy arrived, she attached herself to him like a limpet mine.

Warhol later wrote that Dennis Hopper's party was the most exciting thing that had ever happened to him. Still, the Hollywood Warhol visited that year was dying. You only had to look at the year's most ballyhooed films—*Cleopatra, It's a Mad, Mad, Mad, Mad World, How the West Was Won*—and note that the top box-office stars were still Doris Day, John Wayne, Rock Hudson, and Elvis Presley, to see what the trouble was. Moreover, the young stars Hopper had gathered to fête Andy—among them, Sal Mineo, Suzanne Pleshette, Troy Donahue, Peter Fonda, and Dean Stockwell—seemed every bit as square. What Andy was going to do in the cinema was so far removed from their view of things that he must have realized there was little point in pursuing the "new Hollywood." Andy may have enjoyed himself that night, but he made no effort to contact any of them, apart from Hopper, again.

The opening the following night was a big disappointment. In a last-minute decision that puzzled Mead, Andy decided to withhold the Elizabeth Taylor paintings and show only the Elvis Presleys. The work was coolly received by the local critics and collectors, and not one painting sold. Although Andy was by now adept at masking his reactions, he resented the bad reviews and what he considered the flat-out stupidity of the movie stars who had failed to snap up his work. He was convinced that these paintings, which could have been purchased for a mere one-thousand dollars, payable in installments, would soon be worth a great deal more. As far as he was concerned, they were money hanging on the wall.

They were also among his best works. Stephen Koch would later identify the source of their extraordinary immediacy: "It is worth noticing just how startling and suggestive pictures like *Triple Elvis* once were and how powerful they remain. Ordinarily when we look at any given image, there is a certain passage of time—five, maybe fifteen seconds—during which the mind is simply identifying precisely what it is looking at. In Warhol's case, the time span of recognition is invariably reduced to a flash."

Despite the failure of his show, Warhol turned up, in apparently high spirits, at Oldenburg's opening the following night, as well as at Marcel Duchamp's opening on October 8 at the Pasadena Art Museum, at which he spent a good deal of time talking with Duchamp, one of the century's seminal art figures. Andy was so excited by the show and the party afterwards that for one of the few times in his life he drank too much, and was sick on his way back to the hotel in the early morning. Bored by the formality of the Beverly Hills Hotel, Warhol and company had moved to the Santa Monica Beach Motel and were spending the rest of their visit with the street people and emerging hippies, whom Mead knew.

One night when Mead was preparing to give a poetry reading, Andy mistook his contemplative warm-up for a depression. According to Mead, "Andy said, 'Oh, you should calm down. Here!' and he pulled out this big gray cock and tried to make me blow him. I said, 'You gotta be kidding! I have to think about my reading,' and I walked off. It was a totally evil thing to do—cold-blooded and ruthless shit. The dumbest peasant wouldn't be that cruel or misread a state so much. I couldn't handle it, because Andy usually had a certain amount of consideration, but he was just being a dirty little kid."

Malanga too was seeing a side of Andy that startled and upset him. Throughout the trip he had shared hotel rooms with Andy, with no hint of sexual overtures, so he felt he was doing nothing inappropriate when, after a party, he brought a girl back to their room and put the chain on the door for privacy. Andy returned unexpectedly early: "I was only in bed with her for half an hour when, all of a sudden, Andy's at the door of our hotel room. He was so angry that I had put the chain on the door and he couldn't get in, he literally tried to break the door down. He was banging on the door, shouting, 'Why is this door locked? Who's in there? Come on! Open it! Open this door up!' We put on our clothes and I let him in. As soon as he saw the girl, that just made him more annoyed, and he reprimanded me. He was really pissed off."

The same week, Naomi Levine, who had decided that Andy's work "was all an excuse to be with people," had a tantrum. Andy had made a film during the California visit starring her and Taylor Mead called *Tarzan and Jane, Regained Sort of*. The filmmaking had gone remarkably well, particularly several nude scenes with Naomi during which she was filmed "swimming" in the hotel bathtub. She felt she was making progress at winning Andy over, but at the same time, she said, she was beginning to see "how he provoked people with his passiveness into becoming freaky." She later recalled: "He had obviously decided he liked me, and he was very sweet. One night he took a big bag of sugar and opened it and poured it down my arm."

As Malanga saw it, "Andy was putting up with Naomi. She was a very sensitive person and he went out of his way not to hurt her feelings. Andy's passive state made women feel they could approach him. Women felt that Andy was almost asking them to take care of him."

But once the filming was completed, according to Malanga, Andy got tired of Naomi's needy presence. Things came to a boil after a day spent at Disneyland when she flirted with him during a boat ride through a tunnel. Finally, she snatched at his wig in an attempt to break his composure. Anybody who wanted to make Andy get angry had only to try forcing him to do something. Stunned by his rage, Naomi flew back to New York.

Tarzan and Jane taught Andy an important lesson: If he was going to work with groups of people, he would have to be even more detached to control them. That he hadn't quite mastered this was apparent on the way back to New York. In a North Carolina motel room, he made a pass at Malanga: "We were horsing around in the room when Andy suddenly turned around and put his hand on my crotch over the sheets. I didn't say anything but I shook it off, turning over. He suddenly turned quiet and that was the end of the incident." When they got back to New York, however, Andy, who had usually been generous in this matter, refused to give Gerard cab fare, obliging him to carry his heavy suitcase all the way to the Bronx on the subway.

The next day, Andy and Gerard went straight back to work silk-screening photographs of car crashes and suicides. After painting in the morning, they spent the afternoon looking for a new studio. Gerard wanted a place where he would have a room of his own to live in. Andy wanted a large, open space where he could paint, make movies, and "do everything." In the six months they had been working together, Gerard had made himself indispensable as Andy's assistant and sidekick, so much so that the two had become an entity, a kind of Gertrude Stein and Alice B. Toklas of the art world. A Sam Montana cartoon in the *Village Voice* that winter depicted Warhol commenting on a painting, saying, "I dunno, Jerry, it's not boring enough," and Malanga replying, "Golly, will it hurt us, Andy?"

Although they were widely assumed to be lovers, according to Malanga they were not: "It was almost as if he was sexless. He cringed from physical contact. I think that celibacy gave him enormous manipulative power over the magnificently beautiful people he brought together. But it was congenial. We were like two teenagers hanging out together. I don't think Andy was consciously trying to hide something about himself so much as he was attempting to maintain a mystique, partly for control and partly as a cover for his own inadequacies."

That November, *Art News* ushered in another phase of Andy's career, the Warhol interview. Conducted by Gene Swenson as part of a series of talks with pop artists, it revealed yet another talent that would set Andy apart from his rivals—his gift for the eminently quotable and shocking utterance, such as: "I think everybody should be a machine. I think everybody should like everybody." In time, such declarations would become "sayings," as much keynotes of the sixties as the lyrics of the Beatles and Bob Dylan.

But the mask of blankness was not yet fully in place. On a more conventional level, Andy also told Swenson that he had a grand theme: Everything he painted was about death. Soon he would have the most sensational death of the century for a subject. Of John F. Kennedy's assassination on November 23, Warhol would later claim: "I thought Kennedy was great, but I wasn't shocked by his death. It was just something that happened. It isn't for me to judge."

John Giorno, who rushed over to Andy's house upon hearing the news, remembered quite a different reaction: "We sat on the couch, watching the live TV coverage from Dallas. Then we started hugging, pressing our bodies together, and trembling. I started crying and Andy started crying. Hugging each other, weeping big fat tears and kissing. It was exhilarating, like when you get kicked in the head and see stars. Andy kept saying, 'I don't know what it means!' "

With uncanny intuition he found the perfect image to express that meaning: his *That Was the Week That Was* portrait of Jacqueline Kennedy, based on eight newspaper head shots taken in the minutes before and after the assassination and funeral and metamorphosed into a sixteen-panel work. Andy had admired Mrs. Kennedy enormously, and his dignified setting of her image in golds and blacks heightened the presentation of her as a transcendent figure above the horror.

Later, Stephen Koch wrote what may be the most perceptive description of this work's power:

> These images have a frontality that would hit us smack in the eyes were it not for Warhol's countermove: his voyeur's transformation, his anesthetizing stare. *This* distance is uniquely Warhol's own. The game here is power—the back and forth of Warhol's work is always a subtle eroticized interplay of active and passive terms. This is why soup cans can come from the same artist who shows the images of a man leaping to his death; why the duration of an entire film can sink into the voyeuristic absorption in the face of a man asleep. . . . [The art produced in this period] trafficked in themes of major dimensions: what it means to see feelingly, what it means to fear what you want to see; the struggle with the visual power of fame, beauty, death, and terror.

10

A T THE END of November 1963, a truck containing Warhol's painting equipment from the firehouse and 1342 Lexington Avenue pulled up outside a warehouse and factory building on East Forty-seventh Street. Andy was pleased with his new location. It was just down the block from the United Nations and overshadowed by the Chrysler Building—not at all the sort of neighborhood where an artist might be expected to have a studio. The new space, on the fifth floor of 231 East Forty-seventh, could be reached by a rickety open freight elevator or a flight of stairs. It was a large single room, about one hundred by forty feet, with a couple of toilets in the back and a pay phone. Metal columns stood four-square, defining its central area. The floor was concrete and the brick walls were crumbling. There was little natural light, since most of the windows facing south had been painted black, and the ceiling was low. It had previously been a hat factory.

Without missing a beat, Andy continued painting, turning out electric chair pictures and *White,* twenty repeated images of a 1947 *Life* photograph showing the body of a young fashion model who had jumped out of the Empire State Building and landed, still elegant, on the roof of a car.

Summing up Warhol's career in a catalogue of the Saatchi Collection in London, Peter Schjeldahl perceptively noted the almost ecstatic aura of such a work:

> Like most modern artists, the halcyon Warhol was both radical and conservative, looking both forward and backward in cultural time. Initially appearing to ridicule the preciousness of art with a technique of mass production, Warhol and his silk-screening—actually a clumsy and messy artisan device—finally mocked mass production and exalted painting. This was possible because, for a while, he was on to something serious: chaos—systems entropy, human madness, and death—as a crack in the world through which could be glimpsed a violent bliss.

Andy's next idea may have been at least partly inspired by the hope that Eleanor Ward would reject him again, thus making it easier for him to leave her gallery: He would make four hundred sculptures of grocery boxes for Campbell's tomato juice, Kellogg's cornflakes, Del Monte peach halves, Brillo pads, and so on out of plywood, silk-screening them to look as much like the originals as possible, except that they would be nailed shut.

Mrs. Ward was aghast: The idea sounded like a disastrous departure for someone who had only just been accepted as a painter. How much would he sell them for? she asked. Three hundred to six hundred dollars each. Finally, his enthusiasm won her over.

He and Malanga got to work. For three months, rows of wooden boxes were stacked the length of the studio as they toiled in what one observer described as "a production line in a surrealist sweatshop." Although the results were intended to look as though they had come off an assembly line, making the boxes was the hardest work they had ever done. They had to hand-paint six sides of each box, wait for them to dry, and then silk-screen at least four of the sides.

At the same time, Andy was increasingly turning his attention to film. As soon as he had returned from Hollywood, he had thrown himself into getting *Sleep* developed and edited while Taylor worked on the finishing touches of *Tarzan and Jane*. Andy had watched television replays of the famous Zapruder film of the Kennedy assassination that November, and had been fascinated by the "replay" of the event in slow motion. Perhaps because of this he insisted that these early films be projected several frames per second more slowly than they had been shot, a scarcely noticeable shift that enhanced their hypnotic effect.

Naomi Levine proved a great help in getting Andy into the New York underground film scene by screening the six-hour *Sleep* in Wynn Chamberlain's loft at 222 The Bowery for Jonas Mekas, who ran the Film-Makers' Co-operative and published *Film Culture* magazine. Many people were to dismiss *Sleep* as an insult to their intelligence, but Mekas saw it as an important work. To him the displacement created by running the film at sixteen instead of twenty-four frames per second was the essence of Warhol's art, the "one little choice that shifts the whole to a totally new angle." Warhol was presenting a new vision of the world, Mekas declared, "celebrating existence by slowing down our perceptions."

In late 1963 and early 1964, Andy filmed *Kiss*. He would get a couple like Marisol and Robert Indiana to pose in a mouth-to-mouth kiss, and hold the pose for three minutes. In many cases he mated couples who were not at all compatible. Several segments were filmed at Naomi Levine's apartment on Avenue B in the East Village. One day when Naomi felt uncomfortable with a partner, Gerard Malanga stepped in and began his movie career as a Warhol star.

Sleep was followed by three shorter, minimal films: *Haircut,* which showed one man ritualistically cutting another man's hair; *Eat,* in which Robert Indiana took thirty-three minutes to eat a mushroom; and *Blow Job,* in which the camera stayed resolutely on the twitchings of an actor's face while his penis was being sucked off-camera, again for thirty-three minutes. (The climax of the film, and presumably that of the star, was signaled by the lighting of a cigarette.) Suddenly, as much as pop art was coming to be virtually defined in the public eye by Warhol, so "underground film" now seemed to have been entirely made over by him. Even Stan Brakhage, one of the movement's masters, a filmmaker whose style was as kaleidoscopic as Warhol's was stark, came around. At Mekas' invitation, he had sat through *Sleep* and *Eat* and gone into a rage, announcing that they were all being taken in by a charlatan. When it was discovered that the films had been mistakenly projected at twenty-four frames per second instead of Andy's desired speed of sixteen, he was persuaded to sit through the films again—and was won over. Here, he announced to Mekas, was an artist whose films were achieving as great and clear a transformation of reality as were his.

Andy, typically, adopted a less exalted view. "My first films using the stationary objects," he told the perceptive journalist Gretchen Berg, "were also made to help the audience get more acquainted with themselves. Usually, when you go to the movies, you sit in a fantasy world, but when you see something that disturbs you, you get more involved with the people next to you. . . . You could do more things watching my movies than with other kinds of movies; you could eat and drink and smoke and cough and look away and then look back and they'd still be there. . . . I made my earliest films using, for several hours, just one actor on the screen doing the same thing; eating or sleeping or smoking; I did this because people usually just go to the movies to see only the star, to eat him up, so here at least is a chance to look only at the star for as long as you like, no matter what he does, and to eat him up all you want to. It was also easier to make."

While Andy was working on the Brillo boxes and the early films, a twenty-one-year-old hairdresser and lighting man, Billy Linich, arrived to help design the studio. Attractive and intense, a self-proclaimed Buddhist and black magician, Linich had been living with several other young men in a Lower East Side apartment in which everything was painted or tinfoiled silver. Andy had met him there and had immediately seen Billy and his friends as the precursors of a new style. Would Billy, he asked, do the same thing to the studio that he had done in his apartment? "It must have been the amphetamine but it was the perfect time to think silver," Andy wrote. "Silver was the future, it was spacey—the astronauts. . . . And silver was also the past—the Silver Screen. . . . And maybe more than anything else, silver was narcissism—mirrors were backed with silver."

Andy was drawn at once to Billy. "Andy took to a lot of people who were shy," said Malanga. "He would sit right next to the person and budge up to them, listen intently, and maybe ask questions, always like a little boy. Andy was really good at making people feel important. He always sat down with somebody who didn't have an identity for himself. He found these people because he needed them."

From January to April 1964, Linich toiled away, meticulously transforming the dark, crumbling room into a giant, silver reflector. In the meantime, he was living in the studio, having built himself a nest in a back corner next to the toilets, where he slept on the floor like an ascetic. Indeed, with his strong, sinewy arms, washboard stomach, handsome, serious face, and close-cropped hair, Billy looked very much like Hollywood's idea of one of the twelve apostles.

As soon as he started working there, a number of Billy's downtown friends began to show up—talented misfits, most of them gay and heavy users of amphetamines, and all of them given to theatrical extravagance in costume and manner. With *noms des guerres* like "Rotten Rita," "the Mayor," "the Duchess," "Mr. Clean," and "the Sugar Plum Fairy," they might have crept off the pages of Jean Genet. They were called the "amphetamine rapture group." (Later, they would be referred to in the gay lexicon as "mole people," homosexuals who remained underground throughout most of the sixties, only to emerge as pioneers of gay liberation toward the end of the decade.) Outstanding among them, as far as Andy was concerned, were Freddie Herko and Ondine.

Of Herko, an aspiring dancer in Broadway musicals whom he filmed roller-skating all over New York on one bleeding foot, Andy wrote: "The people I love were the ones like Freddie, the leftovers of show business, turned down at auditions all over town. They couldn't do something more than once, but their once was better than anyone else's. They had star quality but no star ego—they didn't know how to push themselves. They were too gifted to lead 'regular lives,' but they were also too unsure of themselves to ever become real professionals."

Ondine (born Robert Olivo) was a self-described "running, standing, jumping drug addict" and brilliant verbal acrobat. Silent Andy was fascinated by the intensity of this crazy rapper. "And Ondine," said Billy Linich, "was also a high-power intellect. He could be so cruel and didactic about what he thought was wrong or right, sometimes people just looked at this dragon monster and missed the whole point of the aesthetic dissertation he was giving them. One day, Ondine, Andy, and I were trying to think of what to call his studio. We said, we'll call it either the Lodge or the Factory, and since it was a factory before, let's call it the Factory. And everybody just said, 'Yeah, that seems right.' We were the prime movers, the catalysts, the destroyers, taking away people's façades. Saying, 'Are you really telling me this is your true self or are you just putting on shit?' "

Billy persuaded Andy to bring his big Harman Kardon hi-fi system from his house to the Factory, and Billy, Ondine, and friends often stayed up for several days at a stretch taking speed, listening to opera recordings, and talking nonstop.

As traffic increased, Billy became studio manager. Under his watchful supervision, the paraphernalia of drug use were kept out of Andy's sight. "They didn't want to offend him, and I was constantly aware of his security, safety, and well-being," said Linich. "He didn't know that people were shooting up because they were very discreet. And anyway, once he had his Obetrol he would be joyously in tune with everything they were doing."

Brigid Berlin was one of the few women among the mole people. Brigid's claim to fame, apart from her high-society heritage (her father was president of the Hearst Corporation) was that she was said to have squirted Nikita Khrushchev in the face with a water pistol when he visited the United Nations in 1960. She was known as "the Duchess," or "the Doctor" because, she boasted, she would give anyone who asked for it a poke of amphetamine through the seat of their pants (her new name at the Factory soon became Brigid Polk). She shot speed several times a day, gorged on food, and was at times grotesquely overweight. She was also highly emotional, given to screaming tirades. Nonetheless, she seemed to bring out a protective instinct in Andy, who was entertained by her informed gossip, delivered in a broad society accent, about everyone from J. Edgar Hoover to the Duchess of Windsor. She got rid of a lot of anger against her parents by yelling at Andy, who would listen blankly, and she adored him from the moment they met. For the rest of his life she remained one of his closest friends.

Three other women in the amphetamine rapture group were self-styled witches: Dorothy Podber, Orion de Winter, and Diane di Prima. Their attitude, according to Linich, was, "how dare you come into my presence and not be exquisite and perfect and know exactly what you're doing because if you don't I'm going to find out and destroy you!" Naomi Levine was back in Andy's good graces, but she had been eclipsed as a "superstar" by a young society woman, Mrs. Leonard ("Baby Jane") Holzer.

Baby Jane, who had appeared in *Kiss* and had been hanging out with Andy since then, witnessed with a degree of alarm the transformation of the Factory by the mole people into a perpetual happening, although she thought some of their drugged-out performances "brilliant." With her leonine mane of hair, the latest in high-style clothes, and her friendship with the Rolling Stones, this beautiful Park Avenue socialite, the wife of a wealthy businessman, had been thrust into the fashion spotlight by the British photographer David Bailey and been profiled by Tom Wolfe as the "Girl of the Year, 1964." Andy designated her a "superstar" and escorted her to parties, openings, and rock shows, thereby doubling his attention from the press. Indeed, Andy seemed to love the press so much that some of his friends decided that he felt really alive only when he saw a photograph of himself in a newspaper.

The moment the Factory opened its doors, it became a cultural mecca, part atelier, part film studio, part experimental theater, part literary workshop, and a Salvation Army for all the artists and would-be artists who couldn't find shelter elsewhere. "I don't think anybody ever had a studio like the Factory on Forty-seventh Street," said Emile de Antonio. "There were political people, radicals, people in the arts, disaffected millionaires, collectors, hustlers, hookers. It became a giant theater. I once said to Andy, 'You're making a film of a film, aren't you?' He laughed."

Billy Linich ran the place like a theater, vacuuming up after each performance or poetry reading, continually repainting the silver. When Andy gave him a 35-mm camera, he became the unofficial recorder of all that went on, developing the film in a darkroom converted from one of the lavatories. Over the years he built up an extraordinary document of life at the Silver Factory that would be collected in the catalogue for Warhol's first European retrospective in Stockholm's Moderna Muséet in 1968.

The Factory was undoubtedly a man's world, and a gay man's world at that. It quickly took on a style and attitude of its own. Ondine remembered that "Andy was always so provocative sexually.

I think he knew that everybody was really thinking about big cocks. When people came to see him at the Factory, like foreign journalists or art dealers, he would say quite blandly, 'Check him out, see how big his cock is,' and these people would be horrified." According to Malanga, one of Andy's favorite fantasies of himself was as the proprietor of an all-male brothel. His idea, Malanga recalled, "was that he would sit at a table with a cash register on it in a large dormitory with rows of beds without partitions between them. People would come in and have sex with a boy in a bed and then pay Andy the money on their way out."

As the sixties developed, so did Andy's new look. He now dressed like an SS guard in a B-movie about the Second World War, with a few embellishments of his own: black leather jacket, tight black jeans (under which he wore panty hose), T-shirts, high-heeled boots, dark glasses, and a silver wig (to match his Silver Factory). Sometimes he emphasized his pallor and Slavonic features with make-up and wore nail polish. He was now very thin, and the general "look" he was after was clean, hard, and arrogant. He hardly ever laughed and rarely spoke in public. But when he did speak it was in a new, disembodied voice that sometimes sounded like Jackie Kennedy on television, laced with sarcasm and contempt. The British social commentator Peter York wrote: "The absolute flatness [of his voice], the affectlessness, meant you couldn't see behind it at all. Drawing on druggie and toughie and gay styles, it forged an adoptive Manhattan occupational tone for the sixties. The drug voice meant: I'm so far away you can't touch me. The ethnic tough-bitch wisecracking voice said: No quarter given and none expected. The New York fag voice said: Oh, c'mon."

Stephen Koch noted: "Warhol's hypnotized voyeuristic stare of smarmy whitened worminess inspired much fascinated talk about what you find under rocks." His followers, though, told him he looked magnificent.

As his image changed, as he surrounded himself with a bodyguard of flagrantly gay, shameless young men, many old friends began to back away from him. Charles Lisanby said: "I warned him to stay away from that kind of thing, but he was fascinated to be in a room where somebody was shooting drugs. I never got the idea from talking to Andy about it that he was doing any of this himself, but I thought it was terrible. I once accused him of just doing things for effect and of trying to be different, doing things that would disturb people because he thought 'different' was better. He always denied this and insisted that what he was doing was really what he wanted to be doing. But I said to him, 'Andy, if you hang around with these kind of people one of them's going to kill you!' "

Suzi Frankfurt was also getting turned off: "I hated the way he dressed, and I said so. He said, 'Ooooohhhh, Suzi . . . you don't like it?' And he really got into having bad manners and he got tougher on the exterior. For example, I'd have a dinner party for someone Andy liked because they were so rich. He would ask if he could bring ten people, and then they'd arrive two hours late."

Ruth Kligman was confused by Andy's new ways. At his request she had invited some friends to a showing of *Blow Job,* which she regretted: "I showed the film but I didn't like it. Even the word *blow job* offended me. There were all these strange people I couldn't relate to who were all on speed. And there was a kind of prurience I didn't like. Andy took his lack of sexuality and put it into his voyeurism, watching people. He would provoke people who I thought had no ego to get into their dark side, into their homosexuality, even if they weren't gay. He remained the master and he would make all sorts of promises to these people, like to Freddie Herko and all these pathetic souls who hung around, and I thought that was very negative."

In fact, many of Andy's old friends thought he had changed so much that he no longer even recognized them at parties. "It was as if," recalled George Klauber after one such occasion, "he just looked right through me."

To the mole people at the Factory, Andy had become a demonic hero. They started calling him Drella, an amalgam of Dracula and Cinderella. "It was a homosexual campy fairy-tale thing, like the Wicked Witch of the North, and Andy was cast as the bad guy," recalled Malanga. One day, one of the mole people "witches," Dorothy Podber, arrived at the Factory with her dog, Carmen Miranda, and asked Andy if she could shoot his Marilyn paintings. When he said he didn't mind, Dorothy put on a pair of white gloves and pulled a small German pistol out of her pocket, aimed at a stack of Marilyn Monroe paintings, and fired. After she left, Andy went over to Ondine and said, "Your friend just blew a hole through . . ." Ondine said, "But you said she could."

"Andy really was playing with a loaded pistol in everything he did," said Ondine, "but everytime I saw him witness real violence, he was completely surprised. He didn't suspect violence on other people's parts, and violence shocked him. He didn't have street smarts."

But he did have business smarts. When he saw that the bullet had passed cleanly through four Marilyns, he retitled them *Shot Red Marilyn, Shot Light Blue Marilyn, Shot Orange Marilyn,* and *Shot Sage Blue Marilyn,* and later sold them.

Now Andy became openly confrontational. In April 1964, Warhol had a disagreement with the architect Philip Johnson, who had commissioned him to do a mural for the American pavilion at the World's Fair in New York. Andy had delivered a twenty-by-twenty-foot black-and-white mural called *The Thirteen Most Wanted Men,* based on a series of mug shots of criminals. It had been installed beside works by Rauschenberg, Lichtenstein, and Indiana. On April 16, however, Johnson informed Warhol that he had twenty-four hours to replace or remove the piece. Word had come from Governor Nelson Rockefeller that the painting might be insulting to some of his Italian constituents, since most of the thirteen criminals were Italian. When Andy suggested he replace it with large pictures of the fair's organizer, Robert Moses, Johnson "forbade that because I didn't think it made any sense to thumb our noses at Mr. Moses and I thought it was in very bad taste. Andy and I had a little battle at the time." The next day, Andy went out to the fair with Malanga and Geldzahler and instructed that his mural be painted over in silver. "That," he said, "will be my art."

A few days later, Warhol's *Brillo Boxes* show opened at the Stable Gallery. Andy had said he wanted the gallery to look like the interior of a warehouse, and Alan Groh had lined the boxes up in rows and stacked them in corners. The show was immediately a cause célèbre, another rallying point for those for and against the new art. "The most striking opening of that period was definitely Andy's *Brillo Box* show," said Robert Indiana. "You could barely get in, and it was like going through a maze. The rows of boxes were just wide enough to squeeze your way through." Passage was made harder by a man who had passed out between a row of boxes and was left sleeping there.

Robert and Ethel Scull immediately put in an order for a large number of the boxes, and there were long lines waiting outside the gallery. But the presentation of the boxes as sculpture confounded many people, not least among them the abstract expressionist painter James Harvey, who had actually designed the original Brillo box. "When Andy's show happened," said the art chronicler Irving Sandler, "Harvey's dealer at the Graham Gallery came out with a press release saying that while Andy was selling these for three hundred dollars, here this poor starving artist James Harvey had to support himself by making commercial things like Brillo boxes." The press had a field day. Photos of Warhol and Harvey appeared in *Newsweek* with their respective products. Andy called Harvey and offered to trade one of his sculptures for a signed original, but before the trade could be arranged, Harvey died of cancer.

The night after the opening, the public got its first view of the Silver Factory. Andy had decided to throw a party, and Billy had been up for several nights putting the finishing touches on the ceiling and lighting the room with white, red, and green spotlights.

"Reynolds wrap is what hits you," wrote a reporter of the first great art party of the decade. "The whole place is Reynolds wrap, the ceiling, the pipes, the walls. The floor has been painted silver. All the cabinets have been painted silver. The pay telephone on the wall is silver. The odd assortment of stools and chairs are silver. And the bathroom is silver-lined and painted, including the toilet bowl and flushing mechanism."

The party also marked a turning point in Andy's career, for it was the last time he would be photographed in a group with Oldenburg, Lichtenstein, Tom Wesselmann, and Rosenquist. From now on he would appear surrounded only by his own people.

From the point of view of the socialite Marguerite Lambkin, who gave the party with the Sculls, the event was not a success: "First of all, Bob Scull wanted detectives at the door to turn away people who weren't on the list, but, as Andy and I said, how can we keep out an artist bringing someone he'd had dinner with? What should have been frivolous and fun was for us a nightmare. We had everyone from Senator [Jacob] Javits to the New York police, who dropped in. The detectives gave up. Bob Scull was furious because Ethel hadn't been photographed by *Vogue*. The next day Andy rang to ask if I wanted any Brillo boxes."

The Sculls, it turned out, had canceled their entire order. According to Nathan Gluck, who was still laboring away on Warhol's commercial work at 1342 Lexington Avenue and who witnessed the return of the boxes, Andy was devastated by the rejection.

It didn't make sense. Here he was, famous beyond the art world, his name synonymous with pop art, and his work was not selling. Very few of the "death-and-disaster" series had sold, and while the Brillo boxes were an artistic success—even Jasper Johns had to admire "the dumbness of the relationship between the thought and the technology"—actual sales, as Eleanor Ward had feared, were sparse.

Andy's relationship with his dealer had already deteriorated, and now it fell apart. He had begun making overtures to Leo Castelli, and Mrs. Ward was extremely hurt when she found out, accusing him of ingratitude after all the time and money she had invested in his two shows.

Castelli was glad to take him on, once the delicate negotiations had been completed by Billy Linich. The final bitterness between Andy and Mrs. Ward occurred over the ownership of Warhol's *Colored Mona Lisa,* which Mrs. Ward insisted he had given her and Andy insisted he had not. The matter was finally settled in court by a judge who ruled that they each owned fifty percent. But, as Alan Groh pointed out, "the monetary value of the early paintings was not something he took too seriously because the largest painting in the first show was only about $1,200. It wasn't a matter of major concern to anyone. He had paintings he would throw away. He'd say, 'Oh, I don't want that one,' and throw it out."

As Taylor Mead saw it, the move to Castelli ensured Andy's success: "Their grand plan was already in operation. They were taking over the art world, with Geldzahler's help. They were all wheeling and dealing like crazy, with the fine Italian hand of Castelli maneuvering. It was in the cards that they were making it. There was no two ways about it. They were all too cool to be struggling anymore. They were all on a power trip."

11

IN THE SUMMER of 1964, Andy started making large-cast films. The hothouse atmosphere of the Factory sufficed for most of the scenes, but he also began asking friends to lend their houses and apartments as locations. This they did at some risk, since it was a point of honor among the amphetamine addicts to steal as much as they could. "The drugs may have been responsible," Ondine wrote later. "[They] enabled you to commit crimes with relish." ("They were like a fucking crowd of locusts," recalled one observer, describing the hangers-on. "They stripped everything—there certainly wasn't a pill of any kind left in the bathrooms.")

Andy's casting method was simplicity itself: You submitted to a screen test that consisted of letting his Bolex stare at you for three minutes. As Baby Jane Holzer recalled: "You never had to go through the tense part when you were being filmed by Andy—it just happened. He'd say, 'Look at the camera and don't blink.' " Malanga remembered the process less rosily: "These screen tests were studies in subtle sadism. The results were often brutal." And as Taylor Mead recalled, "The more destroyed you were, the more likely he was to use you."

During the spring and summer of 1964, Andy filmed a number of three-minute segments for *Couch.* The title was a play on both the psychoanalytical and Hollywood uses of that piece of furniture; the action consisted of scenes of people having, or trying to have, sex on the Factory sofa. Naomi Levine was photographed writhing naked as she attempted to attract a young man who appeared more interested in his motorcycle than her breasts. Another actress was filmed appearing to be anally penetrated by Malanga as she lay atop the black dancer Rufus Collins. Several scenes involved sex between men. In all of them, the camera was as unblinking as the performers. Whatever else Andy intended by it, *Couch* made the case that heterosexual coupling was not the totality of human intimacy, that homosexuality was just as "normal."

In any case, it was hard to know just what Andy hoped to achieve. According to one observer: "He would sit watching the sex with his legs crossed, wrapped up in himself like a little child. I thought I was in the presence of a Buddhist who had achieved the desired transcendent state."

That July, Andy gathered Malanga, Jonas Mekas, Henry Geldzahler, and another filmmaker, John Palmer, in an office on the forty-fourth floor of the Time-Life Building and filmed *Empire,* an eight-hour study of the Empire State Building at night. "It was John Palmer," said Malanga, "who came up with the idea for *Empire.* Jonas Mekas and I changed the reels for Andy. He barely touched the camera during the whole time it was being made. He wanted the machine to make the art for him. We started shooting around 6 P.M.—it was still daylight—and stopped around 1 A.M. The first two reels are overexposed because it was all guesswork. What happens in the course of the first two reels, and partway through the third, is that the building slowly emerges out of a twilight haze, while the darkness slowly blankets the sky." Andy had initially intended *Empire* to be a sound movie, and after the camera was turned on by Mekas, he encouraged Henry and John to "say things intelligent." Later, upon seeing the rushes, he opted for the purity of a silent soundtrack. He was ecstatic with the results: "The Empire State Building is a star," he announced. "It's an eight-hour hard-on. It's so beautiful. The lights come on and the stars come out and it sways. It's like Flash Gordon riding into space."

But for most audiences, hip or not, it wasn't much of a turn-on. "At the premiere screening of *Empire* at the Bridge Cinema," recalled Malanga, "we were standing in the rear of the auditorium. Andy was observing the audience rather than film, and people were walking out or booing or throwing paper cups at the screen. He turned to me, and in his boyish voice said, 'Gee, you think they hate it? . . . You think they don't like it?' *Empire* was a movie where nothing happened except the audience's reaction."

Like the "death-and-disaster" series, *Empire* was a work inspired by a Warhol "speed" vision. One observer recalled: "Among the younger artists, alcohol got almost completely phased out by marijuana in 1964, and then a few months later by LSD, which made alcohol seem gross. But while everyone else mixed speed and grass and LSD, which made everything softer and more confused, Andy didn't give up the speed for a second."

Expressionless behind his omnipresent sunglasses, apparently fueled only by Obetrol, Andy seemed determined to dehumanize himself as much as possible. He declared that the best movie he'd ever seen was that year's *Creation of the Humanoids*, in which survivors of World War III solve their labor shortage by creating robots. (Its denouement was the hero and heroine's discovery that they, too, were machines.) Now, with his own camera, he set out to portray three men who had given him great nourishment: *Drunk* was a seventy-minute study of Emile de Antonio downing a quart of whisky; *Henry Geldzahler* was seventy minutes of the curator smoking a cigar; and *Taylor Mead's Ass* was a seventy-minute meditation on exactly what it said it was.

De Antonio and Mead both felt bruised by their experiences in front of his camera. Said the star of *Drunk*: "I liked the idea of the risk involved, but Andy lied to me, which was fairly disagreeable. I told him I didn't want anybody there except the people who were necessary, but once the film started, I could see through the lights that a lot of people were looking on. I was very angry—but still moderately sober. Then Andy had a lot of trouble changing the reel, so by the time reel two began I was on the floor and couldn't get up. The next day I called Andy and said, 'My lawyer is so-and-so and the film can never be shown.' He had no reaction."

Mead was even more upset, and shortly after working with Andy, he left New York for Europe. "I was going to kill him," he said. "He was manipulating people like crazy, lying to everybody too much, being too cold-blooded."

Many who were close to Andy at the time were beginning to see him as a power monger. Said Malanga: "Andy is often commented about as being a voyeur, and I suppose his desire for power was initially realized through the voyeuristic distancing of himself from what he was watching with the use of a movie camera." "He became very royal," said Henry Geldzahler. "It was like Louis XIV getting up in the morning. The big question was whom he would pay attention to that day."

Just as his mother had manipulated her sons so that the older two were still debating which of them was "her favorite," so Andy pitched everybody around him into competition for his approval. Billy Linich and Malanga were constant rivals. At one point Billy drew up a list of people who were not allowed in the Factory and put Malanga's name on it. Andy wouldn't let him post the list, but he did nothing to cool the enmity. Recalled Ondine: "Warhol used them both beautifully."

Perhaps the character of Mel, based on Warhol, in Stephen Koch's novel *The Bachelor's Bride,* best illuminates Andy's motives: "If Mel felt uncertain about some aspect of himself, if he felt doubtful of himself intellectually, artistically, socially, sexually, any way—he was in the habit of adding to the Bunch somebody who reflected that anxiety in some way. Then he would play that person off their opposite number. And when the panic began, he'd feel strengthened, reassured. It was as though the two contending people somehow invalidated each other, and left him autonomous, free."

There was always the threat of exile from the court. John Giorno, with whom Andy had finally become fed up, was the first to be dismissed. His memory of that expulsion is still painful: "I totally loved Andy. At the same time he could arouse one's worst feelings and fears."

For most of these young, beautiful, psychologically unstable performers, what they felt was the powerful love of followers for a cult leader: The girls wanted to marry him, the boys to serve him. There was so much to "learn," as artists, as acolytes. Here was no more "theorizing" but real, often exhausting, work. Here were lessons in style: how to appear aloof, to create a mystique. "The Factory was a church," wrote the critic Gary Indiana. "The Church of the Unimaginable Penis. Andy was the father confessor, the kids were the sinners. The sanctity of the institution and its rituals was what was important, not personal salvation."

Certainly there was no hope of financial reward. Only Malanga was actually on the Factory payroll during this period; the others "worked" for free. Why, then, did so many flock to Andy, and feel so devastated when he dropped them?

Warhol would later write: "The Factory was a place where you could let your problems show and nobody would hate you for it. And if you worked your problems up into entertaining problems, people would like you even more for being strong enough to say you were different."

De Antonio saw a darker side: "Andy was like the Marquis de Sade in the sense that his very presence acted as a kind of release for people so they could live out their fantasies, get undressed, or in some cases do very violent things to get him to watch them. He was able to get a lot of people to do weird things in his early films who wouldn't have done it for money or D. W. Griffith or anybody else. He loved to see other people dying. This is what the Factory was about: Andy was the Angel of Death's apprentice as these people went through their shabby lives with drugs and weird sex. Andy just looked, and Andy as voyeur par excellence was the devil, because he got bored with just looking."

On October 27, 1964, the first of several sensational deaths associated with Warhol took place when Freddie Herko, who had danced briefly near Andy's flame, went to a friend's apartment in Greenwich Village, put on Mozart's *Coronation Mass*, and danced naked out of a fifth-floor window, high on LSD. When Andy heard the news he said, "Why didn't he tell me he was going to do it? Why didn't he tell me? We could have gone down there and filmed it!"

The remark, which spread throughout the art and media worlds, confirmed many people's suspicions about how cold and callous Andy had become. Warhol's supporters were quick to spring to his defense, calling it the "complex statement" of an artist who reserved his "pain" for his art. Ondine thought that Herko's death was the "completion" of an elaborate performance: "He had prepared himself for that moment. Released by Andy, he was able to die as he had wanted to, all his life. I don't know how else to say it, but working with Andy gave one a great sense of completion."

Geldzahler continued in his role of Andy's painting mentor. After the fiasco of Andy's *Thirteen Most Wanted Men* mural at the World's Fair, he had suggested that Warhol had looked at death enough in his pictures; perhaps it was time for some "life." To explain what he meant, Geldzahler picked up a magazine and opened it to a centerfold of flowers. With a Castelli opening in the offing for the fall, Andy took the hint and told Malanga to get some silk screens made of a photograph of four poppies by Patricia Caulfield in *Modern Photography*.

During the summer of 1964, with the Supremes and the Rolling Stones blasting away on the stereo, Andy and Gerard made some fifty flower paintings, using silk screens of the Caulfield photograph on a dark jungle-green background. They ranged from four by four inches (a set of six in a box was priced at thirty dollars) to single images measuring nine by twelve feet. In November the paintings were displayed in Warhol's first show at Castelli. They sold out. At the opening Malanga stood by the door receiving congratulations, while Andy sat quietly in a corner. Despite their vibrancy, critics persisted in seeing them as a continuation of his obsession with death and sex, making much of the fact that the flowers were poppies, "flowers of death" (though they were not, in fact, opium poppies). Carter Ratcliff wrote in *Andy Warhol* that they were "a distillation of much of Warhol's art—the flash of beauty that suddenly becomes tragic under the viewer's gaze." In the *Village Voice*, David Bourdon pulled out all the stops: "The artist is a mechanical Renaissance man, a genius." Ivan Karp, overjoyed that his four-year tracking of Warhol had at last paid off, crowed in *Newsweek*: "While the other pop artists depict common things, Andy is in a sense a victim of common things; he genuinely admires them. How can you describe him—he's like a saint. Saint Andrew."

Said Andy of the flower paintings in *Newsweek*: "They look like a cheap awning."

The year 1964 ended in another film triumph for Andy, marked by considerable bitterness, when Jonas Mekas presented him with *Film Culture* magazine's annual award for contributions to the cinema. In his citation Mekas wrote: "With his artist's intuition as his only guide, he records, almost obsessively, man's daily activities, the things he sees around him. A strange thing occurs. The world becomes transposed, intensified, electrified. We see it sharper than before. . . . A new way of looking at things and the screen is given through the personal vision of Andy Warhol; in a sense, it is a cinema of happiness."

Andy did not attend the awards ceremony, sending in his place a silent film of himself and friends that showed them vapidly handing around a large basket of fruit (a reference to the actual prize) and staring into the camera with a bored, surly attitude. Not a few veterans of the New York underground film world were outraged. One of them, Gregory Markopoulous, was quoted as saying: "Here I spent ten years studying my craft, perfecting my craft, understanding, thinking, theorizing about movies and how they're made and what a movie really is, and this guy comes along who does absolutely nothing and knows absolutely nothing. Other people have to set his camera up, load it, focus it, and he just shoots nothing and he's the biggest thing going!"

The most influential of them all, Stan Brakhage, had another change of heart about Andy and resigned from the Film-Makers' Co-op in a stinging letter to Mekas: "I cannot in good conscience continue to accept the help of institutions which have come to propagate advertisements for forces which I recognize as among the most destructive in the world today: 'dope,' self-centered Love, unqualified Hatred, Nihilism, violence to self and society."

Undaunted, Andy closed out the year by shooting his first "talkie," *Harlot*, based on the cult of that time around the 1930s movie goddess Jean Harlow. This film brought to the Factory a gifted young novelist and playwright, Ronald Tavel (later, a founder with Charles Ludlam of the Theater of the Ridiculous), who would become a close collaborator with Andy. *Harlot*, at least overtly, offered more "comment" than the previous Warhol films: In Jean Harlow they saw, said Tavel, "a transvestite like Mae West and Marilyn Monroe, in that their feminineness was so exaggerated that it became a commentary on womanhood rather than the real thing." Still using the stationary camera, Andy staged a tableau in which Mario Montez, a male transvestite performer (whose name derived from that of another camp favorite, the 1940s B-movie queen Maria Montez), was sitting on the all-purpose couch dressed as Harlow and lasciviously eating a banana. Next to him sat an aspiring actress,

Carol Kishinskie, staring into the distance, with a small dog on her lap. Philip Fagan and Gerard Malanga, looking like a cross between Rudolph Valentino and George Raft, stood behind the couch. Tavel's "script," a last-minute improvisation, involved Tavel, the poet Harry Fainlight, and Billy Linich talking off-camera about great female movie stars.

Of that time with Andy, Tavel recalled: "I saw him as a continuation in art of Samuel Beckett, and when I was a kid there was no arguing with Beckett: his was the last horrifying, unarguable word. That was the tradition Andy belonged to—the icy classicist, unapproachable, air-tight, very negative. I do not remember him as somebody well-loved; I remember him in point of fact as somebody hated. But I was objective about it. I was learning a great deal. That was a true artistic period in which nobody would dare ask you to be anything less than your best as an artist, and Andy was uncompromising—he didn't give an inch. When I knew him he was a pure artist, certainly a great artist."

A few weeks later Andy used Mario Montez again as the subject of *Screen Test #2*. One early viewer recalled: "The enormous, out-of-focus head of a sultry, attractive girl [Montez] flashes on the screen. She is brushing her hair. Then sound. The kind of sound you expect from a very old, used-up army training film, garbled, filled with static. An occasional word filters through. An off-screen voice is telling the girl that if she wants to become a movie star, she must master the art of saying certain words with the right inflection. The voice starts drilling her on a word, over and over. The word was 'diarrhea.' 'Di-ah-rii-aaa'—and her lips formed the syllables lovingly and obscenely, her eyes darkened under lowered lids."

Mocking the thing they seemed to "adore," both films had a steely edge that Warhol's previous films had lacked, and their acceptance by young artists was gleeful. The February 1965 issue of *Artforum* carried an article entitled "Saint Andy: Some Notes on an Artist Who, for a Large Section of a Younger Generation, Can Do No Wrong." It reported:

> Art critics who cannot find the art in Warhol, who are mystified at the virtual idolatry with which he is regarded by a younger generation of painters, might have been even more astonished at the roar of

approval which greeted the award given to Warhol's three-minute "Banana Sequence" [in *Harlot*] at the recent Los Angeles Film Festival. For this was an audience of the young, disaffiliated filmmakers making movies on nickels and dimes, film buffs who do not, for the most part, tend to concern themselves with doings in the art galleries, an audience seeking not the chic but the subversive, not the elegant but the destructive, not satire but nihilism. "Banana Sequence," with its blatant and hilarious assault on that world of what Allen Ginsberg has called the "heterosexual dollar," met all the requirements.

12

WHEN ANDY MET Edie Sedgwick in the apartment of the film producer Lester Persky in January 1965, he "could see that she had more problems than anybody I'd ever met." She also had exactly what he was looking for to mold into a "super-star." A slip of a girl with blonde, elfin, androgynous beauty, Edith Minturn Sedgwick, then twenty-two, was the youngest daughter of an eccentric, blue-blood, New England WASP family. She had money (she lived on Sutton Place and drove a gray Mercedes), social position, and a madcap spirit out of the Roaring Twenties. Above all she had an aura—an electric glamour—for which there was no keener eye in New York than Andy's. They would not meet again for two months, when she and her companion, Chuck Wein, began turning up at the Factory.

In the meantime, Andy was perfecting his gift for laconic out-rageousness. Setting himself in front of a remote-control camera for the benefit of a reporter from the *New York Herald-Tribune,* he said: "Why this is marvelous. I mean, if a person were dying he could photograph his own death." To *Vogue* he declared: "Food does not exist for me. I like candies. I also like blood." Canada's National Gallery of Art in Toronto had scheduled a show of the "Electric Chair" pictures and painted Brillo boxes for March, but the museum director had ruled that the grocery boxes were not art and were therefore subject to a twenty percent import duty. When the *New York Times* called up to get his reaction, Andy said: "I really don't care. I think with some of the important things happening they must have more to worry about than some dumb little boxes." Said Ronald Tavel: "People asked why he was so famous. Every morning when we came to the Factory he would go to the phone and call his press agent."

In the Warhol-Tavel films, any remaining barriers of taste were falling fast. That spring they embarked on *Suicide,* the Factory's first experiment with color. Tavel recalled: "[Warhol] had met this guy who had tried on twenty-three different occasions to kill himself by slashing his wrists, and Andy told me to meet him and get the story. I was to act out the people who had provoked him, the guy was to reenact the suicide attempts. On March 6 this guy came to the Factory and he cooperated completely, as suicides will. It was Andy's idea to just focus in on the wrists with all these slashes and to have not blood but water spilled from a pitcher onto the wrists after each 'story.' You would never see the guy's face. Andy's last-minute inspiration was to get gorgeous flowers from a local florist since the hands would get kind of dull just being there. So you saw this wringing of hands tearing apart the flowers, and in the middle of it the guy freaked out and took the water and threw it in my face. Andy came up and said, 'Oh, Ronnie, shall we stop? Oh, how awful!' I said, 'No, I'm fine, the script is still legible.' The guy calmed down and we finished it. But then he took out lawsuits against us and the film was never shown."

After *Suicide* they made *The Life of Juanita Castro,* a spoof of revolutionary rhetoric inspired by the diary of Fidel Castro's sister. Two weeks later, they assayed *Horse,* a "Western," for which an enormous stallion was rented and brought to the Factory. The theme, said Tavel, was implicit cowboy homosexuality in the Old West. "What I really wanted was to see how easily a group of people under pressure could be moved to genuinely inhuman acts toward each other and perhaps the horse." Malanga and Tavel held up directions for the actors on cue cards. The first one read: "Approach the horse sexually." Things disintegrated in a few minutes when the horse kicked one actor in the head, and the whole scene erupted in a brawl.

Their next film was *Vinyl,* inspired by Anthony Burgess' novel *A*

Clockwork Orange, with Gerard Malanga cast as the juvenile delin-
quent antihero. Tavel found the book boring and wrote a script
about the rage and dehumanization of sadomasochism. The results,
however seriously intended, were a farce. "The monotonous and the
ridiculous skitter all over the screen like the peal of a long embarrassing giggle," wrote Stephen Koch. Most of the actors were stoked
up on amyl nitrate, marijuana, and alcohol, and only Malanga had
bothered to learn his lines. But in *Vinyl* Andy found his Marilyn
Monroe: Edie Sedgwick had shown up at the Factory with her hair
cut short and dyed silver to look like his, and he had put her in the
film at the last minute. She did nothing but sit on a trunk in the
foreground smoking one cigarette after another, but her impact was
unforgettable.

Malanga gave this description of Andy's new superstar: "Her features, slight and symmetrical with no outstanding facial bone struc-
ture, were brightened by the vivid and penetrating eyes, full of small
timidities, which recorded perhaps the shock that too great an hon-
esty expects from life. Most of her wardrobe consisted of shirts with
tails hanging out and leotards. She knew how to wear them with a
style and grace unachieved by anyone else. She liked to wear large
earrings. She applied a great deal of makeup before going out.
When she spoke she made sense. She could not be the fool or be
made to look foolish." She was, at the beginning, virtually insepara-
ble from Chuck Wein, a young would-be filmmaker from Harvard.
According to Henry Geldzahler, "He seemed to be controlling and
molding Edie."

"Chuck and Edie's coming to the Factory," said Tavel, "was a
matter of class. Andy wasn't taken in by Chuck for a minute. What
he liked was his blond hair and blue eyes. If he was to be seen with
Edie on his right hand, then on his left he wanted Chuck, the little
look of aristocracy, of class. I thought, Andy! You're an artist. Why
do you care about that shit?" It soon became clear that that was one
of the things Andy did care about: through Edie, Andy would move
up in society.

At the beginning, Andy and Edie's nights on the town were, as
Gerard Malanga said, something "you'd read about in F. Scott Fitz-
gerald." Edie would take Andy, Gerard, and the entourage to din-

ner, then on to various clubs; she either signed the check or paid cash. "Edie made it happen," said Malanga. "She added something to the ambience of every public place or private home she entered. She was an archetype."

Andy saw her as his mirror image: Like him, she craved love but acted as if she didn't care about anybody. (According to the testimonials in Jean Stein's biography *Edie,* her feelings about her parents were deeply ambivalent. Moreover, two of her brothers had recently committed suicide.) She was the quintessential "poor little rich girl," with her big Mercedes, her fur coats and credit cards, a husky little-girl voice that always made her sound as if she had just stopped crying, and huge eyes that one observer described as being the color of "twice-frozen Hershey bars." Edie had, as Warhol wrote, "a poignantly vacant, vulnerable quality that made her a reflection of everybody's private fantasies. Edie could be anything you wanted her to be. . . . She was a wonderful, beautiful blank."

"Vulnerability exuded from every pore of her skin," noted another new friend of Andy's, Isabelle Collin-Dufresne, who, as Ultra Violet, would become another of his superstars. "Like a precocious preppie puppet, she rocked and rolled unconsciously to the sound of a radio station inside her head. She was always high. Andy liked high people."

Edie's first starring role in a Warhol movie was in *Poor Little Rich Girl,* Andy's "Shirley Temple film," in which there was no father to arrive on the scene and spoil the fun. Andy worked without scripts, explaining, "I only wanted to find great people and let them talk about themselves and talk about what they usually liked to talk about and I'd film them." If Edie had needed a script, he said, she wouldn't have been right for the part. For seventy minutes she lay on her bed, talked on the phone, and walked around her room, showing off her clothes and describing how she had gone through her entire inheritance in six months. Gerard Malanga remembered: "We shot two reels. When they came back from the lab, we previewed them and, to our horror, found them to be extremely out of focus—not even close to salvageable. After replacing the lens, we reshot the two long takes a week later and got it right. We took the first reel, from the [first version, and sequenced it with the second reel, from the] second version, so the film opens with an out-of-focus thirty-five-minute take. That takes a lot of guts." When *Poor Little*

Rich Girl was shown at the Film-Makers' Co-operative, Edie immediately became an underground star.

At the beginning of her relationship with Andy, Edie seemed to be happy, at least when she was around him. According to her roommate, Genevieve Charbin, most of the day was taken up talking to Andy on the phone. "Andy was a real blabbermouth on the phone. He told her every little thing he did from the second he woke up. He would compose exercises with Edie. Andy did one hundred pull-ups every morning—which does not surprise me because he had an incredibly strong back." Almost every evening she went out with him or worked on a film.

"Andy couldn't have been nicer," noted one Factory observer. "He never asked her to say bad words. He never asked her to take her clothes off or have sex or do anything. He just said, 'Now the camera's on. Talk. You're great. Just be great. Most of the time it wasn't very good and he didn't care. He didn't criticize her. He gave her an identity."

Edie's rise to star status delighted the gay contingent at the Factory. She was gorgeous, campy, always up, always ready to go, and she seemed to despise straight men. But her arrival was noted with chagrin by the other women. Baby Jane Holzer stopped coming in. One day Naomi Levine screamed at Andy for ignoring her and was hauled to the stairwell by Billy Linich, slapped in the face, and told to get out.

Andy and Edie quickly became the royal couple of the underground, the coolest, prettiest characters on the New York scene. "They were both these pale, frail, glamorous people," Henry Geldzahler later said to Jean Stein. "Andy had always felt himself to be unattractive and to be with Edie was to be Edie for a season. He loved running around with her, appearing in public. She was one of his ego images. And Edie thought she was Andy's. She felt possessed." That spring they attended the opening of *Three Centuries of American Painting* at the Metropolitan Museum of Art and were photographed for the society columns with the First Lady, Lady Bird Johnson. The *New York Times* reporter noted that there was something "seamy" about Andy Warhol in paint-spattered work pants, a dinner jacket, and dark glasses, and his fragile consort with cropped, silver-rinsed hair. But as Andy told Leo Lerman in *Vogue*: "Success is expressing yourself. It's participation-liberation."

When he stood next to his alter ego, Andy felt beautiful. "Andy enjoyed acting, being other than himself," the artist James Rosenquist pointed out. "He wanted the escape of being in another life." He lusted after people, another friend observed, lifting enormous chunks of other people's personalities and making them his own. In most women Andy looked for mothers. In Edie he found himself.

"Andy Warhol would like to have been a charming well-born debutante from Boston like Edie Sedgwick," said Truman Capote. According to Andy's nephew James Warhola, Andy was soon prancing around the house wearing black tights and a T-shirt or long-tailed striped shirt, just like Edie.

Andy's flower paintings were to open in Paris in May 1965. When Ileana Sonnabend offered to pay his round-trip fare to France by sea, Andy asked her to spend the money on four plane tickets instead. He was going to Europe for the first time since he had become famous and he wanted to make as much impact as possible. He decided to take Gerard, Edie, and Chuck Wein. The foursome arrived in Paris in the early morning of April 30.

Warhol's first visit to France was perfectly timed. "Pop art" had entered the Franglais lexicon, and it was the talk of Paris. The poet John Ashbery, who was living there at the time, recalled: "Reporters were always asking Brigitte Bardot and Jeanne Moreau what they thought of it; it was the theme of a strip-tease at the Crazy Horse Saloon, and there was even a pop art dress shop in the Rue du Bac called Poppard."

The Warhol opening at the Sonnabend Gallery broke all attendance records, and critics raved about the work. Peter Schjeldahl, the American art critic, recalled the impact: "It was as if, in a dark, grey atmosphere, someone had kicked open the door of a blast furnace. The beauty, raciness, and cruelty of those pictures seemed to answer a question so big I could never have hoped to ask it: something about being, as Rimbaud had declared one must be, 'absolutely modern.' The future breathed from the walls like raw ozone."

Andy went to nightclubs, gave interviews, and posed with Edie for *Paris-Match* and *Vogue*. He thought the French were terrific because they didn't "care about anything," and he loved Paris because "everything is beautiful and the food is yummy." In fact, he was having "so much fun" that he decided to make a bold gesture. He told the French press that he was retiring from painting to make films.

This was not a pose but a carefully planned strategy. Andy's prices were climbing, but they were still low. A flower painting, for example, sold for around two thousand dollars, depending on its size. Moreover, Andy felt the pop art explosion was spent. His plan was to stop painting, make it big in films with Edie, then go back to painting—by which time he felt sure the prices for his work would have increased greatly.

Gerard noted in his diary that Andy was letting himself be too easily influenced by Edie and was being "very silly" because he had started taking Seconal to go to sleep. One morning Gerard left a snappish note in the luxurious room where they were sharing one very wide bed: "I'm not scheduling myself for a pill head. I took $6 because I had no money and I wasn't going to stay in the hotel till you decided to wake. There's no reason in the world why *you* have to take sleeping pills. This only proves my theory that you are a very impressionable person. If someone told you to jump in fire you probably would."

On certain levels Andy must have enjoyed this. Malanga's position as Andy's prime minister was being threatened by the Sedgwick-Wein team. Andy was happily pitting them against one another for his attention, and Gerard's diary was full of complaints.

From Paris, Andy and his entourage flew to London, where they visited the art dealer Robert Fraser, went to a poetry reading by Allen Ginsberg, and were photographed by David Bailey and Michael Cooper in a series of pictures in which they looked more like a superhip rock group than an artist and his assistants. It was the sort of exposure that was increasingly making him an idol to young people. In the United States, in fact, he already had five fan clubs.

From London they flew to Madrid, then traveled to Tangiers, where Andy took his first vacation since 1956, staying for a week at the luxurious Minza Hotel. He complained that the city smelled too much, but everybody else was happy because of the supply of drugs. They spent their days having lunch by the pool and walking around the city walls while Andy dreamed up the movies he was going to make with Edie.

Back in New York, Edie was passed through customs without

incident, but Andy and Gerard, whose long hair and clothing made them obvious targets, were taken to separate rooms to be strip-searched by customs agents. As he walked off, Gerard saw Andy surreptitiously drop a stream of pills onto the floor. Apparently he was not sticking to Obetrol, or else his prescription had run out and he had bought extra speed illegally.

A limousine took them from the airport straight to a double bill of *A Hard Day's Night* and *Goldfinger* in Greenwich Village. As he watched the movies, with Edie at his side and his car waiting to take him to a party at Sybil Burton's disco, Arthur, Andy must have felt more than content with the movie of his own life.

The next day Warhol astonished Ronnie Tavel with his directness. He was going to make Edie the queen of the Factory, he said, and he wanted a script for her. "Something in a kitchen. White and clean and plastic."

"Do you want a plot?" asked Tavel.

"I want a situation," Andy said.

A soundman, Buddy Wirtschafter, offered his pristine white studio apartment, and the film *Kitchen,* starring Edie with René Ricard and Roger Trudeau, was shot there in June. It consisted of the three of them sitting around a table in a small kitchen making idle talk on a largely inaudible soundtrack. At the end, Edie was "killed" for no apparent reason. Andy said the film was "illogical, without motivation or character, and completely ridiculous. Very much like real life."

Kitchen got extraordinary critical reaction. "It was a horror to watch," wrote Norman Mailer, who told a reporter he thought Andy Warhol was the most perceptive man in America. "One hundred years from now they will look at *Kitchen* and see the essence of every boring, dead day one's ever had in a city and say 'Yes, that's why the horror came down.' *Kitchen* shows that better than any other work of that time." (Mailer would be influenced by the chaos in Warhol's films when he made his own a few years later.)

"Being with Andy and Edie was like running with a teenage gang," recalled the writer Bob Heidie. Genevieve, Chuck, or sometimes Ondine would deliver Edie to the Factory late in the afternoon, and, if there wasn't a film to be shot, the evenings would be spent making the social rounds. For Andy these evenings were as much a part of his work as painting or giving interviews. He always took several people with him wherever he went and used the occasions to make contacts and discuss projects.

"Edie was not only very beautiful," said Heidie, "but there was a lot of sensitivity. She had a kind of Judy Garland quality with the legs, the deep, penetrating childlike eyes, vaporous skin; people would stop and stare. It wasn't the real bad drug period, although she was taking drugs like everybody else. I remember one party at the Factory that summer: Everybody was there—Tennessee Williams, Nureyev, Judy Garland—and Edie was very high up on a rafter doing the twist for the longest period of time, alone. She often talked about trying to get close to Andy. She had some kind of fascination that bordered on sister-brother incest crush, but she was always frustrated that she never could get close to him on some emotional level."

Beauty #2 cut to the quick of the Andy-Edie relationship. While she sat on her bed in her underwear, drinking vodka with Gino, a male hustler in jockey shorts (her "Beauty #2"), Chuck Wein, her "Beauty #1," who had replaced Tavel as "writer" on the project, sat several feet away, just off camera, and interrogated her. Edie emerged as a slightly perverse Hayley Mills until Wein's questions about her father began to stab. As Chuck took Edie apart, Andy's camera recorded her twisting and turning in his grip. At one point Gino tried to make love to her, although it soon became obvious that he was not as interested as she seemed to want him to be. By the end of the film, Edie was reduced to the victim she saw herself as.

It was a disturbing piece of work, perfectly executed. The image of Edie flickering with softness against the hardness of the Silver Factory was like a window into the soul of Andy Warhol. By capturing the "death" of Edie's every little moment, he "completed" her just as he had "completed" Freddie Herko.

Beauty #2 was released at the Co-op on July 17, billed as an "untraditional triangle (without love)." Critics compared Edie's screen presence to Monroe's: She was vulnerable, delicate, dynamite. As one reviewer wrote, "She knew how to eat up a camera alive."

"The films would have an instant audience," said Malanga. "Reviews would appear in the press; and Edie's career was launched, so to speak, but she wasn't getting paid. She thought Andy was making money with the films, because of all the hoopla, but he wasn't. The sales of his paintings were supporting a highly speculative venture into filmmaking. If anything, the films were a drain on him financially. Nevertheless, Edie wanted to get paid, but Andy never indicated that any payment, however small, would be forthcoming, except to say to her every so often, 'Be patient.' Andy assumed, wrongly perhaps, that if he started paying everyone for whatever the work involved, the end result would be of a lesser quality."

Edie became the envy of every hip girl in town. "She was acting out the repression of her mother's generation by blasting out each day constantly," one of her sisters told Jean Stein. "In a way, she was a metaphor for the young of that time who were not political."

Andy's ambitions grew concomitantly. He told journalists that Edie could "change the way movies looked" and that he wanted Edie to play him, "because she does everything better than I do."

The success of *Kitchen* and *Beauty #2* marked the height of Andy's collaboration with Edie. Now they started thinking about making a real hit film with Edie in it, maybe, Andy thought, by stringing several of the shorter films together. When Jonas Mekas offered Andy a week at the Cinémathèque to do anything he wanted, Andy suggested an Edie Sedgwick retrospective.

Once *Beauty #2* made Edie the certified queen of the New York underground, a lot of people began to give her conflicting advice, the sum of which was: "Get away from Andy Warhol. He's just using you. You don't need him. He doesn't even pay you. You could go to Hollywood!" Foremost among them was Bob Dylan's right-hand man, Bobby Neuwirth, with whom she was having an affair. He drew her into the Dylan enclave in Woodstock, where Dylan's manager, Albert Grossman, dangled offers of recording contracts and movie roles with Dylan on the condition she leave "that madman Warhol." This grew into a tug of war between the Warhol and Dylan entourages—the two poles of the New York underground, one homosexual, the other heterosexual, both heavy users of drugs. The two camps despised each other. At the Factory, Dylan was known as "the creep." For the twenty-two-year-old cult object in the middle— Edie—the battle was devastating.

Henry Geldzahler remembered: "I went to her apartment, which I thought very grim, a couple of times. It was dark and the talk was always about how hung over she was, or how high she was yesterday, or how high she would be tomorrow. She was very nervous, very fragile, very thin, very hysterical. You could hear her screaming, even though she wasn't screaming—this sort of supersonic whistling."

In late July, just before Dylan released "Like a Rolling Stone," which contained some acerbic comments about the Warhol-Sedgwick relationship (Andy is "Napoleon in rags"), the two contenders for the underground throne met for the first time when Dylan went to the Factory to sit for a Warhol screen test. Andy took his usual refuge in the humble position of the fan, chewing his fingernails and squealing, "He's here! He's here!" when Dylan, accompanied by bodyguards and a film crew, swept in. There was an immediate standoff between the two opposing entourages. Andy's loyalists wanted nothing to do with Dylan; for their part, the singer's people looked at the gays with cold contempt. As for Dylan and Warhol, it was, one observer noted, as if "two incredible people-users had come together to see who could take a bigger chunk out of whom."

"They were like oil and water," said Gerard. "There was just bad friction. Dylan immediately hated Andy, and Andy thought Dylan was corny." Visibly annoyed, Dylan sat still and silent through the screen test and even went so far as to share the ritual toke on a marijuana cigarette on camera with Warhol and Malanga. But according to Bob Heidie: "After being filmed Dylan said, 'I think I'll just take this for payment,' and walked off with an Elvis painting. Andy didn't say a word, but his face could have fallen through the floor." Shortly thereafter, Andy heard that Dylan had used the painting as a dart board, then traded it for a sofa. "When I'd ask, 'Why would he do that?'" Warhol later wrote, "I'd invariably get hearsay answers like, 'I hear he feels you destroyed Edie.' He blamed me for Edie's drugs." Andy's protests were not without foundation, for manipulative drug use may have been more pervasive among Dylan's followers than among his own, and it was not until after she left the Factory that Edie got heavily into heroin.

By August, even Andy could see how badly off Edie was. She was, he realized, a compulsive liar and a bulimic, who constantly made herself vomit after eating. She rarely took a bath unless he forced her, and she was heavily dependent on amphetamines and barbiturates.

"One night when the parties were over," he told Jean Stein in *Edie,* "I guess she didn't want to sleep with somebody, so she asked me to share a room with her. She always had to have her glass of hot milk and a cigarette in one hand. In her sleep her hands kept crawling; they couldn't sleep. I couldn't keep my eyes off them. She kept scratching them. She just had nightmares. It was really sad."

Another night Edie asked Andy to meet her at the Russian Tea Room, where she finally confronted him. "Everybody in New York is laughing at me," she said. "I'm too embarrassed to even leave my apartment. These movies are making a complete fool out of me! Everybody knows I just stand around in them doing nothing and you film it and what kind of talent is that? Try to imagine how I feel!" She added that she was broke, and if he didn't give her some money, she would refuse to sign a release and he could not show any of the films again.

"But don't you understand," he replied, "these movies are art! If you wait another year or two, a Hollywood person might put you in a real movie. You just have to be patient."

"Then she attacked the idea of the Edie Retrospective specifically," Warhol recalled, "saying that it was just another way for us to make a fool of her. But now I was getting red in the face; she was making me so upset I could hardly talk. Around midnight I was so crazy from all the dumb arguing I walked out."

They patched it up later, but things were never the same. "The fact that Edie couldn't understand that Warhol was her benefactor, the fact that she mistrusted him, by putting him down, was something which I don't think he got over," said Ondine. "He was really hurt."

As Edie lost her footing at the Factory, Chuck Wein made his move. "Chuck was sly and slippery in his own way," Malanga recalled. "He realized Edie was being drawn in by the Bob Dylan group and he was losing his grip on her." That August, Wein came up with an idea for a film about an aging homosexual who rents a boy from Dial-a-Hustler, then has to protect his "property" from his friends.

Andy loved the idea. He decided to shoot it in a beach house on Fire Island with Ed Hood, the black-sheep son of a wealthy southern family, as the old queen and Paul America, a weirdly charismatic bodybuilder, as the hustler. Just to make sure Edie got the point, he cast her roommate, Genevieve Charbin, as the female lead.

That September, without saying a word to Edie, Andy took his cast and crew to Fire Island. Among them were Malanga, Wein, and Paul Morrissey, a hyperactive young man with a high-pitched voice and a fast mouth, whom Malanga had introduced to Andy as a possible technical assistant.

Andy was so fearful that someone might drug his food that he had brought his own private supply of candy bars, on which he planned to subsist throughout the weekend.

He began shooting the movie the night everyone arrived, with Wein "directing"—setting up the scene—and Morrissey on sound. When Andy insisted that the camera remain stationary, Wein took Morrissey aside and explained that this was *his* movie. He asked Paul and Gerard to help him shoot the movie without Andy. "It was a mutiny of sorts," Morrissey recalled, "and I said, 'I'm not going to do that to Andy.' " To make matters worse, somebody spiked the food with LSD.

For the rest of his life Andy adamantly denied that he got dosed that night. According to Malanga, however, it was obvious to him that Andy was stoned when he found him picking thoughtfully through the garbage in the kitchen at six in the morning. When Malanga asked, "What are you doing?" Andy replied whimsically, "Oh, I'm just looking for something."

Andy planned to shoot on the beach that afternoon. The camera would be trained on Paul America lying on the beach, while off-camera the other performers could be heard talking about him from the sun deck. Morrissey pointed out that it seemed a pity that Ed Hood, who was extremely funny to watch as well as hear, would consequently not be visible in the film. "I never move the camera," Andy insisted, slightly annoyed. "I don't like to pan." Finally, Morrissey managed to persuade him to shoot the reel twice. The first time the camera would remain on Paul America, the second time it would pan back and forth.

When *My Hustler* was screened the following month, it was shown with a long pan-shot across the sand from the beach to the house that was sharp and funny and in focus. It was, moreover, the first Warhol film in which the sound was audible, thanks to Morrissey, and it drew a large audience and good reviews. "*My Hustler* had, despite an essentially frivolous air, a real dramatic form, and a hellish dramatic compactness," the film critic Neal Weaver wrote. "The ugly face of rapacious sensuality was delineated with a fierce economy almost Balzacian. And the second half of the film, a long scene in a tiny bathroom, largely between the two hustlers, was rather remarkable in itself. For an unrehearsed scene, filmed in a single long take, it achieved an inordinate degree of psychological subtlety, and a good deal of dramatic tension."

Morrissey's arrival on the scene was one of the many fortuitous accidents in Andy's career. A Catholic social worker from the Bronx, Morrissey thought the art world pretentious and boring, and he believed that the only real artists in America were working in the movies. He immediately understood what Andy was up to: "Andy wasn't doing experimental photography; he was experimenting with people. From the very beginning I could see what he was doing was very interesting because it left the camera on human beings who were characters, and the basic ingredient of all dramatic fiction is character. It was very simple. Andy wanted films that weren't directed. Andy just said, 'Come to the Factory every day.' I was able to provide the framework in which a film that was basically undirected had some direction."

Edie was angry after her exclusion from *My Hustler,* but she agreed to go with Andy to the opening night of the New York Film Festival in September. "Clip-coiffed Edie Sedgwick upstaged the *Vampires* on screen at the Lincoln Center Film Festival last night as she swept in on the arm of pop artist Andy Warhol," noted *The World-Telegram.* "Edie's outfit included her usual black leotard plus a trailing black ostrich-plumed cape like a camp version of Mme. Dracula."

Two weeks later, Andy and Edie reached their zenith as a pop couple when they went to the opening of his first American retrospective at the Institute of Contemporary Art in Philadelphia. The show's curator, Sam Green, had painted the floors of the museum silver, played loud rock music in the background, hoping to turn the ambience into something like the Factory's. But he was unprepared for what happened. The space, which normally held seven hundred people, was jammed with a crowd of two thousand, most of them students. When Andy, Edie, Chuck, and Gerard walked into the room, pandemonium broke out. Two students were pushed through windows. Dressed from head to foot in black, wearing eight safety pins on the collar of his turtleneck sweater and a pair of wraparound sunglasses, Andy was engulfed in waves of ecstatic young fans. "It was," said Leo Castelli, "just a howling . . . like the Beatles."

Sam Green became concerned about safety. "I looked at Andy and he'd turned white with fear. It wasn't anger the crowd was expressing, it was hero worship. They wanted to touch him. It was as if Mick Jagger had been stuck on the subway and discovered by teenage girls. He was pinned against the wall. I think it was the moment that Andy knew he was a star."

While the students stood below and chanted, "We want Andy and Edie! We want Andy and Edie!" the campus security police escorted the Warhol entourage upstairs to a balcony. Edie Sedgwick seized the moment to address the crowd through a microphone: "Oh, I'm so glad you all came tonight, and aren't we all having a wonderful time? And isn't Andy Warhol the most wonderful artist?"

Andy watched the proceedings "in awe," Malanga recalled. "He kept saying, 'Look how exciting this all is.' "

Other members of the group were less thrilled. "It was the peak of media insanity about pop art and I thought it was quite dangerous," remembered Henry Geldzahler, who joined Warhol on the balcony. "My attitude was, 'Let's get out of here.' " From the balcony they were finally taken up to the roof through a hole in the ceiling and down a fire escape to the street, where they were whisked away in police cars. The event made the local television news and enhanced Andy's reputation in New York, where the story of his being mobbed by screaming teenagers grew out of all proportion. As Warhol commented in his memoir of the period, "Now things were getting really interesting."

That Halloween, Roy Lichtenstein and his wife went to a party dressed as Andy and Edie, because as Lichtenstein explained, Andy had made himself and his consort into living works of art. But the changes in the real Edie were now all too obvious. Her eyes were black sockets. She had started wearing long-sleeved floor-length dresses to hide the scratches on her arms and legs; to mask her face, she made herself up like a death's-head. Increasingly in public she seemed to be more Andy's zombie than his partner. He directed her every movement with whispered commands to "stand up," "move around," "pose."

The underground journalist John Wilcock, who was on the set of her next film, *Bitch,* recalled that the shooting ended when Edie threw a drink at a light and it blew out. Warhol's technique of just pointing the camera at somebody and turning it on would often cause this kind of explosion, because the undirected pressure to perform was so great.

To spite her, Andy began to develop a new superstar. "The Warhol people felt Edie was giving them trouble," said the actor and poet René Ricard. "They were furious with her because she wasn't cooperating. So they went to a Forty-second Street bar and found Ingrid von Schefflin. They had noticed: 'Doesn't this girl look like an ugly Edie? Let's really teach Edie a lesson. Let's make a movie with her and tell Edie she's the big new star.' They cut her hair like Edie's. They made her up like Edie. Her name became Ingrid Superstar . . . just an invention to make Edie feel horrible."

Andy's last film with Edie was *The Death of Lupe Velez,* based on a script by Robert Heidie. The film was about the last night in the life of the "Mexican Spitfire" Lupe Velez. Edie acted out a scene in which she tried to commit a beautiful suicide by lighting a circle of candles around her bed and composing herself on it after taking a handful of barbiturates, only to have them make her nauseated. The film ends with Edie sticking her head in the toilet and pretending to drown in her own vomit.

It was filmed in color on a December afternoon in 1965 on a tense set at the socialite Panna O'Grady's apartment in the Dakota apartment building on Central Park West. Edie had been fighting with a lot of people at the Factory, complaining loudly to Andy that his films were trying to make her look like a fool. Urged on by Chuck Wein and unscrewed by drugs, she had been ripping up scripts and throwing tantrums like a diva.

As they began to shoot, Bob Neuwirth arrived and took Edie into a side room. "That was where the separation really took place," recalled one spectator. "Andy was fuming because somebody had invaded his domain." Bob arranged for Edie to meet Dylan later that night, downtown at the Kettle of Fish.

Warhol asked Robert Heidie to be at the restaurant. According to Heidie, "Edie arrived before anybody else, so I sat with her. Then Dylan's limousine pulled up outside and he came in all dressed in black. Edie said something like, 'I've tried to get close to him but I can't,' and Dylan said, 'Who?' She said, 'Andy,' and he muttered, 'Oh.' Andy was the last to arrive. It was almost as if he had been somewhere watching. It was really dramatic. I had the feeling Edie was on the verge of tears. She seemed estranged from Andy and he wasn't expressing anything. Right after Andy came in, she more or less turned around and said good-bye. After she and Dylan left together, Andy showed no sign of reaction. He just said something like, 'Edie's on the road down. I wonder who the next girl will be.'

"He was in the drama, but outside it, and I think that's probably the key to the whole thing. Andy was destructive because he gave nothing, and that's what Edie had been complaining about: What did he *want* from her? After we left the Kettle of Fish, we walked up to Cornelia Street. I showed Andy the spot where Freddie Herko had jumped out the window and he said, 'I wonder if Edie will commit suicide. I hope she lets me know so I can film it.'"

13

OH, WHEN ARE we going to find someone for A. W.?" cried Andy to Ondine in the back of a cab one day in the summer of 1965. (At the Factory, "A. W." stood for "All Witch," "All Woman," "Andy Warhol.") Despite protestations that he no longer "believed in love," Andy's yearnings for a lover were more acute than ever. A year earlier he had "latched onto" (to use Malanga's phrase) a good-looking, vulnerable young man named Philip Fagan, whom he had met at a concert and whom he had invited to move into his house—the first time he had done so with an object of desire. Fagan agreed, but to many at the Factory he and Andy seemed more like childish friends than lovers ("two little girls who baked cakes together," said one observer). Six months later, the relationship ended when Fagan presented Andy with an ultimatum, a sure way to sever ties with Warhol. Andy had planned to take both Fagan and Malanga to an opening in Toronto, but Philip had said that if Gerard went, he wouldn't. Andy had replied, "It's up to you," and the young man, as Malanga recalled, "packed his bags and split. He never came back, and I don't think he would have been allowed back, because once a boy walked out on Andy, that was it."

A few months later, he met another "Fagan," a young Harvard

graduate to whom he was introduced by Chuck Wein. Danny Williams was just the sort of sweet, easily dominated young man Andy was looking for, and like Fagan, he soon moved into the Lexington Avenue house. In no time he was wearing the same boat-neck striped shirts Andy and Edie were wearing and regularly accompanying Warhol on his social rounds. After several months the relationship began to break down. Heidie was with Andy and Danny at a restaurant on Christopher Street one night, when he witnessed one of their fights: "Danny was very angry with Andy," said Heidie, "and I sensed that Andy was afraid of him. Danny jumped up at the table and pulled off Andy's wig. Andy screamed, 'Danny! Stop it!' For a second we all saw him bald, then he popped it back on."

By October, Andy had kicked Danny out of his house, but, unlike Fagan, he was allowed to stay around because he could work the lights and sound for the films. He moved into the Factory, set up a workshop for himself, and lived there through the first months of 1966. Billy Linich had been opposed to the arrangement because "Danny had a tendency to have nervous breakdowns, to become soft and physically unreliable in our working space. As far as I was concerned, that was dangerous and placed us in jeopardy." Danny began taking amphetamines, but he did not handle them well. The handsome Harvard preppie turned into an addict, his hair matted and stringy, his skin coated with the silver dust that crumbled from the walls of the Factory, his glasses broken and taped together. When he fell into one of his funks, sometimes threatening suicide, Andy screamed at him to "shape up." Everyone joined in. Danny Williams became the Factory's whipping boy, and he retreated behind what one observer described as "a gay farm-boy-exposed approach, like, 'If you don't watch out I'll hurt myself and it'll all be your fault!' to which the typical response was, 'Well, fuck you, Danny. Nobody gives a shit!' "

As Henry Geldzahler saw it: "Andy was a voyeur-sadist and he needed exhibitionist-masochists in order to fulfill both halves of his destiny. And it's obvious that an exhibitionist-masochist is not going to last very long. And then the voyeur-sadist needs another exhibitionist-masochist. There were always more people around than Andy could use in any one situation. Therefore there was constant fighting to get into the royal enclave."

"It was as if he was collecting people," said Malanga. "Andy had a hypnotic power to create a personality for someone."

Paul Morrissey was one of the few newcomers to the Factory who had a strong personality of his own. A self-styled "square," Morrissey was determinedly anti-intellectual and (making an exception for Andy) anti–avant-garde. He adored John Wayne, Katharine Hepburn, and the films of John Ford. Consequently, the others looked down on him as "not an artist." But he had the ability to act as a buffer between Warhol and the more volatile people at the Factory, and by the end of 1965, he had become Andy's chief lieutenant, responsible for passing on Andy's orders and handling requests for money. Morrissey's withering sarcasm, delivered in a high-pitched voice, didn't win anyone over, and he was soon the object of general dislike among his co-workers, who viewed his commercial instincts with alarm. Among such notions was Morrissey's conviction that the name Andy Warhol was now eminently marketable.

In December 1965, Andy and Paul were approached by a theater producer, Michael Myerberg, who had brought the first production of *Waiting for Godot* to New York. Myerberg told them he was opening a discotheque in an abandoned airplane hangar in Queens to compete with the popular club Arthur, and he was willing to pay Andy a small fee to bring people to the club.

"I had this idea," Morrissey recalled, "that Andy could make money not only from underground films but from putting the movies in some sort of rock-and-roll context." Paul suggested that Andy also supply the music. Under those circumstances, Myerberg agreed to call the club Andy Warhol's Up. An informal agreement was reached on a proposed fee of forty thousand dollars for four weekends the following April, and the Factory "squirrels," as Geldzahler called the younger kids, went out looking for a band.

Just before Christmas, the filmmaker and squirrel extraordinaire Barbara Rubin heard a group called the Velvet Underground at the Café Bizarre on MacDougal Street. The group was comprised of Sterling Morrison, the lead guitarist, a self-styled "nasty rock-and-roll biker type" who was in fact the friendliest and funniest member of the band; Maureen Tucker, the percussionist, a tiny, androgynous figure who kept a metronomic machinelike back beat on timpani and cymbals; John Cale, who played electric viola and bass guitar, a Welsh music scholar and disciple of the avant-garde composer La Monte Young; and Lou Reed, the hard-edged vocalist and songwriter, who, at twenty-one, was already a rock-and-roll veteran.

The next night, Rubin took Gerard, Paul, Andy, and a bunch of hangers-on, including the rapidly fading Edie, to see her discovery. According to Morrissey, their first impression was that you couldn't tell if the drummer was a boy or a girl, and that the band sang songs about drugs and had the word *underground* in their name, all of which gave them an affinity to the Factory. Bob Heidie, who was also present, said that at one point Andy whispered to him, "Gee, do you think we should, uh, buy them?" Afterward, Andy hit it off with Lou Reed and invited the Velvets to the Factory to discuss ways of working together.

A few days later, Malanga got a phone call from a German singer he had met several years earlier. She was called, simply, Nico. Nico had a fairly glittering résumé. She had had a part in Fellini's *La Dolce Vita.* She had studied acting and singing at Lee Strasberg's Actors Studio. She had a son, Ari, by the French actor Alain Delon. And she had been hanging out with the Rolling Stones in London. Andy immediately proposed that she sing with "his" band. Nico, he wrote in *POPism*, "was a new type of female superstar. Baby Jane and Edie were both outgoing, American, social, bright, excited, chatty—whereas Nico was weird and untalkative. You'd ask her something and she'd maybe answer you five minutes later. When people described her, they used words like memento mori and macabre. She wasn't the type to get up on a table and dance, the way Edie or Jane might; in fact, she'd rather hide under the table than dance on top of it. She was mysterious and European, a real moon goddess type."

Andy's idea was to take the black-clad, scruffy young band with its rock-and-roll music about heroin and sadomasochism, put the icy blond white-on-white Nico up front, and have them play as loud as they could behind male and female go-go dancers while his films were projected in the background and strobe lights roamed the audience. He understood the need to express distress in the culture: Why shouldn't rock and roll be disturbing?

When the Velvet Underground visited the Factory a few days later, they were presented with an offer they could take or leave. Andy would manage them, give them a place to rehearse, finance their equipment, support them, and make them famous, in return for which Warvel, Inc., the cover company, would receive twenty-five percent of their earnings. There was another condition: Nico must sing with the band. Persuading the Velvets to play with Nico was not easy. First of all, she wanted only a back-up band so that she could sing all the songs, and the multitalented Velvets had no interest in simply providing back-up. Besides, some of their best songs, like "Heroin" and "Waiting for My Man," weren't as well suited for Nico's voice as they were for Lou Reed's. Still, everybody was eager to do something, and the Velvets finally agreed to Andy and Paul's proposal that Nico be allowed to sing a few songs and, when not singing, just stand on the stage looking beautiful.

Lou Reed remembered: "Andy told me that what we were doing with music was the same thing he was doing with painting and movies, i.e., not kidding around. To my mind nobody in music was doing anything that even approximated the real thing, with the exception of us. It wasn't slick or a lie in any conceivable way. The first thing I liked about Andy was that he was very real."

All the Velvets were excited about working with Andy. "It was like bang!" the Factory actress Mary Woronov recalled. "They were with Andy and Andy was with them and they backed him absolutely. They would have walked to the end of the earth for him." But it was Lou Reed who was the most affected.

Like Billy Linich and Gerard Malanga, he was ripe for being molded by the master. Self-effacing and vulnerable offstage, a heterosexual who said he wanted to be a drag queen, he was a rock-and-roller around the bend, a wild man on the guitar who, onstage, couldn't be "mean" enough. As one verse of "Heroin" went: "When the smack begins to flow / Then I really don't care anymore / About all you jim jims in this town / And everybody putting everybody else down / And all the politicians making crazy sounds / And all the dead bodies piled up in mounds." Most of Reed's songs were like that—sharp, cool, on target—and he delivered them in a static-electric voice filled with contemptuous rage.

During the following weeks they all worked hard together. Andy gave Lou ideas for songs and asked him how many he had written every day. He taught him that work was everything, and Lou came to believe that his music was so beautiful that people should be willing to die for it. "It was like landing in heaven," said Reed. "I would hear people say the most astonishing things, the craziest things, the funniest things, the saddest things. I used to write it all down."

The Velvet Underground immediately became a part of Warhol's entourage. "New York was based on parties then," Morrissey recalled. "There were twenty parties a night, some of them given by public-relations companies, and Andy started to find his way onto some of those lists." He also became famous for crashing parties, with a dozen people in tow. For example, on New Year's Eve, 1965, Andy, Gerard, the Velvets, and Edie, who was still on the scene, started off the evening by crashing the traditional party given by the playwright Edward Albee and the producer Richard Barr. When they got to the top of the stairs, Barr pointed at them across the room and said, "You! Out!" They all exited quickly, half-amused, half-perplexed by the strength of the rejection. Bob Heidie, who was at the party, was stunned. "Edie was the Girl of the Year," he said, "and it would have seemed absolutely right that they be there along with Noël Coward and John Gielgud. Apparently, however, they didn't want a woman there!"

In preparation for the opening of Andy Warhol's Up discotheque, a test run was scheduled at the Cinematheque. Jonas Mekas had given Andy a free hand to do anything he liked in place of the Edie Sedgwick retrospective, which had been canceled after she refused to sign releases for her films. For the show Billy changed his surname from Linich to Name, which Andy thought was "so cute." One of Andy's ambitions was to have an art show "with people on the walls instead of paintings," so it was decided to present the Velvets and Nico with Andy's films in the background. Barbara Rubin was to run up and down the aisles screaming threatening questions at people while Billy photographed their reactions. And Gerard Malanga was to lead a company of "interpretive dancers" pretending to shoot up, whip one another, and perform crucifixions in front of the band.

The show went as planned, and "left nothing to the imagination," said Ronnie Cutrone, a teenage art student and one of the dancers. "We were on stage with bullwhips, giant flashlights, hypodermic needles, and wooden crosses. It was very severe. It scared a lot of people."

"It's ugly," said Andy, "a very ugly effect, when you put it all together. But it's beautiful—the Velvets playing and Gerard danc-

Andy, age 3 (right), with his mother and brother John: "Being born is like being kidnapped. And then sold into slavery." (Courtesy of John Richardson.)

Andrei Warhola on a Pittsburgh construction site: An arch-disciplinarian with an enormous appetite for work. (Courtesy of John Warhola.)

The house on Beelan Street where Andy lived from age 2 to 4: Flames from the surrounding steel mills sparked conflagrations in such dwellings, giving him a lifelong fear of fire. (Photo by Victor Bockris.)

Andy (in front) with relatives on the day of his father's funeral in 1942, outside the Warholas' house on Dawson Street: This may have been the only funeral he ever went to. (Courtesy of Justina Swindell.)

At age 14 with his brothers John (left) and Paul on Dawson Street: Now he was compulsive about drawing pictures. (Courtesy of Paul Warhola.)

Andy as a college senior in 1948: According to Philip Pearlstein, he was "extraordinarily talented . . . like an angel in the sky." (Courtesy of Archives Malanga.)

THE FIFTIES

In New York, 1950: Within days of his arrival he had found his commercial calling card—ladies' shoes. (Courtesy of Arthur Elias.)

With his mother in their fourth-floor apartment at 242 Lexington Avenue, 1958: As the litter mounted, so did the population of cats. (Photo by Duane Michals.)

Practicing to be famous—à la Capote—in 1958: "He used his shyness like a little boy—playfully." (Photo by Duane Michals.)

Andy (at rear) in 1963 with Henry Geldzahler (left), David Hockney (middle), and Geoffrey Goodman: "Andy was pop and pop was Andy." (Photo by Dennis Hopper, courtesy of Tony Shafrazi Gallery.)

With Irving Blum (rear), Billy Al Bengston, and Dennis Hopper in Los Angeles, 1963: Young Hollywood, from Troy Donahue to Peter Fonda, turned out to fête him. (Courtesy of Irving Blum.)

Shopping in New York, 1964:
Eleanor Ward, his dealer, was
horrified that he was making
sculpture out of grocery boxes.
(Photo by Bob Adelman.)

With Gerard Malanga in Paris in 1965: Andy's desire
for power was intimately linked to his voyeurism.
(Photo by Harry Shunk.)

With Edie Sedgwick in 1965: This poor little rich girl was his mirror image, "a wonderful, beautiful blank." (Photo by Bob Adelman.)

Filming *Beauty #2* with Edie and Gino Piserchio in 1965: By capturing the "death" of his superstar's every moment in this "untraditional triangle (without love)," Warhol reduced her to what she saw herself as—a victim. (Photo by Bob Adelman.)

From *Andy Warhol's Index Book,* published in 1965 (with Diane Hall pointing a toy pistol in the Factory): Foreshadowing 1968. (Photo by Stephen Shore.)

The Factory workers, 1965: (top, left to right) Nico, Brigid Polk, Louis Waldon, Taylor Mead, Ultra Violet, Paul Morrissey, Viva, International Velvet, unidentified person; (bottom) Ingrid Superstar, Ondine, Tom Baker, Tiger Morse, Billy Name, Warhol. (Courtesy of Archives Malanga.)

Andy being put into an ambulance outside the Factory after being shot, 1968: "It hurt so much, I wished I were dead." (Photo by Jack Smith, courtesy of the *New York Daily News*.)

In Positano in 1973 with (left to right) Susan Johnson, Bianca and Mick Jagger, Fred Hughes, and Jed Johnson (holding Jade Jagger): No party was complete without Andy. (Photo by Paul Morrissey.)

With Paulette Goddard at the Whitney Museum opening of his celebrity portraits in 1979: A more glamorous stand-in for his mother? (Photo by Toby Old.)

At Studio 54 in 1979 with (left to right) Lorna Luft, Jerry Hall, Debbie Harry, Truman Capote, and Paloma Picasso: Where the stars were "nobody because everybody's a star." (Photo by Anton Perich.)

Doing a celebrity portrait at the Factory, in 1973: The final result was embalmed expressionism. (Photo by Victor Bockris.)

With Jon Gould (left) in a helicopter over New York, 1983: In love. (Photo by Christopher Makos.)

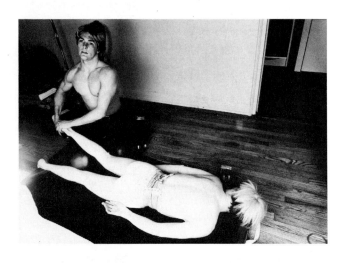

With private masseur: "Muscles are great. Everybody should have at least one they can show off." (Photo by Christopher Makos.)

With Joseph Beuys, Heiner Bastian, and Robert Rauschenberg in Berlin, 1982: "A naive revolutionary." (Photo by Christopher Makos.)

Invitation to a party after the opening of Warhol's joint show with
Jean-Michel Basquiat, showing the two artists: "I think I helped Andy
more than he helped me." (Photo by Michael Halsband, courtesy of
Tony Shafrazi Gallery.)

(Copyright © 1987 by *New York Post*.)

The burial in St. John the Divine Cemetery in Bethel Park: Among the mourners (left to right), Gael Love (head down), James Warhola (hands folded), Brigid Berlin, and Warhol's Filipino housekeepers Nena and Aurora Bugarin. (Photo by Wilfredo Rosado.)

ing and the films and the lights, and it's a beautiful thing. Very vinyl. Beautiful."

The show, which was renamed Andy Warhol Uptight, was designed to provoke the performers as well as the audience. "They were a very bitchy, competitive crowd at the Factory," noted one observer, "and Andy tricked them along. He was always saying, 'You're going to be a star!' and they got involved with him to the point where if they pulled out, they lost everything they had put in. So Andy could just screw people over left and right. No one got paid. He was eating people! It was straight-out exploitation."

Edie danced with Malanga at the Cinematheque, but a few weeks later in February she staged another "final exit" from Andy. They were all dining at the Ginger Man restaurant across from Lincoln Center, when she demanded hysterically, in front of the whole entourage: "What am I supposed to be doing in the Velvet Underground? What's my role? When am I going to get paid?"

Pale and shaking, Andy repeated what he always said, "I don't have any money, Edie! You'll have to be patient."

Edie left the table and made a phone call, ostensibly to Bob Dylan. Then she came back to the table and told Andy she was leaving for good.

Of Edie's "defection" Malanga said: "The people advising Dylan had this illusion that they could develop Edie into a singer. So it was easy for her to finally leave Andy. She was the product of a heterosexual milieu, whereas Andy was very much part of a homosexual sensibility, and the Dylan group was staunchly heterosexual. Edie's talent was totally undeveloped. She thought she could further herself by being associated with Dylan, but this was merely an optimism based on hopes and dreams."

Paul Morrissey explained it this way: "Dylan was a creep. I think he was doing it to spite Andy. He had some sort of dislike for Andy. Andy didn't care about that. He just felt very upset that Edie would be so cruel."

Indeed, Andy had rarely been so upset, and he became more so when he heard that Edie was putting him down as a "sadistic faggot" and making fun of his films. She had, he wrote, "fascinated me more than anybody I had ever known. And the fascination I experienced was probably very close to a certain kind of love." "I still care about people," he told an interviewer, "but it would be so much easier not to care. . . . I don't want to get too involved in other people's lives. . . . I don't want to get too close. . . . That's why my work is so distant from myself." He was, he wrote, a victim of the times: "During the sixties I think people forgot what emotions were supposed to be. And I don't think they've ever remembered. I think that once you see emotions from a certain angle you can never think of them as real again. That's what more or less happened to me. I don't know if I was ever capable of love, but after the sixties I never thought in terms of love again."

Meanwhile, Morrissey was pressing Michael Myerberg about the discotheque in Queens. Morrissey recalled: "There was, let's say, an Italian influence in this club, and I think they had their own plans for the opening. Somehow, even Myerberg lost control of it. About a week before the club was scheduled to open, this lawyer called and said, 'They've changed their mind; they're going to open this weekend with the Young Rascals.' I remember going down to the Café Figaro, where Gerard had taken Andy to see Allen Ginsberg. I said, 'Andy, they're not going to sign the agreement, we don't have a club for the Velvets.' Sitting at the table behind me were Jackie Cassen and Rudi Stern, and they heard me talking. They said, 'You're looking for a dance hall to present a rock-and-roll group? We know a wonderful place.' I went over to St. Mark's Place with them and saw the Dom. We signed the rental deal on Friday, and that afternoon the Velvets moved their equipment in, and Gerard was up on the back, painting the wall white. At eight o'clock, all these people showed up. It was packed."

The advertisement in *The Village Voice* had read: "COME BLOW YOUR MIND. The Silver Dream Factory Presents The Exploding Plastic Inevitable with Andy Warhol/The Velvet Underground/and Nico." There was no question who the main attraction was: The Dom was packed because of curiosity about Andy. Not that anyone could see him. Seven nights a week for the next four weeks, he sat high above the deafening din up in the balcony of the former Polish meeting hall, running the film and slide projectors, conducting, as Jonas Mekas saw him, "light symphonies of tremendous emotional and mental pitch . . . somewhere in the shadow, totally unnoticeable but following every second and every detail of it." The last thing he wanted people to do was relax. Whenever he thought the audience was getting too loose, he ordered the projectionist to "Change it! Change it!"

Throughout April, the Exploding Plastic Inevitable packed the Dom with a cross-section of straights and gays, art tramps and artists (including Salvador Dalí, who was advertised as a member of the group), the thrill-seeking rich, the drugged and the desperate, beautiful girls in miniskirts, and beautiful boys, for all of whom Andy had created a kind of religious spectacle. This was the first time Andy had combined all his different worlds under one roof. Lou Reed said: "Andy created multimedia in New York. The whole complexion of the city changed. Nothing remained the same after that."

According to Morrissey: "It was almost the first time a strobe had even been on a dance floor. And Andy had bought the old mirrored light ball in a junk shop. It was part of his own collection of Americana, and pretty soon every hippie in the world had one in their living room. I always thought we were just reflecting what we saw about us, but people looked on it as some sort of a political movement. The West Coast hippie movement *was* a political movement. People used to say, 'Well, aren't you hippies too?' People outside New York don't understand that the New York sensibility doesn't take anything seriously. Everything's just grist for the mill. It was only provincial attitudes, like in Germany or England or California, that took this stuff seriously."

But the art pundits waxed ecstatic: "The sound is a savage series of thrusts and electronic feedback," wrote the *Voice* critic Richard Goldstein. "The lyrics combine sadomasochistic frenzy with free-association imagery. The whole sound seems to be the product of a secret marriage between Bob Dylan and the Marquis de Sade." Marshall McLuhan, the cultural seer, found the Exploding Plastic Inevitable's performances remarkable enough to include a photograph of one of them in *The Medium Is the Message*, with its celebrated assertion: " 'Time' has ceased, 'space' has vanished. We now live in a global village . . . a simultaneous happening."

The EPI provoked its share of hostility as well. On more than one occasion, members of the group were attacked by bottle-throwers as they left the Dom. It was only to be expected, for, as Stephen Koch would later write: "Seeing [the Exploding Plastic Inevitable] made me realize for the first time how deeply the then all-admired theories attacking the 'ego' as the root of all evil and unhappiness had become for the avant-garde the grounds for a deeply engaged metaphor of sexual sadism, for 'blowing the mind,' assaulting the senses; it came home to me how the 'obliteration' of the ego was not the act of liberation it was advertised to be, but an act of compulsive revenge and *resentment* wholly entangled on the deepest levels with the knots of frustration. Liberation was turning out to be humiliation; peace was revealing itself as rage."

During his first week at the Dom, Andy opened a new show at the Castelli Gallery. There had been an eighteen-month hiatus since the *Flowers* show, during which time he'd devoted himself almost exclusively to filmmaking. Having announced in Paris that he was retiring from painting, having insisted to Leo Castelli and Ivan Karp that he had run out of ideas, he conceived this show as his farewell to art.

Karp had suggested that he paint something "pastoral, like cows" and so he wallpapered one room of the gallery with the repeated images of a cow's head, resembling Elsie, the friendly trademark of Borden's dairy products. The other room he filled with free-floating helium-filled silver pillows.

As a "happening," the show was powerful, and the critics were suitably puzzled: "The ways his materials were deployed demonstrated, in a single show, extremes of stability and mobility; the full implications of that show are still to be worked out," wrote the British art historian Richard Morphet. For Calvin Tomkins, the show was apocalyptic: "With awesome timing, Andy declared Pop Art dead."

Indeed, it would be eleven years before Andy had another show of new work at Castelli.

"You just gave them what they wanted," said the actress Mary Woronov, "and it was like this run. Man, we had a run." With the EPI taking in eighteen thousand dollars its first week at the Dom, with *My Hustler* making a profit at the Cinémathèque, Andy branched out again by producing his first record album, *Velvet Underground and Nico*.

A recording studio was rented for $2,500 for three nights, and conflicts erupted about what Nico could or could not sing. In the end The Velvets, at least, were happy with the arrangement. "Andy was like an umbrella—he was just there," Lou Reed recalled. "He made it so we could do anything we wanted; we made the record ourselves."

Everything was going well until Warhol and Morrissey made the kind of mistake that would undercut a good deal of their work together in the coming years. They did not watch out for the sharks in the booming rock business, who would move in on a good thing as soon as they saw it make money. When a genial booking agent named Charlie Rothchild approached Morrissey and persuaded him to turn over the Dom's box office to him and let him get other bookings for the band, Morrissey agreed. Consequently, at the beginning of May, the Exploding Plastic Inevitable, numbering some fourteen performers in all, found themselves flying out to Los Angeles for a month-long engagement at a club called the Trip that promised to put them over the top and get them a big record deal. They established themselves in the Castle, a large imitation fortress in the Hollywood Hills, where many rock stars put up their entourages at five hundred dollars a week. There, things began to fall apart.

Their opening act, the Mothers of Invention, set out to ridicule the Velvet Underground whenever they could, and the old jealousy between the East and West Coast entertainment businesses broke out in the open. Lou Reed was heard to say that Frank Zappa, the leader of the Mothers, was "probably the single most untalented person I've heard in my life." In rebuttal, Cher, queen of the local rock hierarchy, commented that the EPI would "replace nothing except maybe suicide." The local critics were equally dismissive, and on the group's third night, the Trip was closed down by the local sheriff's department for disturbing the peace. Andy did not want to spend a month in L.A., supporting fourteen people who were doing nothing, but the musicians' union informed him that if the band stayed in town for the duration of the engagement, they would have to be paid the entire fee. Tensions were running high, and Reed was already looking for a way out of his contract with Andy, but EPI decided to stay and sell their tapes to a record company. After several rejections, they got a positive response from the producer Tom Wilson, who was about to move into an executive position at

MGM. But now Reed refused to sign the contracts unless all money from sales came first to the band, not to Warhol as originally agreed upon. Morrissey started to think that Reed too was a creep, just like Dylan.

The moment of truth came when the band was booked to play a weekend at Bill Graham's Fillmore West in San Francisco at the end of the month. By then tempers were so frayed that the New York contingent could no longer hide their contempt for the West Coast scene. Morrissey sarcastically asked Graham why the West Coast bands didn't take heroin, since "that's what all really good musicians take." It was a put-on, but Graham exploded: "You disgusting germs! Here we are trying to clean everything up and you come out here with your disgusting minds and whips!" That night Gerard was arrested in the street for carrying the leather bullwhip he danced with, and spent a nervous night in jail. Everyone split up after that: Andy returned to New York—the trip was over.

Looking back on the whole experience, which coincided with the surge of the West Coast hippie movement, Lou Reed reflected: "It was very funny, until there were a lot of casualties. Then it wasn't funny anymore. That flower-power thing eventually crumbled as a result of drug casualties and the fact that it was a nice idea but not a very realistic one. What we, the Velvets, were talking about . . . *was* . . . realistic."

14

ANDY HAD NEGLECTED to renew his lease on the Dom, and when he returned to New York, he found, much to his dismay, that none other than Charlie Rothchild and Dylan's manager, Albert Grossman, had taken over the place and turned it into a lucrative rock club called the Balloon Farm. (A year later, drawing on the concepts Warhol had pioneered, it would become one of the seminal and most lucrative rock clubs of the sixties, the Electric Circus.)

Andy bewailed the collapse of the Exploding Plastic Inevitable. "Other people succeed who have no talent," he would say. "Here we are with all you gorgeous people and we can't make it. How come? Oh, it's so hard." Still, he never let failures stop him in what Malanga called his relentless drive for "*la gloire.*" The Exploding Plastic Inevitable had spread his name to a much larger, younger audience than he had had as an artist and filmmaker. Now was the perfect time to put out a new film this audience could eat up. The feelings that had erupted around the disintegration of the EPI were, he thought, perfect material.

Rather than focusing his camera on one "star," he would turn it loose on the whole bunch—Ingrid Superstar, Mary Woronov, Nico (whom he was promoting as his new "Girl of the Year"), a newcomer who called herself International Velvet, Malanga, Ondine, and Brigid Polk. And in the process, he would expose the reverse side of the sixties, challenging the corny flower-power philosophy of the hippies and their messiah, Dylan.

Ever since he had been commissioned to do *Ethel Scull 36 Times,* Andy had been aware that painting portraits was a quicker and surer way to make money than painting works like the "death-and-disaster" series. After pausing briefly to knock off several commissioned portraits (of the gallery owner Holly Solomon and Lita Hornick, a socialite), he embarked in mid-June 1966 on the busiest three months of his movie-making career.

"Andy tried to film a sequence a week," Morrissey recalled. "To buy the film, to develop it and get a print was about a thousand to fifteen-hundred dollars a week, depending on whether it was black and white or color. He wasn't making a fortune then, so these experiments, which everybody except us thought were idiotic, had to prove themselves in some popular way."

Between June and September, he shot some fifteen one- and two-reel films at the Factory, in various apartments, and at the old bohemian Chelsea Hotel on West Twenty-third Street, where several of the performers were living. His general idea was to film people in conflict with one another or, if alone, with themselves. The dynamic behind the films was like that of the EPI: tense and confrontational.

No one in the cast was fully aware of what Andy was up to, but they were all primed to perform. The films had no plots and, in most cases, no scripts, except for a few sketches mailed in by Ronnie Tavel, who had finally become so upset by what he saw as Warhol's cruelty that he had removed himself to California. As with previous Warhol films, the scenes were shot in one take until the thirty-five-minute reels ran out, the idea being that if he aimed the camera at interesting people and kept it running, *something* was bound to happen. "This way I can catch people being themselves instead of setting up a scene and shooting it and letting people act out parts that were written," he explained. "Because it's better to act naturally than act like somebody else. These are experimental films which deal with human emotions and human life. Anything to do with the human person I feel is all right."

Naturally, this put all the burden on the performers, and this pressure was invariably compounded by personal hostilities and the effects of drugs. "All these people were used again and again in his films," Ondine pointed out, "but in ways that would lead them to really dislike each other, because of the dialogue. Also because of the drug taking—an enormous amount of drug taking—most of the people were off the wall with their own versions of what was happening." To turn the pressure up, Andy and Paul would plant rumors about unpleasant remarks someone had made about someone else.

The films were shot under the most primitive conditions. The sound was recorded optically, which was inexpensive but often created almost inaudible soundtracks. Warhol's attitude was not to care. When the soundman on one set protested that the sound was hopelessly unbalanced and the batteries were dying, Andy shot the film anyway. It was this reckless, driven, edgy, "Just do it!" attitude along with everything else that inspired his actors to give him everything they could.

The results were often explosive. For Ondine's scenes, it was decided that he would play the "Pope of Greenwich Village." In one reel, desperate to be magnificent, he began by shooting up amphetamines on camera, confessing his homosexuality, and lambasting the state of the Roman Catholic church. As his exposition became more searing, Ondine uttered what would become one of his most controversial lines: "Approach the crucifix, lift his loincloth, and go about your business!" A girl named Rona Page, who had been sent by Jonas Mekas, came in to "take confession." On camera she made the terrible mistake of calling Ondine a phony. Flying into a rage, he slapped her in the face, tore into her, jumped up and slapped her again. Andy, who hated violence but was too fascinated to stop it, ran to the other side of the room, followed by Rona. Ondine stormed off after them, screaming, "Turn off the fucking camera!" but the camera stared obdurately at the empty couch and ground on. Off set, Ondine could still be heard yelling, "You phony! You fool! You moron! You misery! You're a disgrace, a disgrace to yourself. May God forgive you!"

Andy's methods were unpleasant, Ondine said, "but he pulled out of these people, including myself, some of the best performances *ever* on screen."

In August, Jonas Mekas asked Warhol for a film to show at the

Cinemathèque, and Andy and Paul started reviewing the footage they had shot over the summer. As they screened the twelve to fifteen reels, they realized that the films related to one another in a compelling if unintended way. In addition to the Pope/Ondine story, there were harrowing reels of Brigid, playing a drug dealer, shooting up amphetamines through her blue jeans, of Gerard Malanga being called an irresponsible hippie by Marie Mecken in the role of his mother, of Mario Montez being reduced to tears by two bitchy homosexuals, of Eric Emerson stripping and telling his life story, of a lesbian torture sequence, and of Nico cutting her hair and crying. They quickly assembled twelve of them into a sequence and gave it the umbrella title *Chelsea Girls.*

With a running time of six-and-a-half hours, the film was too long for theatrical distribution. To solve the problem Andy decided to show two reels simultaneously on a split screen with only one side of the screen "talking" at a time, thereby cutting the running time in half. The juxtaposition of actors and action, color and black and white, sound and silence heightened the schizoid effect, particularly when the same players appeared in adjacent scenes exposing differ- ent aspects of their personalities. Ingrid Superstar, who appeared in more scenes than anyone else, emerged as the comic heroine of the film. Morrissey explained: "With us everything is acceptance. Noth- ing is critical. Everything is amoral. People can be whatever they are, and we record it on film. The one Andy loves is Ingrid Superstar, because Ingrid can't dissimulate. She couldn't *not* be Ingrid. She can do her thing for us because she thinks we're trash. We treat her like dirt and that's the way she likes to be treated."

Above all, *Chelsea Girls* stood out as a harrowing portrait of what Andy Warhol's world had become by the summer of 1966, for by the time the filming began, even his greatest champion had walked out. Recalled Henry Geldzahler: "I finally understood what Andy was doing with people and I had to get out of there to save myself. There was one tense moment. There was a blackboard in the studio and I wrote: 'Andy Warhol can't paint anymore and he can't make movies yet.' He never forgot it."

By the time *Chelsea Girls* was finished, the Factory was seething, and casualties were beginning to mount. Danny Williams had re- joined the EPI as a technician one last time for a week of shows in Chicago in June, but after an argument with Morrissey during the sound check had resulted in a fistfight, he had returned to his parents' house on Cape Cod. On September 8, the week before *Chelsea Girls* was to open at the Cinémathèque, word arrived at the Factory that Danny had driven to the shore, undressed, left his clothes in a neat pile by the car, plunged into the ocean, and drowned. Among those who had watched Andy's rejection and constant belittling of Danny, the general attitude was, "If that's what he wants to do, that's cool." When Williams' parents sent Andy two doorknobs that Danny had left him with his suicide note, everyone at the Factory pretended they didn't grasp the message about where Andy should shove them. According to Ronald Tavel: "Andy's reaction was appalling. I was there the day [Williams'] mother called and I said, 'You must speak to her.' He said, 'Oh, I don't care, what a pain in the neck, he was just an amphetamine addict!' "

"You couldn't blow your cool ever," remembered Ronnie Cutrone. "You were not allowed even to be a human being. Everything worked through guilt and paranoia."

Billy Name said that he got so sick from exhaustion that he was reduced to lying on a couch for several days, "urinating this black and red stuff and crying because it was so painful." Andy advised him to "see it all as a movie so you don't have to experience all that pain."

Even Gerard Malanga's relationship with Andy was reaching the breaking point. Morrissey's involvement had increasingly subverted Malanga's position as Warhol's closest associate, and he began keeping a daily tally of rebuffs in a "Trip Book," which he described as a "chronicle of love-hate conflicts," mostly with Andy. A typical entry, dated September 4, 1968, was an imaginary letter: "Dear Andy," it began, "it seems I'm always writing you letters to explain myself, as you find it easy to say nothing. . . . I feel that you will do nothing in your almost absolute power to correct the mess you are responsible for."

On September 15, the day *Chelsea Girls* opened at the Cinémathèque, Warhol upbraided Malanga for not getting copies of all the film reels finished on time. Gerard noted tersely: "Andy is sometimes beneath contempt and his contempt came out in full force today."

Despite this and other last-minute problems, *Chelsea Girls* was an immediate success, a cause célèbre that became the first underground film to capture the interest of the general public. The press had a field day: *Chelsea Girls* was variously hailed as "the *Iliad* of the Underground" (*Newsweek*), as a metaphor for "burning Vietnam" (the *Village Voice*), as "a grotesque menagerie of lost souls whimpering in a psychedelic moonscape" (the *New York Times*), and as "a three-and-a-half hour cesspool of vulgarity and talentless confusion which is about as interesting as the inside of a toilet bowl" (the critic Rex Reed).

"Don't you make no dirty movies!" his mother had admonished Andy. And there was a bad moment in Max's Kansas City, one of his favorite late-night hangouts, when a drunk attacked the entourage, pouring a bottle of beer over Andy's head. But *Chelsea Girls,* which in two months had moved out of the Cinemathèque to "legitimate" theaters in New York, was making Andy more money than anything else ever had before.

Andy's associates scoffed at his constant complaint that he didn't have any money, but in fact it was much closer to the truth than any of them, even Malanga, would allow. Since the beginning of the decade, Andy had been earning less than he had during his peak years as a commercial artist in the fifties, while at the same time maintaining a much more expensive style of life and work. His financial demands included the monthly tab for the Factory and the entourage of fifteen to twenty whom he fed and transported around with him, as well as the upkeep of his house, supporting his mother, and sending contributions to relatives in Pittsburgh. All of this was being paid for by the sale of paintings from which he might see at most two thousand dollars each, and a monthly stipend from Castelli. Moreover, apart from *My Hustler,* the films had so far earned him absolutely nothing, and the profits from the shows at the Dom had gone into supporting the act, taking everyone out West, and making the record (a deal had finally been made with MGM), which would not be released for almost a year.

The film's astonishing success was widely publicized (it earned three hundred thousand dollars in six months, of which Andy, owing to a bad business deal, got only half), which brought the long-simmering money problem at the Factory to a boil. Mary Woronov's mother sued Andy for showing the film without having gotten a release from her daughter, and he settled out of court. This paved the way for the others to complain, and eventually Andy was forced to pay everyone in the film one thousand dollars each. Getting the money from him was a humiliating process, and it took a long time to collect.

Others who had made marginal contributions to the film, like Ronnie Tavel, thought of suing too, but changed their minds. "My lawyer said, 'Did you learn something from working with Warhol?' " recalled Tavel. "I said, 'A great deal.' He said, 'Then write it off to a learning experience.' "

In November 1966, a lawsuit was leveled against Andy by Patricia Caulfield, whose photograph he had used to make his flower painting. She had been prompted to sue him when she heard that Andy was "rich." A long, costly court case resulted, out of which Andy ultimately agreed to give Caulfield several paintings and a percentage of all profits resulting from any future reproduction of the paintings as prints.

Other enmities began crowding in on Andy. Ivy Nicholson, a fashion model who had been at the Factory since 1964, was so desperate for attention that she had begun making noises about "marrying" Andy. On one occasion, when Ondine went over to her apartment, she opened the door and threw a cup of hot coffee in his face. Another time, after Billy had ejected her from the Factory, she left a pile of her excrement in the elevator.

And Edie Sedgwick had reappeared. Dismissed from the Dylan entourage after his motorcycle accident, and injured in an apartment fire, she had begun coming around the Factory asking for pills and money. Andy always gave her a few dollars and Obetrol if he had one to spare. In November 1966 he put her in one last movie to "help her out." It was called *The Andy Warhol Story,* an attempt by Andy to turn the camera on himself.

Paul Morrissey recalled the filming: "René Ricard was supposed to be Andy, and Edie was in it with him. She was in a bad way, and we thought we could help her, even though she had been so mean to do what she did. We thought it might work, but it wasn't any good. All René did was look in the camera and say nasty things about Andy, and it was really embarrassing because he thought he'd be funny. I remember very well Andy not finding it funny at all. Anybody else would have turned the camera off, but he wouldn't."

The Andy Warhol Story was such a painful document of Edie's disintegration that the one time it was shown at the Factory, those watching begged Andy to turn it off.

Andy blamed drugs for what was happening to his "superstars." "On drugs everything is like a movie," he wrote. "Nothing hurts and you're not the way you used to be or would have been." Even so, he continued to play off his performers against one another. That autumn he squired around his latest find, Susan Bottomly (International Velvet), another poor little rich girl with an allowance from her father that enabled her to pick up the tab at discotheques. Another Malanga diary entry reveals just how shrill the competition among Warhol's entourage had become: "Ingrid is very unhappy because she feels that she's fading. Mary was someone I invented, put a whip in her hand, and spread her name around and made her a star, but she did not really show any interest and because of her passiveness allowed herself to be eclipsed by Ingrid Superstar, Nico, and Susan. Nico is the true star because she keeps her distance and is socially professional. Andy and I go to meet Susan and Edie and Mary at El Quixote Restaurant in the Hotel Chelsea. We have a lot to drink. Mary keeps her cool although she's as insecure as Susan, and Edie is doing nothing to help herself. I bring up the fact that when Nico comes back from Ibiza she'll eclipse all the underlings. Susan is very stoned—gets uptight and leaves the table to go to her room."

The journalist Gretchen Berg pinpointed the way in which Andy fuelled so much insecurity around him: "He believed you should not alter the way things really are. They have to happen just the way they happen, even if it happened to himself. He handled people by not handling them. A lot of people became very petulant and uncontrollable as a result. . . . He was living in the middle of a vortex and he really put up with a lot of shit. . . . It was like walking around in a gasoline-filled room holding a match, but I had a feeling he was very tough and would outlast us all."

One of those around Andy who was feeling particularly uptight was Gerard Malanga. He felt increasingly replaceable, particularly after he met an Italian fashion model named Benedetta Barzini and fell obsessively in love. Andy did not like it when his associates fell in love because it took their attention away from him. "I sense that

Andy is going to do something chemically destructive between Benedetta and me," wrote Gerard in his diary. "Andy should learn not to interfere in other people's private lives."

Malanga was convinced that Andy was trying to "dump" him. After Benedetta abruptly ended their affair, he heard that Andy had said, "She was only seeing him so she could be in one of my movies." The distance between Andy and Gerard seemed especially gaping when he was left behind while Andy took Henry Geldzahler (who had become friendly again) to the social event of the decade, Truman Capote's Black and White Ball at the Plaza Hotel.

Even Julia Warhola was complaining about her famous son in public. In *Esquire,* she told an interviewer that she was lonely and ill but Andy was never at home. (Paul Warhola had nearly died in a car crash that October, and she prayed for him night and day.) Andy had removed her still further from his life by forbidding her to answer his phone. (Brigid Polk recalled that often when she was talking on the phone to Andy he would suddenly cry, "Hey, Mom, get off the phone!") In November 1966, Andy starred Julia, in a movie shot in her basement apartment, as an aging peroxided movie star with a lot of ex-husbands. "We're trying to bring back old people," he said.

Earlier that year, in San Francisco, Andy had met an attractive young man at a cocktail party given for a screening of his film of Michael McClure's play *The Beard,* about Billy the Kid and Jean Harlow. (McClure had originally agreed to Andy's making the film but before a contract was signed had withdrawn permission. When Andy filmed it anyway with Malanga and Mary Woronov, McClure was furious. The cocktail party had been planned to mend relations, but it was not successful. In the end, Andy gave the print to McClure as a gift.) The meeting with the young man had led to an "erotic correspondence," and in October, Andy had flown him to New York and moved him into Lexington Avenue. The day he arrived, Malanga noted ominously in his diary that the young man was "obvious about his feelings and will be needing much of Andy's attention."

Andy's latest love object came from a well-to-do San Francisco family. He was tall, gangly, and still carrying his baby fat—another shy, egoless postpubescent on whom Andy could assert his will. Andy cast him in an occasional small part, but he had no gift for the kind of dramatic self-expression Andy's movies required. Publicly he commanded little of Andy's attention: When Andy went out in the evenings, he was *working*. But Andy was possessive of his new love—vengefully so.

One evening in December, Andy was coming home with Malanga around midnight when they encountered the young man walking toward the Lexington Avenue house with Randy Borscheit, a youngster Andy had used in a movie called *Closet*. Gerard recalled that Andy turned bright red when he saw his lover and Randy together and blurted out, "What are you doing with him if you're my boyfriend?" Muttering some excuse to Malanga and dismissing Randy, he followed the young man into the house and slammed the door. The following day Andy changed all the locks to his house and told his San Francisco "catch" to move out.

The success of *Chelsea Girls* had put the Factory under siege. The police, looking for drugs, had raided the place so many times that winter that Andy asked his lawyers for emergency phone numbers where they could be reached in case anybody needed to be bailed out of jail.

The establishment press was on the attack as well. "It has come time to wag a warning finger at Andy Warhol and his underground friends and tell them politely but firmly that they are pushing a reckless thing too far," wrote Bosley Crowther, the *New York Times* film critic. "It is time for permissive adults to stop winking at their too precocious pranks. . . . It is particularly important to put a stout spoke in Mr. Warhol's wheel." Another article about *Chelsea Girls* in the *Times* declared: "More disturbing than the contagious lethargy of the movie is the deeper message: These dreamy swingers, playing their little games, clearly question the most basic assumptions of our culture—namely that heterosexual coupling, happy or unhappy, moral or immoral, is a socially significant enterprise worthy of the closest possible scrutiny. Hollywood's tinsel titillation and the art-house film's hard bedrock fornication are replaced by a new sexual mythology, a cool, low-keyed playful polymorphism. The message flashed . . . is utterly subversive."

15

BUT HOW TO go beyond *Chelsea Girls?* At the beginning of 1967, Andy began working on three new films in the *Chelsea Girls* mode, using the same actors, improvised dialogue, and one-take filming. *Loves of Ondine* was to be a series of confrontations similar to the Pope/Ondine sequence. With Ondine and Brigid Polk, he was also shooting scenes of *Imitation of Christ*, portraying a married couple up against a host of problems centering on their son, who, among other things, wants to wear a dress to school. The third movie, *Vibrations*, was about the Kennedy assassination, black magic, and "love situations," as Andy described them, in which such performers as René Ricard and Ivy Nicholson were thrown together to insult and hit one another. *Loves of Ondine* and *Imitation of Christ* were to be eight hours long; *Vibrations* was to be *the* Warhol endurance test—forty-eight hours of film that would run for twenty-four hours on a split screen.

The Factory was still attracting an ever-expanding company of actors, and the new movies presented several fresh faces: Patrick Tilden, known for his imitations of Bob Dylan; Andrea Feldman, who would become a superstar and another Warhol suicide; the raven-haired French heiress Ultra Violet, who had abandoned Salvador Dalí's entourage at the St. Regis Hotel to "find" herself in Warhol films; and a striking young visionary named Allen Midgette, who had made some early films with the Italian director Bernardo Bertolucci.

Despite Andy's determination to push on with these ambitious new projects, 1967 would be a year of unending problems, beginning in March when MGM released the long-delayed *Velvet Underground and Nico* album. The record was clearly billed as an Andy Warhol production in both its packaging (the sleeve featured a banana that could be "peeled") and advertising. One ad in *Evergreen Review* read: "What happens when the Daddy of Pop Art Goes Pop Music? The most underground album of all! It's Andy Warhol's new hip trip to the subterranean scene." But the popularity of Warhol's art and film efforts could not guarantee air play for the Velvets. Although the Beatles had just released their LSD-inspired hit "Strawberry Fields Forever," songs like "Heroin" were still too controversial for radio. The album fizzled; it has sold steadily ever since, but Warhol never saw a cent of his royalties.

"Back then we were surprised at how vast the reaction against us was," recalled Lou Reed. "I thought we were doing something very ambitious and I was very taken aback by it. I used to hear people say we were doing porn rock."

Andy genuinely tried to push the record by opening a new club called The Gymnasium in a rented Czechoslovakian meeting hall on the Upper East Side, but this time the magic did not happen, the crowds were sparse, and Andy quickly dropped the expensive project. Eric Emerson, one of the EPI dancers and a star of *Chelsea Girls*, put the final nail in the album's coffin when, in need of money to go to London, he sued MGM for including a photograph of him on the album's back cover without a signed release. Andy remained completely passive and refused to lift a finger to stop Eric, with the result that MGM withdrew the record from the stores, and the Velvets began looking for new management.

A few months into the start of shooting, problems were developing on the set of *Vibrations*. "Things weren't working," recalled Allen Midgette. "People were not being themselves, the way it was supposed to be." As Midgette saw it, the aggressive, amphetamine-fed histrionics of people like Ondine and Brigid had become a "cheap trick." Midgette himself was taking LSD before his scenes, and practicing a discipline of calmness in the face of on- and off-screen chaos.

Billy Name had talked Orion, one of the three so-called witches, into performing with Midgette in one sequence. The "location" was the classical guitarist Andrés Segovia's elegant apartment, the set a sofa under a magnificent crystal chandelier. Allen Midgette recalled: "When I arrived, Orion was already on pretty strong acid and then I took acid. I knew that this was one of those scenes that was going to be heavy duty. Orion was a very strong woman. Orion was sitting on a couch and I was sitting on a chair and there was a huge bouquet of flowers and we were just staring at each other through the flowers and we weren't saying a word. She insisted on playing Maria Callas at full volume and Paul kept whining, 'Well, you know, uh, we don't have the rights to that music and, uh, you know, at least turn it down.'

"Orion said, 'Darling, the stipulation was that I could do anything I wanted to do so just shut up and listen to the music.' And we continued to look into each other's eyes.

"Finally, Paul started saying to Orion, 'It's very boring. We gotta do something. You gotta have sex or something or fight with each other.'

"Orion just looked at him and she said, 'Oh, really?' There was a machete on the wall and she picked it up and hit the chandelier and the glass went flying. I will never forget the image of Andy standing behind the camera, whiter than he normally is, frozen behind the camera with little pieces of glass on his shoulders and he could not even speak, he was so terrified."

The day after Andy threw his California lover out of his house and changed the locks, he started hanging out with a nineteen-year-old king-size Alabamian who called himself Rod La Rod. According to Ultra Violet, Rod La Rod claimed to have two gods, the governor of his home state, George Wallace, and Warhol, whom he called "the Great White Father." It was an unspoken rule that nobody touched "Drella," yet Rod and Andy regularly got into bizarre fights in which they would slap and punch each other. "It appeared to be a physically violent relationship," said Malanga, "but Rodney was always very corny about his physical overtures toward Andy. It wasn't like he slugged him; they were always love taps, or Andy pushing him away or trying to block the punches."

"They'd have these fistfights right on the set," said Ondine. "Then they'd make up. It was just wonderful. They'd found each other."

Rod was neither one of Andy's impossible-to-attain beauties nor one of his quiet, easily dominated houseboys. He was not much to look at, an ungainly hippie hick in his bellbottom trousers, which were always too short, and shirts with clashing stripes. Paul, Gerard, and most of the others in Andy's inner circle found him unsophisticated and oafish. ("It was like the king taking the cowgirl, the shepherdess into the royal chambers," said one of Warhol's friends.)

That May, Andy flew to France for the screening of *Chelsea Girls* at the Cannes Film Festival. With him on the three-week trip was an assortment of superstars, including Malanga and International Velvet, Paul Morrissey, Rod La Rod, and the producer Lester Persky—who had persuaded Morrissey that they needed him to "make the deal." Cannes was a fiasco. Word of mouth had labeled *Chelsea Girls* a perverse celebration of madness, homosexuality, and hard drugs, and without even seeing it, Louis Marquerelle, the official in charge of the "Critics' Choice" programs, ruled against showing the film. Andy and company got a lot of publicity but spent a boring week at Cannes, enlivened only by a dinner at Brigitte Bardot's villa, and parties honoring Antonioni's *Blow-Up*.

In Paris, the premiere of *Chelsea Girls* was memorable largely because the French critic Jean-Jacques Lebel led a walkout in the middle of the screening. Taylor Mead, who had been living in Europe, showed up at the Paris Cinemathèque and was "awed" by the film. Andy asked him to come back to the Factory and Mead accepted, ending what had been three years of self-exile.

A final stop was scheduled in London so that Warhol and Morrissey could meet with Paul McCartney and the Beatles' manager, Brian Epstein, to explore film projects and get their backing for a British tour by the Velvet Underground. Epstein and McCartney, while interested in the Velvets' banana album, were involved with the imminent release of *Sgt. Pepper's Lonely Hearts Club Band*. McCartney brought along the album's cover by the British pop artist Peter Blake to show Warhol, but seemed otherwise mainly concerned about soliciting their help in getting Nico out of his house before his future wife, the photographer Linda Eastman, arrived for a visit from America. Little else of substance was discussed, and Warhol and Morrissey came away empty-handed. To McCartney's relief, Nico left with them for the return trip to New York, where new disappointments awaited.

On the night of their arrival, Andy, Paul, and Nico flew up to a Velvet Underground concert in Boston, but by then Lou Reed had hired a new manager, Steve Sesnick, and the band refused to let Nico join them onstage. The aftermath was bitter. Warhol told Reed over the telephone that he was "a rat" for breaking their agreement, and Morrissey accused him of stealing the Factory's share of the banana album's profits. Reed, for his part, told reporters that he "was never a great friend of Andy's" and "I fired Warhol!" Thus ended the collaboration that had sparked the firestorm of the Exploding Plastic Inevitable.

By the end of May, the bloom was off Andy's friendship with Rod La Rod. Taylor Mead, who had returned as promised, was astounded by Rod's behavior. "I almost punched him out because he came on to Andy in such a terribly rough way. He would grab Andy and hug him and Andy would look pleadingly and I'd scream at Rod. Then Brigid would say, 'Oh, they love each other.' "

Ondine, too, had begun telling Andy to "get rid of that boy." "Andy would start crying. Finally, he actually approached us and said, 'Do you think I should?' And we said, 'Yeah, plain dump him because he's a monster.' Andy was the only person I've ever met who took his friends' advice about love, and he dumped him."

To another friend Andy confided that he had been hurt so often he didn't even care anymore. "It's too sad to feel," he said. "I'm really afraid to feel happy because it never lasts."

16

NDY'S POLICY HAD always been to take whatever was offered, so in July 1967, when Paul Morrissey got a phone call from the owner of the Hudson Theater, Maury Maura, asking if they had any exploitation films he could run, they gave him *My Hustler*. Now, almost a year after *Chelsea Girls*, the mainstream New York press showed up, as they would for any serious filmmaker. "Warhol is adept at using non-actors whose lack of theatrical skill makes the realism of their being wholly convincing," wrote Archer Winsten in the *New York Post*. That same week, the *New York Times* reviewed with remarkable objectivity highlights of the *24 Hours Movie* screened at the Factory: "The method is superimposition: three projectors are focused simultaneously on a single screen. As one projector reels off a far-out party scene, for example, another projects the oversized face of a man eating. On those two images may be superimposed a third scene involving an amorous couple. The sound track has superimposition, too, so that electronic squawks can be mingled with murmured dialogue."

Three weeks later Maura was back on the phone. "Give us something like *I, a Woman*," he said.

"Oh," said Andy, "we'll do *I, a Man*."

Thus began a trilogy of feature-length Warhol-Morrissey comedies, *I, a Man, Bikeboy,* and *Nude Restaurant,* which would lead to the team's ultimate movie success in 1970 with *Trash.*

I, a Man, while not particularly good or funny, was memorable for one performance—that of a radical feminist and lesbian, Valerie Solanas. She had founded an organization called the Society for Cutting Up Men (SCUM) and was publisher of a mimeographed anti-male rant called "The SCUM Manifesto," which she hawked on the streets. "All the evils of the world emanate from this male incapacity to love," she proclaimed, and she advocated the elimination of the male sex as a means to world peace. Earlier that year, Solanas had come to the Factory with a script called *Up Your Ass.* "I thought the title was so wonderful and I'm so friendly that I invited her to come up with it, but it was so dirty that I think she must have been a lady cop," Andy told the journalist Gretchen Berg. "We haven't seen her since and I'm not surprised. I guess she thought that was the perfect thing for Andy Warhol."

By the time he returned from Cannes, Solanas had become impatient and wanted her script back. When Andy told her he had lost it, she started calling regularly, asking for money. Finally, he said she could come over and earn twenty-five dollars by being in one of his movies.

Many people who knew or worked with Andy over the years said that he was almost incapable of saying no. He had never had any intention of doing anything with Valerie Solanas' script: People sent him proposals every day, and most of them ended up in the slush pile of unanswered mail and other papers scattered around the Factory like a teenager's forgotten homework. Valerie's script had joined them.

Valerie was good in *I, a Man.* Andy liked her performance because she was honest and funny. Valerie, too, had seemed pleased. When, a few days later, she brought the French publisher Maurice Girodias to the Factory to see a rough cut of her scene, he noted that "she seemed very relaxed and friendly with Warhol, whose conversation consisted of protracted silences." Soon, however, Valerie started up her diatribe against Andy again. He was a vulture and a thief, she told Girodias, adding, "Talking to him is like talking to a chair."

Andy had been spending a lot of time with Nico, who was also in *I, a Man*, pushing her as a solo act and doing publicity stunts with her. She had recorded a solo album called *Chelsea Girl*, and now was singing on her own in the basement of the Dom. "Andy likes other people to become Andy for him," Nico said. "He doesn't want to be always in charge of everything. He would rather be me or someone else sometimes. It's part of pop art, that everybody can impersonate somebody else. That you don't always have to be you to be you."

Andy never developed the kind of rapport with Nico that he had had with Edie. For all his interest in beauty and glamour, he liked good talkers best. Nico had a wonderful presence. She was mysterious and fascinating to be with, but she was not Brigid Polk in the rap department. Edie and Andy had been able to communicate on speed. Nico's use of LSD and heroin made her more remote. Moreover, Nico was a star in her own right. She was not completely dependent on Andy; she spent a lot of time with Jim Morrison, Bob Dylan, and Brian Jones. She was beginning to get sidetracked by drugs, and it was time, once again, for Andy to find a new girl.

He did, that summer, in Susan Hoffman, who was renamed Viva, and who took the Factory spotlight as Andy Warhol's latest super-star in *Bikeboy* and *Nude Restaurant*. A painter who had given up painting for acting when she met Andy, a talented writer who began collaborating with Paul on scripts, Viva was strikingly beautiful. Her features were delicate and aristocratic, her hair was worn in an individual frizzed-out style. Best of all, as far as Andy was concerned, she complained endlessly about personal subjects that no respectable woman talked about in public, and with a kind of mock-upper-class languor that Andy began to imitate in his own speech. As Ultra Violet wrote in her memoir *Famous for Fifteen Minutes*: "Viva complained about having no sex, she complained about restaurants and lousy food, she complained about being depressed, she complained about the word *artist*, she complained about people hanging up on her, she complained about male chauvinism, she complained about getting phone calls from weirdos, she complained about Andy's way of stirring people up to fight, she complained about being called a brainless nincompoop."

Viva was a natural—more self-possessed than Edie—and, at least for a while, she had some idea of how to handle her new fame.

Unlike Edie, she also had a real understanding of what Andy was up to. "The Warhol films," she wrote in the *Village Voice*,

> were about sexual disappointment and frustration. The way Andy saw the world, the way the world *is*, and the way nine-tenths of the population sees it, yet pretend they don't. In Andy's movies, women are always the strong ones, the beautiful ones and the ones who control everything. Men turn out to be these empty animals. Maybe the homosexuals are the only ones who haven't really copped out.
>
> The feeling that we were on to something good led us to approach this seemingly random improvisational method with a contagious enthusiasm and a deadly seriousness that we tried hard to hide. In actuality the whole scene, including Andy's direction, was extremely stiff. Andy's role was like that of all directors, to play God.

The mood at the Factory was heating up. Morrissey's attempt to run the place in a more businesslike fashion—he had installed office-style cubicles—was having a divisive effect. Malanga and Billy Name were chafing the most—the former because he was tired of being in Andy's shadow, the latter because he wanted the Factory to stay the way it had been. Malanga was trying to make movies on his own, as well as getting his poems published, and demanding rights to certain Warhol projects. Billy's habit of spraying everything silver was driving Morrissey crazy. "It was hideous," Paul recalled. "There was silver powder in your hair and lungs and you couldn't ever get clean." In August, Andy didn't invite Malanga to the San Francisco and Los Angeles premieres of *Chelsea Girls*, and his former right-hand man flew off in a huff to Italy, where one of his own films had been accepted by the Bergamo Film Festival.

That summer, there had been an ugly scene at Max's when Ivy Nicholson erupted at Andy, screaming and throwing food. Andy ran out, hopped into a cab, and told the driver to take him home. The part-time cabbie happened to be an art critic, Ted Castle, whom Andy knew and who tape-recorded the bewildered artist without his knowing it: "So Ivy was, you know, she called me up and said, uh, you know, uh, I'm going to Mexico right now and, you know, can you give me some money? I'm getting a divorce and I'm coming back and marrying you, and I said, 'What? You know,' and I decided that, you know, everything is wrong and I decided that we're going to get organized and really do things right . . ."

Andy's hope of "doing things right" was beginning to drive Ondine crazy, too. The problem came to a head in San Francisco, when Morrissey rebuked Allen Midgette for not wearing shoes to a press lunch at Trader Vic's, after which Ondine blew up at his idol: "What's the big deal about someone not wearing shoes? You make your own rules! You're the original American genius!"

In the autumn of 1966, Warhol had been asked to screen a film and give a talk to the film society of Columbia University in New York. He chose to show them *Blow Job*. The screening drew an enthusiastic, standing-room-only crowd. The critic Rex Reed described what happened:

> Warhol himself was in the audience and had promised to speak at the end of the film. The audience sat attentively during the first few minutes of the film, which showed a boy's face. That's all. Just a face. But something was obviously happening down below, out of camera range. The audience got restless. The put-on was putting them down and they didn't like it. (Some of them began to sing "We Shall Never Come.") They finally began to yell things at the screen, most of them unprintable. Total chaos finally broke out when one voice (a girl's) screamed: "We came to see a blow job, and we stayed to get screwed!" Tomatoes and eggs were thrown at the screen; Warhol was whisked away to safety through the raging, jeering, angry mob and rushed to a waiting car.

Thus it was that Andy, who knew better than anyone else the value of negative publicity, agreed to tour college campuses around the country in the fall of 1967. By then, he had worked out a program that would annoy the students even more.

The controversy over the war in Vietnam was at its height, and the universities had become the storm centers. Radicals like Abbie Hoffman, Timothy Leary, and Allen Ginsberg, were crisscrossing the country giving lectures for one to two thousand dollars per engagement. Just as most students had never read a line of Ginsberg's poetry or taken the LSD that Leary was promoting, few had ever seen a Warhol film or painting. But they all knew who he was, and he had no trouble pulling them in.

The Warhol road show typically included a segment of his dullest film, the *24 Hour Movie*, after which Paul Morrissey gave a brief speech and Viva answered questions. Andy stood onstage, togged out in his uniform of leather jacket and dark glasses, saying nothing even when questions were insistently shouted at him. In Viva's view they were like "Spanky and Our Gang, with Andy as Alfalfa": "Andy stood on the stage, blushing and silent, while Paul Morrissey, the professor, delivered a totally intellectual anti-intellectual rapid-paced fifteen-minute mini-lecture putting down art films, hippies, and marijuana, saying things [ironically] like, 'At least heroin doesn't change your personality.' Then I, as Darla the smart ass, answered questions—'The reason we make these movies is because it's fun, especially the dirty parts'—and advised them to drop out of school."

For this they were regularly hissed and booed. "They really hated all of us," said Viva, "but they especially hated Andy. They were always hostile. But afterwards there would usually be a little clique who would come up and say, 'Come to our house.' Once, on the way to one of these parties, students on the roof of a college dorm picked up huge chunks of ice and threw them down at us. Andy was totally blasé. I think he liked it. He always said, 'Everything is magic!' That was his favorite *explication de texte*. I think Andy was totally in the clouds."

Back in New York, Andy was going to Max's Kansas City every night. He always occupied the corner table in the back room—"the captain's table," Malanga called it. There he would hold mostly silent court among the faithful in a grouping that one photographer thought of as *The Last Supper*. "I used to see him every night in Max's," the artist Richard Serra recalled. "Warhol was already a historical figure. His people were making up their own tradition, and it freed all of us. He gave us a larger permission, a greater freedom to look at a larger reference in American culture. Everybody understood that he was right on the edge, completely awake. He was a strange and wonderful presence."

By now, even the back room of Max's had been politicized into two camps, with a popular New York disc jockey named Terry Noel on the right side of the room and Andy's crowd on the left. There were frequent chick-pea fights between the two contingents. Noel, as the self-appointed leader of the anti-Warhol forces, had visited the Factory several times with urgent appeals that they reform their wicked ways, saying to Andy: "Don't you know what you're doing is wrong? Don't you think there's such a thing as right and wrong? Why are you letting all this negativity be your driving force?"

Andy would listen impassively, but the Factory dog pack didn't take kindly to sermons. Noel had finally given up trying to save Andy after Paul America crashed a party at his apartment and systematically slashed all the guests' coats with a hunting knife: "I'd had it up to here telling Andy how I felt. It was all over by then. We were on opposite sides of the line. Everybody I knew thought he had no talent whatsoever. He had acquired this unbelievable mystique by letting insanity go on around him, but he absolutely destroyed everybody around him and the hatred for Andy got real serious."

One night, Andy saw Valerie Solanas huddled at another table at Max's and encouraged Viva to go over and talk to her. "You dyke!" Viva said. "You're disgusting!" Valerie immediately told Viva about a childhood experience of forced incest. "No wonder you're a lesbian," Viva responded.

The noise at Max's was often laced with threats. One night the poet Gregory Corso, who was friendly with Edie Sedgwick, came up to Andy's table and said: "I know you, mister, and I don't like you. I know all about how you use people. How you make them superstars of New York and then drop them. You're evil. And you know what else? You never give anything away. You know what's wrong with you? Too many lonely women are in love with you. You use them. You give them dope and then you leave them. I'm glad I'm not in your faggoty scene. It's all show. I see that beautiful blond, angelic face of yours and it's got a snarl on it. It's an ugly face."

Andy sat staring straight ahead as if he hadn't heard a word, but, as the journalist Jane Kramer reported, Allen Ginsberg, who was sitting next to him, noticed that "a trace of a sad expression had settled on his face. Flinging his arms around Warhol and enveloping him in a long, happy hug, Ginsberg shouted, 'You've got feelings!'"

Many of Andy's friends were struck by the fact that he never seemed afraid of the explosive people he hung around with. Back in 1964, when Dorothy Podber had stalked into the Factory, pulled out a pistol from her black leather jacket, and fired a bullet through a stack of Marilyn portraits, it had been the kind of "event" that was accepted in those days, and Andy had hardly reacted. In 1967, however, there were several instances of people coming into the Factory and shooting off guns.

One of them was a wealthy eccentric who wanted to produce a film. According to Ronnie Tavel: "At Andy's request I wrote a three-hour film called *Jane Eyre Bear* that never got produced because the guy who was supposed to put up the money came in throwing around guns and shooting at the ceiling at ten o'clock in the morning. I knew he was drunk because I had had breakfast with him and he had been drinking. I thought, well, he likes me, but don't bullets bounce off the ceiling? Something's going on here that's too weird."

Early one evening in November, a friend of Ondine's known only as "Sammy the Italian" ran in waving a gun and made Andy, Paul, Billy, Taylor, Nico, and Patrick Tilden sit in a line on the couch. Telling them he was going to play Russian roulette, he put the gun to Paul Morrissey's head and pulled the trigger. When nothing happened, they all thought he was just auditioning for a film role. "You're just so absurd, you're not even good," Mead told him, but when Nico got up to leave, Sammy fired the gun at the ceiling, and this time it went off.

Andy had been sitting silently on the couch staring at the gunman as if he were watching a movie. "It was so awful," recalled Mead. "Andy was such a fucking schizophrenic I just don't think he believed it."

Sammy then demanded money and started to cry. He said, "I don't want to do this, Andy. Here, someone take the gun," and he handed it to Patrick Tilden, who said he didn't want it and handed it back.

The most frightening moment came when Sammy put a woman's plastic rain hat on Andy's head, made him kneel, and said he was going to take a hostage. At that point Mead "got so offended that this little punk had Andy, whom I loved and considered a genius, kneeling on the floor with a gun pointed at his head that I jumped him from behind." After a struggle, the gunman ran down the stairway to the street, while Mead broke the window and screamed, "Call the police!"

The police arrived minutes later. They didn't seem to believe the story of what had happened. One of them wisecracked, "Why didn't you film it?"

After the police left, it was decided to give the story to the *New York Times*. "We wanted it to be known that this had happened to us," recalled Billy Name. "But the *Times* said, 'No, we don't necessarily believe you. It wouldn't be an important story anyway.' The occurrence itself was very disturbing, but the real thud was that no one cared about us. The *New York Times* was constantly saying, 'Andy Warhol, get off the stage, you have had your time, you're not really art.' Andy was very hurt by it."

The *Times* was hardly alone in its disdain. *Time*'s art critic, Robert Hughes, expressed a particularly scathing view of Andy's "superstar" business:

> They were all cultural space-debris, drifting fragments from a variety of sixties subcultures (transvestite, drug, S&M, rock, Poor Little Rich, criminal, street, and all the permutations) orbiting in smeary ellipses around their unmoved mover. . . . If Warhol's superstars as he called them had possessed talent, discipline, or stamina, they would not have needed him. But then, he would not have needed them. They gave him his ghostly aura of power. . . . He offered them absolution, the gaze of the blank mirror that refuses all judgment. In this, the camera (when he made films) deputized for him, collecting hour upon hour of tantrum, misery, sexual spasm, campy, and nose-picking trivia. In this way the Factory resembled a sect, a parody of Catholicism enacted (not accidentally) by people who were or had been Catholic, from Warhol and Gerard Malanga on down. In it, the rituals of dandyism could speed up to gibberish and show what they had become—a hunger for approval and forgiveness. These came in a familiar form, perhaps the only form American capitalism knows how to offer: publicity.

Imitation of Christ was released in November 1967. Jonas Mekas declared that "the protagonist and the feeling and the content is pure Warhol. . . . Andy Warhol is the Victor Hugo of cinema!" But Andy withdrew the film from circulation after one performance, and did the same thing to the *24 Hour Movie* after it was shown once in mid-December.

Many of the superstars were outraged that a year's work, for which they had been promised stardom beyond their wildest dreams, had been negated so arbitrarily. "It was unforgivable what Andy did to people!" said Taylor Mead. "Patrick Tilden could have been a superstar! He was the James Dean of the underground. But just on a whim Andy decided not to pursue it." Perhaps because of his dismissal in establishment quarters such as the *New York Times* and *Time*, perhaps because he was rising as a collectible in the art market, Andy, they felt, was pulling back, chickening out.

That December, Random House published *Andy Warhol's Index Book*. A collector's item today, the book was a pop art presentation of the Factory life style, consisting mostly of high-contrast black-and-white photographs. It included a transcribed conversation between Nico and Andy talking about the Velvet Underground album and a desultory interview with Andy that ran through the book. Two images stood out. The first, spread over two pages, was a pop-out medieval castle in whose windows could be spotted Brigid, Andy, International Velvet, and others. Underneath was the caption: "WE ARE CONSTANTLY UNDER ATTACK!" The second image was a large photograph of Andy sitting in the Factory with a woman who looked like one of Charles Manson's followers standing behind him and pointing a silver pistol at the back of his head.

17

I N THE AUTUMN of 1967, while lecturing in Tucson, Warhol and Morrissey had conceived of a Western with Viva as a bareback rider. So enamored were they of the idea that Paul had jabbered to the local press that their next project would be a Western, filmed on location in Tucson, called *The Unwanted Cowboy*.

By the time Andy was ready to shoot his Western in the last week of January 1968, the title had been changed to *Lonesome Cowboys* and the story line had Viva playing a rich rancher who runs into trouble with a local gang of cowboys. The rest of the cast included Taylor Mead, in one of his best roles, as her nurse, Eric Emerson, Allen Midgette, and the newcomers Joe Dallesandro, Julian Burroughs, Jr., Tom Hompertz, and, as the gang's leader, Louis Waldon. Andy had the "sheriff" played as a drag queen by Francis Francine. The picture was to be shot on location in Old Tucson and at the Rancho Linda Vista dude ranch twenty miles outside the city, where John Wayne had made pictures. It was to be in color, follow a real story line, and be sharply edited.

Just before Andy left for Arizona, Gerard Malanga, who had escaped arrest in Italy for forging and attempting to sell a Warhol portrait of Che Guevara, returned to the Factory. Andy was surprised to see him. "Gee, how was Rome?" he asked. Cutting straight to the point, Malanga apologized for the forgery and tried to explain why he had done it, but Andy's eyes turned to slits of stone as he looked directly into Gerard's eyes and said, with a hard, flat finality, "You should have known better!"

Transporting the Factory to Arizona at the beginning of 1968 seemed foolhardy: The rednecks of the Southwest would not look kindly on their life styles being spoofed by the likes of Andy Warhol and his gang. By now, wherever Andy went it was not so much with an entourage as an army. In addition to the actors, he took Morrissey and a gaggle of witnesses, including David Bourdon, who was covering the event for *Life* magazine, the sculptor John Chamberlain, and a car thief named Vera Cruise, who sometimes toted a gun. And a thickset young stud from San Diego known only as Joey had been flown in to stay with Andy.

The local press, television, and radio had made sure that everyone within fifty miles was aware of the presence of this ragtag army of cultural terrorists. On the first day of shooting in Old Tucson, a crowd of 150 people showed up. The sight of Francis Francine as the sheriff and Eric Emerson teaching Joe Dallesandro ballet steps "to tighten the buns" can have done little but confirm their worst suspicions. That night Taylor Mead made a scene in a restaurant, calling a local businessman a "big queen." Leaving the place, they were followed by several cars. David Bourdon said: "I can't tell you how scared I was. Andy was in the front seat. He wasn't saying anything, but somebody else and I in the back were getting more and more agitated. We tried all kinds of things to shake [the cars]. We lost one of them, but the other one stayed behind us. It turned out they were just school kids who had recognized us at an intersection and started following us."

Andy's primitive method of focusing a camera on a group of people, turning it on, and keeping it going until the film ran out would no longer work. He began to abdicate his role as director, gradually letting Morrissey take over. "Paul was doing most of the directing," said David Bourdon. "Andy was at the camera doing the actual shooting, filming all the crazy zooms and missing all the action, and Fred [Hughes] was holding the microphone, but it was always Paul on the sidelines saying, Now do this, now do that. A lot of the actors objected, and I thought they had a good point. Paul was too heavy-handed, not letting them improvise freely."

With Andy in charge, his actors had felt completely safe and let themselves fall into whatever transpired. With Paul giving directions like "You gotta fight!" or "Take your pants down!" they were prone to lose faith in themselves, with the result, as Viva saw it, that nobody was relating to anybody else in the film.

On the second morning, Andy awoke to the acrid stench of gas in his cabin and sprang out of bed to discover that Joey had tried to commit suicide. One onlooker recalled: "He was another of Andy's hunks. He was a funny kid and he was sort of in the way, but there he was. Andy was disconcerted by it; he didn't like it one bit, but judging how upset Andy was was always difficult. He would get very upset about little things and stamp his foot and have rages, but he did not show that he was terribly upset about big things." Bourdon remembered Warhol being embarrassed by the incident: "The kid was just a little groupie and he was put on the plane right away."

That evening the whole gang was sitting watching television in the main cabin when the door swung open and two real cowboys strode in. Expecting them to whip out shotguns and execute the entire cast on the spot, Bourdon froze again, but it turned out they just wanted to see what was going on and had been hoping to catch Viva in the act. Asked who would have defended them in case of such an attack, Bourdon paused before answering—seriously—"Taylor Mead."

Viva's reputation as a vamp was not unearned. According to Bourdon, who shared the main cabin with her and could hear everything that went on in her room, she slept with every available male in the company, causing even Andy to remind her that she was supposed to "save it for the film." As far as Viva was concerned, the conflict between Andy, who wanted to maintain an esoteric approach to his films, and Paul, who wanted to commercialize them, was causing tension between the actors. The characters they were playing in the film began to take over their "real selves," resulting in an unplanned scene of simulated gang rape. According to one observer, Viva was "being punished for being too 'temperamental.'" After the "rape," she stormed off the set screaming, "Get Ultra Violet for the part. I quit!" (There was a simmering competitiveness between Ultra and Viva for Andy's attention. Moreover, Ultra had been having an affair with John Chamberlain, who was sleeping with Viva during the making of the film.)

It was the gang rape scene that drove the locals around the bend. Ever since the first day of shooting in Old Tucson, the Warhol crew had been under surveillance by the police and a self-elected vigilante group who had warned them on several occasions to "leave town," only to be told by Viva, "Fuck you!" Almost every day the sheriff would drive up, screech to a halt in front of the main cabin, haul himself out of his cruiser, and proceed to "check out" the situation. Amazingly, they never bothered to bust anyone for drugs, which would have been dead easy since virtually everybody—except Andy and Paul—smoked so much marijuana that Bourdon had to sweep the seeds and stems off his porch every morning. After the "rape," however, the surveillance became so disruptive that Warhol decided to return to New York and finish the film there.

The rape scene also prompted an official complaint to the FBI. The local office of the agency contacted their New York office to see if they might be able to arrest Warhol on grounds of interstate transportation of obscene material, and Warhol was at once put under FBI surveillance.

But his most immediate problem was Viva, who was beginning to believe her own publicity and who was demanding more and more attention from Andy. When she threw a fit at the Tucson airport, storming out of the bar after the barkeep refused to serve her, Warhol turned to Waldon and moaned, "Oh, Louis, please do something about Viva, I just can't take it anymore!"

In fact, Viva was going through the Edie Sedgwick experience. Ever since *Nude Restaurant,* in which she had appeared virtually naked, complaining in her tired, comic voice about the problems of being a woman in America, Viva had seized the attention of the media. In the four months she had been working with Andy, she had become almost as famous as he. She was his spokesperson; she traveled with him on lecture tours; she even made a lightning visit to Sweden, immediately after returning from Tucson, for his first European retrospective at the prestigious Moderna Muséet in Stockholm. (It was in the Swedish catalogue that Andy's best-known aphorism—"In the future everyone will be famous for fifteen minutes"—first appeared.) In the view of the media, Viva was Andy's "woman," just as Edie had been. Indeed, her parents were convinced they were having an affair. They weren't—and they were: According to Waldon, Viva was in love with Andy—but he was untouchable. He was in love with the idea of *being her*. And, like Edie, Viva had never seen a penny for her work.

One cold morning in mid-February, standing outside the Factory in the pouring rain and unable to get in because she did not have a key, Viva flipped out. Grabbing the nearest telephone and almost pulling it out of its socket, she called up the Factory and started yelling into the mouthpiece, "Get down here right now, you fag bastard, and open the door or—" at which point the "fag bastard" in question (Paul Morrissey) hung up. Viva had crossed her Rubicon. You did not call anybody at the Factory a fag bastard without becoming subject to instant excommunication. But she hadn't finished yet. Spying Andy himself climbing out of a cab outside the building, she ran down the street hollering, "Why don't I have a key to this place? I'm not treated with any respect around here because I'm a woman!" According to the writer Barbara Goldsmith, "Warhol regarded her, bland as farina, whereupon she flung her handbag at him catching him across the side of the face. 'You're crazy, Viva,' he said dispassionately. 'What do you think you're doing?' "

Andy ducked into the building, slammed the door, and rode up in the elevator, shaking with rage. It upset him terribly to see Viva lose control, he wrote: "After a scene like that, you can never trust the person in the same way again, because from that point on, you have to look at them with the idea that they might do a repeat and freak out again."

In the fall of 1967, when business was not going well for Andy Warhol Enterprises, Andy became involved with the man who would play the largest role in his career for the rest of his life.

Frederick W. Hughes was utterly different from most of the characters who hung around Andy at the Factory. A Rudolph Valentino look-alike, dapper, charming, and worldly, he had been born and brought up in the most ordinary of circumstances in Houston, Texas, until the art collectors Jean and Dominique de Menil had taken him under their wing as a teenager, recognizing his good taste and sharp eye for a picture. By the time he met Andy Warhol, Hughes, the son of a traveling salesman, had transformed himself into a patrician snob who claimed to be related to Howard Hughes and to be descended from aristocracy. Warhol—who once said, "I prefer to remain a mystery, I never like to give my background and anyway, I make it all up different every time I'm asked"—must have recognized something in Hughes, for shortly after their meeting, he drew Fred into his world like an octopus sucking in food. Before long, Fred Hughes was running the business.

Andy must have breathed a sigh of relief as he climbed aboard Jean de Menil's Learjet that fall for a fast trip to Montreal to see his new self-portraits hanging in the American pavilion at Expo: At last he had somebody selling his art who knew what he was doing. For although Andy had always claimed to be happy at the Castelli Gallery, Eleanor Ward had apparently been right in warning him that Leo would not treat him with the same care he lavished on, say, Jasper Johns. During 1967, when Warhol's fame was at its height, Castelli sold only twenty thousand dollars' worth of Warhol paintings, less than artists like Johns and Rauschenberg were getting for a single canvas. Fred Hughes arrived just in time.

"Castelli never sold a lot of Warhol paintings," explained Hughes. "That's where *I* came in. What I did is *do*. It wasn't like a normal corporation, taking over the reins and that kind of rubbish. I came in and I was doing. I had a very interesting job with the de Menils' art foundation and I continued to work with that foundation."

Furthermore, Hughes seemed to understand Warhol better than anyone else who had ever worked for him. Whereas Billy Name, Ondine, and Gerard Malanga were absolutely devoted to Warhol and would have died for him under the right circumstances, their understanding was limited by their own needs as artists. To them he was a film director who had made Ondine and Malanga superstars and promoted the photographic aspirations of Billy Name. Hughes had no longings to be an artist himself, and the picture he saw was much broader and deeper.

The first thing he did was sell the de Menils several of Andy's early works that had been ignored—the hand-painted pictures of advertisements and cartoons and the "death-and-disaster" series. He also got a commission from them for Warhol to film a sunset. Next, he started getting Warhol portrait commissions at twenty-five thousand dollars a shot. "The first portraits that got going were through the de Menils or through a particular friend of mine, Doris

Brynner, Yul Brynner's ex-wife," Hughes recalled. "She was a social friend, and she got a lot of great people for us to do it just for the fun of it." Warhol's career suddenly shifted into high gear. With Hughes at the helm, painting could pay the bills.

As a mark of his esteem for Fred, Andy immediately introduced him to his mother. Julia Warhola was so taken with the well-groomed, polite young man, who was so different from anybody else Andy had brought around, that she dubbed Fred "the Priest." This was her highest accolade, and it showed that her intuitions were as sharp as ever: Fred Hughes was going to help her Andy.

At the beginning of 1968, Andy had found a new space for the Factory, downtown on the fifth floor at Thirty-three Union Square West. The new place looked more like an office than an artist's studio. It consisted of two large rooms. The front one had clean white walls and polished wooden floors and was furnished with identical glass-topped desks on which stood white telephones and IBM typewriters. The back room, slightly less formal, was reserved for painting and screening films.

The new Factory was the creation of Hughes and Morrissey, as opposed to Name and Malanga. Paul hired a new full-time employee from Sacramento, Jed Johnson, to replace Gerard. Jed and his twin brother, Jay, were the epitome of what the new Factory was about. Very young, soft-spoken, sweet, and elegant, they looked more like European fashion models than cultural revolutionaries.

The only assistant from the old place who made the move to Union Square was Billy Name. There he was reduced to a kind of spectral janitor, and he spent most of his time alone in the tiny darkroom he built for himself behind the screening room. Andy was still playing the latest rock songs on his stereo, screening films constantly, and people flowed through. But some of the old hands found themselves made to feel very uncomfortable when they dropped by uninvited.

The move had been brought on by the Russian roulette scare. Andy, Paul, and Fred wanted to remove themselves from the druggies and crazies who were spinning out of control as the fun of the sixties turned to horror. But Andy could not shake off Valerie Solanas, who was soon calling with all kinds of outrageous charges and demands—and an occasional threat. Nothing infuriated Warhol so much as a threat. He would shoot his persecutor the kind of look his father had used to freeze his three sons with if they laughed on Sunday. "Andy could *slice* you with a glance," Malanga wrote. As soon as Valerie started threatening him, he stopped taking her calls.

That winter she was interviewed in the *Village Voice*. Warhol, she told the reporter, was a son of a bitch: "A snake couldn't eat a meal off what he paid out." The reporter got her to admit that there was no SCUM organization, that she had no followers, that she was operating completely on her own without a friend in the world. But yes, she pathetically concluded, Andy was still planning to produce her lost script, *Up Your Ass*.

The media had a new dish to feast on that February when *Time* and *Newsweek* revealed that back in 1967, Andy had sent out an actor (Allen Midgette) to pretend he was Andy Warhol and five colleges had swallowed the bait, paid the fees, and never known the difference. Now the smoldering outrage at Andy Warhol and all his works flared up. What an insult! How dare this creep put on institutions of learning like the University of Rochester and Salt Lake City College! Who did he think he was? Scribes across the country reached for phrases like "the pooped artist" and "puke's bad boy." There was also the suggestion that Warhol might be liable to lawsuits for fraud.

To make amends, Andy was forced to trundle back out on the lecture circuit, only to be booed and hissed by students more hostile than any he had faced before. On one occasion, according to Viva, he was held in a locked room for half an hour while university authorities determined that he was in fact Andy Warhol.

In May, Andy and the crew headed west again, this time to the exquisite town of La Jolla, on the edge of the Pacific Ocean just north of San Diego, where he rented a luxurious mansion for the three-week shoot of the *Surfing Movie*, or *San Diego Surf*, as it was also called. The police were all over them as soon as they arrived. It seemed that every time Viva went out the door, she was stopped by a cop.

San Diego Surf had little of the questionable content of *Lonesome Cowboys*. Its "plot" was a spoof of the Annette Funicello-Frankie

Avalon beach party movies. Nonetheless, Warhol's mere presence had become a threat to red-blooded, middle-class America. One day the filmmakers' car was pulled over as they were scouting locations, and all six passengers were spread-eagled against it and questioned. "So you're Andy Warhol, huh?" snarled the cop. Louis Waldon felt "very sorry for Andy. I thought it was very undignified to see Andy spread-eagled. But Andy sat back down and they interrogated each of us. They were looking for drugs and nobody had anything. They must have asked each of us twenty or thirty questions over and over again, and I happened to hear Andy's questioning. Andy was so brilliant at saying nothing. Finally, he would say, 'Oh . . . I don't . . . uh . . . yeah . . . uh . . . yeah . . . uh . . .'

" 'Well, were you born there? Is this your age?'

" 'Oh, oh, yes, uh, no . . . ' until finally the whole idea of questioning got turned around and the cop ended up answering the questions for him."

The real problem lay in the relations between Warhol and his cast. If Andy had begun to remove himself in Tucson, he was even more detached in La Jolla. Taylor Mead, Louis Waldon, and Viva resented Morrissey's controlling direction, and Viva began to hound Andy, trying to get him to take charge. At one point she yelled at Louis, "If you're a real man you'll beat the shit out of [Paul] and save this film from his cheap commercial tricks." Once again the shoot was aborted ahead of schedule and the troupe returned to New York.

Flying across the country with Taylor Mead, Andy was supremely confident about the future and full of grandiose promises to his volatile cohort. "He said that this was to be '*my* year,' " recalled Mead. "He described how we would use the Factory to make my own films, publish my book, make a record—everything. I was snowed, although he would probably have canceled it all on a whim. He was just a liar, a terrible liar. He'd say anything that was convenient. You cannot be that cool with people, as Andy was. You can't pull that shit of kings forever."

18

ON MONDAY, JUNE 3, 1968, Andy spent the morning sitting on the edge of his canopied bed in a dark room on the second floor of his house on Lexington Avenue, talking on the phone to Fred Hughes. Hughes reported that he had been mugged the previous night in front of his own apartment building on East Sixteenth Street directly across Union Square from the Factory. Fred's wallet and a watch he'd inherited from his grandmother had been taken, and he was bitter about the way the neighborhood was deteriorating. Andy was mildly sympathetic. Before leaving home, he said his daily prayer with his mother in her basement sitting room, then made a few stops: checking in with his lawyer, Sy Litvinoff, renewing a prescription from his doctor for Obetrol, doing a little shopping at Bloomingdale's.

At the same time, Valerie Solanas had arrived at the Factory looking for Andy Warhol. Paul Morrissey told her that he wasn't there and wasn't expected that day and that she could not hang around. Solanas left and took up a position down the block, leaning against a wall. When Fred Hughes went out for lunch an hour later, he noticed she was still there.

Before heading downtown, Andy knocked on the door of his

friend, the interior designer Miles White. Finding no one at home, he headed for the Factory. He had a couple of appointments to keep there, if he felt like it, so he hailed a Checker cab.

It was 4:15 when the cab pulled up outside Thirty-three Union Square West, and Andy, wearing his basic uniform of brown leather jacket over black T-shirt, pressed black jeans, and black Beatle boots, emerged. Union Square Park was jammed with the usual crowd. Assorted merchants juggled for space on the sidewalk, drug dealers milled around the statues of Washington and Lincoln and the monument to Jefferson inscribed with these words from the Declaration of Independence: "How little do my countrymen know what precious blessings they are in possession of and which no other people on earth enjoy."

At the same time, Jed Johnson, one of the new assistants at the Factory, glided down the block carrying a bundle of fluorescent tubes. Solanas strode up from her position near Sixteenth Street and joined Andy on the sidewalk as Jed arrived. The three of them walked into the building together.

As they waited for the elevator, Andy noticed that Valerie was wearing a thick turtleneck sweater beneath her coat, and it crossed his mind that she must be awfully warm. As they got into the elevator he also noticed that she was nervously twisting a brown bag in her hands, and, moreover, that she was wearing lipstick and makeup, unusual for a radical feminist.

Upstairs, across the polished wooden floor of the Factory's front room, Fred Hughes sat at his black glass-topped desk next to an open window that overlooked the park, punctiliously writing a memo in a black leather notebook. Opposite him at an identical desk, Paul Morrissey was listening to the telephone and tugging at his mane of curly hair. Viva was on the other end of the line, uptown at Kenneth's hairdressing salon, telling him about her part in the film *Midnight Cowboy* as she prepared to have her hair dyed for the role. The art critic and curator Mario Amaya paced between the two desks. He had been there for an hour, waiting to talk with Andy and Fred about an upcoming retrospective in London. Amaya had removed his jacket and was in shirtsleeves, smoking a cigarette. He had been leery of the leather freaks, with their sex and drugs, who hung around the Silver Factory. He couldn't understand what a man of Andy Warhol's tasteful sensibility was doing with such a damaged crowd, and he was relieved to note that there were no such creatures, nor any signs of their presence, in these austere, businesslike quarters.

The elevator door opened and Andy wandered into the room, followed by Jed and Valerie, chatting. Jed crossed to the private office in the rear corner of the room. Andy acknowledged Amaya's presence and nodded to Hughes, who came out from behind his desk to remind his boss of the need to discuss the retrospective. Morrissey told Valerie she looked awfully well; she said something witty and nasty in reply; he said something mean to her, and everybody laughed. He told Andy that Viva was on the phone and put the receiver on the desk, then excused himself to go to the lavatory. Andy went over to Paul's desk to talk to Viva, and Fred turned to Valerie and asked her if she was still writing dirty books.

Sitting in Paul's chair, half-listening while Viva rattled on about the various dyes they were going to apply to her frizzy filaments, Andy leaned forward and looked down into the black glass desktop, inspecting his own coiffure in its reflection. He saw a ghostly visage looking back at him, and smiled. He then signaled Hughes to get on the line and continue the conversation with Viva. He was bored. Valerie reached slowly into her paper bag and drew out a .32-calibre automatic pistol. She pointed it at Andy. Nobody paid any attention. She raised the gun slightly. Hughes leaned forward to pick up his phone receiver. Andy leaned forward. Solanas fired.

Amaya, who thought a sniper was shooting at them from another building, yelled, "Hit the floor!" Fred Hughes thought a small bomb had gone off in the office of the American Communist party two floors above them. Sitting at the beauty parlor, Viva thought someone was cracking a whip left over from the more outrageous Velvet Underground days. In that frozen second only Andy saw what was really happening. He dropped the phone, jumped from the desk, and started to move, looking directly into the woman's pinched face.

"No! No! Valerie!" he screamed. "Don't do it!"

Solanas fired a second time. Warhol fell to the floor and tried to crawl underneath the desk, but she moved in, placed the paper bag on the desk and, taking aim more carefully, fired again. Her third bullet entered his right side and exited the left side of his back. He later said that he felt "a horrible, horrible pain, as if a firecracker had exploded inside me." Blood pumped from his chest, soaking through his T-shirt and splattering the white telephone cord. "It hurt so much," he told friends later, "I wished I was dead."

Believing she had killed Warhol, Valerie Solanas crossed rapidly to the crouching figure of Mario Amaya. Their eyes met as she stood over him, fired a fourth time, and missed. He watched her take aim again and whispered a rapid prayer. Her fifth shot hit him in the flank, just above the hip; it passed through the flesh and exited his back. With a shock of adrenaline, he scrambled to his feet and crashed through the double doors leading into the back room. Once inside, he turned quickly and tried to lock them against her, but found that he'd broken the latch, so he held the doors closed with the weight of his bleeding body. It was in this position that Paul and Billy Name, who had been developing prints in the darkroom, found him. They had rushed up to find out what the "firecrackers" were all about.

"Valerie shot Andy," Mario gasped. "She shot Andy!"

They could hear her trying to open the door. Billy threw himself against it, while Paul slipped into the glass projection booth that overlooked the front room.

Believing that the door was locked, Solanas turned to hunt down another victim. Paralyzed with fear, Fred Hughes stood behind his desk, staring. Solanas crossed the room to Andy's office, where Jed Johnson was standing, desperately clutching the doorknob with both hands. She tried and failed to open the door, then turned toward Hughes. The thin, dapper businessman epitomized the kind of people who laughed at her poverty and beliefs. She strode up to him. She stopped several feet away and raised the gun. Hughes begged her not to fire. "I have to shoot you," she said and aimed the pistol at his chest.

Hughes fell to his knees. "Please don't shoot me, Valerie," he pleaded. "You can't. I'm innocent. I didn't do anything to you. Please, just leave."

Whether it was the urgency in his voice, the uselessness of shooting him, or a loss of confidence, the words "just leave" made contact. Solanas backed away and pressed the elevator button. Then she walked back, aimed at Hughes's forehead, and pulled the trigger. The .32 jammed. She whirled toward the brown bag, which contained a back-up .22. At that moment the elevator doors opened and Hughes cried out: "There's the elevator, Valerie. Just take it." Solanas bolted into it and the doors closed.

Now, Billy Name, Morrissey, Johnson, and a limping Amaya rushed in. Hughes crawled over to Andy to give him mouth-to-mouth resuscitation, but because of the wounds in Andy's lungs it was too painful. "It hurts, Fred, it hurts," he croaked. Hughes picked up the phone and called for an ambulance and the police.

Blood was spreading to the floor. "I can't . . . " Andy kept gasping, "I can't . . . breathe." Billy Name started to cry, which made Andy laugh. "Oh, please don't make me laugh, Billy," he whispered. "Please. It hurts too much."

"I'm not laughing, Andy," Billy replied, cradling the silver head in his lap, "I'm crying."

Jed Johnson stood over them, choking back tears. Morrissey paced the room yelling, "Call an ambulance! Call the police!" even though Hughes had already done so. Amaya hadn't yet realized that he had been shot.

The telephone rang. Viva was calling from Kenneth's to find out what was going on. She had heard screaming and thought Andy had been kidding. Hughes said, "Valerie Solanas just shot Andy. There's blood all over the place. I've got to hang up. Good-bye." Putting the receiver down, Viva still thought it was a Factory prank, and she decided to get her hair trimmed before having it dyed. She told the hairdresser to charge it to United Artists.

Morrissey was terrified that Solanas would return. He tried to jam the elevator but could not. It suddenly opened, and everybody spun in horror. Gerard Malanga emerged, accompanied by the drummer Angus MacLise and his wife, Hettie, hoping to borrow forty dollars. As Malanga recalled: "There was chaos—telephones ringing, people running back and forth. Andy lay in Billy Name's lap, gasping, 'I can't . . . I can't . . .' " Gerard believed he meant "I can't die," and thought of Julia hearing on television that her son had been murdered. Turning aside, he told Morrissey, "I'm going to get his mother."

"That's a good idea," Paul replied, and pushed some bills into his hands for cab fare.

At Kenneth's salon, the hairdresser asked Viva if she was going to call back and find out if what Hughes had said was true. She hesitated, then dialed. This time Jed Johnson answered. He cried out, "Yes, it's true and there's blood all over the place." Viva hung up. She still couldn't believe it. A friend who was with her called back and asked for Andy. "Andy isn't here," a terse voice replied, "and he may never be back."

It was 4:35. Andy was conscious again. He had been lying there for fifteen minutes when two members of the Emergency Medical Service stepped out of the elevator with a wheeled stretcher. They would not administer a painkiller, saying that pain was a valuable sign of what was going on in the abdomen. They picked Andy up, placed him on the stretcher, and wheeled him across the room. But the stretcher would not fit in the elevator. The medics decided that they would have to carry him down the stairs.

Lit by bare bulbs suspended from the ceiling, the stairs were steep, narrow, and smooth with age. The last flight was the steepest but somewhat wider. They pushed through a broad steel door, past two sets of glass doors, and into the sunny street, where a crowd had gathered. As Andy was lifted from the stretcher and placed beside Mario Amaya in the ambulance, he lost consciousness. The ambulance sped away.

Viva came out of the Fourteenth Street subway and ran across the park to the Factory. Before she was halfway there, she saw the police cars and the crowd. She bumped into Jed Johnson on the sidewalk, saw the empty stretcher, and started screaming. She went up in the elevator and burst into the Factory. The rooms were being searched by eight plainclothesmen, one of whom had stopped to pore over stills from *Lonesome Cowboys*. One of them looked up. "Okay, lady," he said, "tell us what you know." Only then did she fully realize that this was not a movie. Andy really had been shot. She saw the tape marking the bullet holes. She threw herself into Billy Name's arms, crying hysterically. Fred Hughes crossed the room and slapped her, saying, "Stop it! Now stop it!" She saw the blood on the telephone cord, and then she fainted.

In the ambulance, the driver said that for an extra fifteen dollars he could turn on the siren, and Mario Amaya told him to do it: Leo Castelli would pay. Amaya was afraid to look at Andy, dreading that he might be dead.

Warhol was wheeled into the emergency room at Columbus Hospital in Cabrini Medical Center on East Nineteenth Street at 4:45, twenty-three minutes after he had been shot. A call had been placed from the ambulance to announce his estimated time of arrival and his condition—critical. An emergency operating room had been prepared; three nurses and a team of doctors headed by Dr. Giuseppe Rossi, a crack surgeon who had been on his way home when the report had come through, were standing by. None of them had any idea who their patient was.

The stretcher was wheeled straight through to the operating room. The doctors clustered around Andy and began to take his vital signs. The pulse was faint. They attached him to an electrocardiogram machine and inserted a catheter in his penis to empty his bladder and determine the state of his kidneys, then began to examine his wounds. During these first few moments in the operating room, Warhol was semiconscious again, and he heard voices muttering, "Forget it," and "No chance."

Mario Amaya, who was lying on an operating table across the room, suddenly sat up. "Don't you know who this is?" he cried. "It's Andy Warhol. He's famous. And he's rich. He can afford to pay for an operation. For Christ's sake, do something!"

Paul Morrissey and Viva were on their way to the hospital. Valerie Solanas was wandering through Times Square in a daze. Uptown, Gerard Malanga was hammering on the door of Andy's house, trying to reach Julia before she heard the news. He could hear a phone already ringing in the front room.

At 4:51 Andy was pronounced clinically dead, but Dr. Rossi was determined to try to save him. He began to cut open Andy's chest. The first step was to massage the heart.

As Andy Warhol lay on the operating table, detectives from New York's Thirteenth Precinct continued to ransack the Factory, examining stills of naked men, slides of "death-and-disaster" paintings, and files of receipts—looking, they said, for "evidence." Fred Hughes insisted that they should be out looking for Valerie Solanas instead, but the police were suspicious of everyone at the Factory. They took Hughes and a weeping Jed Johnson to the station house and held them as suspects. When Hughes asked if he could call the hospital to check on Warhol's condition, they said no.

By the time Andy reached the hospital, the shooting had been announced on the radio. Now, reporters, photographers, and members of Warhol's entourage converged on the emergency waiting room. Leo Castelli and Ivan Karp arrived and stood with a reporter in one corner. Another reporter took down a quote from Ingrid Superstar: "Andy's shooting was definitely a blow against the cultural revolution. We're constantly being attacked." Nearby was Ultra Violet, declaring to two reporters: "Violence is everywhere in the air today. He got hurt in the big game of reality." The photographers snapped.

Viva arrived to find Louis Waldon talking on the phone to Ivy Nicholson: She was threatening to kill herself the minute Andy died. Taylor Mead, who would later say that if Valerie Solanas had not shot Andy, he might have, was there weeping. Minutes later, Gerard Malanga escorted Julia Warhola into the room. Stooped and gray, she was wearing a threadbare black coat, black stockings with runs in them, and a babushka.

"Why did someone harm me Andy?" she cried. "Why did they shoot me Andy?" Breaking down, Julia was put in a wheelchair and taken away to be sedated.

"How do you feel, Viva?" barked a radio reporter, shoving a microphone at her.

"How would you feel," she snapped, "if somebody you love was shot?"

Ultra Violet closeted herself in a cubicle with one reporter after another. As the hospital's public relations officer escorted Viva and Gerard to the upstairs waiting room so that they could stay with Julia, they heard Ultra saying to a reporter, "Well, I always thought that he was a great artist. . . . I have made three movies for him, the first was called . . . " Upstairs, the PR man blankly asked Viva if she was Valerie Solanas.

At 8:00 that evening, in Times Square, Solanas walked up to William Shemalix, a twenty-two-year-old rookie traffic cop, and said, "The police are looking for me and want me." She reached into both pockets of her trench coat, drew a .32 automatic from one and the back-up .22 pistol from the other. She handed them to Shemalix and said that she had shot Andy Warhol, explaining, "He had too much control of my life." Shemalix placed her under arrest and phoned in a report, requesting further instructions. Hughes and Johnson were released.

Brought handcuffed into the booking room at the Thirteenth

Precinct, Solanas grinned at the crowd of reporters and photographers. Asked what her motives were, she said, "I have a lot of reasons. Read my manifesto and it will tell you what I am." The photographers jumped onto the booking desk, pushing cops out of the way, yelling at her to look at them. The noise of clicking cameras and shouted questions was so loud that the booking officer could not hear Valerie's voice. Eventually, the police hustled the journalists out of the station house and took her off to be fingerprinted. She was charged with felonious assault and possession of a deadly weapon.

In the operating room, the surgical team had been surprised to discover the amount of damage the bullet had done to the interior of Andy's chest. It had entered his right side, passed through his lung, and ricocheted through his esophagus, gallbladder, liver, spleen, and intestines before exiting his left side, leaving a large, gaping hole. The doctors removed the ruptured spleen and shortly after 10:00 P.M., five and a half hours after they had started, sprinkled some antibiotics into his wounds to ward off infection. They needed to know if he was allergic to penicillin. Julia could not remember the name of his private physician, but Gerard did. They located him and discovered that Andy was indeed allergic. They would have to use some other kind of antibiotic. The surgeon poured it into the open cavity and sewed the wound closed.

The emergency waiting room was now jammed with people eating sandwiches and giving out "exclusive interviews." Viva later said, "All that was missing was the booze."

Gerard and Viva wheeled Julia out through the crowd of photographers and put her, still weeping, into a cab. Paul and John Warhola, who had come from Pittsburgh, arrived and were taken to the recovery room. "It didn't look like the same person," said Paul. "His head was as big as a watermelon! The doctor says, 'Andy was lucky. I thought he was a goner.' I says to him, 'What's the chances?' He says, 'You gotta figure fifty-fifty.' "

"He couldn't talk," John recalled. "He wrote it down: 'Who shot me?' I says, 'A girl.' He wrote, 'Did she say why?' "

That night there were vigils for Andy. Nico went to International Velvet's apartment, where they lit candles, sat on the floor, and prayed. Ivy Nicholson continued to call the hospital every ten minutes asking if Andy had died so she could jump out the window. At Andy's house, Julia Warhola, clutching her son's bloodstained T-shirt, had calmed down with the arrival of Paul and John and was at her private altar in the basement, where she would pray for hours. After leaving the Warholas, Gerard went with Viva to her apartment, where, according to Malanga, they made love for the first time.

"I never even knew Andy was so famous until he was shot and got all those headlines," said his brother John. Indeed, the next morning, the early editions of the *New York Post* and *Daily News* carried the headlines: "ANDY WARHOL FIGHTS FOR LIFE" and "ACTRESS SHOOTS ANDY WARHOL, CRIES, 'HE CONTROLLED MY LIFE.'" All day long, as Andy remained in critical condition, Fred Hughes, Paul Morrissey, and Billy Name replayed the whole scene over and over again into ringing phones at the Factory.

Valerie Solanas, wearing tan jeans, a yellow sweater over a black turtleneck, and torn sneakers without socks, was brought before Judge David Getzoff in Manhattan Criminal Court. "It's not often that I shoot somebody," she said. "I didn't do it for nothing. Warhol had me tied up, lock, stock, and barrel. He was going to do something to me which would have ruined me." Could she, the judge asked, afford an attorney? "No, I can't," she said. "I want to defend myself. This is going to stay in my own competent hands." Then she shouted out: "I was right in what I did! I have nothing to regret!" Getzoff ordered the court stenographer to strike the outburst from the record, and Solanas was remanded to the psychiatric ward at Bellevue Hospital for further observation.

At Columbus Hospital, one of Andy's vivid memories as he slipped in and out of consciousness was, as he later wrote in *POPism*, of hearing "a television going somewhere and the words 'Kennedy' and 'assassin' and 'shot' over and over again. Robert Kennedy had been shot, but what was so weird was that I had no understanding that this was a *second* Kennedy assassination—I just thought that maybe after you die, they rerun things for you, like President Kennedy's assassination."

Bobby Kennedy, who had been shot after winning the Democratic presidential primary in California, was also on the critical list. Andy's headlines had been eclipsed.

Of his recovery, Andy remembered the first days in intensive care as "just cycles of pain," interrupted only by the surprise appearance of Vera Cruise, disguised as a nurse. As he gained strength, he was able to brood on his would-be assassin. "I couldn't figure out why, of all the people Valerie must have known, I had to be the one to get shot," he wrote later. "I guess it was just being in the wrong place at the right time. That's what assassination is all about. I realized that it was just timing that nothing terrible had ever happened to any of us before now. Crazy people had always fascinated me because they were so creative—they were incapable of doing things normally. Usually they would never hurt anybody, they were just disturbed themselves; but how would I ever know again which was which?"

Early in the second week, Gerard and Viva were allowed a ten-minute visit with Andy by the hospital authorities, who treated them, said Viva, like "lepers." As she remembered it: "A white cloth was tied in four small knots at the corners of [Andy's] head, an electrocardiogram machine monitored his heartbeat, intravenous tubes dripped solutions into his forearms, and in the next bed a drug overdose patient was deliriously raving."

"Hi," Andy whispered. His voice was so weak that Viva had to bend down to hear him. "Look at that guy next to me. Don't tell anybody, but the nurse is in love with him. They kiss and hug when they think that nobody can see them. Look at that cabinet full of drugs. I'm afraid if Brigid gets in here she'll steal all the drugs. Don't tell her about them."

Uptown at the house on Lexington, Warhola relatives were in and out, taking care of Julia. Viva and Brigid Polk, who were amazed at all the religious statues, especially the crucifix over Andy's four-poster bed, visited her several times the first week, and she talked their ears off. Between handwringing lamentations for her son, mixed with emotional flashbacks to the death of her infant daughter in Mikova, Julia told Viva, "You are an angel and I pray to the good Jesus that he will save me Andy so he can marry you. Work for other people. Me Andy don't pay you enough. You need money for the wedding."

One day, Andy's sixteen-year-old nephew, George, was startled to see his grandmother throwing Andy's leather jacket into the trash. He rescued it and wore it on his next visit to Columbia Hospital. "Andy," he recalled, "said 'Hey! I want that, you can't have it!' I said, 'Gee, Bubba was throwing it out.'"

Throughout his six-week hospital convalescence, Andy received numerous gifts of delicacies, cakes, and boxes of candy. Afraid he might be poisoned, he insisted that his nephews sample the food first; they eagerly complied.

On June 13, ten days after the shooting, his doctors reported that he was "on his way to complete recovery."

That day Valerie Solanas appeared in the State Supreme Court with two representatives of NOW (the National Organization for Women): the New York chapter president, Ti-Grace Atkinson, and Florence Kennedy, a lawyer who had represented the black militant H. Rap Brown after the Newark riots that previous spring. Atkinson testified that Solanas would go down in history as "the first outstanding champion of women's rights." Kennedy called her "one of the most important spokeswomen of the feminist movement" and maintained that her client was being prejudicially treated because she was a woman. Kennedy moved for a writ of habeas corpus on the ground that Solanas was being improperly detained in a psychiatric ward, but State Supreme Court Justice Thomas Dickens denied the motion and sent Solanas back to the hospital for further tests. On June 28 she was indicted on charges of attempted murder, assault, and illegal possession of a gun.

As had happened so often in his life, the shooting polarized feelings about Andy Warhol. At one extreme were those for whom he had now attained a Christlike martyrdom. At the very least, having been attacked for "political" reasons, he must now be viewed as a political artist. At the other pole were the feminist revolutionaries. One group calling itself the "Up Against the Wall Motherfuckers" brought out a pamphlet entitled "Valerie Lives," in which Solanas was described as a "chick with balls" and her victim as a "plastic fascist." Andy followed the media reaction to his shooting with keen interest, and he was especially hurt by the article in *Time* under the headline "Felled by SCUM," which sermonized: "Americans who deplore crime and disorder might consider the case of Andy Warhol, who for years celebrated every form of licentiousness. . . . The pop art king was the blond guru of a nightmare world, photographing depravity and calling it truth."

And what had been "underground" was now moving into the mainstream: John Schlesinger's *Midnight Cowboy* was being filmed that summer in New York, and not only was its subject—male hustlers—a "legitimization" of Warhol's concerns, but the British director had proposed filming a party scene in the Factory, with Viva in the role of an underground filmmaker. (Before the shooting Andy had been asked to play himself but declined.) Andy was flattered by Hollywood's attention, and a little jealous of all the money being poured into the film. "Why don't they give us the money?" he complained. "We would have done it so *real* for them."

Paul Morrissey took up the idea: Why not do their own version of the hustler story? He drafted a script about a day in the life of a male prostitute, and assembled a cast featuring Geraldine Smith and Patti d'Arbanville, two aspiring teenage actresses, along with Joe Dallesandro. For four thousand dollars, Morrissey shot *Flesh* over two weekends in July. Andy's input was minimal, consisting of daily gossip with Morrissey at the hospital about doings on the set. (He was especially amused to hear that Dallesandro had got an erection on camera and allowed Geraldine to tie a bow around it.) He also heard less cheerful news: Edie Sedgwick was in a New York hospital, suffering the effects of a drug overdose.

On July 28 Andy went home. He spent the first ten days, including his fortieth birthday on August 6, in his four-poster, watching television, especially the news reports of the Soviet invasion of Czechoslovakia and the riots at the Democratic Convention in Chicago. He called up his friends, many of whom cried at the sound of his voice. When he was able to move around a bit, he started work on a commissioned portrait—one hundred faces of Governor Nelson Rockefeller's wife, Happy. Since Julia was spending most of her time in bed as well, Jed Johnson did much of the looking after him, fixing up the pack-rat mess of the house, shopping, and making dinner.

On September 4 Andy went out in public for the first time since the shooting. With him at Casey's, a fashionable restaurant in Greenwich Village, were Viva, Paul Morrissey, and Letitia Kent, a reporter from the *Village Voice*. At one point, Kent asked: "Do you think you had any complicity in the shooting, in the sense of encouraging those around you to act out their fantasies?"

"I don't know," said Andy. "I guess I really don't know what people do. I just always think they're kidding. I don't think Valerie Solanas was responsible for what she did. It was just one of those things."

"We are constantly under attack," Viva put in. "Andy's shooting was part of a conspiracy against the cultural revolution."

"Well, it's our year for crazy people," said Andy. "But I can't feel anything against Valerie Solanas. When you hurt another person you never know how much it pains."

Kent asked whether he was still in pain.

Andy replied: "It slows you up some. I can't do the things I want to do, and I'm so scarred I look like a Dior dress. It's sort of awful, looking into the mirror and seeing all the scars. But it doesn't look that bad. The scars look pretty in a funny way. It's just that they are a reminder that I'm still sick and I don't know if I will ever be well again. Before I was shot, I always suspected I was watching TV instead of living life. Right when I was being shot I knew I was watching television. Since I was shot everything is such a dream to me. I don't know whether or not I'm really alive—whether I died. It's sad. Like I can't say hello or good-bye to people. Life is like a dream."

"Are you afraid?" asked Kent.

"That's so funny. I wasn't afraid before," said Andy. "And having died once, I shouldn't feel fear. But I'm afraid. I don't understand why. I am afraid of God alone, and I wasn't before."

Andy was still extremely fragile when he starting coming into the Factory again in September. He would seclude himself in his tiny office off the main room, as far as possible from arriving visitors, and emerge briefly only when harmless-looking friends dropped by, to tape and photograph them with his new Uher-400 recorder and Polaroid camera. The sound of the elevator doors opening made him tremble, and Morrissey tried to ban anyone who, in his view, operated on "tenuous mental health." On this issue Andy was ambivalent. He later wrote, "I was afraid that without the crazy, druggy people around jabbering away and doing their insane things, I would lose my creativity. They'd been my total inspiration since 1964. . . . I didn't know if I could make it without them."

Apart from his personal safety, he was most concerned with money. He told friends that his hospital bill for eleven thousand dollars had wiped out most of the year's profits, but according to Hughes, Andy had made a lot of money in 1968 and was doing fine.

One benefit of the shooting was to boost the value of his paintings. Works that had originally sold for two hundred dollars were now fetching fifteen thousand and more. "People were willing to buy them at any price," commented one art dealer. "It was like holding on to IBM stock." Of course, he saw none of the money from the resale of his old work, but he still owned many of his early pieces, for which Hughes was able to command high prices.

In October, *Flesh* opened for what would turn into a smash seven-month run at the Garrick Theater on Bleecker Street. While *Flesh* lacked the innovativeness of the early Factory films, its comparatively formal editing and story-shaping made it much more accessible than Andy's own movies. Despite a badly recorded soundtrack, the reviews of *Flesh* were good, and the film, along with its "strong, silent" star, Joe Dallesandro (whom Morrissey compared to John Wayne), gained a cult following.

A lot of people at the Factory criticized Morrissey for taking advantage of the situation and trying to promote himself as a filmmaker on his own. When the film was released, however, Paul chose to play down his own role, and he listed Andy's name as director in the credits. A "Warhol film" was comparable in his mind, he said, to a Walt Disney production. Besides, the idea of a "director's cinema" was "snobbish and trashy." He was, he said, "just doing a job for Andy."

That fall Andy told Viva and Louis Waldon that he wanted to make a movie with them and asked them "to think of something." They came up with the story of a couple who meet in a borrowed apartment to make love for the last time.

Andy had always wanted to make a movie about two people having sex, and he decided to call it *Fuck*. According to Viva, "because Andy was so shy and complexed about his looks, he had no private life. In filming as in 'hanging out' he merely wanted to find out how 'normal people' acted with each other. And I think my own idea about *Blue Movie* [as *Fuck* would be called] wasn't, as I believed at the time, to teach the world about 'real love' or 'real sex' but to teach Andy."

The ninety-minute film was shot in a single day at David Bourdon's apartment in long takes with a fixed camera, from which Andy, at one point, walked away during the shower scene. Paul stood by uncomfortably on the sidelines and finally walked out during the lovemaking scene. Viva attributed Paul's behavior to "embarrassment," but according to Malanga, Paul was unhappy at having failed to "sanitize" Andy.

Afterward, they all headed for Casey's, but as they were approaching the restaurant Andy stopped and said, "Oh no, we can't go in there, there's only two women and there's eight men. It won't look good. They'll think we're gay!" When everybody assured him it would be all right and urged him to go in, he said, "Oh, okay." He was very quiet during dinner, Waldon remembered. "He just kept saying over and over that he thought the film went really well and was 'beautiful.' "

A week later Andy and Billy Name gave an interview to the authors of *The Complete Book of Erotic Art*. Andy said he did not think his films were erotic because "we show everything and the way we show it, it doesn't look sexy." Then he took off on a long rap about pornography: "The people who used to do girlie movies copy our movies now and they're really good. Oh, it's really dirty, I mean I've never seen anything so dirty. They copy our technique." ("I think it should be noted," said Billy Name, "that Andy's sort of beyond sophistication.")

To another interviewer, he said that *Blue Movie* was about the war in Vietnam.

Blue Movie would be Viva's swan song with Andy. When she saw the rushes, she was appalled, particularly by the sex scene, which she felt was flat, quite unlike the balletic sequence she had envisioned. Andy had to plead with her to sign a release so he could "show it once at the Whitney."

And Andy seemed to have tired of her. "After Andy was shot he became really terrified of women," Viva recalled. "He was very much changed toward me, much cooler. He was sexually afraid of women before; I mean you couldn't touch him, he would cringe. That could have been an act, but afterwards he seemed deeply afraid."

In November she decided to leave New York for Paris and a romance with the actor Pierre Clementi. Andy had originally encouraged the match, but now he tried to persuade her to stay. In the end, he accompanied her forlornly to the airline office, paying for her ticket and adding seven hundred dollars—"for my Clementi dowry," Viva said.

Although her romance with Clementi soon fizzled, Viva's career away from the Factory prospered. She married a French filmmaker, Michel Auder, and starred in *Lion's Love,* a film by Agnes Varda. When it opened in New York, Andy wrote to tell her, "You were great . . . you looked beautiful. We can't wait till you come back to us. If you need money just ask for it." She did, on several occasions, and Andy sent it to her. Yet frequently during this period Viva made bitter remarks about Warhol and the Factory, and once sent a letter stating that if he did not send more money, she would work as effectively against him as she had worked for him.

In March 1969 she announced that she had begun work on an autobiographical novel called *Superstar,* which would be an exposé of the underground. Andy correctly interpreted this to mean of him. She also threatened to sue Andy for having allowed Grove Press to publish the text of *Blue Movie,* complete with photographs. "We compromised on a two-thousand-dollar payoff," she said. "I was always a cheap date. But I guess I learned from Andy that if you consider yourself an artist, everything you do is equally valuable."

Since the shooting, the Factory hierarchy had become more rigid. Paul Morrissey increasingly assumed the role of spokesman for the Warhol films, expounding to reporters on the role of the artist as "supervisor" in the age of mass communication, on the influence of television and home movies on his cinematic style. He also assumed the role of antidrug propagandist, telling the press that drugs were "obvious, boring, and old hat."

With Andy operating at diminished capacity, tensions were running high again. In his *Secret Diaries,* Malanga saw them as stemming in part from the struggle to see who would "be chosen to be part of the future the second time around." Brigid Polk, the one woman who had become closer to Andy after the shooting ("She was the wife-figure in his life," sneered Viva), would accuse Paul of being a "power-mad puritan." Someone else would say of Brigid, "She's an evil pig, but Andy likes to have her around. I don't know why." But for many who were still there, the Factory remained what it had always been—the most stable element in their lives, a home.

The poet Jim Carroll, who was living in Brigid Polk's hotel room and working part-time for Andy that fall, described the Factory in his journals as a "medieval monastery" with Andy as the "Pope in Exile" and Paul as "the abbot and Grand Inquisitor." The favored choirboy was unquestionably Jed Johnson. "I never knew Andy to be so satisfied in a love relationship until he met Jed," said Malanga. "Somehow I felt that Andy might have actually got somebody he could love in Jed. Whatever companions Andy had prior to Jed were distractions from his art, but Jed was very helpful. He would set up the projectors, put the film in the projectors, sweep the floor. Jed was a real sweetheart."

With Viva gone, the spotlight was now grabbed by two transvestites, Jackie Curtis and Candy Darling, who had made a cameo appearance in *Flesh*. "Among other things," Andy wrote in *POPism*,

> drag queens were ambulatory archives of ideal movie-star womanhood. I'm fascinated by boys who spend their lives trying to be complete girls, because they have to work so hard—double time—getting rid of all the telltale male signs and drawing in all the female signs. I'm not saying it's not self-defeating and self-destructive, and I'm not saying it's not possibly the single most absurd thing a man can do with his life. What I'm saying is, it is very hard work to look like the complete opposite of what nature made you and then to be an imitation woman of what was only a fantasy woman in the first place.

A third transvestite superstar, Holly Woodlawn, was introduced to Warhol in 1969. "I was expecting one of those loud, boisterous, imposing, assuming big shots," Holly recalled of the meeting. "He was a quiet little nothing, but I thought he was cute."

The drag queens made an intriguing trio: Holly Woodlawn was the sultry Hedy Lamarr figure; Candy Darling was the super-feminine Kim Novak-Marilyn Monroe type; Jackie Curtis, whose stubble showed through the pancake makeup, was Joan Crawford, vicious and strong. Andy developed the routine, when visitors arrived, of introducing everyone on staff, regardless of sex, as a transvestite.

Warhol's stable also included a group of rambunctious, sexy teenage girls: Dallesandro's co-stars in *Flesh*, Patti d'Arbanville, a green-eyed honey blonde who would go on to make it in Hollywood, and the Garboesque Geraldine Smith; Andrea Feldman; and, later, Jane Forth. "We all had a big crush on Paul even though he seemed so asexual . . . because he was the director, he had the power," recalled Smith. "And Andy really represented New York to us. Everytime we went to a party and Andy showed up, it was *the* party."

To Andy, they were "post-pop," and in the movie lot tradition, he called them "the kids."

All summer long there had been a frenzy of typing at the Factory: Andy's "novel," based on twenty-four hours of tapes recording a day in the life of Ondine, was to be rushed into print by Grove Press to cash in on his new notoriety. Billy Name supervised the typesetting, making sure that every spelling mistake and typo was left intact so that Andy's intention of making a "bad" book would be realized. Andy had always wanted to call such a book *Cock,* but it was published that November as *a* in a classy hardback edition at the relatively high price of ten dollars.

Paul Carroll, writing in *Playboy,* praised Andy's answer to James Joyce's *Ulysses* as a "genuine microcosm of the world of words, fractured sentences, grunts, giggles, and blablabla that surrounds us." But most of the other reviews were sharply negative, notably in the *New York Review of Books,* where Robert Mazzocco tore into the book at dizzying (and flattering) length, calling Warhol "a *haut* vulgarian," and the book "a bacchanalian coffee klatsch." The mole people, wrote Mazzocco, were "ghouls"—"spook-hour hysterics smothered in sedatives, non-stop gabbers on a Transylvanian talk show. If Warhol were a genius, they would be devastating. As it is, the characteristics of *a,* like many of the other characters of Warhol films, suggest the final touch, or the final solution—they represent the bizarre new class, *untermenschen* prefigurations of the technological millennium, as insulated from the past, from pleasure and pain, from humanism and the heroic tradition, as were pygmies and dwarfs from knights in armor." *a*, the review concluded, "is [so much] about the degradation of sex, the degradation of feeling, the degradation of values, and the super degradation of language, that in its errant pages can be heard the death knell of American literature."

Undaunted, Andy delighted in his "novel," reading it over, he estimated, at least forty times. And so did the "ghouls": The book was important because there had never been one like it before.

For one of them, however, *a* marked one of those "final acts" that Andy's closest associates were inevitably driven to. In this case it was not a walkout but a walk *in*. After finishing the galleys, Billy Name retired into his darkroom at the back of the studio. "After Andy was shot," he recalled, "it became obvious to me that Paul was almost completely taking over the management position. Whenever anyone came from the media, Paul would tell people that he was in charge up there. I did point out that I was also one of the people in charge there, but I felt that Andy didn't really need me anymore."

With a stack of books on "white magic," he remained secluded, refusing to come out of the little back room, letting his hair and beard grow. He was, he said, trying to "clear the air of all the hecticness that had gone on. I never bothered to tell anyone because they would just have made something silly out of it." During that winter, the only evidence of Billy's existence was the empty takeout containers left in the trash overnight.

"Everybody expected me to try to somehow get Billy to come out, but I didn't," Andy later wrote. "I had no idea what made him go in, so how could I get him to come out?"

It was a wonder that Andy didn't go into seclusion himself. For him, 1968, America's most turbulent year since the Second World War, ended on several disturbing notes. Tom Hedley, a young editor at *Esquire*, witnessed the first at a party given by Larry Rivers in the Hamptons: "Warhol saw [the painter] de Kooning, made a pilgrimage to him, said, 'Hi, Bill,' and offered his hand. De Kooning was drunk and he suddenly turned to Warhol and said, 'You're a killer of art, you're a killer of beauty, and you're even a killer of laughter. I can't bear your work!' It was a very dramatic, ugly moment, face to face, and became the talk of the party. Andy smiled, turned away, and said to Morrissey, 'Oh, well, I always loved his work.' "

The second occurred on Christmas Day. In August, Valerie Solanas had been declared incompetent to stand trial and was committed to a mental institution. As far as everyone at the Factory knew, she was still safely locked away. Then, the night before Christmas, Andy answered the phone. It was Valerie. He must, she demanded, drop all criminal charges, pay twenty thousand dollars for her "manuscripts," put her in more movies, and get her booked on Johnny Carson. If he didn't, she said, she "could always do it again."

19

THE YEAR 1969 began with a flurry of ideas. What about a television show, Andy suggested, called "Nothing Special," consisting of six hours of people walking past a hidden camera? (He had recently had one installed in the Factory to improve security.) Or a film called *Orgy,* a large-cast version of *Blue Movie,* which would be shot on a journey around the world? Another nutty notion was to "figure out a way to make a ten-foot mural that will turn brown in three days, like a Polaroid print." Another, to parody "systems art" by renting out his superstars to do anything asked of them for a thousand dollars a day. At Brigid Polk's suggestion, he had started taking Polaroids of penises—of any Factory visitor he could persuade to drop his trousers. He later estimated that he had taken thousands of such pictures: "Whenever somebody came up to the Factory, no matter how straight-looking he was, I'd ask him to take his pants off so I could photograph his cock and balls. It was surprising who'd let me and who wouldn't." Indeed, Andy's desire to record everything around him had become a mania. As John Perrault, the art critic, wrote in a profile of Warhol in *Vogue:* "His portable tape recorder, housed in a black briefcase, is his latest self-protection device. The microphone is pointed at anyone who approaches, turning the situation into a theater work. He records

246

hours of tape every day but just files the reels away and never listens to them."

In May, *Lonesome Cowboys* opened at two theaters in New York, with Morrissey doing most of the talking to the press about "Andy's intentions" behind this first "pornographic Western." It was all meant to be funny, Morrissey said, nothing more. To *Variety* he explained: "Sex is the stuff of comedy. The big commercial sex pictures are just like the underground newspapers, they take the whole thing absolutely seriously." As for the absence of traditional characterization in the film, Morrissey said, "When they leave the theater, people don't say, that was a great movie, they say those were great people." That summer at the San Francisco Film Festival, *Lonesome Cowboys* won the Film of the Year award. Agents from the FBI attended a showing, and filed a report saying that the "White Female" (Viva) had not in fact been raped, thus putting an end to the agency's year-and-a-half surveillance of Warhol.

Had Andy "sold out"? That May, *Esquire* ran a cover with the line "The Final Decline and Total Collapse of the American Avant-Garde." The composite photograph showed Andy drowning in a can of Campbell's tomato soup. In fact, his chief preoccupation now seemed to be money. "If only someone would give us a million dollars" had become his daily litany, and he was looking to Hollywood for that pot of gold. Gerald Ayers, an assistant to the president of Columbia Pictures, had been encouraging Morrissey to submit a film proposal, and Paul had come up with an idea (in collaboration with a reporter for the *Los Angeles Times*, John Hallowell) for a movie about a celebrity interviewer called *The Truth Game*. He sent Ayers the screen treatment, and in late May, Columbia flew Warhol, Morrissey, Joe Dallesandro, Geraldine Smith, and Jed Johnson to Los Angeles, putting them up at the luxurious Beverly Wilshire Hotel.

According to Hallowell, Andy and company arrived half an hour late for a conference at the studio: "Somehow we got ourselves into the inner sanctum where the studio head himself greeted us from behind an enormous desk with various executives assembled. Oscars shimmered from one wall and, instinctively, Andy placed himself in a chair below Hollywood's beloved gold statues. Morrissey did the talking. So much so, that at one point the studio head called him 'Andy.' That produced a Warhol smile. Otherwise, throughout the entire madly inconclusive meeting, Andy simply sat there swathed in black leather and uttered not a word. Beneath all the money talk, the studio was petrified. How could they explain all this to the stock-holders? Where was the script? But on they went, through days of talks and telephones and meetings."

During their stay, Andy and his entourage were fêted at a discotheque called the Factory, where Jane Fonda took them under her wing, and they went to a celebrity-packed screening of *Easy Rider*. After four days of waiting for another call from Columbia, Andy got fed up and took everyone back to New York.

The first anniversary of the shooting brought the news that Valerie Solanas had been sentenced to three years in prison for "reckless assault with intent to harm" (she had already served one of those years in a mental institution). "You get more for stealing a car," said Lou Reed, reflecting the general Factory view that the judgment was a sign of the "hatred directed toward Andy by society." According to John Warhola, the short sentence was in part the result of Andy's refusal to appear in court to testify against Solanas: "He was so thin and weak, he just didn't want to bother."

In fact, Andy was still in pain from one wound that had not healed properly and needed regular draining. His natural pallor had become more ghostly than ever. Zipped tightly into his surgical corset and black leather jacket, he struck Cecil Beaton, who arrived to take photographs at the Factory, as "a zombie, more dead than alive." The *New Yorker*'s Calvin Tomkins wrote: "At the moment, what we seem to see reflected in that strange face is a sickness for which there may be no cure. Andy, in what one fervently hopes is just another put-on, begins to look more and more like the angel of death."

Asked by a reporter for *Vogue* how he felt, Warhol replied: "Maybe it would have been better if I had died. I mean, it's so-o-o awful. Everything is such a mess. I don't know. It's too hard." "But you seem so cheerful and active," said the reporter. "Yes, I know," said Andy. "But you have to . . . you know, you have to pretend."

In an attempt to generate some fast money that summer, Warhol rented the dilapidated Fortune Theater at 62 East Fourth Street and showed a series of gay porno films. Gerard Malanga was in charge of the operation, and the paperwork was done under his name and that of his company, Poetry on Film. The hardcore house was called Andy Warhol's Theater: Boys to Adore Galore. Renting the place was Morrissey's idea, as was the admission price of five dollars, more than double the price of watching the same ten-minute loops in Times Square. Gerard Malanga managed the theater and ran the music behind the silent reels; co-managing the venture and taking tickets was Jim Carroll, who wasn't sure if his new job "was a promotion or a demotion from Studio della Warhol."

One of Warhol's actors, in addition to running the projector for several weeks, was also, according to Carroll, "making a nice piece of change for himself by taking the wealthy swills of our clientele into a small sofa-filled room beside the projection booth and packing their fudge for them for prices only a true superstar could demand." Jim briefly considered reporting him to Paul, but then realized that he, too, could make a nice piece of change by taking a percentage at the door.

In spite of the inflated ticket price and the complaints of a few customers who expected to see Warhol films, the six-week venture seemed a success, particularly on Tuesdays and Thursdays when the features were changed and the 150-seat auditorium was packed. On a good night they could take in $1,500, although Morrissey, who would stop by punctually after the last show each night to collect the day's take, quickly began to suspect that Carroll's uncharacteristic possession of pocket money was the result of skimming the proceeds. Carroll was taking out two or three hundred dollars on a good night. His justification: Andy and Paul were "making out like bandits on this layer of obscenity." Andy, in fact, realized little profit, and when plainclothesmen started sniffing around, he pulled out.

Blue Movie opened at the Garrick Theater on July 21, and the premiere was celebrated at Max's, where Andy gave away the "bride," Jackie Curtis (in a white taffeta gown), at his "wedding" to "groom" Stuart Lichtenstein. During the bridal feast early in the morning, one of the "kids," Andrea Feldman, jumped up on a banquette and, shoving a fork into her breast, shouted at Jackie, "This is what a real woman looks like!"

Blue Movie opened well, but it was seized by the police on the grounds of obscenity. In one of his few public protests, Andy later wrote: "They came all the way down to the Village and sat through Viva's speeches about General MacArthur and the Vietnam war, through Louis calling her tits dried apricots and through her story about the police harassing her in the Hamptons for not wearing a bra, and then they seized the print of our movie. Why, I wondered, hadn't they gone over to Eighth Avenue and seized things like *Inside Judy's Box* or *Tina's Tongue?* Were they more socially redeemable maybe? It all came down to what they wanted to seize and what they didn't, basically. It was ridiculous."

The following week, *Lonesome Cowboys* was seized by the police in Atlanta. Asked by Letitia Kent in an interview for *Vogue* what he thought about the film being labeled hardcore pornography, Andy replied, "I think movies should appeal to prurient interests. I mean the way things are going now—people are alienated from one another. Hollywood films are just planned-out commercials. *Blue Movie* was real. But it wasn't done as pornography—it was an exercise, an experiment. But I really do think movies *should* arouse you, should get you excited about people, should be prurient. Prurience is part of the machine. It keeps you happy. It keeps you running."

Asked about his laissez-faire approach as a filmmaker, he replied, "Scripts bore me. It's much more exciting not to know what's going to happen. . . . Years ago, people used to sit looking out of their windows at the street. Or on a park bench. They would stay for hours without being bored although nothing much was going on. *This is my favorite theme in movie making*—just watching something happening for two hours or so. . . . I still think it's nice to care about people. And Hollywood movies are uncaring. We're pop people. We took a tour of Universal Studios in Los Angeles and inside or outside the place, it was very difficult to tell what was real. They're not-real people trying to say something. And we're real people not trying to say anything."

By November, Billy Name had been living in his darkroom for nearly a year, and Paul was getting worried. "Andy, he's going to die in there," he said, "and the papers are going to say 'ANDY WARHOL LOCKS MAN IN TOILET.' " Andy replied that Billy "would work it out for himself." Billy had become more legendary than real. Stories abounded that he had shaved his head and was caked with scabs from lack of light, that his eyes had turned yellow and he had grown clawlike fingernails. The only person who saw him with any regularity was Lou Reed, who eventually "freed" him by arranging for a payment of two hundred dollars for one of Billy's photographs to appear on the cover of a Velvet Underground album. As Billy later explained, "I said, 'Well, I've done this for about a year now and I've accomplished what I wanted to and Andy doesn't need me any more, especially since Fred does a nice job of managing things, I think I will just go out into the world.' "

One morning Warhol found Billy's door open and a note tacked to it reading, "Andy—I am not here anymore but I am fine. Love, Billy."

In short order the walls of the darkroom were painted white and a newly leased Xerox machine was installed.

Excited by the success of *Easy Rider,* Andy had been urging Morrissey to make a film about drugs. "I thought drugs were bad and at first I didn't want to do it," said Morrissey. "But then Andy said, 'You know, it hasn't been done. Nobody's really made a movie about drugs,' and I thought, That's true. Well, I'll show how silly it is." The result, *Trash,* would be the most expensive Warhol movie to date (it was budgeted at twenty to thirty thousand dollars) and by far the most successful.

Trash, shot during the first two weeks of December, starred Joe Dallesandro, repeating the role of "the hunk" he had played in *Flesh,* but with one difference: He was supposed to be unable to get an erection because of the character's heroin habit. (Off-screen, Dallesandro lived quietly with his wife and child in the same apartment building as Morrissey, "in an atmosphere weirdly and powerfully controlled by Paul," noted Malanga in his diary.) Geri Miller, the "supergroupie" who had appeared in *Flesh* as a girl who was thinking of having her breasts inflated with silicone, was cast as the first of several unsuccessful sirens, the others being Jane Forth, a sixteen-year-old socialite with shaved eyebrows and hair slicked back with Wesson Oil, and Andrea Feldman as an LSD-crazed teenybopper. The female impersonator Holly Woodlawn was cast as Joe's wife, who was given to cruising the Fillmore East rock palace and hunting for home furnishings in garbage cans.

John Russell Taylor, the British film critic, later noted the film's antidrug message:

> The true subject of *Trash* is presented neatly, as a sort of formal statement of theme, in the opening sequence, during which Geri Miller . . . tries everything she can think of to excite Joe Dallesandro, who remains resolutely, and not too concernedly, as unaroused by her manipulating as by her elaborate go-go dance. Geri is worried in an almost maternal fashion about Joe: the trouble she says, is the drugs he takes. Why can't he trip on sex instead? It's cheaper, nice, and a lot healthier. Can you trip on sex? asks Joe. Of course, says Geri; isn't it great when you come? No, says Joe; it's over.

Andy gave the performers twenty-five dollars a day and free meals at Max's. The atmosphere on the set was, for a Warhol film, disciplined (although Andrea Feldman complained that Dallesandro had gone too far when, in one scene, he threw her on a bed and ripped off her clothes—she had wanted her parents to see the movie). Jed Johnson, who worked the camera some of the time, recalled: "Andy and Paul wanted it to be successful. Everything was ad-libbed, but ad-libbed with some framework and direction for the actors to work in. Andy was occasionally on the set, but not much. But even when he was away you felt a real strong influence of his presence. You thought, 'Well, how would Andy do this?' I still feel that today." (As Jonas Mekas would write about Andy's role in the process, "The mystery of it all remains how it all holds together. It's like the United States—the idea, the concept, the essentials came from Warhol, and the particulars, the materials, come from everywhere and they are held together by the central spirit.")

Of all the ideas Andy had for films, his next effort, *Women in Revolt,* was perhaps closest to his heart. Made sporadically over a period of two and a half years, it starred the three drag queens, Candy Darling, Jackie Curtis, and Holly Woodlawn, playing women in different stages of "liberation": Jackie played a virgin schoolteacher from Bayonne, New Jersey; Candy a Long Island socialite longing to be a movie star; and Holly a struggling bohemian. The comic high point was the scene in which Jackie paid a former Mr. America to have sex with her so that she could "find out what we're fighting against." After gagging through an awkward blow job, Curtis ad-libbed (in one of Andy's favorite lines): "This can't be what millions of girls commit suicide over when their boyfriends leave them."

Attacking the women's movement was hardly the point: Fred Hughes later told a reporter, "We are for equal pay, day-care centers, free abortions . . ."

"And lipstick for both men and women," Andy added.

In January 1970, while Andy, Paul, and Jed were editing *Trash,* a showing in London of *Flesh* was raided by the police. In addition to confiscating the film, they took the unprecedented action of arresting the entire audience of two hundred people. The raid sparked a debate in the House of Commons and a ruling by Britain's official film censor, John Trevelyan, that *Flesh* was not objectionable, and that the theater could resume showing it: "This is an intellectual film for a specialized audience," he said. "I have seen it, and while it is not my cup of tea, there is nothing at all corrupting about it."

Meanwhile, the Factory was busy with plans for the first major American retrospective of Warhol art: It would open at the Pasadena Museum in California in May and travel to Chicago, Einhoven in Holland, Paris, and London, before ending up at the Whitney Museum in New York in the spring of 1971.

The show's curator, John Coplans, asked Andy if he had any special recommendations. Andy insisted that his early hand-painted works be excluded and that the exhibition be restricted to his series—soup cans, disasters, Brillo boxes, portraits, and flowers— the representative works of his high-pop oeuvre, completed before his "retirement" from painting in 1966. Recalled Coplans: "I said, 'Anything else?' He said, 'No.' It was the briefest conversation I've ever had with an artist on his retrospective."

"Andy thought [the retrospective] was so old-fashioned, so ridiculous, so conventional," said Leo Castelli. And to another acquaintance Andy complained that he would "rather have done something new and up-to-date" for the show. Yet, when asked what sorts of things he might paint, he said, "Well, I like empty walls. As soon as you put something on them they look terrible."

In fact, Andy seemed less interested in painting than in maintaining a Duchampian distance from painting. His ambition now, he told Malanga, was "to do nothing." "The critics are the real artists. The dealers are the new artists, too," he told Emile de Antonio. "I don't paint anymore. Painting is dead." To the photographer David Bailey he said, "I haven't stopped painting. I paint my nails. I paint my eyes every day." In reality, all this posturing was purely in jest. Andy had long planned to return to painting, when the price was right.

Andy attended the opening on May 12 in Pasadena with a bevy of superstars, one of whom cooed when she saw the show, "Gee, Andy, you really are an artist!" This was underscored the following day when one of the soup can paintings was bought by a German collector at the Parke-Bernet auction house in New York for sixty thousand dollars, the highest price ever paid at auction for a work by a living American artist. "At first there was quite a scandal," recalled Leo Castelli. "People suspected there had been some sort of foul play and the auction had been rigged. But the price turned out to be quite correct."

In a 1971 profile of Warhol, Calvin Tomkins tried to define the phenomenon Andy had become:

> Andy is the first real art celebrity since Picasso and Dalí. . . . The word, I think, is resonance. From time to time an individual appears, often but not necessarily an artist, who seems to be in phase with certain vibrations—signals not yet receivable by standard equipment. The clairvoyance with which Andy touched the nerve of fashion and commercial art, the energy emanating from God knows where, the inarticulateness and naiveté, the very mystery and emptiness of his persona—all this suggests the presence of an uncanny intuition. Always somewhat unearthly, Warhol became in the 1960s a speechless and rather terrifying oracle. He made visible what was happening in some part of us all.

Overnight, the worldwide trade in Warhols boomed. The soup cans fetched the highest prices, followed by the disasters, many of which had already been acquired by European collectors and museums after their initial lack of success in America. A few days after the Parke-Bernet auction, John Giorno sold a suicide painting to a German collector for thirty thousand dollars in cash. Philip Johnson, who in 1962 had bought his first Warhol, *Gold Marilyn,* for eight hundred dollars, purchased a disaster painting privately from Andy for thirty-five thousand, feeling reasonably sure that he was getting a bargain. "Painting isn't dead," he commented. "Not with the prices artists are getting."

The astonishing rise in his prices and the traveling retrospective pulled Andy back into the art world. He had wanted to focus on films, but the financial lure could not be ignored. In New York the art scene had become politicized. An "Artists' Coalition" had been formed, which was demanding a voice in the running of the Museum of Modern Art, and a protest had been organized at the museum. Andy was indifferent to all this. "The new art is really a business," he announced. "We want to sell shares in our company on Wall Street." In fact, his lawyers and accountants were busy establishing Andy Warhol Enterprises, Inc., as a bona fide corporation. Lest it be perceived by the Internal Revenue Service as a "personal holding company," one of the stipulations to Leo Castelli was that nowhere in future contracts should it be called for "a painting to be executed by Andy Warhol the individual."

Andy was proving himself an astute businessman. Vincent Fremont, a young man whom he had met in Los Angeles and who had replaced Billy Name as Factory manager, recalled: "All our lawyers and business advisers were always amazed at how good Andy was at really understanding the basic concepts of a deal. There was no question that he knew what he wanted."

In Fred Hughes he had someone who could make it happen. "Factory Fred," as Malanga dubbed him, took the widest view of Warhol as an artist, seeing it as perfectly likely that Andy might move into theater, television, or whatever, depending, he would say, on "the people you meet who take you one place or another." Hughes understood that Andy was an instinctive, intuitive person, whose habit was to go to his office every day and wait for something to happen. He also dreamed of elevating Andy and company to a world where they could "splurge on limousines and nice restaurants instead of waiting around for taxis." To attain that, Andy would have to start painting again. Andy responded by doing a new portfolio of flower prints, commissioned by the art dealer David Whitney, to be sold through the Castelli Gallery. He also completed a portrait commission, arranged by Hughes, of Dominique de Menil. As a result of Hughes's old connection to the Houston family, the de Menils had become the biggest collectors of Warhols in America. And there were ways beyond the art business to bring in money: In 1969 Andy appeared in an advertisement for Braniff Airlines with Sonny Liston. The copy read: "It happened on a Braniff plane: world heavyweight champ meets pop guru. Big ugly bear meets short chic painter. Silent spade meets honkie bullshitter. Meanest man alive meets strangest artist alive."

With Hughes as a companion, Andy had started collecting again. "I soon realized that Andy was an avid collector," recalled Hughes. "At his house on Lexington, I found rooms stacked with an extraordinary diversity of objects, from circus figures and carousel equipment to eccentric Victorian furniture, as well as the work of contemporary artists—a combination of the influences of his background: on the one hand, that of his mother with her whimsical sense of humor and love of buying little things from dime stores; on the other, that of so many European immigrants to New York who were amassing important art collections. When Andy discovered a new area of interest, he would become extremely covetous, forcing me to intercede in an attempt to dampen his frenzy. He had no pretensions to connoisseurship, and if American Indian baskets attracted him, he suddenly wanted lots of them. To him it was all so much fun—he would act like an excited child."

At the time, Andy's collecting frenzy was directed mainly at Art Deco objects and furniture and American Indian arts and crafts, both shrewd anticipations of the marketplace. (He was equally astute about real estate, which was then skidding into a postwar low in Manhattan. In 1970 he bought two buildings on the Lower East Side for fifteen thousand dollars. They would be worth a million dollars by the time he died.)

Collecting got Andy involved with a new social world, people like Peter Brant, a businessman and collector, and his wife, Sandy, who would become important business partners in the seventies. Hughes recalled: "On a trip to Paris in 1969, we and the Brants indulged in a rather well orchestrated treasure hunt for Art Deco pieces. The Brants led the way in finding the names of collectors from old exhibition catalogues and calling them up out of the blue."

After that trip, Andy began making Paris almost a second home, finding French society much more open to him than New York society had been, loving the emphasis on glamour, the easy mingling of art, aristocracy, and fashion. In time, Hughes developed a Warhol coterie that included Paloma Picasso, Eric de Rothschild, Yves Saint Laurent, and his partner, Pierre Bergé. When Andy and his entourage returned to Paris in September 1970 to film *L'Amour*, the fashion designer Karl Lagerfeld lent them his apartment as a set. ("We had run out of New York apartments," quipped Morrissey.) A vehicle for Jane Forth, playing an innocent abroad, *L'Amour* also featured Donna Jordan, another American waif, whose 1940s outfits—wedgies, padded shoulders, bright lipstick—helped inspire Saint Laurent's 1971 "look." Always a harbinger of fashion himself (his leather look in the sixties would become the uniform of punk rock), Andy was now wearing Saint Laurent, creating the role of the dandy (silk shirts, velvet jackets, designer ties) that he would maintain throughout the seventies—with his own touches (jeans, tie askew).

The year ended with a double triumph. In October, *Trash* opened at the thoroughly aboveground Cinema II in New York and was an immediate hit. Even the *Times* had come around: "*Trash*," wrote Vincent Canby, "could simply not have been made in any time or place but Spiro Agnew's America, which, in effect, the movie celebrates. . . . Its heart is counter-revolutionary." Holly Woodlawn was applauded as a "comic-book Mother Courage." *Trash* eventually did better than any other Warhol film, grossing $1.5 million. (One of its marketing innovations was Andy's use of consumer feedback: Moviegoers were interviewed as they left the theater, and their responses were used in the ads.)

In November the Warhol retrospective opened at the Musée d'Art Moderne in Paris and was heartily acclaimed: "The only great event," wrote one critic, "in an otherwise bleak period."

Paris was followed by London in February—with even greater success. For the Tate Gallery's catalogue of the retrospective, Richard Morphet noted the work's surprising "grandeur," its "tenderness and great passion." Andy himself afforded the British press great amusement: "He looks like a corpse which has somehow raised itself up off a cold stone slab and walked out of the mortuary," wrote Geoffrey Matthews in the *Evening News.* "He really ought to go back to the mortuary." The public was extremely disappointed not to find him on display after the opening reception: Andy and his entourage had flown to Germany for the Munich premiere of *Trash.*

"Andy was greeted in Germany with an enthusiasm bordering on adoration, more like a popular monarchist than a pop artist," wrote Bob Colacello in an article about the trip for the *Village Voice.* It was not much of an exaggeration. The first major study of Warhol had just been published, written by the German art historian Rainer Crone, and Colacello wrote of "Frankfurt boys of fifteen or sixteen [chasing] after us in the street clutching [the book], beaming ecstatically as Andy signed each and every one, 'To Mary—Andy Warhol.' " Moreover, *Flesh* (thanks partly to a sensational advertising campaign by its German distributor) had recently been one of the top-grossing films in German movie houses. *Stern,* the leading magazine, had no trouble getting special permission to pose Andy in the golden alcove of the castle at Neuschwanstein, intended for the throne of Ludwig II, the "mad" king of Bavaria. (The irony of Andy, the archcapitalist, being "crowned" in Germany was not lost on Robert Hughes, who later wrote: "The idea that Warhol could be the most interesting artist in modern history has regularly been echoed on the left—especially in Germany, where Warhol's status as a blue chip was largely underwritten by Marxists praising his 'radical' and 'subversive' credentials.")

Finally, after what a press release described as "a triumphal four-star tour of world art capitals," the Whitney Museum in New York performed the canonization. On April 26, 1971, the Whitney opened its version of the Andy Warhol retrospective and drew the biggest crowds since its Andrew Wyeth show in 1967. At Warhol's insistence, the huge fourth-floor space was covered from floor to ceiling with magenta and green "cow wallpaper," on which his mammoth serial paintings of soup cans, car crashes, electric chairs, flowers, Marilyn, Jackie, and the rest were hung in billboard size. The play of color and form reflected in the lights and polished floors was dizzying. Andy had wanted to create a show that "anyone could just get a flash of in a second as the elevator doors opened—and then split."

When the elevator doors opened that night and Andy stepped into the room, looking, in the words of one guest, "like an Andy Warhol doll in his corduroy jeans, DeNoyer jacket, and straw hair," and surrounded by his rag-tag harem of sexy boys and girls, and others less identifiable by gender, applause broke out—as well as hissing. The opening had turned into a happening. For the first time in New York, the reviews were unequivocal. "The plain inescapable fact, which will give pain to his enemies, is that Andy looks better than he has ever looked before," wrote John Canaday in the *Times*.

John Perrault in the *Village Voice* noted the aptness of the wallpaper: "He is, like a cow, whatever you need. To minimal people, he is minimal. To publicity art people, he is publicity. To boring people, he is camp. To lyrical abstractionists, he is lyricism. To decorators, he is decoration. To poets, he is poetry. To art critics, he is criticism. To filmmakers, he is film. To junkies, he is junk. To motherlovers, he is mother . . ."

Asked how he felt about all the attention, Andy said he was changing his name to John Doe. Then, opening his jacket, he pointed to his chest and said, "Here. Wanna feel my scar?"

20

FOR SEVERAL YEARS after the shooting, Andy had been a semi-invalid, looked after by the tireless, sweet-tempered Jed Johnson. In March 1969 he had had a follow-up operation to remove part of the bullet the doctors had left inside him. It was such a frightening experience that, according to his brother John, he developed a phobia about hospitals, announcing, "I never want to go in again, because I'll never come out alive." The doctors had sewn his stomach muscles back together in a way that obliged him to wear a surgical corset the rest of his life to prevent his stomach from blowing up like a balloon when he ate.

In the meantime, Julia Warhola's health had greatly deteriorated. Gerard Malanga had been struck by what a "spunky" character Julia was when he first met her in 1963. "She wasn't an old lady slugging along; she was very crisp. Don't forget she supported Andy through times of doubt. Of all the people who spent any time with him over a period of years, Julia was the only one who was there every day regardless of what happened. Andy was always the little boy with Julia."

By 1971, however, when Paul and John Warhola arrived for a visit, they found a different person. "On one occasion," Paul remembered, "she says to me out of the clear blue sky, 'Take me down to the other place. I don't wanna stay here. Take me to the other place.' She put her coat on. We went outside and I walked her around the corner maybe fifty feet, because she sort of shuffled, then came back to the house. She said, 'We're here. Oh!' she says, 'Thank you! It's so good to be back here.' She was beginning to be forgetful. She was having hardening of the arteries and getting Alzheimer's disease. Andy told me mother had to take fifteen pills at three different times a day. Andy took good care of her. It wasn't that easy. She was the type that wouldn't take the pills. She hid 'em and pretended she had. You had to say, 'No, you take it right now,' and even then she'd try not to swallow 'em."

She had begun wandering, disoriented, in the streets. "She would go out and leave the door open, forget where she went," recalled Jed Johnson. "We were afraid she'd get lost." John Warhola's wife, Marge, remembered being called in Pittsburgh on one such occasion by the New York City police: "They found her wandering on the street and knew who she was by the pills in her purse. It was getting to be hard for Andy. We suggested he maybe get a full-time nurse for her, but he didn't like having anybody in the house all the time, and she was fussy, too. She didn't like the maid Andy had, saying 'She's not doing this right!' And then there were all those kids climbing over that high fence in the backyard trying to get in to see Andy. It was really a difficult time."

Julia told Marge: "If Andy ever wants you to take me to Pittsburgh, don't do it, because I want to stay here and someday Andy's going to come home and he'll find me and I'll just fall asleep and die in my sleep. That is the way I want to die."

In February 1971, Julia suffered a stroke and was hospitalized in New York. When she was released, a semi-invalid, Andy decided she had to go home to Pittsburgh to be looked after by his brother Paul. John Warhola felt that this was a terrible thing to do: "Andy thought he was doing her good because Paul had the place out in the country. Well, the worst thing to do is take an older person like that from the environment she knew. She stayed with Paul for about a month. By then she was in a state of confusion where she didn't know where she was at."

At Paul's, Julia suffered a second stroke and was hospitalized for about a month. When she was released, Paul and his wife, Ann, put her in a nursing home. Paul Warhola recalled the family discussion over their decision: "Well, John called up Andy and says Andy was mad because we put her in a home. But we couldn't keep her. She was wandering too much and her mind was gone."

For the next year and a half, from New York or wherever he was in his travels, Andy called his mother regularly. But he never came to visit her, and he never saw her again.

Andy was now constantly on the move. In June 1971 he and Morrissey made several trips to Los Angeles to film *Heat,* a takeoff on Billy Wilder's *Sunset Boulevard,* with Sylvia Miles sending up Gloria Swanson as the aging screen goddess and Joe Dallesandro as a "former child star." The film also included a vivid performance by Andrea Feldman as a disturbed young mother who kept her baby quiet with sleeping pills and couldn't decide if she were a sadist or a masochist.

August was spent in a rented house in the Hamptons on eastern Long Island, where Paul and Jed edited *Heat.* In another farsighted real-estate move, Andy and Paul bought an estate, consisting of an old, high-ceilinged "lodge" and several smaller houses, at the easternmost end of the island in Montauk. Andy's attitude toward his new status as gentry permitted no illusions. "Montauk," he later wrote with Bob Colacello in *Exposures,*

> is a little town at the end of Long Island. The next stop is Lisbon, Portugal. Montauk is about one hour past Southampton, where I should have bought a house. At least there are people to go to lunch with. There's nothing in Montauk but a bunch of motels where the locals play pool all night long. Between Montauk Village and Montauk Point is Ditch Plains, Long Island's leading trailer park. All the people there look like they've taken too many hamburgers. . . . I never go [to the house] except as a guest. I rent it to friends every summer and wait to be invited. Actually I hope I'm never invited. I dread going there. I hate the sun. I hate the sea. I hate slipping between those damp wet sticky sheets.

"Everyone's back to beautiful clothes," Andy told Truman Capote. "The hippie look is really gone." And Andy, as always, was in vogue. His black leather had been replaced by velvet jackets, under which he wore European-designed shirts and even a tie. He had bought a miniature dachshund, Archie, which he carried around as part of the "look"—like Oscar Wilde's lily. He had "fallen in love" with Archie, he said, and was convinced the dog could talk.

Andy was also, that summer and fall, in the forefront of another trend: the fusion between fashion and rock. He designed the notorious "zipper cover" for the Rolling Stones' classic *Sticky Fingers* album, adding gay prurience to the steamy aura around rock's favorite bad boys. He joined the celebrities at the concert for Mick Jagger's twenty-ninth birthday at Madison Square Garden in the company of his new best friend, Bianca Jagger. And he was part of the vanguard at David Bowie's sold-out Carnegie Hall concert in September with another new best friend—Jackie Onassis's sister, Lee Radziwill.

In Bowie, he had inspired his first famous clone. Bowie, long a fan of Andy's for his myth-making abilities, had seen *Andy Warhol's Pork* in London that fall and been impressed by the trashy glitter of its costumes and gender-bending. Put together out of taped conversations between Andy and Brigid Polk by Anthony Ingrassia of the Theater of the Ridiculous, *Pork* centered on the curious character of one "B. Marlowe" (Andy) as he taped the scatological comments and snapped the obscene poses of "Amanda Pork" (Brigid), "Vulva" (Viva, played by a transvestite), and the "Pepsodent Twins," two nude boys with pastel-powdered genitals (based on Jay and Jed Johnson). Its "explicit" sexual content and "offensive" language (as the ad cautioned) had made it as scandalous a hit in London as it had been at its original venue, Café La Mama in New York. Bowie immediately befriended Anthony Zanetta, the young actor who had played B. Marlowe, who arranged for him to visit the Factory.

The meeting was tense. Bowie had brought along a recording of his new song, "Andy Warhol," which he insisted on playing for his idol. Andy responded, "That was great, thank you very much," but he was upset. "He thought it was horrible," recalled an observer. "Particularly the line about him looking 'a scream'—because he was very sensitive about what he looked like."

That evening Bowie had dinner with Lou Reed at Max's. The Velvet Underground singer was amused by Bowie's account of how "fascinating" the meeting had been because Andy had "nothing to say at all, absolutely nothing." Reed told the English rocker that the Velvets had once considered producing an Andy Warhol doll: You wound it up and it did nothing at all. But his encounter with Andy left its mark: By the autumn of 1972, Bowie's Warholian persona as "Ziggy Stardust" had become the focus of his show.

Led by Bowie, "glitter rock" (or "cock rock," as it was also called) became an enormously popular trend in the early seventies. One rock critic called 1972 "the year of the transsexual tramp," when "all of a sudden almost everyone in rock 'n' roll wanted to be—or at least suggest the possibility of being—a raging queen." "It was the homosexual time," recalled *Esquire's* Tom Hedley. "The faggots were our new niggers. Homosexuality was chic. There was a kind of angry gayness going on and we were very open to making faggots and lesbians our brothers. . . . They were the most stylish people in town, they ran the galleries, they had the best clubs, they had the best dinners. Andy was very involved with all that."

And it wasn't merely a New York phenomenon. Perhaps the clearest sign of Andy's impact on pop culture was the success of Lou Reed's hit single "Walk on the Wild Side" (produced by Bowie) with its caustic verses about Holly (Woodlawn), Little Joe (Dallesandro), the Sugar Plum Fairy, and Jackie (Curtis). The Factory was now a legend to be broadcast on radio stations around the world.

Once again, old Warholians were dismayed. Brigid Polk spoke for many when she told David Bailey in his 1971 documentary on Warhol: "I don't know a thing of what [Andy] is about, because since Fred Hughes came along about five years ago, Andy completely changed. Now I believe Andy to be a businessman, perhaps beginning an empire, and he is a man who goes to Grenouille for lunch every day. . . . He doesn't believe in art, yet he sneaks away to Switzerland to do prints, and he will say to you, 'Oh can't you find somebody to get me a forty-thousand-dollar portrait commission? I'll give you a good chunk, dear.'"

Andy's habit of using and discarding people without rewarding them financially was beginning to catch up with him. In 1971 Ronnie Tavel, who was broke, sued Andy for payment he believed was owed him for his fourteen "scripts" that had been made into Warhol films (including his contribution to *Chelsea Girls*). Back in 1965 Andy had proposed that they split any profits from the films three ways— among himself, Tavel, and the cast. Tavel had never been paid a dime, and his memory of trying to bring Andy to account tells much about the psychological "glue" of the Factory: "Andy was shocked that I would betray him as an artist—this is why he felt hurt when I brought suit against him. He assumed that I should excuse all faults and all shortcomings, and he plunked down $25,000 to get the lawyers of Princess Radziwill to represent him because he would rather beat me out of this than give me what I deserved.

"One morning, he said, 'Ronnie, can't we settle this another way? I can give you a painting or something. Let's go to Hollywood and make a movie—you know I like your work.' I said, 'Andy, it's too late to talk about that.' The hurt in his face! I can't describe the sense of betrayal that was in his face. It was like saying to me, 'I know I've screwed you left and right, but you ought to understand this as another artist. This is the way I am and this is the way it has to be.' And I felt very guilty about it. There were so many people who didn't understand and who attacked him, the least he could expect from me was to understand and not say anything, be exploited, be shit upon, be used for my talent. His face said, I was hurt because you have gotten benefits out of this, you have been privileged to move in a charmed circle and rub shoulders, plus you got fourteen of your scripts done and learned enormously from it. It was one artist saying, If there is anything we can hold onto it is that another artist will not betray us in this world! And now you are doing that.

"The legal hearings just drained me. I dropped the suit because I couldn't take it; it was destroying my life; the hatred was making me into a hateful person. I also saw that it wasn't going to work. Some-time afterward I was walking up Park Avenue in the snow, a bitter cold night, and something told me to stop and just let the snow come down. There he was just standing in a doorway absolutely alone. I moved a few steps toward him. He must have been waiting for some people but there wasn't another person around, and we stood for a while and said nothing. Then I went on. That was the last time I ever saw him."

In November 1971 Edie Sedgwick died, choking on her vomit after a night of drinking and drug-taking in Santa Barbara, California, where she was living with her husband, Michael Post. Brigid phoned Andy to tell him the news. Andy asked: "How could she do a thing like that?" Then he asked whether he would inherit Edie's money. When Brigid said that Edie didn't have any money, Andy changed the subject.

With the success of the traveling retrospective and the enormous surge in his prices (the early works now averaged thirty thousand dollars), it was time to make a major—and well-publicized—return to painting. Richard Nixon had just made his world-opening trip to China. What better image for 1972 than the revolutionary chic of Chairman Mao? Working from a frontispiece of the famous "Little Red Book," *The Quotations of Chairman Mao,* Andy executed enough Mao paintings—more than two thousand—to fill a small museum. They ranged in size from seventeen by thirteen feet to six by six inches and included a number of rolls of purple-and-white Mao wallpaper. He completed the Mao paintings in three months.

As always, the color combinations of the silk-screened images were striking, transforming the chairman's inscrutable mask into an attractive, at times comic caricature. To give the paintings more "style," Andy was now adding hand-painted squiggles and free-form brushstrokes reminiscent of the mock action painting of his earliest cartoon and advertising canvases. Quickly and seemingly haphazardly adding these touches to rows of Mao portraits on the floor at the Factory, he explained to visitors that "it's easier to be sloppy than to be neat." The "hand-painted look," he declared, was now "in fashion."

Henry Geldzahler, for one, was delighted by the Mao paintings: "The irony that is obvious and front-row center in these images is the fact that they are produced cheaply to be sold dearly by an artist in the capitalistic capital of the world."

Fred Hughes had played a key role as a middleman between Warhol and Bruno Bischofberger, a Zurich-based art dealer and Warhol collector who had commissioned the Maos and who arranged for the first exhibition of the new paintings in Basel, Switzerland, that fall. At Hughes's instigation, Andy's return to painting would be characterized by two important changes: From this point on, all new Warhol artworks would also be reproduced as prints to be sold in signed portfolios; moreover, he would work mostly on commission.

About charges that Andy had begun to prostitute himself, Hughes said: "Andy did like the idea of making money, but he had a rather sweet, childish idea of how that's done. I was about the only person who could say, 'Andy, you're full of shit on this one!' But then you had to be careful, because some of his craziest ideas when they first hit you were the best ideas."

Although he was now a major player in the New York art scene, Fred Hughes was seemingly content to remain in the shadow of his famous boss and friend, which is one of the reasons he lasted longer than just about anyone else around Andy. At one point he appeared on the best-dressed list and was squiring some of the most fashionable women around town. But soon he ducked back into his hole, where he labored, invisible to the public, as chief architect of Warhol's career. The kind of subtle humiliation he had to endure over those years was bound to take its toll on anyone, perhaps accounting for Hughes's tendency to easy inebriation. Under the influence of a few drinks, his impeccable mask would dissolve to reveal the soul of an English public-school boy boasting of his lineage—in his case fictitious.

Brigid Polk, the only person from the "right" background at the Factory, was particularly contemptuous of Hughes's phony bearing and accent. So was Suzi Frankfurt: "Fred sounded like such a jerk most of the time with the art dealers, but Andy must have liked it because there was never any criticism. He used to say how cute Fred was: 'Oh, Fred gets so drunk!' Maybe Andy thought that was the aristocratic thing to do. It was real convenient for Andy to believe that Fred was such an aristocrat and was so rich because then Andy didn't have to pay him very much."

And, as everyone around Andy realized, if Fred exaggerated the importance of his role, well, that *was* his role—to exaggerate the importance of his role.

Simultaneously with the Mao images, Andy finished another series, this one commissioned by supporters of the Democratic presidential hopeful, Senator George McGovern. "Vote McGovern," as the set was called, was a portrait of his Republican opponent, Richard Nixon, painted in pointedly repellent colors—yellow mouth, blue jowls, green upper face. Henry Geldzahler declared the work "a latter-day disaster painting. The anger and horror Warhol feels for Richard Nixon is sharp and unrelenting." Over the summer of 1972, the poster raised forty thousand dollars for the McGovern campaign (but, as one writer noted, it may have promoted *both* candidates).

After Nixon's landslide victory that fall, Warhol—like Norman Mailer, Terry Southern, Robert Rauschenberg, and other writers and artists who in one way or another had criticized the president— was audited by the Internal Revenue Service. As Rauschenberg remembered, "Andy Warhol and I were on the IRS list because we were politically involved. It nearly made me bankrupt. The guy from the IRS said that if I didn't just sign the agreement, he would go and do the same thing to all the artists and friends that I had ever paid or known."

Andy, recalled Factory manager Vincent Fremont, was "hit with a gift tax. Although he gave the poster as a gift to the McGovern campaign, we ended up having to pay money on top of it. After that we looked into the legal ramifications of whatever contributions we made and made much tighter contracts. Whether Andy was on Nixon's hit list or not we didn't know, but he was audited up until the time he died."

To keep a better account of his deductible expenses, Andy began dictating a daily diary to his secretary, Pat Hackett. She had been with him since 1969 and would stay until he died. Pat was not a glamorous Warhol superstar but a trusted and reliable friend. She was also a good writer. She would record his diary every morning for the next fifteen years, and came to know more about his personal life and opinions than anyone else. In addition to documenting all his tax deductions, she was keeping an oral history of his increasingly glamorous life.

Women in Revolt finally opened in February 1972, getting some of the best reviews ever received by a Warhol film. The *Time*'s Vincent Canby wrote: "Probably no man, not even Norman Mailer, will ever have the last word on women's liberation, but until one does, perhaps the Andy Warhol–Paul Morrissey *Women in Revolt* will do." Because of a bad distribution deal, the film achieved none of the success of *Trash*, but the Warhol–Morrissey team's "auteurship" was now widely recognized, and both the Venice and New York film festivals accepted their newest collaboration, *Heat*, for fall premieres. Andy, Paul, Fred, Joe Dallesandro, and Sylvia Miles attended the celebrity-studded affair on the Lido in September, and prepared themselves for the even splashier showing of the film in New York in October. Between the two events, however, Andrea Feldman, one of the film's stars, committed suicide.

She had been showing signs of being disturbed throughout the summer, calling herself "Andrea Warhola," apparently in the hope that Andy would marry her. The success of *Trash* had gone to her head. She would screech, "They come to see meeee! Not you, Andy Warhooool!" On another occasion, she exploded with "You fag! You asshole! You Warhole!" until finally Andy, in one of his rare rages, screamed back, "Get out of here! Get out of here! And never come back!" One day she had come to the Factory, her face covered with scabs and small sores. Someone said to Andy, "She's very sick. Andrea should go to a hospital. Did you see her face?" Andy replied matter-of-factly: "Well, she's putting cigarettes out on her face. She always does that," adding (his stock response to such situations) that Andrea was "just going through a phase."

One night in September, after writing letters to people with whom she had been fighting ("I'm going for the big time—Heaven," she wrote her mother), she made a date with several friends, including Jim Carroll, to whom she promised: "You'll see something special." By the time Carroll arrived to meet her at her apartment on Fifth Avenue at Twelfth Street, police cars and an ambulance had already converged: Andrea had jumped out of a top-story window, clutching a can of Coca-Cola and a rosary.

The media would make much of Feldman's suicide, with Andy cast as Satan disguised as the Pied Piper. Dotson Rader wrote in *Esquire*: "It is appropriate that Andrea died clinging to two symbols of Western Culture, and leaving behind letters addressed to a third. Because Andy Warhol is nothing if not a symbol to the young. He represents limitless tolerance, deliverance from loneliness and alienation. He is a parental figure, a father to the young, to this present generation which cannot connect with its parents or with the world in which it grew up." Clouded by Feldman's suicide, *Heat* was seen by some as the rankest form of exploitation. Said Peter Schjeldahl in the *New York Times*: "Miss Feldman, with her twisted little face and frightening laugh, was clearly in a bad way, and the pitiless exposure of her suicidal mood makes *Heat* a repellent document."

Most of the Factory people refused to blame Andy. Vincent Fremont said: "Andy was always concerned about people. He'd give them advice and was very kind, but they don't listen. I don't think people realize he had that compassion; they just thought he was a cold stone. But with someone like Andrea, I don't think you could do anything."

Andrea's best friend, Geraldine Smith, agreed: "I don't think Andy ever destroyed anybody. That's such a crock of shit. Andrea was fucked up in her childhood. Her mother left her alone when she was two years old and she never got over that. She was obsessed about getting her mother's love. She was hospitalized a couple of times. She always planned to commit suicide. But she would blame Andy and say terrible things about him."

As for Andy himself, Smith recalled that he "didn't say much about Andrea's death." But he later told Truman Capote: "She seemed so strong and if I'd thought she was really going to do something like that I would have really tried to help."

Andy was in Los Angeles for the opening of *Heat* when his mother died on November 22. "Promise me you'll take care of Andy," she said to Paul Warhola, her last words to her eldest son. "I want you to look after him because sometimes I wonder if he don't have a childish mind."

John Warhola had been unable to find Andy to give him the news, and he didn't hear about his mother's death until he was back in New York. "I talked to him on the phone," recalled John. "I told him, 'I have some bad news.' I was broken up, but he took the death pretty good. He says, 'Uh . . . aaahh . . . well, don't cry.' He didn't want to let me know how bad he felt."

Julia left nine thousand dollars, to be divided equally among her three sons, and a five-hundred-dollar life insurance policy. She was buried under the same tombstone as her husband in Saint John the Divine Cemetery in a suburb of Pittsburgh, on a grassy sloping hill overlooking a highway. Andy paid for but did not attend the funeral. Paul Warhola remembered: "I covered up for him. I told relatives he happened to be out of the country. Andy didn't want to see nobody dead. He was deathly afraid. He says to me one time,

'You know what, Paul, I don't want you to feel bad that I didn't come, but, uh, you know, I want to remember Mother as she was.' "

To his associates at the Factory, Andy was close-mouthed about his mother's death. It was many weeks before Jed Johnson heard that Julia had died, and "a couple of years" before Vincent Fremont found out. "I knew Andy for twelve years," said Johnson, "and he never talked about anything personal to me, *ever*." Fred Hughes recalled being "aware" of Julia's death. "But it was a big thing and Andy was very private about that. One *suspected* it had a particularly strong effect on him, but Andy couldn't or wouldn't show it."

To his family, however, Andy seems to have been more open about his feelings. George Warhola, one of his nephews, came to stay with his uncle in New York for a month after Julia's death. "He almost had a nervous breakdown," he recalled of Andy. "He had a handkerchief of [Julia's], and he didn't want anybody to see him, but he'd take off his wig and put the handkerchief on his head. Someone sent him a picture of my grandmother in her coffin and he was very upset about that. When Uncle Andy was by himself, he was very unhappy. He was like lost—he always had to be around people to lift him up."

Marge Warhola, George's mother, recalled Andy's telling her that Julia's death was "always on my mind" and adding: "I should never have sent her to Pittsburgh. I feel so guilty."

Two years later, Andy painted several portraits of Julia—smiling, wise-looking, bespectacled, and surrounded by agitated brushstrokes. One critic called it "a haunting memory, at once closed and distant." To others it looked strikingly like Andy himself, dressed as an old woman. Andy's brothers were unaware of the picture until Paul spotted it on the cover of *Art in America* in January 1975. Andy made several copies of the painting but didn't give one to Paul even though he knew he would have liked one.

In the winter of 1972, Andy cultivated the friendship of two of New York's most glamorous older women—Paulette Goddard and Diana Vreeland—in an attempt, perhaps, to replace his mother with more dazzling stand-ins. Goddard he admired for being "one of the smartest of all the Hollywood stars because she didn't end up broke." Vreeland, the fashion guru, he described as "the most copied woman in the world . . . like a Campbell's soup can." Both women responded warmly to Andy's attentions, propelling him into social echelons he had only dreamed about. He was now moving in the worlds of high gossip and high fashion, and surrounding himself with a new breed of acolyte, young men who were well scrubbed and socially, if not artistically, ambitious.

Chief among them was Bob Colacello, who had studied international affairs at Georgetown University and had now become Andy's diplomat. Old Warhol admirers deplored the new clique: "I saw Colacello as a symbol of the social butterflies who were about to take over the culture," said Tom Hedley of *Esquire*. "He also struck me as the kind of guy who was sucking Andy dry. There was a moment when Andy created interesting reflections of his own vanity and confusion and moral ambiguity. But then he began creating parasites on his own energy, which is very deadening and boring for an artist to do."

"It was the end of the underground," one Warhol associate noted. "The people at the Factory were becoming yuppies, but nobody knew what a yuppie was yet." Indeed, the Factory itself now looked like a hip advertising agency on Madison Avenue: Art Deco desks, a receptionist's nook, and Dutch doors near the elevator. The installation of a receptionist and the new doors was as much a matter of security as of corporate image: Andy had been lax about access to the Factory after the shooting, but in the spring of 1972, there had been a robbery in which personal effects were stolen. One of John Chamberlain's crushed-car sculptures was brought down from Andy's house to block the way "in case girls came in and wanted to shoot Andy," Morrissey said, although another factory worker saw it as "a marvelous place to stash drugs."

That winter Andy took a holiday with Suzi Frankfurt, Jed Johnson, Fred Hughes, and the Brants at the ski resort of Saint Moritz in Switzerland. They stayed at the grand Palace Hotel, where Andy spent most of his days in the lobby. They hobnobbed with the Gianni Agnellis and the Stavros Niarchoses and other European plutocrats—"the sort of people [who] generate more portraits," Hughes noted.

"Switzerland," Andy declared, "is my favorite place now because it's so nothing. And everybody's rich."

21

I<small>N THE SUMMER</small> of 1973, Andy was in Rome working at the Cinecittà film studio on *Flesh for Frankenstein* and *Blood for Dracula*. As a filmmaker, he was now big-time: His co-producer on both films was the Italian movie mogul, and husband of Sophia Loren, Carlo Ponti. Andrew Braunsberg, the London producer who had set up the deal, had raised $700,000 from Ponti, Cinerama in Germany, and Jean-Pierre Rassam in France. Roman Polanski was a silent partner.

Ponti had welcomed the hard-working, efficient team to his fold. When Morrissey had met with Braunsberg and Ponti earlier that year to discuss making a 3-D version of *Frankenstein*, they quickly reached an agreement for Morrissey to make the film on a $300,000 budget. He and Warhol would receive a fee in advance and have a share in the profits, but Ponti would control all distribution. Ponti then asked Paul how long the film would take to shoot. "Three weeks," said Morrissey. Sensing an easy mark, Ponti said, "Why don't you take six weeks and make two films? What could the second one be?"

"*Dracula!*" suggested Braunsberg.

Besides Morrissey, the Warhol entourage included Joe Dallesandro, who was to star in both films, Jed Johnson, who had already been in Rome for several months doing the complex pre-production work, and Fred Hughes, who was to be the art director of both movies (which may have accounted for the casting of the German actor Udo Kier, who was the spitting image of Fred, as Count Dracula). They moved into Roman Polanski's house, the Villa Mandorli, on the Via Appia Attica, where they were soon joined by Bob Colacello. Polanski was so repulsed by their taste in friends, which, he wrote, "was snobbishly confined to the ultrachic and aristocratic upper crust of Rome society," that he got himself another place and abandoned the Villa Mandorli to the Roman Factory.

The acting troupe was an international hodgepodge, including Dallesandro and Kier, the distinguished Italian director Vittorio de Sica, the actress Monique Van Vooren, the English socialite Maxine McKendry, and Polanski in a cameo appearance. Because English was a second language for many, improvised dialogue wouldn't work, and Morrissey, in addition to coping with the technical problems of directing his first 35-mm film in 3-D, found himself typing scripts into the early hours of the morning until Andy sent Pat Hackett over as a script collaborator. She wrote a good deal of dialogue for *Dracula*, which was much the wittier of the two films.

Andy's international life style crystalized that summer. He jetted back and forth from Rome to New York, where he was doing a number of commissioned portraits. He talked like a star-struck kid about the publicity shots his actors made with Sophia Loren, about the excitement over Jed's sixteen-year-old sister Susan's having been with Paul Getty, grandson of the oil billionaire, the night he was kidnapped. Paulette Goddard, Anita Loos, Franco Rossellini, Gina Lollobrigida, the French actress Anna Karina, the fashion designer Valentino, and other high-flyers came by the big house on the old Roman way. Bob Colacello roped in the socialites; no party was complete without the presence of Andy and friends.

"In Rome I discovered a new Andy," the Factory's Italian connection Daniela ·Morera, recalled: "He was social, he was glamorous. He said, 'This is the real Hollywood, Cinecittà in Rome, *La Dolce Vita*, everybody fantastic!' Andy's photograph was in all the gossip magazines. And he also had the respect of the intellectuals. I always heard very high level people in Europe, especially in Italy, talking about Andy in a way I never heard in America."

Frankenstein was shot first. With its scenes of 3-D gore popping out at the audience, it was not just a parody of blood-guts-and-vomit movies such as the popular *Exorcist*; it was also, in its scenes of Udo Kier caressing human spare parts, a kind of acting-out of Andy's death demons. "Andy once told me that he felt as if he would pop open someday," Morrissey recalled. "When I finished *Frankenstein*, I thought it might be a kind of exorcism for Andy and all the people who are crippled and haunted by some nut case. And then I added laughter, because that's the only way we survive." One of Dr. Frankenstein's memorable lines in the film touched directly on a personal problem of Andy's: "To appreciate life, you must first learn to fuck death in the gallbladder!" For just like his father before him, Andy had earlier that year developed a problem with his gallbladder. His doctor had strongly advised him to have it taken out, but Andy's fear of hospitals was as strong as his mother's had been, and he refused. In *Dracula*, there were unavoidable suggestions of Andy as well: This was no lusty Transylvanian aristocrat but a pale, passive ascetic, embarrassed by his roots, lost in the modern world. While Paul and Jed stayed to edit *Frankenstein* and *Dracula* at Cinecittà, Andy flew back to New York.

In early August he returned to Rome to film a cameo appearance as himself in a movie called *The Driver's Seat*, which starred Elizabeth Taylor, who had just broken up with Richard Burton. Andy celebrated his forty-fifth birthday on August 6 practicing his lines for his first scene with Liz the next day. "Let's go. Let's go. I fear I am already dangerously late" sounded nothing like him, but the scene went smoothly enough after a few takes, and the star invited him for a drink in her trailer. Assured that he wasn't carrying his tape recorder, she latched onto Andy as a confidant. They met again for lunch a few days later. "The whole time Liz was talking, she was pulling leaves off a bush next to the table," Bob Colacello recalled. "One by one she plucked every leaf off that tree and then stacked them all in the middle of the glass table. It was such bizarre behavior. She kept telling Andy how much Richard meant to her and how important it was to her to be married to him and how destroyed she was by the breakup. When she started getting really agitated, Andy looked nervous. So I went over to him, but Liz screamed at me, 'Get out of here! Just get the hell out of here!' "

Back in the fall of 1969, Andy had casually started an underground movie magazine called *Interview*, edited by Gerard Malanga. During its first few years the monthly publication had crept along, acquiring a small, loyal audience, but it had yet to establish a distinctive style and voice. By 1973, the magazine had gone through twelve editors, caused a lot of friction among its staff, and was losing enough money to make Andy consider dropping it. Hughes suggested: "Let's get rid of the idea of doing an underground film magazine written by poets and artists and make a whole different magazine. Let's make it a magazine for people like us!" By that Hughes meant people dedicated to the pursuit of conspicuous consumption and fashion—fashion in clothes, in the new "hot" faces of the entertainment industry, in clubs and hangouts, in expensive decoration. He rounded up investors, including Bruno Bischofberger, Andy's Swiss art dealer; Peter Brant, who now owned *Art in America* and *Antiques* magazines; and Joe Allen, Brant's partner in the company that sold *Interview* its paper. Rosemary Kent, who had been with *Women's Wear Daily*, was brought in to edit the new *Interview*, but she and Andy did not get along, and she was soon replaced by Bob Colacello. "We're trying to reach high-spending people," announced Colacello. "The trend in our society is toward self-indulgence and we encourage that. We're not interested in journalism so much as taste-setting. We're the *Vogue* of entertainment."

Produced in an outsize format, *Interview* pioneered the "style" magazines that would proliferate in the eighties: elaborately lit, studio-shot photography of celebrities on the newsprint of a tabloid; ads pushing the latest in personal adornment; close-up views of the newly rich and famous going about their lives. Chief among its innovative features were Fran Lebowitz's column "I Cover the Waterfront," which became the basis of her best-selling *Metropolitan Life*, and the totally unstructured celebrity interview, whose best practitioner was Andy himself.

Arriving at the subject's hotel suite or home without any agenda of questions to be asked, turning on his tape recorder and just letting it run, then printing a virtually unedited transcript, he achieved a Warhol voice-portrait, as in this exchange with the singer-comedienne Bette Midler:

BETTE MIDLER: Have you ever been to Hawaii?
ANDY WARHOL: Yes. As soon as you get off the plane it smells like sex.
BETTE MIDLER: Is that what your sex life smells like? Gee . . . Where've you been hanging out?
ANDY WARHOL: No, but it does smell like sex, doesn't it? And everybody goes there for sex because it smells that way. Don't they? I think they do.
BETTE MIDLER: Well, Hawaii doesn't smell like sex to me. It's the only place in the world that smells like that to me, but it's not sex, it's freedom.

And as the Midler conversation shows, the magazine was a vehicle for Andy not only to meet the most interesting people of the day but also to advertise himself. In Bob Colacello's diary column "Out," readers were treated to a monthly chronicle of Andy and the gang's every social appearance, complete with reports of *their* conspicuous consumption. For example, the November 9, 1973, issue ran a description of them all having dinner at Pearl's, the fashionable Chinese restaurant, with the following information: "Bob Colacello in his emerald green corduroy suit by Polidori of Rome, Yves Saint Laurent silk shirt, Givenchy cologne; Vincent Fremont in his dark brown custom tailored gabardine jacket, tan pants, white Brooks Brothers shirt; Jed Johnson in blue Yves Saint Laurent blazer, light blue Brooks Brothers shirt, striped tie from Tripler's, New Man pants; Andy Warhol in his chestnut DeNoyer velveteen jacket, Levis, boots by Berlutti di Priigi, Brooks Brothers shirt, red and gray Brooks Brothers tie, brown wool V-neck Yves Saint Laurent pullover."

The Hughes-Colacello approach soon began to pay off: *Interview's* circulation rose from thirty-one thousand to seventy-four thousand in six months, and its ad revenues increased from $1,800 to $7,000 an issue in the same period. Daniela Morera, who commuted between Milan and New York as the magazine's European correspondent, saw *Interview* as Andy's way of bringing "the life he discovered in Europe back to New York." To earlier toilers around the Factory, it marked a new, unattractive snobbishness in Andy. As Ronnie Tavel observed, "There was an underbelly to Andy that was very ugly—bigotry, racism, class."

As a painter, Andy continued to shine more brightly in Europe than in America. In Paris at the Musée Galliera in February 1974, he showed the Mao paintings in a spectacular installation, lining up the painted variations in horizontal rows and mounting them on "Mao wallpaper"—a sea of Mao images larger in scale than the painted ones. As the critic Charles Stuckey wrote: "Altogether, 1,951 images of Mao loomed and receded as painting and decoration in tandem orchestrated the gallery space."

Arriving to inspect the show, Andy commented to Fred: "Gee, these paintings are great."

"Now, don't forget you painted them," Hughes advised.

The critical reaction was, once again, positive—most eloquently a month later in a London *Times* review of an exhibition at the Mayor Gallery of eight preparatory drawings for the Mao series that hailed Andy as "the most serious artist to have emerged anywhere since the war, and the most important American artist. . . . Warhol is in some ways like Oscar Wilde. He hides a deep seriousness and commitment behind a front of frivolity."

The Mao paintings also showed, as Carter Ratcliff noted, the artist's uncanny sense of irony about himself: "Having arrived at the upper levels of the consumer worlds . . . Warhol opened his art to an icon from China, a nation dedicated to eradicating whatever vestiges of bourgeois consumerism might linger in its citizenry. . . .Warhol showed uncanny acuteness in introducing the Mao image into his art at a time when the artist himself was just coming to enjoy, full-scale, the benefits of Western 'decadence.' "

Andy Warhol's Frankenstein had proved a hard sell to American film distributors, but eventually a deal was cut with the leading distributors of pornographic films in the United States—known to the Factory only as "the Purino brothers"—who had recently made a killing with *Deep Throat*. On May 19 *Frankenstein* was given a lavish champagne and caviar premiere at the Trans Lux East Theater in New York. Among the notables who watched the flying gore through 3-D glasses were the socialites Patricia Kennedy Lawford, Mrs. William F. Buckley, Jr., Diane and Egon von Furstenberg, and Princess Yasmin Aga Khan, the daughter of Rita Hayworth and Prince Aly Khan. It did not go unnoticed in the press that two days later, fitting neatly into the Warhol saga, Candy Darling died at twenty-five of leukemia.

The film was a box-office hit, grossing over $1 million during its first two months, despite generally unflattering reviews. By the summer, with bookings scheduled at an additional 150 theaters, *Frankenstein* was projected to earn a minimum of $10 million in the months ahead. "Audiences are laughing at *Frankenstein*, his sexually repressed bug-eyed assistant, and the doctor's sister wife who makes the fatal mistake of seducing a zombie," noted Paul Gardner in the *New York Times*. "When asked what he does, since Morrissey receives credit as writer-director on their films, Warhol says, 'I go to the parties.'"

Andy's euphoria over the fruits of their Roman summer was short-lived. Since Carlo Ponti controlled the film's distribution, Andy looked to him for an accounting of sums due Andy Warhol Enterprises, and it soon became clear that none would be forthcoming. "First," Vincent Fremont recalled, "Ponti claimed that *Frankenstein* did not make any money in North America." The astonished Factory team could not believe the Italian producer's gall. According to the movie trade's bible, *Variety, Frankenstein* had grossed $4 million (on an investment of $300,000). Furthermore, the Purino brothers informed Morrissey that they had collected rentals of $20 million on the film. Over the next four years, the mystery of *Frankenstein*'s profits was to strain Morrissey's relationship with Warhol beyond the breaking point, teach Andy a hard lesson about the realities of the movie industry—and yield no money for them at all.

Another upshot of this debacle was that *Andy Warhol's Dracula*, a far superior film to *Frankenstein*, was unceremoniously dumped; it was released with little fanfare and quickly disappeared. When Hughes and Fremont tried to collect from Ponti the money they believed was rightfully theirs, they discovered what anybody who has ever tried to sue internationally for collection of royalties learns: that it is a fool's game conducted around evaporating lawyers who "cannot be reached."

"Andy," recalled Fremont, "was very irritated. He was not a person to lose money. He didn't understand subtraction, he only understood addition."

Finally, Andy Warhol Enterprises managed to get an injunction preventing both films from doing any business in America, where-upon Ponti's son appeared out of the blue with a deal to return the rights to Warhol. No sooner had Andy regained the rights, how-ever, than the Factory resold the American distribution rights to Landmark Films for "next to peanuts" in a deal that still had Fre-mont shaking his head years later; Landmark made another million dollars on the picture, none of which went to Andy.

Typically, in the face of this fiasco, Andy boldly decided to expand his business. For some time now he had been bursting out of his Union Square offices, renting other rooms in the building to house *Interview* and even an extra space on the tenth floor in which to paint. At one point he considered buying the whole building. When this didn't pan out, he decided the time had come to move again.

One day, gazing across Union Square, Fremont and Hughes noticed a large FOR RENT sign on the corner building at 860 Broad-way. At first the building's agent put them off. He had no interest in renting the space to a freak like Andy Warhol. But when Hughes and Fremont showed up at the office of the owner, Edward Gordon, they discovered that he was married to the sister of the painter Larry Rivers. The ice broke and a deal was made.

The third floor of 860 Broadway consisted of a suite of offices that had been renovated by S&H Green Stamps in the 1920s. It featured a corporate wood-paneled boardroom or dining room equipped with a small kitchen, a large kidney-shaped reception room, and two broad galleries running through to the back, where there were a number of smaller rooms that could be used as offices, storage space, or painting studios. The 12,500-square-foot rental was a per-fect fit for the expanding Andy Warhol Enterprises, and in August 1974, the move began. Ever economical, Andy made it a condition that visitors had to carry at least one item across the street to the new Factory.

Fremont recalled: "We sweated through the move to get the bills paid. Fred and I were on the phone constantly trying to make deals.

Andy rose to the occasion, doing more prints and appearing in a series of advertisements for Pioneer stereo equipment." Still, it was a stretch. His overhead had more than doubled; as ever, he seethed with inner conflicts about the direction he was going in.

The new offices were empty and bleak when the first crates were unpacked in early September. "It was cold, and we were all shivering," Warhol's new silk-screen assistant, Ronnie Cutrone, recalled. "We unrolled a giant old flower canvas—a big bright yellow flower—and we all sat around it as though it was a campfire. Andy said, 'What . . . whu . . . whatever happened to the sixties?' In other words: Whatever happened to bright yellow flowers?"

22

A S THE SEVENTIES shifted into high gear, Andy Warhol Enterprises developed into the best team Andy had ever had. Fred Hughes worked out of a large screened-off space to the right of the reception room. Bob Colacello ruled over *Interview* in a small, elegantly furnished office at the end of a long gallery. Andy had two rooms beyond Bob's. The small one he turned into a trash dump, the other was his painting space. In a cubbyhole between the reception room and the dining room Vincent Fremont, the office manager, kept watch.

Ronnie Cutrone would be Andy's full-time painting assistant for the next ten years. He was another of the angelic-looking hustler types, like Malanga and Giorno, that Andy favored. Swarthy, short, and muscular, with a dancer's balance, he resembled the Silver Factory pioneers more than the middle-class kids who were taking over. His experimental spirit would be a vital arrow in Andy's quiver throughout the seventies. Andy also hired Rupert Smith as his silkscreen printer and art director. Smith would become another lifer.

As personal secretary and diarist he still had steady, enthusiastic Pat Hackett, just the sort of empathic woman, like Ellie Simon and Gretchen Schmertz, in whom Andy had always been able to confide.

And he still commanded the loyalty of Jed Johnson, who was trying to find a new house for Andy. Now, for the first time in his career, every aspect of Andy's needs was in the hands of a competent person. All the Warhol activities were now under Andy Warhol Enterprises and at the "office," as the new generation called the Factory, Warhol was no longer "Drella." He was "the boss."

Andy would usually arrive around noon. After rifling through the telephone messages and mail, he would check in with Hughes, Colacello, and Fremont. Most often, their conversation, laced with bitchy gossip, would begin with a review of the previous night's social rounds and then move on to the central concern of the day: Who was coming to lunch? Arranging the ritual lunches was one of Colacello's responsibilities, and, under his supervision, the midday gatherings took on a stylized format consisting, he recalled, of "two socialites, one Hollywood starlet, one European title, and the victim"—a prospective portrait commission or advertiser in *Interview*. (Andy still paid his staff fairly low salaries but did give them the incentive of commissions if they brought in an ad for the magazine or a portrait-sitter.) Colacello had the special talent (which Andy did not) of remembering who was in town, arranging compatible tablemates, and making the seemingly endless calls to get people to come. The setting was the wood-paneled dining room gone slightly berserk: a large oval French Art Deco table, over which loomed an enormous nineteenth-century painting, *The Wind,* by David Forrester Wilson, a stuffed moosehead, and several Swahili ancestor-worship poles.

It was decided that watercress, smoked salmon, and caviar sandwiches (like those Diana Vreeland served at the Metropolitan Museum of Art) were too expensive, and the menus became formalized: pasta salads from the Greenwich Village specialty store Balducci's for portrait clients, and quiche and pâtés from the Three Little Pigs for advertisers. The bar was stocked with Stolichnaya vodka, Cuervo Gold tequila, and the other fashionable drinks advertised in *Interview.* Throughout lunch, Andy poured wine for his guests while remaining abstemious himself. He had become careful about what he ate, but would often go on eccentric eating jags—for example, having a bean sandwich every day for two weeks, then suddenly switching to something else, like the Filet o' Fish from the McDonald's across the street.

If the banquet did not produce immediate results, clients were invited back for an even more celebrity-packed lunch or flattered by a tape-recorded story on them in *Interview*.

For all the glamour of the guest list and the swagger of the setting, these lunches were usually anxious affairs. Before the guests arrived, Andy, adjusting his wig and putting on makeup, would sometimes start to shake all over. Once everyone was seated, he sat, mostly speechless, while Colacello and Hughes tried to keep the chatter going. Ronnie Cutrone recalled the occasions as "awkward, brittle, and stiff. Most of the people genuinely bored me to tears, and they were so nervous. I would sit there drinking Bloody Marys, watching two sets of people being nervous."

After lunch, Andy would usually spend the afternoon painting, assisted by Cutrone, a talented artist in his own right, who had first joined the Warhol circle as a dancer with the Exploding Plastic Inevitable. The demand for Warhol portraits was booming now that Andy had scored with the likes of Gianni and Marella Agnelli, Saint Laurent, Brigitte Bardot, Bianca Jagger, Brooke Hopper, and the hottest fashion designer of the moment, Halston. By the fall of 1974, the portrait business was well on its way to becoming a million-dollar-a-year operation. Anyone could have a portrait painted by Warhol for twenty-five thousand dollars, the price of a forty-by-forty-inch canvas. A nonrefundable ten-thousand-dollar deposit was all that was required in most cases. Andy usually painted more than one canvas of his clients if he thought there was a chance he could sell them more than one. The second canvas cost fifteen thousand, the third ten thousand, the fourth five thousand. Additional panels held a special incentive for art collectors—where else could you get a comparable Warhol for the price?—and Iolas, Irving Blum, Ivan Karp, Ileana Sonnabend, Lita Hornick, and Yoyo Bischofberger, the wife of Warhol's Swiss art dealer, all commissioned portraits.

The process began with an afternoon photo session in which Andy snapped off Polaroids as Fred or one of his other aides leaped about, advising the client on hair and makeup, saying how "great" the client looked—a style borrowed, in part, from Halston's reassuring fitting-room manner. Additional photo sessions were often required before Andy got what he wanted—generally a three-quarter profile in the style of a television talking head. He was not interested in a "warts and all" approach, preferring images with strong graphic contrast. The chosen snapshot would then be sent to Alexander Heintici at Chromacomp, a fine-arts printer in Manhattan's flower district, to be converted into positive proofs the size of the final painting. "We wanted the middle tones to drop out and wanted to keep the very dark and light ones," Heintici recalled. "Andy got very upset if it was not what he wanted. You had to listen not only to what he said, but be sensitive enough to understand what he really wanted." Andy used the positive proofs to trace the image on canvas. He then painted in the background color, the eyes, lips, and other features, and returned the painted canvases to Heintici, who silk-screened the black-and-white image of the subject on top of each. Finally, Andy embellished the silk-screened canvas with more brushwork.

The impression Andy liked to give of knocking off the portraits "automatically" was entirely misleading. The whole process took at least as much time as a traditional portrait painting. Moreover, Andy gave a great deal of thought to his choice of appropriate colors for the subject—for example, the mock-royal gold and lavender for Mick Jagger. And he used his illustrator's instincts to exaggerate the features he considered important, as in the 1940s Joan Crawford, whose smear of lipstick almost reached her ears.

The results were an embalmed expressionism. As David Bourdon wrote: "Warhol transforms his 'sitters' into glamorous apparitions, presenting their faces as he thinks they should be seen and remembered. His portraits are not so much documents of the present as they are icons awaiting a future."

Andy's energy was prodigious. "His seven-days-a-week work ethic was part of his working-class Eastern European background, and it was contagious—everyone around him adapted to it," said Christopher Makos, a staff photographer for *Interview*. "For years," recalled Rupert Smith, one of Andy's assistants, "we painted on Saturdays and Sundays but would tell people that we were out of town."

Andy was getting rich. And so was Fred Hughes, who was getting twenty percent of every Warhol he sold. It was rumored that much of the profits were put into a Swiss bank. "I was bringing in rolls of portraits of the Italian fashion people under my arm on the plane to Milano and going through customs without paying any duty," said Daniela Morera. "They say, 'What are these?' 'Posters!' I say. And I know that the clients were paying the money in Switzerland. All the paintings that Bruno Bischofberger and his partner Thomas Ammanu sold in Zurich, I'm sure that money stays in Switzerland. If you go to Paris and sell paintings you don't ask the Rothschilds to send you the money in America. It goes to Switzerland. You don't pay any taxes and nobody knows anything. Every good American businessman was doing that."

Vincent Fremont denied this account: "Whatever Andy earned in Europe he brought back to the States because we needed it here. We were expanding all the time. I was never aware of a Swiss bank account."

In any case, getting rich did not alleviate Andy's fear of the poorhouse. "Andy was always afraid he would lose his money or that his checkbook would be overdrawn," Rupert Smith said. He did not have credit cards, preferring to carry his wad of crisp one-hundred-dollar bills in a brown envelope. Rarely ostentatious in his show of wealth, he did, however, feel secure enough that year to buy a new green Rolls-Royce.

Andy usually remained at work until seven while Colacello and Fremont waited for him, a process often prolonged by Andy's habit of getting involved in a long telephone conversation at the end of the day, or deciding to reread all his mail. If Andy wanted to be particularly irritating, he might assign whomever he was picking on that week such last-minute tasks as double-checking to see that there were no burning cigarettes in the ashtrays. He had a profound fear of fire, and anyone who had left a burner on in the kitchen or a lighted cigarette lying around risked his red-faced ire. Most of his assistants were impatient to get home, largely because they would be expected to reappear shortly at the dinners and parties where they were expected to continue working, pushing Andy and his product.

Andy would take a taxi home, where he would eat his "first" dinner of the evening. The gallbladder problems kept him on a restricted diet, but since the shooting he had also continued to worry about food away from home or the office not being "clean." His favorite foods were the simplest—such as turkey and mashed potatoes. And he still loved to rush into a pastry store and buy a birthday cake just because it made him feel good.

From 1974 to 1979, the Factory was heavily influenced by Fred Hughes's anglophilia, and many of Andy's female assistants, or "gals," as he liked to call them, were drawn from the English upper class, such as Ann, Rose, and Isabella Lambton and Catherine Guinness. Andy admired their ability to be haughty or rude while maintaining a fixed smile. Even though Andy had replaced court jesters like Ondine with titled names, he still liked to have at least one unsettling joker in his deck.

"The best dates," Andy would say, "are when you take the office with you." The avuncular, somewhat toadlike Colacello, with his horn-rimmed glasses and fastidiously buttoned-down appearance, seemed at first the least likely of Andy's inner circle to become his most regular social companion, but Bob's aggressive verbosity endeared him to Andy, for whom he functioned as a mouthpiece. "Andy could be very verbal within his inner circle, dishing away like a decadent fishwife," Colacello recalled, "but at dinner parties he would go mute, partially out of shyness, but also because he preferred watching to being watched. Often he would give me the cue to tell an amusing anecdote about Truman Capote, Paulette Goddard, or Diana Vreeland, and I would launch into a long, densely detailed story complete with mimicked dialogue right up until the punch line, which Andy was primed to deliver. 'Gee,' he would say the next morning on the phone, 'they really liked us last night. Maybe we should go on TV and tell funny stories. You could be the straight guy and I could be the nut.' "

As Paul Morrissey had been with Andy's films, so Colacello emerged as the explicator of "the real" Andy. "What I did best for Andy, I think, was sell him. I don't mean his paintings, but him. I explained him to the clients and the ladies, to the press and my parents' friends. When they said he got Edie Sedgwick [hooked] on drugs, I told them how he got Brigid Berlin off them. If they said he was evil, I said he went to church every Sunday. He became my cause."

Andy was now a fixture in the gossip pages (the British press

287

printed rumors of his marriage to Lee Radziwill after she rented his Montauk estate in the summer of 1974), and the central figure in a pack that included Halston, Truman Capote, and Bianca Jagger— or, as Colacello dubbed them, "His Highness," "the Count," and "Queen Bee." (Andy was "the Pope.") Others in the group were Liza Minnelli, the socialite Barbara Allen, and Victor Hugo. A Venezuelan assistant to Halston, Hugo became the Ondine of the seventies, given to long, incomprehensible, and sometimes downright offensive raps that would send Andy into tailspins of silent laughter while visiting dignitaries shifted uneasily in their seats. Victor was instrumental in bonding the friendship between Halston and Warhol that formed the core of the pack.

Once again, there were many in the art world who thought Andy was selling out. By becoming "in" he had violated a canon of modern art: To be serious you must be an "outsider." *Time*'s Robert Hughes was, as usual, scathing:

> To see Warhol entering a drawing room, pale eyes blinking in that pocked bun of a face, surrounded by his Praetorian Guard of chittering ingénues, is to realize that things do turn out well after all. The right level has been found. New York—not to speak of Rome, Lugano, Paris, Tehran, and Skorpios—needed a society portraitist. . . . The alienation of the artist, of which one heard so much talk a few years ago, no longer exists for Warhol: his ideal society has crystalized round him and learned to love his entropy.

23

BUT ANDY HAD higher social worlds to conquer: With Bob Colacello as his Talleyrand, he went after two of the most "royal" targets of opportunity in the world: the Peacock Throne in Iran and the Marcos regime in the Philippines. In Tehran, the Shah's wife, Farah Diba, had begun to spend what would amount to millions of dollars exercising her fantasy of filling a contemporary arts museum with works by Rauschenberg, Johns, Lichtenstein, Oldenburg, Stella, and Warhol in time for the golden anniversary of the Pahlavi regime in 1976.

The first invitation to the home of Fereydoun Hoveyda, the Iranian ambassador to the United Nations, came in September 1974. Dinner was in honor of the Italian ambassador to Russia, and Andy's ladies of the night, Diana Vreeland, Paulette Goddard, and Lee Radziwill, were also in attendance. Gisela Hoveyda, the young German wife of the Iranian ambassador, seemed most interested in Andy, and Colacello made her the target of his follow-up phone calls. By December, "caviar" had become a buzzword in Bob's *Interview* column, and he had maneuvered Andy's way up the protocol chain to an embassy dinner for the premier of Iran and Princess Ashraf Pahlavi, the Shah's twin sister.

The courting of Imelda Marcos, who was on a New York shopping binge that fall for property, art, jewelry, and shoes, began in November, a week after Andy returned from a three-week trip to Paris, Milan, and Japan. (The highlight of the trip had come in Kyoto, when Andy was summoned in the middle of the night to meet another guest at the hotel, Margaret Trudeau, the wife of the Canadian prime minister. He found her sitting on the floor of her room, sucking on a joint of marijuana and blowing smoke rings into a little rock garden. "Hi, Andy," she said. "You're the hardest person to reach in the world.") Back home, Andy and Bob were invited by the Philippines' First Lady to a tea at the Carlyle Hotel, where, amidst chit-chat about how "artists bring people together," Mrs. Marcos extended a special invitation to Andy's dachshund Archie to visit her thirty dogs in Manila. Two days later, Andy, Bob, and their new best friend went to tea at the Chinese embassy, where they watched propaganda films of Mrs. Marcos talking to Mao Tse-tung. Next, they attended the opening of the Filipino Cultural Center on Fifth Avenue, while demonstrators outside chanted, "Imelda, go home!"

Colacello gushed over Mrs. Marcos in his *Interview* column, describing her as "always polite, articulate, politic, and underneath it all, extremely intelligent." Andy later remarked that he was most impressed by her claim that she only needed two hours of sleep a night.

For such toadying after the heads of two regimes whose corruption and brutality were beginning to be aired in the American press, Andy drew fire from a new quarter, the political left. On December 30, 1974, the spotlight on Andy changed colors again when he received a Modern Language Association award from the Popular Culture Association for his "contribution to the understanding of homosexuality." The *New York Times* reported: "Mr. Warhol carried a tape recorder, which led many persons in the audience to suppose that he was fearful lest his words be lost to posterity." Instead he gave a lesson in concision: "Thank you," was all he said, in his tiny, Jackie Kennedy voice.

The new year, 1975, was another banner year for Andy, with a few jolts to keep the public mindful of his "dark side." It began inauspiciously with the flop of his one and only Broadway venture, *Man on the Moon.* This brainchild of Paul Morrissey's had been built around the musical talents of John Phillips, the former leader of The Mamas and The Papas, and his wife, the South African actress Genevieve Waite. Andy had been persuaded to "produce" the musical in name, if not in fact, and was able to watch the unfolding of the fiasco with some dispassion. The strains among the inexperienced collaborators had been considerable, and by the time of the opening in late January, Phillips had numbed himself with cocaine and heroin, and Morrissey, who had worked himself into a shrill frenzy, had been banned from the theater, a turn of events that greatly amused Andy. Two nights before the opening, Genevieve Waite overdosed on pills and was rushed to Lenox Hill Hospital. She rallied for opening night on January 29, but the show was forced to close three days later. Morrissey fled to Hollywood and never worked with Andy again.

In the spring of 1975, the value of Andy's paintings took another quantum leap with the decision of one of Germany's leading collectors of contemporary art, Dr. Erich Marx, to amass the largest collection of Warhols in the world. With the curator Heiner Bastian as go-between, Marx bought more than twenty canvases, dating back to the hand-painted advertisement series of 1960. From then on, Andy would visit Germany regularly, adding prominent burghers—whose company he did not enjoy at all—to his roster of commissioned portraits.

That summer, Mick and Bianca Jagger rented Andy's Montauk place, and the rest of the Rolling Stones moved in to rehearse for their impending American tour. Andy went out to visit: "My favorite Jagger is Jade [the daughter]," he later wrote. "I love Mick and Bianca, but Jade's more my speed. I taught her how to color and she taught me how to play Monopoly. She was four and I was forty-four. Mick got jealous. He said I was a bad influence because I gave her champagne."

John Phillips arrived, too, and according to Vincent Fremont, "There was all sorts of fun out there that summer." Apparently no one was much bothered by the death of Eric Emerson, a star of *Chelsea Girls* and *Heat,* who had been found dead of a heroin overdose in May.

Nothing, in any case, slowed Andy's production of paintings. He had accepted a commission for a portfolio of Mick Jagger portraits to be signed by both him and Jagger; at the same time, he was engaged in another portrait project, "Ladies and Gentlemen," a series of drag queens recruited as paid models by Cutrone and Colacello. He was now using torn paper patches to create a collagelike effect, which greatly complicated the process, requiring up to ten silk screens to complete the final product.

Socially he had reached the pinnacle: He was invited to a White House dinner on May 15 for the Shah of Iran. Jed and Bob helped him check into a huge suite at the Watergate Hotel and escorted him as far as the White House gates, all decked out in white tie and tails, while Andy wailed: "Oh, why can't I dress right? What's wrong with me? I mean, why can't I look good?" Returning to the hotel at two in the morning, Andy reported that he had sat with Nancy Kissinger, wife of the secretary of state, and had stayed hidden in a corner during the dancing out of fear that the First Lady, Betty Ford, or the Shah's Empress would ask him to dance.

Bianca Jagger had developed a White House connection in the person of Jack Ford, the president's twenty-three-year-old son. She introduced him to Andy one night at El Morocco in New York, where Andy was dining with the Marquesa de Portago and the gaga Duchess of Windsor, who spent the evening thinking that Andy was an intellectual and that she was aboard the QEII ocean liner. Afterward, Andy and Bianca took Jack Ford to the gay discotheque Le Jardin, where there was an awkward moment when a man came up and asked Jack to dance. Later, Andy asked Bianca if she could arrange a talk with the president's son for *Interview*.

Betty Ford was initially dubious about the idea, but she finally agreed to it—which resulted in one of the most successful publicity coups of Andy's career. Andy, Bob Colacello, and Bianca Jagger were at the taping session in the White House, where Bianca (a regular interviewer for the magazine) did most of the prodding, getting Jack Ford to blurt out that life in the White House was so "stifling" he would trade places with anyone "for a penny." She also arranged herself for a photograph in the Lincoln bedroom in a provocative pose with the young man, which was subsequently leaked in *Photoplay* magazine, sparking rumors of an international romance. Betty Ford was outraged, but nothing could be done: The scandal was perfectly timed to coincide with the publication of another Warhol product, *The Philosophy of Andy Warhol* (*from A to B and Back Again*).

Culled from Andy's telephone tapes with Brigid Polk and Pat Hackett, transcribed by Pat, and shaped into final form by Colacello, the book was an assemblage of Andy's observations on love, fame, beauty, and money—an entirely "negative philosophy," he told one reporter. The book was immediately hailed as the cry of the zeitgeist, an emblem of what the social critic Tom Wolfe called the "Me Generation," an age of narcissism and self-interest without trust, ideals, or love. But there was no breast-beating in Andy's "philosophy." Its tone was unfailingly lighthearted. "Warhol," wrote the *Newsweek* reviewer Jack Kroll, "often comes on as a perversely funny sage—a pop La Rochefoucauld." As in this acute Warholism: "The rich have many advantages over the poor but the most important one is knowing how to talk and eat at the same time." Barbara Goldsmith, in the *New York Times Book Review,* concluded: "Some people say California is the bellwether of America. I'd say Andy Warhol." And, as Kroll put it: "In his art and his life, both flights from emotional commitment, you hear the laughter and the cry wrenched from a man who heard something go pop in America."

The publishers, Harcourt Brace Jovanovich, had arranged a nine-city book-signing junket that September, the high point of which came in Houston, where Andy and his "bodyguard," Ann Lambton, posed like mannequins in a department store window while the Velvet Underground's song "Heroin" blasted onto the street. To middle America, Andy was no longer a subversive threat; he had become something more palatable—a clown.

The American tour was followed by a swing through Italy, France, and England for fashion shows, art openings, and book parties. In London, society columns ran rumors of the "imminent" engagement of Andy and Ann Lambton, whose parents, Lord and Lady Lambton, gave a book publication party at their house. Prominent among the guests who danced all night was Caroline Kennedy, the teenage daughter of the late president. Her presence was duly noted in the tabloids, and when Andy returned to New York, he ran into her mother, Jacqueline Onassis, who said: "Thank you for taking such good care of Caroline in London." "I wasn't sure what she meant," recalled Andy.

Despite the relentless pitching, Andy's *Philosophy* did not sell particularly well, and Andy bought back a number of copies to give away as gifts.

The year ended with another move: For $310,000 in a depressed real estate market Andy bought himself a five-story Georgian-style mansion at 57 East Sixty-sixth Street in the heart of Manhattan's Upper East Side.

He had long been wanting to move out of his "candy box" house on Lexington Avenue, partly because of memories of his mother, partly because the house had become much too small for his endless accumulation of treasures. He had also decided it was too dark. "Isn't sunlight wonderful?" he had remarked on a visit to Truman Capote's sunny apartment at United Nations Plaza. Jed Johnson had looked at ninety houses before finding the right one. With its wide stairways and large, light, open rooms, the house on Sixty-sixth Street had, as one visitor said, "the traditional old-money look Andy wanted." Jed was immediately put in charge of overseeing the move and decorating the new place.

Jed had a memory for decor, and he started adding touches recalled from the glittering places he and Andy had visited—Saint Laurent's townhouse in Paris, Hélène Rochas's home on the Riviera, Eric de Rothschild's estate at Château Lafite. Andy surrendered to Jed's ideas of grandeur. "Remember, he was in his Shah of Iran phase then," said a friend. New pieces arrived almost daily to supplement Andy's collections of furniture, tureens, serving dishes, and tea sets. Jed's approach combined neoclassical, Art Deco, and Victorian styles. Notably absent among the chintz, the Joseph Barry cabinets, Sheraton tables, and pieces by Duanad and Legrain, were any traces of pop art culture—apart from some Lichtensteins and a Jasper Johns that Andy had purchased early in his career, and one of his own small Maos. This last rested on a dresser in a bedroom in front of walls stenciled in a pattern seen at King Ludwig's castle, Neuschwanstein.

"He told me that the antiques made him feel rich," recalled Johnson. So did the wads of money Jed noticed tucked away under the specially made straw mattress on Andy's bed. "You only feel as rich as the money you have in your pocket or under your mattress," Andy said.

That fall, he moved into Sixty-sixth Street, letting Fred Hughes take over the house on Lexington. He quickly hired two Filipino maids, Nena and Aurora Bugarin, who would run the house smoothly for the rest of his life, and he installed a tight security system. Once several of the main rooms had been furnished, Andy invited Diana Vreeland, Truman Capote, and others to dinner parties. Soon, however, he complained to Jed that entertaining in the house made him uncomfortable. "It was always a disaster," recalled Johnson, "He just didn't enjoy it—I think he was embarrassed. I think he just needed a place to be alone."

From then on, the Sixty-sixth Street house became a private Xanadu, off limits to all but Andy's closest associates. The elegant, stately rooms increasingly became storerooms. The long Federal dining table began to disappear under a heap of cigarette cases, antique watches, and Indian rugs. Like a teenager, Andy shuttled between his favorite rooms, his bedroom and the kitchen, where he ate his carefully prepared meals.

"He kept most of the rooms locked," said Jed Johnson. "He had a routine. He'd walk through the house every morning before he left, open the door of each room with a key, peer in, then relock it. Then at night when he came home he would unlock each door, turn the light on, peer in, lock up, and go to bed."

24

AT THE SAME time that he appeared to be pandering after the world's rich and powerful with almost shameless glee, Andy was recharging the nihilistic side of his "philosophy." His last movie, *Bad,* was filmed in New York in the spring of 1976 after a year of deal-making. Initially planned as a low-low-budget affair, the project had mushroomed into the costliest Warhol effort to date—$1.2 million—with the involvement of the Australian rock-and-roll entrepreneur Robert Stigwood. When Stigwood dropped out, pleading other commitments, Andy decided to produce the film himself, funneling much of the money he had made during six months of doing portrait commissions into the project. Fred Hughes invested some of his own money into it as well and raised additional financing. To direct Pat Hackett's script, Andy chose Jed Johnson, who had been Morrissey's right-hand man on previous films.

Bad was conceived as the blackest Warhol "comedy" yet, the adventures of a sexy, utterly amoral gang of women who are respectable by day and vicious by night, an assassination squad who, for any price, will cut off victims' fingers and kill babies. (In the film's most notorious scene, one of the heroines drops her own baby out of a high-rise window.) It was another satire of women's liberation, depicting conventional marriage as a sham and men as utterly ineffectual. Only now, the "women in revolt" were to be played by real women: the actress Carroll Baker (the famous "bad" girl of *Baby Doll* in the fifties) as the leader of the pack, whose members included Susan Tyrell, Geraldine Smith and her equally stunning sister Maria, Cyrinda Foxe, Susan Blond, and Brigid Polk, happily back in the fold after a two-year absence.

The film was Andy's first entirely "legitimate" project. The crew included thirty to forty members of the Screen Actors' Guild; even the Factory "kids" had to join SAG. Vincent Fremont, the Factory bookkeeper, was dismayed at how *Bad* was chewing up money, but Andy was delighted by the big-time aura of it all, bringing people he wanted to impress to "visit the set" at various New York locations. He was uncharacteristically vocal in his suggestions as well, attending the "dailies" and giving Pat and Jed encouragement and critiques of their progress.

Meanwhile—with typical two-sidedness—he was engaged in a collaboration with the painter Jamie Wyeth, the son of America's favorite traditional artist, Andrew Wyeth. The two artists had been commissioned to paint each other's portraits by the Coe-Kerr Gallery in Manhattan, a decidedly derrière-garde setting. A show, including preparatory drawings, was scheduled for June. Aligning himself with the Wyeths was a daring move for Andy. Jamie Wyeth's hyperrealistic approach to his portraits of celebrated people (including John F. Kennedy and the movie mogul Joseph E. Levine) was utterly alien to the cool chic of a Warhol portrait. Produced in the painstaking, painterly manner of an Old Master, with an almost visceral immediacy, Wyeth's work risked making Andy's approach seem even slicker and more soulless than his critics charged. But the Wyeths were an American legend—"old money" in their appeal (Jamie Wyeth's wife was an heiress to the DuPont fortune)—and for Andy's reentry into the New York art scene, the collaboration was a promotional and social coup.

The show was a success for both artists. Wyeth's portrait depicted Warhol as a scary, spectral presence, clutching his dachshund, Archie, as if for dear life; for his part, Andy showed the handsome younger painter as an all-American art icon, and perhaps also a victim of celebrity. Accompanied by drawings, the show revealed Warhol to be the serious, discerning, and painterly artist he really was. The reviews were good, and the two men continued to see each other. Andy even made the pilgrimage to Chadds Ford, the Wyeths' domain in Pennsylvania, where the other "Andy" of American art greeted him warmly.

Unable to rent out the Montauk compound that summer, Andy stayed there for two weeks in June with Jed, who was editing *Bad*, then turned the place over to his staff and friends as a retreat from the summer heat while he, Fred, and Bob Colacello headed for London on their way to Iran. Colacello's courting of the Iranians had finally paid off with a commission from the Shah to paint his wife, the Empress Farah Diba. They began to catch political flak as soon as they arrived in London. At a party at the poet Stephen Spender's, Colacello was cornered by a *New Statesman* reporter who asked, "How could you go to a police state like Iran?" "By airplane," was Bob's tart reply. They arrived in Iran in early July to a welcoming committee of young girls and were taken to the Hilton. Andy went to take Polaroids of the Empress, who gave him and his entourage a viewing of the crown jewels and a dinner party, after which they headed triumphantly for home.

The visit to Iran drew sharp criticism from the left. Particularly harsh was Alexander Cockburn in the *Village Voice* who lambasted *Interview* for "its exaltation of 'Fascist chic' " and its "moral indifference to its heroes and heroines." "The *Village Voice* and the anti-Iran group like to blow this up as a kind of decadent thing," recalled Fred Hughes. "It wasn't. There were some very interesting people involved around the Pahlavis, very complicated, and it was hard to make the kind of judgment one would normally make."

That August, the *New York Times Magazine* commissioned a Warhol cover portrait of Jimmy Carter, the Democratic presidential candidate. Andy took Fred Hughes with him to Plains, Georgia, where they met the Carters, and Andy took Polaroids of the former governor. As a memento, Carter gave Warhol two signed bags of peanuts, about which Andy commented: "Politicians always want something for nothing, and so do I!" A few weeks later he was asked by the Carter staff to make an edition of one hundred prints of the portrait to be sold at a thousand dollars apiece to raise money for the campaign. Despite his unfortunate experience with the McGovern campaign poster, Andy agreed. He liked Carter's smile and made it the prominent feature of the portrait, telling an interviewer: "Politicians have twenty-four-hour smiles. So do dogs."

His political commissions were one thing, his personal vision another. "There were always a number of portraits to do," Ronnie Cutrone recalled. "That was work. But then there were times when Andy would say, 'Okay, now what are we going to do for art?' " What he did for art that fall was a series of pictures using the hammer and sickle as a subject. As usual, Andy claimed no particular significance for the choice of imagery. He had merely noticed graffiti of the Communist party symbol all over Rome on a visit to Italy and he liked, he said, "the look." His approach was inventively childlike. He began with real objects, a sickle and mallet purchased at a local hardware store, which Cutrone photographed so that their True Temper labels were clearly visible. Whereas the Communist symbol crosses the hammer and sickle to signify the solidarity of workers, Andy chose to display the objects in disarray. The photographs were converted into silk screens, and the painting process began in the back-room studio at 860 Broadway. These paintings were among the largest he had done since the Maos, and he developed a new technique to accommodate them—"mopping"—applying sweeping strokes of paint with a sponge mop. From the "Still Lives," as he called the results, he proceeded to paintings based on a particularly beautiful human skull he had bought in Europe. Among his best works of the decade, they seemed in retrospect to have prefigured, as the art critic Trevor Fairbrother wrote, "the resurgence of skull imagery that accompanied punk culture, escalating threats of nuclear and ecological disasters, and the AIDS epidemic."

The skulls were not shown in New York, but the "Hammer and Sickle" series opened at Leo Castelli's big new Soho space in January 1977, Andy's first major exhibit of new work in New York in more than a decade. The paintings were, as David Bourdon wrote, astutely conceived for the New York audience: "Warhol's hammer and sickle works are probably calculated to titillate certain capitalists, who would rejoice at hanging such trophies in their living and board rooms. But Warhol, being a shrewd strategist, certainly considered the possibility that these works might also appeal to those who lean left. Warhol's hammer and sickle series is strong and brims with wit."

By the mid-seventies, Andy had recovered from the shooting as fully as he ever would, and his strength and determination had inspired a new diligence at the Factory. Now, the highly polished floors shone, sunlight sparkled on the spotless windows, and the aroma of large bunches of beautifully arranged flowers mixed with cologne and perfume to create a slightly aphrodisiac odor. Conformity was the rule, with everyone copying some aspect of Andy's style. The men wore suits and ties or elegant jackets and jeans, and imitated the way Andy talked: "Uh, whu . . . whu . . . oh, really? Oh. Well, see, that's what you should do . . . " They found themselves walking with his curiously choreographed little dancer's step, one hand carefully placed at waist level and jutting out to the side. Nobody would have dreamed of going to the Factory unshaven or in slovenly dress unless he was a star in his own right. It was a little bit like a British boarding school, with Andy as the headmaster, Fred as the head prefect, and Brigid, now free of drugs, as the matron.

Of all the people in his life, apart from his family, Brigid Polk had the longest relationship with Andy. Underneath her dragon image, Brigid was a softy who adored Andy, in part because he had encouraged her to stop taking drugs and had always left the door open for her at the Factory. Brigid was able to connect with Andy on a different wavelength from other people. With her he was neither a little boy nor a vampire but something of an inner voice, calling her in the middle of the night and whispering, "Wasted space, wasted space, what's in your mind, wasted space?" Brigid loved that. Andy in turn loved her attitude toward art. She would take Polaroids and then photograph them being flushed down the toilet or make ink impressions of people's scars. Andy once compared himself and Brigid to Marcel Duchamp and his wife, "Teeny."

She was also remarkably unjealous of his changing cast of supergirls. Chief among them at this point was Catherine Guinness, an offspring of the Mitford family and the Irish Guinnesses, an unthreatening beauty whose fresh humor about New York kept Andy fresh too. Catherine played a key role in the development of *Interview*'s style, impressing would-be advertisers with her aristocratic manner and acting as the worldly foil to Andy's innocence on *Interview* assignments. From 1976 to 1979, she was Andy's date at every dinner, opening, and show. "Andy was incredibly generous, not only with money but with himself, too," she recalled. "I never knew anybody else to pay when we went out to dinner unless it was a client."

With his power not merely to paint but to create celebrities in *Interview*, Andy was now attending all the important movie, rock, fashion, and art openings. Although he was never to be accepted by the movie industry, he was able to befriend, however fleetingly, the stars he interviewed for cover stories. One actor he developed a genuine liking for was Jack Nicholson, whom he considered casting as Jackson Pollock in a film based on Ruth Kligman's memoir of her affair with the artist. He had in mind Nicholson's girlfriend, Anjelica Huston, to co-star as Ruth, but the idea came to nothing after Roman Polanski was arrested in the actress's house for having sex with a minor.

To rock musicians Andy was something of an idol, and New Wave groups such as Talking Heads, Blondie, and The Clash all came to the Factory to pay homage and be publicized in *Interview*. His loyalty to the Rolling Stones remained as strong as ever. In 1977 he did the cover for the group's *Love You Live* album, and after the Jaggers separated, he became as friendly with Mick's new girlfriend, Jerry Hall, as he had been with Bianca.

In the spring of 1977, he found his ideal playground in a new disco club called Studio 54, which within weeks of its opening organized New York's nightlife into two groups: those who were famous, powerful, or beautiful enough to get in, and those who weren't. The brainchild of Steve Rubell, a restaurateur, and his business partner, Ian Schraeger, this former television studio on West Fifty-fourth Street became for Andy what the Moulin Rouge had been for Toulouse-Lautrec. It was the place to observe, with his tape recorder and Polaroid camera, what he called the "bubonic plague of our times," the "social disease" whose symptoms were an obsessive need to go out, the preference for exhilaration over conversation, unless the subject were gossip, and the judging of a party's success by how many celebrities were present. Andy was fascinated by the fact that

Studio 54 was more than just a watering hole for the rich and famous. It was a place where people danced, drank, did drugs, made friends, made love, broke up, did business, even slept. The club's equalizing effect was like that of the old Factory. "The key to the success of Studio 54," he wrote, "is that it's a dictatorship at the door and a democracy on the floor. It's hard to get in but once you're in you could end up dancing with Liza Minnelli. . . . At 54, the stars are nobody because everybody's a star." It was, he said, "the New Society."

Andy became a nightly regular there, using the club as a second office to recruit volunteers for work at the Factory, to entertain potential "victims" like Liza Minnelli and Truman Capote, of whom he made two of his best portraits that year. The New Society's drug of choice was cocaine; according to Catherine Guinness, "little packets" were regularly thrust on Andy, who'd accept them, then throw them away. "He didn't say anything either," she recalled. "He expressed an attitude by not taking the drugs." Andy scarcely drank anything, and his sobriety enabled him to probe the secrets of the many intoxicated people who swirled around him under the club's neon sign of the Man in the Moon, which dropped from the ceiling and "snorted" little twinkling lights up its nose.

His favorite informants were women, and his favorite information was about their sex lives. One night he taped one of Hollywood's biggest stars on the subject of the sexual performance of her husbands. (Years later, after he died, she was on the phone to Fred Hughes, making sure the tape never saw the light of day.) Not that Andy would have tried publishing that sort of thing. He seemed perfectly content merely to have heard what he heard. Before retiring to bed at the usual hour of six A.M.—for the party generally went on to somebody's apartment, hotel suite, or an after-hours' club—he would store away his tapes with the care of an archivist.

Bad was a disaster. It opened in New York in April 1977 and got lost in the disco haze. After three weeks, it was clear that the movie was going to fail. Once again, Andy had landed a bad distribution deal. The American distributors, New World Pictures, had refused to honor the Factory's demand that the scene with the baby being thrown out the window be cut, and *Bad* was advertised alongside the porno films. For a while it seemed that the European engagements would turn a profit, but the Italian distributors reneged on their payments, and *Bad* was confiscated in Germany for its excessive violence. (In addition to the baby scene, offense was given by the shot of a finger being smashed by a Volkswagen.) It was, said Vincent Fremont, the first time Andy had overextended himself—and the last time. By his estimation, Andy's losses amounted to four hundred thousand dollars.

The *Bad* fiasco marked the beginning of the end of Andy's relationship with Jed Johnson, who took the film's failure as his own. Jed retreated into the East Sixty-sixth Street house, limiting his activities to collecting new pieces and decorating rooms. He had developed a reputation as an interior designer, and he was soon at work decorating an apartment for Pierre Bergé and Yves Saint Laurent in the Pierre Hotel. "It was always difficult," said Johnson, "because Andy didn't know what he wanted from other people. On the one hand, he wanted you to be successful, but on the other, he wanted you to be dependent. Success would have meant independence." "They'd been getting on very badly for a long time," recalled Catherine Guinness. "Andy'd say, 'Jed's complaining that I never go out with him, so I've got to go with him.' But in fact, Jed hated going out with Andy because of being in his shade, being his little puppet. And Andy could be very nasty."

Jed, moreover, had grown disillusioned with his mentor: "When Studio 54 opened, New York was at the height of its decadence, and things changed with Andy," he recalled. "I never liked that scene, and I felt that Andy was just wasting his time. It was really upsetting. He spent his time with the most ridiculous people."

In May, Andy flew to Paris with Hughes, Colacello, and his current "Girl of the Year," Barbara Allen, for the French publication of his *Philosophie* and the opening of his "Hammer and Sickle" paintings. The summer of 1977 was the peak of the punk-rock vogue in Europe, and Andy was greeted as the man who had invented it all with his mask of stupefaction, his films of aimless defiance, and his celebrated aphorisms to the effect that everything meant nothing. With their craze for safety pins, the European punks could even point to Andy's having been ten years ahead of his time as a fashion setter, since he had worn safety pins on his lapels back in the sixties. The French punks couldn't get enough of their prophet. They mobbed his book signing, proffering breasts and even penises for Andy to autograph. The French critics greeted his *Philosophie* with their usual bombast: "The Warhol oeuvre," one of them intoned, "transforms itself into destiny. The Warhol personage transforms itself into the Warhol oeuvre, he commands it, he dominates it, and he is the parameter of reference."

From Paris, Andy went to Brussels with Paloma Picasso to attend a Warhol opening at Gallerie D, where he was received by hundreds of punk photographers. Back in Paris, dining al fresco at Monsieur Boeuf's with Philip Niarchos, the Greek ship-owning heir, and Bianca Jagger, he was assaulted by (as Colacello wrote in his diary) "a punk off the street [who] screamed . . . that she was a necrophiliac fresh out of a mental institution and madly in love with A.W.! She was a very real punk and the very real police had to come and take her away."

When he wasn't hobnobbing with high society—attending tennis matches with Bianca or dining with Princess Firyal of Jordan at Maxim's—he was often indulging his passion for French perfume shops. "His interest was as much in the bottles and the way they wrapped them as in the scent itself," recalled a friend. "His favorites were Chanel No. 5, all the Guerlain scents, because they came in Lalique crystal, and mixtures of essence that he'd either have concocted or mix himself."

But the punks seldom let him alone. The "Hammer and Sickle" opening drew hundreds of them. Noted Colacello: "Some punks wrote HATE and WAR on the walls in sorbet. Some punks vomited white wine. One punk knocked another punk's tooth out. One punk peed. Sao Schlumberger [the socialite] said, 'I think I better get going to my dinner at Versailles,' clutching her purse, as she tried to run past the swine."

"It's just fashion," Andy told Bianca. "I don't understand it at all."

Nonetheless, he understood it well enough to try managing his own punk-rock act shortly after returning to New York. Its punk "star" was Walter Steding, an electric violinist who performed in a "bug suit" rigged with blinking lights and electronic gadgetry that modulated his music into a bizarre barrage of squawks and squeaks. Like Ronnie Cutrone, with whom he was sharing an apartment,

Steding worked as a painting assistant to Warhol. As usual, Andy had made rivals of his assistants. "Right away he was saying, 'You can take over Ronnie's job 'cos he's on his way out,'" Steding recalled. "He had all these problems with Ronnie, but he would never speak to Ronnie about them. He would come to me."

Steding occasionally took the brunt of Andy's temper: "He yelled, but he yelled like a mouse." Mostly, however, Walter was nagged at: How many songs had he written? What was he doing? Why wasn't he working? When Steding did begin playing at the New York punk club CBGB's, Andy would typically comment that his music was good, but not good enough. Nonetheless, he was supportive enough to put out a record by Steding on his own Earhol label. As usual, however, Andy had picked a talented misfit: Steding's career went nowhere.

In the meantime, Jamie Wyeth was back at the Factory, where Andy had offered him space to work on a portrait of Arnold Schwarzenegger. Andy loved having the bodybuilder and fledgling movie star sitting around the Factory with his shirt off—a sight guaranteed to startle visitors—and he was energized by Wyeth's daily industry. After a while, however, the presence of another artist working independently of him became an irritant. As much as he might gush about how "great" everybody around him was, there was really only one star at the Factory—Andy Warhol. That was, after all, the point of the whole setup: Everybody was there to cater to some aspect of Andy's needs. Moreover, most of Andy's long-term relationships were not with equals. The "stars" were never around very long, unless they were having a nervous breakdown, in which case they would find Andy in constant attendance. In the absence of a mutual need, Wyeth and Warhol gradually drifted apart.

With the election of Jimmy Carter in 1976, cordial relations with the White House had been restored, and on June 14, 1977, Andy was invited to a special reception honoring the "Inaugural Artists" who had contributed prints to the Carter campaign—the others being Jacob Lawrence, Robert Rauschenberg, Roy Lichtenstein, and Jamie Wyeth. Wyeth brought along Schwarzenegger; Andy was accompanied by Colacello. Summing up the occasion, Andy said: "My favorite thing to do at the White House is look at the furniture."

Behind the disingenuousness, he strengthened his ties with the Carters by latching on to the President's redoubtable mother, "Miss

Lillian" Carter. A few months later, he squired her to Studio 54 for a party promoting tourism in India (where Mrs. Carter had been a Peace Corps volunteer). Afterward, she told Andy that she hadn't known "if I was in heaven or hell, but I enjoyed it," adding that she couldn't understand why all the boys were dancing with one another when there were so many pretty girls around. Later that year, Andy persuaded her to sit for a portrait.

This was an immensely productive time. Apart from the nonstop portrait commission and magazine work, Andy was engaged in a series of business art projects, arranged by Hughes. One was a portrait series of famous athletes—among them Pelé, Tom Seaver, Dorothy Hamill, Kareem Abdul-Jabbar, O. J. Simpson, Willie Shoemaker, Chris Evert, and Muhammad Ali. Each of them, in return for posing for Andy's Polaroids, would receive one of the six resulting portraits and fifteen thousand dollars once all the paintings were sold. (A lucrative print series was also in the works.) "Andy loved the athletes," recalled Catherine Guinness. "It was very exciting—much nicer than painting Bob's rich old ladies." The most exciting of all was Ali, the heavyweight champ, who was photographed that August at Fighter's Heaven, his training camp in Pennsylvania. With his tape recorder going, Andy was greeted with a forty-minute Ali-logue, delivered from notecards, denouncing the world Andy had come from—that of "prostitution," "pornography," "homosexuality," and even angel food cake. Andy later commented: "How can he preach like that? It's so crazy. I think he's a male chauvinist pig, right? . . . He was just torturing us."

The champ would undoubtedly have been meaner had he known what Andy was up to in his "private" work: a series of "piss paintings" and images of "sex parts." For these, his chief collaborator was Halston's window decorator, Victor Hugo, who was game for anything that would cheer Andy up. It was Victor's charm to arrive by seaplane at a Montauk dinner party in a sequined jockstrap, or to show up at Studio 54 in an ambulance, jump off the stretcher, and hit the dance floor. Most people found his Venezuelan accent incomprehensible, but he talked nonstop and he was Andy's court jester. ("The Queen of the Shallow," he called Andy.) Hugo was also Andy's sometime model and chief procurer for the series he began in the fall of 1977.

"Andy," wrote Ultra Violet, "was fascinated by the naked body. He delighted in the fact that every organ of the body varies in shape, form, and color from one individual to the next. Just as one torso or one face tells a different story from another's, so to Andy one penis or one ass told a different story from another."

Hugo would pull in the young men to expose themselves and have sex with one another while Andy clicked away. Steding, who was not gay, found these sessions unsettling: "Someone would come by saying they had a really big dick. Andy said, 'Well, let's take a picture of it,' and he did. Then the pictures came to me as the person who had to put them somewhere. I wrote on the box 'Sex Parts,' which is where Andy got the name for the series. He would take pictures over a couple of hours of two men screwing. I found it difficult, but what am I supposed to do? I realized my position was to be there, but at the same time, you know, I was looking around at the walls."

According to Hugo, Andy would excuse himself to masturbate in the bathroom. But Steding thought otherwise: "I don't think these situations turned him on. In order for Andy to have sex, it had to be separated from his art. The people he was sexually attracted to were sensitive, quiet individuals doing something totally removed from what he was doing."

Hundreds of "sex part" photos were taken over many months, of which Andy selected the least sexually explicit for a series called "Torsos." (The others were never shown.) Simultaneously, he had completed the "piss paintings"—or "Oxidation" series, as it would be called in the art market. This was a revival of an idea dating back to 1961: Victor, Ronnie, Walter, and Andy took turns urinating on canvases coated with wet copper paint that oxidized and turned green and orange where the spatters hit. ("Andy was taking a lot of B vitamins," recalled Vincent Fremont. "During that period the back room stank of piss.") This series was surprisingly well received when it was displayed in Europe the following year, one critic hailing the paintings as "Warhol at his purest." Another critic commented that "anyone who thinks Andy Warhol's society portraits of the seventies verge on piss-elegance will find something more literal in the so-called piss paintings."

The atmosphere at the Factory resembled more than ever that of a feudal court. By the time of the king's arrival around noon, the waiting room was full of petitioners—minions waiting for his instructions or encouragement, portrait-sitters ranging from well-heeled unknowns to the newest flavor in rock stars, dealers or curators there to discuss a Warhol exhibition somewhere around the globe, a journalist or two on hand to get "color" for an article on life at the epicenter of the zeitgeist. Andy would move from courtier to courtier, whispering a few words of assent behind the fixed suggestion of a smile. Out of the *Interview* offices would slide Colacello, plump hand extended, wrapping a "victim" in compliments and laughter.

Making a beeline for the art-world emissary would be Fred Hughes, ready with a stage-British phrase about some shared acquaintance that would set the air buzzing with the syllables "Pahlavi" or "Jagger." Meantime, the phones rang constantly, to be picked up by an assistant who would sing out, "Caroline Kennedy on three" or "Philip Johnson on two." On occasion the atmosphere would become giddily festive if someone utterly out of place, like Pelé the soccer player, was arriving. If the visitor was, say, King Carl XVI Gustaf of Sweden, the mood would be sober and hushed. The Factory would have been sealed by FBI agents for an hour, and finally the king would arrive. Even he would be kept waiting for a few minutes while Andy, hunkered down in his mess in the back, finished his counting of a thousand new sheets of paper or joked with Cutrone and Steding, delaying to the last possible moment his Entrance.

The contradictions between the public and private Andy were now sharper than ever. Of the thousands of people who claimed to "know" him on the basis of a visit to the Factory or a greeting at an opening or a smile across a restaurant, most would never hear him say anything beyond "Gee!" or "Great!" or "I really love . . . " Yet behind the mask of almost goofy good will and approbation was a vituperativeness he freely indulged in private. Some of it was directed at the rich and famous who were sitting in the Factory waiting room, trembling with excitement over the prospect of seeing themselves in an Andy Warhol portrait. Ronnie Cutrone recalled that in the back room, Andy would "scrunch up his face and go, 'Oooo, Nooo! She's going to make me cut her double chin off.'" Walter Steding once asked Andy if he actually liked any of the rich industrialists and their wives who bought their pictures from him. Steding got the immediate reply "I *hate* them."

Every morning before going out into the world as the man who liked everything, he had the compulsive need to call his secretary, Pat Hackett, and dictate into his "diary" the most penetrating put-downs of the "friends" he had been with the day before, the host-esses and guests at the dinner table he had graced the previous night, the artists of his generation who had rival shows on. After an evening out with Truman Capote, he would do a hilarious imitation at the Factory of the writer's high-pitched whine going out of con-trol on booze. He would devastate his target with expressions of "concern": Having mentioned Bianca Jagger's "need" for "three vodkas" at a fashion shoot, he would say, "I mean it's just work . . . I don't understand . . . I mean she's so beautiful but . . . ," all of it punctuated with rubbery grimaces, much fluttering of hands, and childish giggles. About women he hated his favorite put-down was "She stinks." About a man, "He's corny."

Envy fueled much of this scorn: Artists like Cy Twombly and Andrew Wyeth had had it "easy" because they had "married rich women." He had no loyalty to the collectors and dealers who had supported him when he was starting out: Mr. and Mrs. Burton Tremaine, he once said, were a "horrible old couple—they were dogs," and he couldn't "stand" Irving Blum because he was "so Jewish." His longing to be "the most famous artist in the world" was so intense that he once remarked how much he resented the fact that Marc Chagall was still alive and painting in his nineties.

A feeling of having been "let down" often sparked a dismissal. He had "gone out of his way" to help Capote, who had failed him with his writer's block. Anyone who had ever crossed him was never forgiven or forgotten, especially if that person had gone on to suc-cess. A case in point was Lou Reed, who had denied Andy a share of the earnings from the first Velvet Underground album. Reed had continued to come to the Factory, making periodic obeisances to his old mentor, but he never knew how he would be received. On one occasion Andy would be all smiles, on another icily distant, and the singer would leave deflated.

Just as his father had been able to cut his sons down with a glance, Andy let his victims feel the lash with the slightest lessening of approval. Bianca Jagger's fall from grace would eventually cause her to think of her once "magic, beautiful" friend as a "vampire." It was an apt choice of words, for once Andy's suction stopped, his victims felt drained.

But the court was always full: Many of his followers thought of Andy as an "addiction." Belying his public image as "limp" was his pistonlike energy: Something was usually happening around Andy, and if it wasn't, he could *make* it happen. His body was hard, thanks to years of workouts, but he projected such vulnerability that anyone who followed him felt compelled to protect him. One friend recalled seeing Andy jump with fright when a balloon popped at a party; instantly, the friend jumped in front of him, saying, "It's all right, it's all right." But you didn't touch Andy: That was strictly forbidden. If you did, he would cringe as though repelling an invasion.

For invading was, above all, what he did: Many of his followers would say that Andy had got "inside" them. His childlike curiosity about the most intimate details of other people's lives was so avid and so seductively pressed that it was irresistible. How and with whom one had had sex was his obsessive interest, and with his un-threatening manner and voyeuristic pull he invariably learned what he wanted. If he didn't, his reaction was that of a spurned lover. One friend recalled telling, after the most insistent prodding, the details of a homosexual pass: " 'What happened? What happened?' Andy wanted to know. When I finally said 'Nothing,' his face really fell—it was like the most terrible disappointment."

But in the roller-coaster seventies, Andy's crashes could be followed by days and evenings of pure elation. As 1977 raced to a close, he took time out from his work to indulge another passion—Christmas shopping. His spree began, as always, in November, and every morning he arrived at the Factory laden down with shopping bags full of treasures for his staff and friends. The climax was the annual Christmas party, during which he unveiled his cornucopia of presents, ranging from Polaroid cameras to tape recorders to signed prints worth as much as $1,500 apiece.

But the biggest pile of gifts, by far, was always for Andy. With benign detachment he seemed not to notice them. By the next day, though, they had disappeared—to be opened by Andy at home, in private.

25

WEDNESDAY, MARCH 15: Pope [Warhol] and I passed the House of Halston to pick up His Highness, Queen Bee Bianca. . . . Limoed across town to Studio Rubell. Danced with Count Capote. . . . Peter Beard arrived around 3 A.M. I don't remember what happened after that, but a lot did." So went one of Bob Colacello's reports in *Interview* of a typical night on the town in 1978. For Andy and his entourage, it wasn't just a case of "Saturday Night Fever"; it was an every-night binge, and the toll was beginning to show.

"Diana, it gets more like pagan Rome every night," Colacello once shouted into Diana Vreeland's ear at Studio 54. "I should hope so, Bob," came "the Empress's" reply. On April 3, Warhol and Capote hosted an Oscar celebration that was billed as the party of the decade. A few nights later, Halston threw a birthday bash for Bianca Jagger, the highlight of which was the entrance of a naked black man leading a naked black woman on a white pony through a curtain of gold streamers. This was followed by Elizabeth Taylor's birthday celebration, during which the Radio City Music Hall's Rockettes wheeled out a birthday cake replica of the star, all the while kicking with perfect precision. When Andy wasn't at "Studio

Rubell" for these and more mundane events, he could be spotted at the rival discotheque Xenon or downtown at the Mudd Club, a new temple of Punk, looking like a ghostly oracle with his long, white-blond wig, slightly parted lips, hands folded in front of him and clutching his tape recorder, as he stood absolutely still, staring into space, while the party raged around him.

His ubiquitous presence at these and other watering holes was not just recreational. Going out was his way of making business connections, keeping himself in the public eye and abreast of new talent and trends. Staying high on nothing more than voyeurism, he remained firmly in control of his perceptions while Halston, Truman, Liza, Bob, Fred, Ronnie, and most of his other nightly companions were finding it increasingly hard to stay afloat on their intake of drugs or drink or both. Indeed, with the exception of Vincent Fremont, who kept the books in good order, all of Andy's principal stalwarts at the Factory seemed to be coming apart, using the open bar in the dining room as a daytime refuge against hangovers and boredom.

Andy's response was characteristically contradictory—genuine concern mixed with tacit encouragement. Looking back, Ronnie Cutrone concluded that Andy was "attracted unconsciously to people with compulsive problems. . . . Andy was always fascinated by other people's soap operas. It was a way for him to avoid his own problems."

He was especially concerned about Truman Capote, who had been unable to write anything since the infamous opening chapters of *Answered Prayers*. Andy gave him a tape recorder and assigned him several *Interview* pieces. For a while it worked: Capote went on the wagon and produced many of the journalistic pieces that made up his last best-seller, *Music for Chameleons*. But the author's sobriety did not last long. By the end of 1978, when he and Andy were supposed to tape-record a conversation for *High Times* magazine, Capote was too drunk to speak for days at a time. (Perversely, one of Andy's Christmas presents that year was a painting of the Studio 54 complimentary drink ticket. The bigger the friend, the bigger the painting.)

Andy's involvement with the radical, drug-promoting magazine was the result of his new friendship with its extroverted art director, Toni Brown, whose stories about lesbian life he found to be amusing material for his tape recorder. Many of the Factory people were dismayed by his urge to be with Brown virtually every night. Unbeknownst to them, it was not merely her uninhibited company he enjoyed; he was engaged in one of his fruitless attempts to tape-record somebody's life story as the basis for a book or even a Broadway show.

Another controversial new friend was Tom Sullivan, a cocaine smuggler who had blown into town that year to have some fun with $2 million in his pocket. Uneducated and unsophisticated, with a romantic pirate-king aura (one hand, disfigured in a fiery plane crash, was always gloved in black leather), Sullivan was a Studio 54 charmer who swept both Catherine Guinness and Margaret Trudeau off their feet. He had rented three adjoining suites at the elegant Westbury Hotel on Madison Avenue, which he shared with Peter Beard, the playboy-anthropologist, and the French starlet Carol Bosquet. Dinners with Tommy at the Westbury's Polo Lounge became a regular event, with Andy ambiguously present as recorder. Albert Goldman, the biographer of Elvis Presley (and later John Lennon), another recorder of the dark side of celebrity, was sometimes present as well, and he viewed Andy's enjoyment of those dinners as something less than innocent: "Andy would come with his Polaroid and sit there at the table. Everybody was carrying on and he'd say nothing, but periodically he goes *brrr* with the machine and then this long thing comes out *eeee*. I always thought it was just like sticking his tongue out at the company. Puking on them in a way. Now I ogle you . . . now I puke on you. The sense I always got out of Andy was incredible arrogance, contempt, derogation. I thought he was a disgusting human being. Cold and creepy and calculating and manipulative and exploitive and hiding behind all these little-boy, little-girl la-la masks that he had contrived."

That summer, Andy rented his Montauk estate to Sullivan, who used the place for the filming of *Cocaine Cowboy,* a story written by Sullivan and a German director, Ulli Lommel, about a drug smuggler who tries to get out of the business by becoming a rock star. The veteran Hollywood actor Jack Palance was signed up for a starring role, and Andy himself agreed to appear, interviewing Sullivan as the protagonist. The charming drug vendor was sinking fast: He had broken up with Margaret Trudeau in London, and in the course of filming, the local police had raided the Montauk house, looking for drugs. They arrived too late: The night before, Sullivan had paid off his Colombian suppliers, and the only suspicious item the police found was $25,000 in cash. *Cocaine Cowboy* was the nadir of Andy's involvement with films: His interview with Sullivan was banal beyond toleration. By the end of the summer, Sullivan had lost all his money and become a pariah to the New York sharks, who shunned him as quickly as they had moved in on him when his pockets were full.

Andy had long been fascinated by television. The off-register colors of his 1967 Marilyn prints had been influenced by an out-of-focus TV set, and since 1969 he had been talking about creating his own talk show, "Nothing Special." Now, nine years later, he decided that the producer for such a venture might be Lorne Michaels, the free-wheeling inventor of NBC's satirical variety show "Saturday Night Live." Vincent Fremont, Brigid Polk, and a few other Factory "squirrels" whipped up some ideas, and a meeting was arranged.

On the big day, Michaels arrived at the Factory with a hip young assistant, and sat down opposite Warhol and his team at the dining-room table, all smiles. Halfway through Fremont's pitch, Michaels broke in excitedly; he was prepared to give them a hundred thousand dollars in development money immediately, a prime-time Saturday night slot, and complete cooperation. They could do whatever they wanted: He would protect them from the network bosses who might question some of their more experimental ideas.

Fremont turned to his own boss for the go-ahead, but as soon as he saw Andy's face, he knew the meeting had been a disaster. Andy was staring blankly past Michaels, his pale Slavic features a slab of stone. He had not said a word during the forty-five-minute spiel, and now it was obvious that he was completely turned off. But why? Scrambling to keep up appearances, Fremont realized only too well: Andy could not stand paternalism in any form. Behind his passive façade, he always had to be in control. To Andy, Michaels' promise to "take care" of him meant "I promise to take advantage of you." Smashing up against the moonscape of Warhol's face, the meeting ended when Andy got up and left the room without a word.

Six months later, Andy finally produced his own show for cable television. Following the format of *Interview*, "Andy Warhol's TV" appeared weekly for a half hour of chat with friends like Henry Geldzahler and Diana Vreeland, interspersed with fashion shows and at-home visits with up-and-coming rock stars like Debbie Harry of Blondie. Visually innovative in ways that anticipated the music videos of the eighties, the show lasted nine years.

"Warhol's standing in the art market," recalled Leo Castelli of this period, "was a bit down in the dumps." The portrait commissions had kept the cash flow steady (in November, Andy's courting of the Pahlavis had paid off in another royal portrait, this one of the Shah's "dragon lady" sister, Princess Ashraf). But there had been no significant new gallery work since 1976. At the end of January 1979, Andy's "serious" side began to reemerge with a show at the Heiner Friedrich Gallery in New York, based on one of his most mysterious images—a shadow. Ronnie Cutrone recalled the origins of the series: "Andy was always saying how much he liked the corners of his paintings where the screen falls off and it becomes just broken dots. He'd say, 'Oh, that looks so pretty. Why can't we do something that's like that?' The 'Shadows' were a way of doing something abstract that was still really something."

The "Shadows" sold out even before the opening and were critically well received. Typically, Andy deprecated them as "disco decor," but once again he had found the perfect image with which to evoke the emptiness at the heart of so much of the period's gaiety. A few months later, the financial standing of his art picked up when it became apparent that Charles Saatchi, the London advertising tycoon, and his wife, Doris, were amassing a collection of Warhols to rival that of the de Menils and Dr. Marx. "Saatchi wanted certain pieces, rare pieces that were very expensive," recalled Castelli. "When he found a Warhol he wanted—well, we were perfectly aware of the price he had paid for certain previous paintings, and Andy's prices started going up and up."

With the fall of the Shah in Iran that summer, Andy suffered a setback: Along with the Peacock Throne, the dreams of Farah Diba for a museum of contemporary art in Tehran had vanished. But he still had his own home-grown royalty. For his fifty-first birthday that August, he was given a glittering party by Halston at Studio 54, at which he received such presents as five thousand tickets for complimentary drinks and a garbage pail filled with one-dollar bills from Steve Rubell.

That fall Andy celebrated the life he'd been leading since 1974 with the publication of *Andy Warhol's Exposures,* a coffee-table book of his celebrity snapshots, accompanied by a gossipy text. It was published in conjunction with Grosset and Dunlap under his own imprint, Andy Warhol Books, and the *Times* announced: "Andy Warhol, Prince of Pop, has decided now that he has painted pictures, made movies, taken photographs and written books, that he would like to be a publisher, too. With Mr. Warhol, no sooner said than done."

The title was apt. There was nothing fawning in *Exposures* about the garishly lit black-and-white glimpses into the nightcrawls of the rich and famous. Bianca Jagger was shown shaving her armpit; Halston was seen holding falsies up to his chest. But despite a twenty-five-city American and European tour, ending with an ABC documentary on Warhol, sales of the book were disappointing. A gold-embossed collector's edition, accompanied by a signed lithograph and selling for five hundred dollars a copy, did reasonably well, but not well enough for Grosset and Dunlap to continue the imprint. For all its grittiness, *Exposures* seemed too soft. Peter Schjeldahl spoke for many in *Art in America:* "One realizes with a start how crucially Warhol's sixties hothouse of social nomads and street people, the laboratory of his social creativity, contributed to his cultural authority. That strange authority is long gone now, consumed by the anxiety of the rich to think well of themselves."

Was Warhol another "fashion victim"? And the lingering question remained: Were his celebrity portraits "art"?

That November, the Whitney Museum in New York attempted to settle the issue with an exhibition of fifty-six portraits of the famous figures Andy had painted over the decade. Chairman Mao occupied two walls of his own in a series of ten. The others, done in the double-image format of a "Most Wanted" criminal poster, ranged from Golda Meir to Liza Minnelli, Sylvester Stallone to Julia Warhola. Mounted on walls papered a glossy brown like a Madison Avenue boutique, and lining the museum's entire fourth floor, they seemed especially macabre at the opening reception, during which many of the faces on the walls stared down at their "real" faces staring up at them. The high point of the evening came when Andy, arriving with Paulette Goddard on his arm, stripped off his tuxedo trousers to reveal a pair of tight Levis.

Once again, feelings about Warhol the man inhibited inquiry into the merits of the work. In *Time,* Robert Hughes raged that Andy was "climbing from face to face in a silent delirium of snobbery." Hilton Kramer in the *Times* seemed personally affronted: "The faces are ugly and a shade stoned, if not actually repulsive and grotesque. It is probably idle to complain that the work itself is shallow and boring. What may be worth noting, however, is the debased and brutalized feeling that characterizes every element of this style. That this, too, may be deliberate does not alter the offense."

Lita Hornick, a literary patron and editor whose portrait Andy had painted in 1966, was closer to the mark in her book *Night Flight,* in which she noted that "Warhol both glamorized and satirized his subject. The key to the mystification he always evoked is that Warhol was always a double agent. His polarized point of view often seemed like no point of view at all, emptiness or vapidness. Nothing could be further from the truth. Warhol saw our fractured world in double focus."

Looking back on these portraits nearly a decade later in the British journal *Artscribe,* the critic Donald Kuspit pinpointed the source of their disturbing ambiguity in the artist's psychosexual feelings toward his famous subjects:

> Masochistically, Warhol felt inadequate compared to his subjects, whose self-love—the certainty that they were entitled to see and be seen—made them seem adequate in and for themselves. Even as photographically empty appearances they would always have more reality than he felt he would ever have. This feeling confirmed his sadistic treatment of them—his transformation of them into simulations— that is, his "de-realization" of them. But in a vicious circle this also announced his need for and envy of them. Warhol's portrait simulations are the opium he uses to anesthetize himself against the fate of forever feeling inadequate, empty, meaningless, unlovable, even nonexistent. . . . Warhol's portraits are full of vicious passivity.

To another observer, Susan Sontag, that passivity masked Warhol's unfeeling "capitalism":

> Warhol's ironic perceptions of things excluded one enormous emotion—indignation. It wasn't possible for him to say, "That's terrible— that shouldn't be"—which is the attitude of capitalism. Andy thought the Shah of Iran was charming and amusing. He thought it was

glamorous to know a head of state. But he could not think about whether he was a good guy or not. What he did think was, "I don't have to worry about that question. That question is boring." And it was not a boring question if you have feelings.

And the artist himself? Asked by a television reporter what he thought of a critic's remark that the paintings were terrible, Andy replied, chewing gum: "He's right."

It was, no doubt, Andy's comment on where the seventies had come to: the end of the parade. For as the portrait show was opening, the eighteen-month-long party at Studio 54 was ending: Rubell and Ian Schrager were pleading guilty in Manhattan Federal Court to evading more than $350,000 in taxes, a case that had followed in the wake of newspaper rumors (later proved unfounded) that the White House chief of staff, Hamilton Jordan, had used cocaine at the club. Truman Capote was once more in a bad way, having fallen off the wagon again and landed in the hospital. His association with *Interview* had ended after Andy let Bob Colacello edit one of his pieces, and Andy later claimed that he never heard from Capote again. Soon, one of Andy's princesses of the night, Liza Minnelli, would find herself in the Betty Ford Clinic for Alcohol and Drug Rehabilitation.

At the Factory, relations among Andy and his closest aides, Hughes and Colacello, were increasingly quarrelsome. Catherine Guinness, Andy's favorite playmate, had decamped for England to marry a lord, leaving "the supposedly cool artist," as the critic John Richardson noted, "more bereft than he liked to admit." (According to Walter Steding, Andy's only spoken response to Catherine's defection was: "Well, at least I never paid her.") Having an especially hard time was Ronnie Cutrone, who was drinking heavily, experiencing blackouts, and losing his wife. Unlike others at the Factory in desperate straits, he had begun to confide his problems to Andy, who "would genuinely try to care." Andy, recalled Cutrone, was suffering too: "I think everyone, with the exception of Fred and Andy, always knew that they'd have to leave the Factory. But, see, Andy hated people to leave. There was a fear of abandonment—he could never be alone."

That winter Andy seemed to mark the end of an era by painting a series of large canvases called "Reversals," a recycling of some of his best-known work of the sixties and early seventies. Now, the images of Marilyn Monroe, the Mona Lisa, the electric chair, the flowers, and Mao were silk-screened in negative so that the surface was mostly black, as though Andy were throwing a shroud over his art. "Reversals" was followed by "Retrospectives." Inspired by the example of Larry Rivers, this series combined an assortment of old Warhol images on his largest canvases to date, some measuring thirty feet long. Their impact was dramatic, but some observers viewed "Retrospectives" as a sign that Andy had reached a dead end: If before he had made an art out of "boredom," he was now falling victim to it.

In April 1980, he published *POPism,* his memoirs of the sixties. Coauthored with Pat Hackett, the book was hailed in *The New Yorker* as "arguably the best piece of work that Warhol has yet given us in any medium." But others—like Peter Conrad in the London *Observer*—saw it as a dead end:

> *POPism* is a necrotic book, in which the bloodless, undead, silver-maned Warhol broods over the demise of the decade and of his own talent. *POPism* reads like a report from beyond the grave. It recalls the Sixties as a zombified hell, fuelled by speed and acid, fed by junk food, populated by hermaphroditic sadists like Warhol's pop group the Velvet Underground or by cybernetic girls frugging in electric dresses with batteries at the waist and hair slicked down with frying oil—a long and demented binge which at this distance, for all its revolutionary ambition, seems as frivolous as the Twenties. Warhol is welcome to his fond mortuary reflections.

Near the end of 1980, Jed Johnson finally moved out of Andy's house. Andy's outward reaction was typically hard-boiled. When Ronnie Cutrone told him he had bumped into Jed on the street, Andy replied, "Jed who?"

"It was just horrible," Suzi Frankfurt recalled. "I said, 'Oh, Andy, Jed left, you must feel terrible. Is there anything I can do for you?' He said, 'What do you mean? He was just a kid who worked at the Factory.' It was like being slapped across the face."

But others saw the impact of the breakup. Raymond Foye, a friend, remembered that late one night after Jed's departure, Andy called up to say he had just found one of Jed's socks in a drawer. "Do you know how sad it is to find one sock?" he moaned. "I guess the relationship is really over."

A friend recalled this period as a "sick, dirty" one. Andy began seeing a British aristocrat, whom he would take to the back room of the Factory and watch as he masturbated. To the author William Burroughs, Andy remarked: "Entertainment sex is going to be the style of the eighties . . . the S&M thing where you go down to the S&M bars where they shit and piss and it entertains you." (Burroughs pointed out that it entertained *some* people.) Later in the same conversation Andy expressed the contrary view that sex was "too dirty, too dirty."

Andy now began acting out his feelings over the breakup with Jed in an uncharacteristic way: He started drinking. He drank vodka at lunch and champagne in the evenings, getting tipsy, but he was unable to lose control and really get drunk. In bars and restaurants he complained that drinks were not strong enough and ordered doubles. "I don't give a shit anymore," he told Walter Steding.

His collecting became more manic than ever. In the preceding several years he had rediscovered his first assistant, Vito Giallo, who now ran an antique shop on Madison Avenue in the East Seventies. As Giallo recalled, "For Andy, starting a new day meant buying something. He would come in on most mornings around 11 o'clock and stay in the shop for about an hour. He was interested in everything, and I was just floored by the amount of things he bought and the diversity of his interests. Andy's mania for collecting was an extension of his painting. He would buy rows and rows of mercury-glass vases, copper luster pitchers, Victorian card cases, all in one gulp. One couldn't help being reminded of his paintings of multiple images. He was very canny once you got past the 'Oh, this is fabulous' routine—he always had to appear an imbecile because that would give him the edge. Auctions had a fascination for Andy. We would compare notes before a sale and I would do the bidding for both of us. Then when the lots arrived at my shop, Andy would rush up, buy what he wanted, and rush back home only to put all the stuff in a closet."

"What Andy liked about auctions," said Fred Hughes, "was that you saw things without pretensions. You saw bad things as well as good things—things at their best and their worst, without their frames or upside down."

While Jed had been at East Sixty-sixth Street, Andy had stuck to his promise to confine his shopping bags to one or two upstairs rooms. Now, with Jed gone, the place soon overflowed with acquisitions, as though he couldn't bear the thought of being alone in the house. "Every Sunday," recalled the inventor Stuart Pivar, another obsessive collector, "I would pick him up at the local Catholic church and we would head downtown to the flea market. He liked to collect the best of things, the worst of things, and the mediocre. He loved the concept of trashiness, the very idea that there could be an advanced form of mediocrity. He didn't like compartments in his life and he didn't like compartments in his collecting. He just responded to things individually, not because they belonged to this or that category. He didn't collect like an interior decorator either, because he had a niche or a shelf that was empty. And he never collected Chinese art. 'Once I start,' he said, 'I'll never be able to stop.'"

Even Andy's legendary reserve in public seemed to be breaking down. "One night at [the disco club] Area," recalled Daniela Morera, "he was drunk and kissing a blond boy right in front of me! I said, 'Andy, you are so funny tonight!' And he pushed me to the boy he was kissing and said, 'Touch him! Touch him!'"

At times, he seemed in utter despair. He was fifty-two and frightened of spending his life alone. To Raymond Foye one night in a bar he cried: "What am I going to do? What am I going to do?"

In the summer of 1981, Chris Makos, the *Interview* photographer, introduced Andy to Jon Gould, a young vice president of production for Paramount Pictures in New York. Gould was handsome and extroverted, and it soon became clear that Andy had fallen obsessively in love with him. The pace of work at the Factory slackened as Andy chatted girlishly with Jon on the phone. He began to shower him with presents. At one point his assistants found themselves silkscreening hearts as a Valentine's Day gift for Jon. Makos noted: "Andy was intensely absorbed in his work except when he was having a relationship. Then the relationship became his work."

Andy's friends had mixed feelings about Gould. Some, like Vito Giallo, saw him as warm and loving, someone Andy could trust. Others, like Suzi Frankfurt, saw him as a druggie and an opportunist: "He was a fashion victim, the consummate hustler." A good mutual friend insisted that Andy and Jon were not sexually intimate—"just close companions." That Christmas and New Year's they rented a house in Aspen, Colorado, with Makos and his roommate, Peter Wise. Andy skied for the first time and, according to Makos, "loved it, until the last hill, where he became exhausted and just sat down to slide the rest of the way down the mountain." Catching his Rolex watch on a branch, he sprained his wrist and had to have it bandaged at the local hospital. Back in New York, recalled Makos, Andy's bandaged wrist was "like a badge. Everyone was thoroughly fascinated."

Whatever Gould's merits, it was clear that his friendship had lifted Andy's spirits. Andy had stopped drinking and begun a diet of macrobiotic food. He even employed an exercise instructor to come to the Factory every day and work out with him. "Muscles," he said, "are great. Everybody should have at least one that they can show off. I work out every day, and for a while at the beginning I tried to get 'definition,' but it didn't come off that way on me. Now I do have one muscle that appears and then it seems to go away, but it comes back after a while."

In early 1983, Bob Colacello left the Factory, bringing to an end a relationship that had grown increasingly strained. Colacello's influence had reached its apogee after he and Andy attended the Reagan inauguration in January 1981. As a mark of the superficial conservatism into which he had pushed *Interview,* his column burbled about a state dinner he and Andy attended for Ferdinand and Imelda Marcos: "Nancy never looked lovelier, Imelda never looked smarter, the President was as rosy-cheeked as ever, and Marcos impressed guests with his fifteen-minute toast calling for a strong America."

Within months after the inauguration, Colacello had hired Doria Reagan, the president's daughter-in-law, as a contributing editor, and through her had arranged for Andy to tape the First Lady herself for a cover story. The interview took place in October, and Nancy Reagan's soporific monologue on how fascinating it was to be in the White House rendered Andy mute during most of the taping. The Nancy Reagan interview wiped out whatever standing Andy still had as a "radical." The most pointed of the responses to his perceived amorality was Alexander Cockburn's parody in the *Village Voice*, which had Warhol and Colacello interviewing Hitler.

Despite his coup, Colacello had grown increasingly short-tempered in his supervision of the magazine, where the atmosphere was, according to the receptionist, Dona Peltin, "as congenial as being at the South Pole in your underwear." Even Andy had been the target of Colacello's vituperative eruptions. For a while, Andy seemed amused by the outbursts, following them with an imitation demonstrating how out of it his editor had been the previous night on cocaine. But Colacello's restiveness was becoming more and more marked: To a reporter he announced that he was thinking of running for political office, hinting at three or four "wealthy" (but unnamed) supporters.

In his defense, Colacello repeated an old charge against his boss: "Andy adored having three right-hand men arm-wrestling behind his back or, better yet, in front of him. Like a peasant mother, he was expert at keeping his 'kids' in a state of constant competition. I once spent hours selling the great art dealer, Iolas, only to have Andy throw the commission to Fred Hughes, because I had been in the bathroom at the moment Iolas decided between the two canvases I had shown him. Finally, I tired of selling Andy. I wanted to sell myself."

But, according to Vincent Fremont, the final showdown came when Colacello demanded a financial share in *Interview:* "Bob made an ultimatum, and Andy said no. Andy was very decisive if you challenged him on that score. It was his empire and there wasn't going to be any compromise. Bob wrote an official letter of resignation to Fred and myself."

To everyone but Warhol, Colacello's departure had seemed a foregone conclusion. But for weeks after the resignation, Andy complained to all who would listen: "How could Bob do this?"

26

INCE THE EXPLOSION of pop art in the early sixties, there had not been as much excitement in the New York art scene as that being stirred up by a new generation of painters in the early eighties. The artists—Julian Schnabel, David Salle, Eric Fischl, Susan Rothenberg, Francesco Clemente, Sandro Chia, Keith Haring, Kenny Scharf, and Jean-Michel Basquiat, among others—were all in their twenties or early thirties, and they all shared a passion for richly painted canvases, flamboyant color, and disturbing imagery, a style the critics labeled neo-expressionism. The marketplace and media had greeted them with almost unseemly enthusiasm. Here, after the mind-numbing conundrums of conceptual art and the intimidating austerity of minimalism, were real *pictures* once again, painted with energy if not always coherence. Here, once again, was art you could hang on walls, art that reproduced well in magazines, art that was eminently collectible—and with signatures by artists who, for the most part, had no reservations about promoting a public persona.

And here, in the Reagan economy of easy money, was a whole new generation of collectors, mindful of the astronomical leaps in the market value of artists who had been "unknowns" twenty years earlier—Johns, Rauschenberg, Lichtenstein, Warhol, Stella. Overnight, the prices for the smashed-plate paintings of Schnabel, for example, were approaching one hundred thousand dollars apiece; and Haring, a mere twenty-two-year-old, was seeing his graffiti-inspired cartoons fetch anything from two to ten thousand.

In this bullish art market, Warhol's marketability was as strong as ever, but his standing as a "serious" artist remained problematic. His reputation in Europe, always higher than in America, had received another boost, particularly in his stronghold of West Germany, where the revered Joseph Beuys had praised him as a real, if somewhat naive, revolutionary artist. Andy had taken some Polaroids of Beuys during the German artist's retrospective at the Guggenheim Museum in New York in 1979, and he returned the compliment by making one of his few portrait series of another contemporary artist. Over the somber black-ink face of the German, he sprinkled diamond dust—an American's answer to the sorts of materials (animal fat and human hair) Beuys used in his apocalyptic works. The Beuys portraits, among Warhol's strongest, toured several European cities in 1980, with both artists attending the highly publicized openings. Confounding his critics on the left, Andy told a West German newspaper: "I like [Beuys's] politics. He should come to the United States and be politically active. That would be great. . . . He should become president."

But such experiences no longer exhilarated him. Back home, he complained to Emile de Antonio that "Germany was so boring. I had to paint industrialists." (Only when de Antonio asked him how much he charged for the portraits did Andy brighten: "Fifty thousand dollars," he said, "unless they have wives and children. Then it's seventy-five.")

Around the Factory he had been nicknamed "Grandma," and Ronnie Cutrone began to feel that Andy was doomed to go on repeating himself. Aware of the neo-expressionists' return to a more freewheeling and painterly style, Cutrone was determined to prod Andy away from the "anonymous-hand" approach, to get him to "cut loose": "Andy hadn't done anything really important since 1977—only frivolous prints that would sell in Miami and Palm Beach. I wanted to have the respect I'd always had for him, so I started to muscle him. I said, 'Fuck this, let's just go and do it. Come on, let's just *paint* it!' He did one painting loose, *The Wicked Witch of the West*, and it was great, but he couldn't really break out. An artist gets trapped by his own image, and the risk of losing money and clients and getting bad reviews. I just wanted him to break new ground. One day he showed me some lobster paintings, and I said, 'Andy, what the hell are you painting? You're going out to have dinner with Chris Makos in a lobster joint, you take the bib and silkscreen a lobster. So what? That's shit! Come on!' In response to this sort of thing he'd either shut down and walk away, or he'd give me an order and say, 'Look, this is what we gotta do, let's just do it.' Or he'd say, 'No, no, *noooo*. I don't like that idea!' "

There were some new explorations in subject matter. The New York art dealer Ronald Feldman had commissioned "Ten Portraits of Jews of the Twentieth Century"—Sigmund Freud, Albert Einstein, Martin Buber, Sarah Bernhardt, George Gershwin, Gertrude Stein, Golda Meir, Louis Brandeis, Franz Kafka, and the Marx Brothers. (Andy had wanted to include Bob Dylan, with whom he had become friendly, but the singer had recently declared himself a born-again Christian.) A deluxe edition of the series sold for three hundred thousand dollars, and the paintings traveled to various small American museums in 1980. For Bruno Bischofberger's gallery in Zurich, Warhol created a powerful "Zeitgeist" series based on photographs of German stadiums and war monuments. And in keeping with the "appropriationist" thinking of the neo-expressionists, with their overt borrowings from artists of the past, he had begun to "Warholize" such art-history icons as Botticelli's *Birth of Venus, The Scream* by Edvard Munch, and the surrealistic cityscapes of one of his favorite twentieth-century artists, Giorgio de Chirico, these last offering a dazzling counterpoint to a retrospective of the Italian painter's work at the Museum of Modern Art in 1982.

Speaking about his affinity with de Chirico, he was unusually revealing about his own artistic concerns: "I met him in Venice so many times and I thought I loved his work so much. Every time I saw de Chirico's paintings I felt close to him. Every time I saw him I felt I had known him forever. I think he felt the same way. He repeated the same paintings over and over again. I like the idea a lot, so I thought it would be great to do it. I believe he viewed repetition as a way of expressing himself. This is probably what we have in common. The difference? What he repeated regularly, year after year, I repeat the same day in the same painting. All my images are the same, but very different at the same time. They change with the light or colors, with the times and moods. Isn't life a series of images that change as they repeat themselves?"

Still, he seemed stuck in a rut. As Ronnie Cutrone saw it, the measure of how low Andy had sunk was revealed by the *Dollar Sign* show at the Castelli Gallery in 1982: "That could have been a beautiful show. Andy had done some paintings of knives and guns at the same time [the gun was the same .32 snub-nosed pistol that Valerie Solanas had shot him with], and I started to hang the dollar signs and weapons all together so that when you walked into the gallery it looked like you were being mugged. Richard Serra [the sculptor] came in while I was setting it up and said, 'God, this is brilliant.' Then Fred Hughes came in, hung over, and said, 'This is too European. Let's just go with the dollar signs.' I called up Andy and started screaming that if he cared anything about his art, he'd come and take a look. But he thought Fred knew more about business than anyone so he said, 'No, Ronnie, look, I'm sorry you had to go through all that work, but just let Fred take over.' I walked out."

The *Dollar Sign* show was a singular disaster. Warhol suffered not only the insult of Castelli's decision to relegate the exhibit to his least prestigious space, the basement of his Greene Street gallery, but also the shock of not selling a single painting. There were some admirers among the critics, but the general response was summed up by Carter Ratcliff in his book *Warhol*: "Warhol's work has always been empty, but now it seems empty-headed."

He was, in any event, far from empty-handed. From 1982 to 1985, he moved most of the Factory's enterprises into enormous new spaces in a disused five-story Con Edison generator station that stretched an entire block from East Thirty-second to East Thirty-third Street between Madison and Fifth Avenue. The price was $2 million, and the expense of renovating the place would skyrocket from the original estimate of $1 million to $3 million. But the prices for his work were also higher than ever, especially for the earliest work. In 1983 the Blum Hellman Gallery sold a 1961 *Dick Tracy* for more than $1 million, and Robert Rauschenberg got almost as much for a *Saturday's Popeye* of the same year. Under Colacello's successor, Gael Love, a no less abrasive editor who had been working at the magazine in minor capacities since 1975, *Interview* was flourishing with a greater emphasis than ever before on mindless celebritymongering. The cable interview show, "Andy Warhol's TV" was holding nicely. And with his renovated physique, Andy finally felt confident enough in his appearance to accept regular offers to sell his celebrity for television spots. Working first for the Zoli agency, than as a Ford model, he was earning from two to ten thousand dollars a shoot, pitching the rums of Puerto Rico, Barney's clothing store, Sony, New York Air, Coca-Cola, and Golden Oak furniture. In October 1984, when the magazine *Manhattan Inc.* published a profile, "Andy Warhol: Portrait of the Artist as a Middle-Aged Businessman," the estimate of his wealth at $20 million was considered conservative.

Still, as his friend Emile de Antonio noted, "The richer Andy got, the more troubled he seemed to be by money. You sensed that the whole empire was shaky."

Andy was traveling a great deal, back and forth to Europe on the Concorde, and to his associates he seemed tired. In the fall of 1982, he had jetted off to Hong Kong for the opening of a discotheque, then gone on to Beijing. To Chris Makos, who was along on the trip, he had complained that he was too tired to get up the hill to the Great Wall, rallying only when he was told that a film crew was there waiting to photograph him. (According to Makos, "Andy didn't appreciate Chinese beauty, but he did appreciate the people's simplicity and their antlike organization.") Back in the States, when the rock singer Debbie Harry broke up her group Blondie, Andy asked a friend why she had stopped "being Blondie." "Because Debbie's too intelligent to remain in the role of a cartoon character every day," the friend replied. "What do you think I've been doing for the last twenty-five years?" Andy snapped. On another occasion he remarked: "Sometimes it's so great to get home and take off my Andy suit."

In the last years of his life, the person who helped free him from his "Andy suit" more than anyone else was Jean-Michel Basquiat, the wild child of neo-expressionism. The son of a Puerto Rican mother and a Haitian father, he was raised in a middle-class neighborhood of Brooklyn. This precocious, fiercely energetic young man was, as Andy had been, a protégé of Henry Geldzahler, who had been impressed with his work in a *New York/New Wave* group show at P.S.

1 Gallery in Long Island City. (Andy, in fact, had met Basquiat in 1979 while having lunch with Geldzahler in a Soho restaurant. The young man, then nineteen and a street huckster, was selling post-card reproductions of his paintings. Andy had bought one for a dollar.)

With the support of Geldzahler and Bruno Bischofberger, Basquiat soon established himself as the "real thing" among the neo-expressionists. His paintings—raw, frenzied assemblages of crudely drawn figures, scrawled mysterious symbols, and "messages"—were at once menacing and childlike, as free and violent as the graffiti with which he had once disfigured Soho walls. Not only was Basquiat of the streets; he had used the streets: His first paintings had been done on materials foraged from garbage cans. A heavy drug user, he had the personality to match his art: alternately shy and explosive, brilliant and threatening, self-important and self-destructive. His heroes were Picasso, Charlie Parker, and Jimi Hendrix: He would, he said, be the first fusion of artist and rock-and-roll star. Following one of Western art's great traditions, in a fit of rage he had destroyed all the work intended for a show in Italy. After his international "discovery" at P.S. 1, his prices began to soar, and so did his ambition to get close to Andy.

For a long while in the early eighties, Andy would have nothing to do with him. After Basquiat left a graffiti message on the door of a loft Warhol owned on Great Jones Street, Andy instructed Walter Steding, the loft's occupant, not to let him back in. A similar injunction was levied at the Factory. "I'm not sure why," recalled Ronnie Cutrone. "Maybe because Jean-Michel was black and maybe because he was a street kid and maybe because he took too many drugs. People used to have to go to the door and say, 'Oh, Andy's not here right now.' And Andy would be hiding in the back."

Finally, under prodding by Geldzahler and Bischofberger, who had become Basquiat's representative in Europe, Andy relented. Geldzahler was allowed to tape the young artist for *Interview*, and in 1984, when Bischofberger offered to sponsor a three-way collaboration among Warhol, Basquiat, and his more refined Italian counterpart, Francesco Clemente, Andy agreed, and the ban at the Factory was lifted.

Andy's decision to collaborate with two younger artists was both practical and intuitive. In 1970, Leo Castelli had predicted that

Warhol would be "cross-influenced" by what would come later. What he had not been able to foresee was that of all the artists of his generation, Andy would be the one most esteemed by the new generation. "He was my hero, the reason I came to New York in the first place," said Kenny Scharf. "When I was younger I was involved in the club scene—Club 57 in particular. We all wanted him so bad just to walk into that club. He was the father, and we were the children." Keith Haring recalled: "Of all the people I've met, Andy made the greatest impression on me. He was the one who opened things up enough for my situation as an artist to be possible. He was the first artist to open the possibility of being a public artist in the real sense, a *people's* artist." And, according to Julian Schnabel: "His contribution was as great as Jackson Pollock's—maybe even greater. I loved him."

Benjamin Liu, who had become a key assistant at the Factory, recalled that, for Andy, working with younger artists had become almost an obligation: "When the *New York Times Magazine* came out with its cover story about the new kids [February 1985], Andy was called 'the Pope.' He was very well aware of his role. He *willed* himself toward them."

Jean-Michel Basquiat would later say that it was all a matter of timing: "Andy hadn't painted for years when we met. He was very disillusioned, and I understand that. You break your ass, and people just say bad things about you. He was very sensitive. He used to complain and say, 'Oh, I'm just a commercial artist.' I don't know whether he really meant that, but I don't think he enjoyed doing all those prints and things that his stooges set up for him. I think I helped Andy more than he helped me, to tell the truth."

Basquiat did nothing to endear himself to Andy's other associates. Indifferent to Factory protocol, he chain-smoked marijuana as he worked, and Warhol's aides found themselves at a loss when dealing with what Geldzahler described as Jean-Michel's "charming but disdainful" attitude. He would look right through people with whom he had previously been friendly, or maintain an uncomfortable silence in the face of such simple questions as "How are you doing?"

"Andy did get a little nervous when Jean started smoking big spliffs of ganja," recalled Fremont. "That was something which would normally have driven Andy absolutely crazy. But they got along, and Andy would give him some fatherly lectures about health and try to tell him to stop."

Andy himself said that working with Basquiat was the "first time he had really enjoyed himself painting in years." Benjamin Liu saw the "affinity" Warhol felt for the young man as "recognition of his raw talent. Above all Andy was a very primitive artist."

Working with Basquiat, Andy changed his image from Brooks Brothers shirts and ties back to black leather jackets, sunglasses, and black jeans; he looked younger, thinner, no longer like an "old woman."

In 1984, Walter Steding, whose management contract with Warhol had been terminated, was told he would have to move out of 56 Great Jones Street, where he had been living rent-free. Andy rented the loft to Basquiat for four thousand dollars a month.

Basquiat's first one-man show at the Mary Boone Gallery was in May. The night before the opening, he threw Andy out of his house in a fit of nerves. Unperturbed, Andy attended the show, which included the young artist's portrait-homage to his mentor, showing Warhol as a banana. That same spring, in the *New Portraits* show at P.S. 1, Warhol displayed a portrait of Basquiat in a jockstrap, posed as Michelangelo's *David*.

Their collaboration continued through the summer, by which point Andy Warhol Enterprises, including *Interview* and the management staff, had relocated to the new Factory, leaving only Andy behind at 860 Broadway, with Basquiat, Brigid Polk, Benjamin Liu, and a trusted bodyguard, Augusto Bugarin, the brother of Andy's maids.

As with Jon Gould, Andy's relationship with Basquiat never became intimate, but he took the young man along as his date to parties, restaurants, and openings, telling reporters that Basquiat was "the best."

Nonetheless, several friends viewed the relationship with alarm. Emile de Antonio, for example, thought Andy was acting "like an old man in love with a tough young woman. Andy was obviously going to be thrown away at some point, if he didn't destroy Jean-Michel first." To others, the relationship brought out Andy's need to "save" someone. He was insistent that Jean exercise with him, and he counseled him endlessly on the evils of heroin. But to Cutrone, it seemed that Andy was "happy to be around a young drug addict again."

With Clemente, Andy was less personally involved. The Italian artist, who was by temperament more introverted than the other two, joined them on a number of occasions throughout the year, and their three-way collaboration resulted in at least a dozen canvases that were never shown. With Basquiat, Andy produced thirty to forty paintings. The results, unveiled at the Tony Shafrazi Gallery in September 1985, were more amusing than overwhelming: By some mysterious alchemy the paintings had an overall unity, without either artist having lost a trace of his individuality.

By 1985, Andy's relationship with Basquiat had leveled off. He had grown increasingly intolerant of the way Jean-Michel was handling his success. Basquiat had become a wild spendthrift, wearing Giorgio Armani suits to paint in, traveling in limousines, from which he once threw bums hundred-dollar bills, drinking five-hundred-dollar bottles of wine while maintaining his drug habit, and being rude to everyone around him. Andy had begun to needle Jean. On one occasion he goaded him into ordering dinner for six people in Basquiat's suite at the Ritz Carlton Hotel; it cost one thousand dollars. In March 1985, during a lavish dinner at the Great Jones Street loft on the eve of Basquiat's second one-man show, Andy remarked with syrupy irony that Jean-Michel had learned so much about wine. For his part, Basquiat was becoming increasingly vocal in complaining that he and his art were being "used" by the rich—perhaps out of resentment about being used by Andy. According to Emile de Antonio: "To most people Jean-Michel dominated Andy—Andy had been victimized. But I saw it quite the other way. I came to the conclusion that Andy was the prime mover of a fairly evil thing in relationship to Jean-Michel."

According to *Interview*'s advertising director, Paige Powell, the breakup came when the *New York Times* critic John Russell wrote that Basquiat's show was too obviously influenced by Warhol. After this, Jean-Michel stopped seeing Andy and never really talked to him again. From then on, Basquiat made a point of being as late as possible with the loft rent as a way of getting back at Andy. Andy's reaction to the break was ambivalent. On the one hand he was, as always, hurt and upset, but on the other hand he was relieved. He told Paige that it was better not to have Jean around the Factory so much: There was always the possibility he might turn violent.

By September, when their show of collaborations opened at Tony Shafrazi's gallery, the Warhol-Basquiat relationship had disintegrated to the point where they didn't speak to each other at the opening; Basquiat did not even bother to attend the celebratory dinner at Mr. Chow's. The Warhol-Basquiat show was drubbed—unfairly—by the critics, who turned their rancor on Warhol for another of his "manipulations," and on Basquiat for allowing himself to become an "art-world mascot." Andy, complaining that Jean-Michel was "just too peculiar" to work with anymore, returned to his own projects, and Basquiat's career fell into a long, disastrous decline. Finally, in the summer of 1988, he was found dead of a drug overdose in the loft on Great Jones Street.

27

IN LATE 1984, Jon Gould, who had been living at Andy's home on East Sixty-sixth Street, was diagnosed as having AIDS. The disease had already claimed one member of the Factory entourage, the *Interview* editor Robert Hayes, as well as a number of Andy's personal friends. Suddenly, the humor had gone out of Warhol's old adage about the most exciting thing being "not doing it." As Gould's condition deteriorated, so did his relationship with Warhol. According to Dr. Andrew Bernsohn, a chiropractor specializing in stress, whom they were both consulting about their relationship, "Jon was trying to get more in touch with his inner soul and he wanted Andy to do the same, but Andy wouldn't let go of the ego, the glitter, and the fame. He got frightened, and Jon would get mad because he didn't have the balls to let go. Jon felt stifled and choked by Andy."

"Everytime I met Jon he was becoming crazier and drunker," recalled Daniela Morera. "I saw him fighting with Andy, becoming very wild, jumping and screaming and answering Andy in violent ways." Suzi Frankfurt recalled: "Jon Gould became very demanding, and Andy wasn't used to people being so demanding. I think he was very disappointed by that because he was madly in love with Jon."

In early 1985, Gould had a medical crisis and nearly died. He was in New York Hospital for several weeks. Despite Andy's aversion to hospitals, he visited Jon daily, often staying for hours, drinking tea and drawing. He gave a number of drawings to one of Jon's nurses in the hope that she would take special care of Jon. Having no idea who Andy was, she threw them away. When Gould was released, he left Andy and moved to Los Angeles, where he was hoping to produce some films with spiritually positive themes. To his close friends it was obvious that Andy was hurt by Jon's departure, and particularly by the way he left: He told Andy he was going to California for a week, then called to say he was staying for two weeks; he never returned to Andy. Warhol felt betrayed. "When is he coming back?" he would ask Bernsohn, who didn't want to tell Andy that Jon was in fact traveling back and forth between Los Angeles and New York regularly but did not want to see him. "Why doesn't he call?" Andy would plead.

Soon Andy had adopted his old habit of expunging the tormentor from his life, and after a while he no longer mentioned Jon—nor did anyone else. When Gould died in September 1986, Bernsohn, who broke the news to Andy, found his reaction "quite neutral." In an interview later that year, however, Andy made the unusual admission that he was "a romantic": "My heart's been broken several times."

In August 1984, at Jon Gould's suggestion, Andy had begun making weekly visits to Dr. Bernsohn. Bernsohn had a nonprofessional interest in the use of crystals to "tap into" the "healing energy" and "vibrations" of the brain. Now Andy started wearing a crystal pendant around his neck to "tune him in to the cosmos." Crystals, he said, were "full of life force," explaining that the reason women live longer than men is that they wear crystal earrings and jewelry. According to Chris Makos, "He got so hooked on crystals that he even put them in the pot when he boiled water for his herbal teas. He was searching for spirituality."

The visits to Bernsohn became part of a new routine of obsessive concern about his health. On Mondays, he went to another chiropractor, Dr. Linda Li, for counseling on nutrition. She got him interested in eating raw garlic, a throwback to his Czechoslovakian ancestors, who used garlic to cure everything. The smell was unbearable at times, mingling oddly with the heavy perfumes he wore. On Tuesdays, he visited a dermatologist, Dr. Karen Burke, for collagen shots to keep his face wrinkle-free; on Wednesdays, Bernsohn adjusted his spine; on Thursdays, he had *shiatsu* massage; and on Fridays, he kept a regular appointment with his internist, Dr. Denton Cox. Naturally, Andy involved all his doctors with one another and was soon accompanying Bernsohn on dates with Burke and Li, getting them to compete for his attention. "He loved doctors," Bernsohn recalled. "He told me he wanted to stay youthful and live forever in his body. He loved life and he loved people. He really was quite different from the image he projected. He was seeking the fountain of youth."

As a result of the new regime, his appearance changed dramatically. He became thinner than he had ever been, his skin glowed, and he adopted a costume that seemed to bring together all the old and new influences in his life: wilder, bushier wigs; big, black-framed bullet-proof glasses; black Brooks Brothers turtleneck sweater; red L. L. Bean down vest; black Levis; black leather car coat designed by Stephen Sprouse; white or black Reeboks; and a big crystal around his neck. "Andy's look," said Makos, "always made a statement, and the overall effect of this one was that he'd accomplished everything imaginable in his lifetime."

But he had lost something crucial—the capacity to shock. In the fall of 1985, Andy went to Los Angeles to play himself in a segment of the hugely popular television series "The Loveboat." He fretted that when his friends saw "how terrible I am, my whole career will fall over," but he needn't have worried. At the end of the episode, one of the "Loveboat" characters said, "I just want to say how honored I am that you chose my wife to be the subject of your portrait." To Middle America, Andy Warhol was no longer a New York weirdo. He was a star.

The trip was lucrative (in addition to the "Loveboat" appearance, he painted Lana Turner's portrait and filmed a Diet Coke commercial) but his spirits seemed low. To a friend in New York, he referred to his Hollywood fans as "idiots." That fall, a week after his poorly received collaborative exhibit with Jean-Michel Basquiat at the Shafrazi Gallery, he opened a portrait show at the uptown Castelli Gallery, where he had first exhibited his "Flowers" in 1964. Called *Reigning Queens,* and depicting the monarchs of Great Britain, Denmark, the Netherlands, and Swaziland, the series had been executed almost entirely by his assistants, following his instructions. Standing at the opening in a ripped tuxedo jacket, black jeans, white sneakers, and a paint-spattered turtleneck, Andy told a friend: "They're trying to say I was a bad influence on Jean-Michel, but those paintings were good. Better than this junk. This is just trash for Europeans."

"Getting rich isn't as much fun as it used to be," Andy reflected during the complicated financing of the new Factory on East Thirty-third Street. "You spend all your time thinking about making the payroll and moving the cash flow and knowing everything about tax laws, which seem to change every year." To assistants like Benjamin Liu he complained that the new headquarters were too officelike, not enough an artist's space, and he moaned about all the prints he would have to make to pay for the renovation. To his brother Paul he complained about the sixty-thousand-dollar monthly mortgage payments, sounding so beleaguered that Paul offered him a loan. It was Paul's last meeting with Andy, who also complained bitterly about having to pay taxes to a government that had been auditing him since 1972.

Fred Hughes was the target of much of his irritation. There was no doubt about his feelings of gratitude to Hughes. "Andy said many times that if anybody deserved what he had made through his career it was Fred," remembered Liu. "He would also say to me, 'Oh, you know when I got shot, it was Fred who gave me mouth-to-mouth resuscitation.' Behind closed doors they could still get past their differences and down to business." But the strains were obvious to many. Hughes seemed to be using stimulants and alcohol more heavily than ever, and his behavior had become erratic. Often he would mysteriously disappear, apparently chafing under the burden of organizing Andy's complicated schedule now that Jed Johnson was no longer around, a task exacerbated by Andy's increasing forgetfulness. "It was like an old marriage," recalled Daniela Morera. "Fred had gotten really disrespectful of Andy. He'd say 'Don't listen to *him!*' His attitude was, 'He's an old, pathetic creature.' "

What most people did not know was that both men were seriously ill. Fred had had a minor attack of multiple sclerosis in 1983, but hadn't told anyone about it. Andy's gallstones, which had bothered him on and off since 1973, were acting up so badly that on at least one occasion he had to cancel a series of interviews because of the pain. Both men tried to ignore their physical problems, as if that would make them disappear.

The mood at the Factory was ugly: the old habits of vying for Andy's approval had given way to selfishness and indifference to any common goal. Of the old guard, only Vincent Fremont was solidly dependable. (Brigid Polk, manning the reception desk, had stopped drinking, but that hadn't softened her sharp tongue.) Andy's nephew George Warhola, who worked at the Factory as a maintenance man in 1985, recalled that "everybody was grabbing. Andy had a lot of money—that was the general attitude. They didn't take Andy for himself, they always wanted something from him. *Interview* was a mess; there was no control whatsoever. A package would come and nobody knew who had ordered it, and I said, 'Well, send it back.' They said, 'Naaa, it's okay. Just leave it.' "

Two of Andy's mainstays, Christopher Makos and Gael Love, were widely disliked for their abrasiveness. Andy himself was not above the general bitchiness. He was furious at one *Interview* editor's practice of going out in designer clothes that had been lent to the magazine for fashion shoots. When she was raped one night, he wondered aloud whether the rapist had liked her Armani gown.

Among the new staff members, Andy became friendliest with a young *Interview* assistant. Andy would take him along as his date to art openings and evenings at the new clubs like Area and Limelight, which had opened in the vacuum left by Studio 54. The young man enjoyed the attention, if not all of Andy's antics. Phoning him and finding him upset over something his boyfriend had done, Andy would call the boyfriend, get *his* story, then call the young man back to stir up more trouble. On one occasion, the man felt that Andy had purposely embarrassed him by inviting him to a party at Yves Saint Laurent's apartment in the Hotel Pierre without telling him that dress was black tie. Arriving in jeans and a leather jacket, the young man spent an uncomfortable evening with the leaders of fashion while Andy teased him about his beautiful lips and eyes. On another night, Andy took him to dinner and, with apparent sympathy, listened while he agonized over how to tell his parents he was gay. Then Andy suggested flippantly: "You don't have to say you're gay. Just say you don't like women because they smell."

Andy's social pace now included the suddenly fashionable author of *Slaves of New York,* Tama Janowitz, the fashion designer Stephen Sprouse, and the pop star Nick Rhodes of Duran Duran. "I love him, I worship him," he told a reporter. "I masturbate to Duran Duran videos." He attended the weddings of Madonna and Sean Penn in Los Angeles, and Maria Shriver and Arnold Schwarzenegger in Hyannisport. He was still astonished by celebrity. Sitting at the new club Nell's one night with Bob Dylan and the rock idol Sting, he turned to Paige Powell and whispered, "Do you believe who we're sitting with?"

For all the going out, he was increasingly alone. Evenings often ended early as he returned to his bedroom to watch television, experiment with his makeup, or try on one of his four hundred wigs before the large oval mirror at his dressing table. It was, noted his friend John Richardson, "a megalomaniac's mirror that would overpower anyone who wasn't wearing a full-dress uniform or ball gown." Another detail that caught Richardson's eye was "the basket by the fireplace overflowing with dog's toys—rubber mice and squeaky bones—belonging to Archie and Amos, the two miniature dachshunds that were regularly shuttled between Andy and Jed Johnson, after the latter moved out. The dogs were his boon companions, poignant relics of Andy's private life, and the only living things to share his bed."

To his friend Victor Hugo and others, Andy complained that he was suffering "the worst pain of all—the pain of boredom."

"Everything's boring" was his stock response when asked how he was feeling. "Terrible," he said, when asked how his painting was going. At private film screenings he invariably fell asleep, snoring loudly. He now spoke wistfully of old "first boyfriends." To a close friend like Chris Makos, he behaved like a "mad old queen," tormenting him like a lover (which Makos wasn't) with jealousies and unreasonable demands. To Benjamin Liu he seemed obsessed by the loan he had taken out to finance the new Factory. "Money was always on his mind. Money *was* his mind," recalled Liu. And always he seemed "let down." "More than anyone I ever knew," said Heiner Bastian, "Andy talked about being disappointed by someone."

At the end of 1985, Harper & Row published *America,* a cheaply printed album of snapshots of the American social and physical landscape culled from Andy's extensive crisscrossings of the country. Now, not everything was "so great." Now, he wrote, "one thing I miss is the time when America had big dreams about the future. Now . . . we all seem to think that it's going to be just like it is now, only worse."

"The inanities had ceased to charm, having reached a brutal apotheosis with the picture book, *America,*" wrote the critic Gary Indiana.

It was eerily, if unpleasantly, symbolic when, during a book-signing at Rizzoli's bookstore in New York, a young woman ripped off Andy's wig and made a clean getaway in a waiting car. With scarcely a change of expression, Andy, according to Victor Fremont, "just put his Calvin Klein hood up, didn't move, and kept writing."

He did seem to want closer ties to his family, with whom, apart from a brief weekly phone call from John, he had had little contact since Julia's death in 1972. When his nephew George announced he was going back to Pittsburgh, he said, recalled George: " 'I'll pay you to stay, I'll take care of you, whatever.' I said, 'Oh, Uncle Andy, it's not the money, I'd do anything for you if I could.' And he says, 'Once you go back, you'll stay home.' To be honest, I don't think Uncle Andy was very happy at all, even with all that money and fame."

After George left, Andy got another nephew, John's son, Donald, to come and work at the Factory. But he left soon too. As John remembered it: "Andy felt so bad Don didn't want to stay. Four Sundays in a row he says, 'Didya ask Don why he went back home?' He says, 'Gee, if Don hadda stayed I was going to put the *Interview* business over in his name.' "

Quietly, Andy had been going to Catholic mass at least weekly, if not daily, at Saint Vincent Ferrer at East Sixty-sixth and Lexington—"after which," recalled Catherine Guinness, "he was a lot nicer and less cynical." Knowing how much he hated holidays, Paige Powell suggested he help out that Thanksgiving and the following Christmas and Easter, serving dinners to the poor and homeless at the Church of the Heavenly Rest. With Wilfredo Rosado, an *Interview* staffer, and Stephen Sprouse, "Andy dragged around garbage cans and poured coffee," Powell recalled. "And he did something that wasn't on the program: He brought Saran Wrap so people could take the food home."

"That was the first time I ever saw him in an environment where no one knew who he was," said Rosado. "He just loved it."

28

ON JULY 8, 1986, Andy opened a show of self-portraits at the Anthony d'Offay Gallery in London. "When Andy walked into the reception," recalled d'Offay, "lots of people burst into tears. Andy Warhol was not just the world's most famous artist; he was an art hero, someone in whose life you perceive something extraordinary and brave."

"Warhol has always been much more than a magnet," wrote Polly Devlin in the *International Herald-Tribune*. "He is like a terrible prophet of doom, like that rock which the ancients thought an oracle, and through which the perpetual wind boomed the sound 'endure.' "

In his vast, doom-haunted oeuvre, these last portraits were the most electric with a sense of imminent demise. Based on a photograph of himself facing the camera, hollow-cheeked, eyes wide open but blank, white hair flying off in all directions, they were silkscreened, for the most part, behind a variously colored pattern of military camouflage, a brilliant metaphorical "scrim" that he used with other imagery of his last works, including the Statue of Liberty (a series in commemoration of the statue's one-hundredth anniversary that year), a final portrait of Joseph Beuys, and Leonardo's *Last Supper.*

It was a face that, in person, had become as famously ravaged as any in the world. As the German filmmaker Rainer Werner Fassbinder had remarked: "In Warhol's face you see the horrifying price he has to pay. To exist as a shell. Destroyed by one's own work." And Andy had done himself justice. "The new painting is like Warhol's great self-portraits of the sixties, candid and disturbing," wrote John Caldwell, who purchased one for the Carnegie Museum in Warhol's hometown of Pittsburgh. "It is, in a sense, too self-revealing; he looks simultaneously ravaged and demonic, blank and full of too many years and too much experience. . . . Warhol's face seems over-lit, almost dissolving in light, like a photograph on a sheet of news-paper held over a fire and about to burst into flames. Along with the obvious coldness and matter-of-factness of the image there is about it a kind of poignancy and we feel that Warhol himself, like his self-portrait, is imminently perishable."

In London, where the show was widely publicized, and where he was fêted at glittering parties, he proved, too, that his wit was as sharp as ever. "I paint pictures of myself to remind myself that I'm still around," he said. And: "It's hard to look at yourself. This is just weird stuff. If it wasn't me in the pictures, the exhibition would be great."

When he returned home from London, he seemed to have found new serenity—and energy. "Things were really moving on lots of fronts," recalled Vincent Fremont. "He wanted to put money into making movies again. We had bought the rights of Tama Janowitz's *Slaves of New York,* and Andy wanted to get the rights to some other books."

"The great unfulfilled ambition of my life is to have my own regular TV show," Warhol had said repeatedly for nine years. "Andy Warhol's TV" had been on cable since 1980 but had never taken off. Now the project was showing commercial promise. The producer Fred Friendly wanted to do a big daily television show on Andy, and Andy was interested. Other Warhol television projects now included making rock videos for bands such as The Cars for the popular

MTV cable channel, some of which featured Andy in cameo appearances that introduced him to a whole new audience of pubescent fans. Said Vincent Fremont: "We got tons of letters from high school teachers saying one of the first names that came up in art classes was Andy Warhol." *Interview* was continuing to expand—not without criticism from the serious art world. ("Now *Interview*," wrote Carter Ratcliff in *Artforum*, "is [Warhol's] greatest triumph: the vehicle of his constant presence in the media, the sign that he is part of the machinery generating the *now* that absorbs and degrades so much of our energy and our history.")

There was enormous interest in early Warhol. The Whitney Museum was organizing a retrospective of his films from the sixties. The de Menils' DIA Foundation had reached back to the early sixties, exhibiting the little-seen "disaster" paintings from 1963 and an assortment of "Hand-Painted Images" from 1960–1962. In 1986 the auction price for a Warhol reached a new high with the sale of *200 One Dollar Bills* for $385,000. John and Marge Warhola visited Andy in New York just before Christmas and found him in fine spirits, eager to hear about their day and looking extremely well.

He was most consumed by new work. Inspired by a plaster mock-up of *The Last Supper* found in Times Square, he was completing his last great series, using pop advertising imagery (the G.E. and Dove soap logos) to "energize," as John Richardson would later say, a sacred subject. Moreover, in the figure of the Soviet revolutionary Lenin he had found the subject for one of his most powerful celebrity portraits.

In January 1987 he had his most successful New York show in years, his first foray into fine-print photography, at the Robert Miller Gallery. Consisting of from four to twelve repetitions of images ranging from a James Dean fan with a "portrait" of Dean on his T-shirt to a self-portrait to skeletons, the photographs got excellent reviews. Their "aesthetic distance," wrote Andy Grundberg in the *Times*, was "just beyond the reach of either passion or resolution. If this essential quality has seemed diminished by repetition since the sixties, with these photographs he has found a way to restore its contemporaneity." Andy had recruited an assistant, Michelle Loud, to hand-stitch the prints into a group of multiples, and his old collaborator Gerard Malanga, writing in the *Village Voice*, saw in "those dangling threads . . . an eroticism . . . as if they were symbolic pubic hair."

At the opening, Andy stood behind the counter, signing catalogues. It was the last time David Bourdon saw him: "The place was jammed, and the shoulder-to-shoulder crowd extended all the way to the elevator bank. He was thinner than I had ever seen him, but he looked terrifically healthy, and that nervous little smile still darted about his lips."

Two weeks later, Andy flew to Milan for the opening of his last show. Capping a career driven by greater rigor and development than anyone suspected, it was organized by the man who had given Warhol his first show back in 1952 in New York—Alexander Iolas. Its subject was Andy's *Last Supper*. As the Milanese thronged the Palazzo della Stellina in the glare of television lights, as much to see Andy as to see what he had done with Milan's greatest painting, he was in benign spirits, telling one interviewer: "I think an artist is anyone who does something well—like if you cook well."

Behind the spectacle, friends felt a sense of foreboding. One, Pierre Restany, described Andy as "very moving in his platinum state wig with a mauve sheen, making him look as if he were in half-mourning." Iolas remarked: "As Christ said to all those priests, 'Suffer the little children to come unto me,' and Warhol is a horrible child. He has helped America to get rid of its puritanism. . . . Probably some day he will be considered a saint." It was not lost on his entourage, which included Fred Hughes and Chris Makos, that Andy made a comparatively early evening of it, returning to his hotel, the Principe e Savoia, before midnight.

The last two days in Milan, Andy did not leave the hotel. "He was very much in pain," recalled Daniela Morera. "He was in bed."

In fact, death seemed to be circling him, and he was characteristically both prescient and fearful. Earlier that year he had told an interviewer for the British magazine *The Face* that he liked a certain kind of Italian lip stain because it was "the stuff morticians use on dead people." Asked what would happen to his collection when he died, he replied, "I'm dead already." From Milan, he and his party flew to Zurich, where they were scheduled to be wined and dined for a week. But Andy became so frightened by the sight of a woman who attended a number of the dinners that he returned to New

York two days earlier than planned, claiming that she was trying to kill him.

The toll of AIDS was beginning to mount among old friends and colleagues; yet when they died, Andy maintained his usual reserve. In 1984 he had been the only person from the Factory not to attend the memorial service for the popular *Interview* editor Robert Hayes. He had made no comment when Ted Carey and Mario Amaya succumbed to the disease in 1985 and 1986, when Jackie Curtis died of a drug overdose in May 1985, or when news reached him of the death (from other causes) of Joseph Beuys in 1986. He had even refused to attend the celebrity-studded memorial for his boyhood idol, Truman Capote, in 1984.

By the end of 1986, his gallstones had become so enlarged that he was warned they could be life-threatening if he didn't have them removed. Still, he did nothing, paralyzed by his fear of hospitals. (Indeed, passing New York Hospital on his way to an auction at Sotheby's, he would turn his head to avoid seeing it.) In the first week of February, the illness stopped him in his tracks. For the first time anyone could remember, he abandoned friends in the middle of an evening on the town and hurried home to his canopied bed, doubled up in pain.

On Friday afternoon, February 13, he watched Brigid Polk wolf down a box of chocolates. "I'm dying for one," he said, "but I can't. I have a pain." On Valentine's Day, Wilfredo called him at home to say he didn't want to go out that night as planned. He was amazed when Andy replied, "I don't want to go out either." That day he had complained of abdominal pain to his dermatologist, Dr. Karen Burke; she made a sonogram which showed that his gallbladder was enlarged but not infected. He spent much of the weekend in bed, refusing to acknowledge his increasing discomfort to friends. When Victor Hugo called to complain of a three-week cold, Andy was sympathetic. Asked how *he* was feeling, Andy changed the subject.

On Monday, as he came down the stairs of his home, he remarked to an aide, "I feel funny—it's my stomach." He canceled all his appointments that day and did not go to work. That afternoon at the Chiropractic Healing Arts Clinic, Linda Li gave him a *shiatsu* massage. Andy subsequently claimed to Dr. Burke that the treatment had sent one of the gallstones into the "wrong pipe," causing him greater pain.

He was able to keep a Tuesday appointment to appear with Miles Davis as a model in a fashion show at a new downtown club called The Tunnel. His friend Stuart Pivar recalled that he was kept waiting for an hour in a cold dressing room "in terrible pain. You could see it on his face." Nonetheless, to the applause of his entourage, Andy clowned his way down the runway, carrying Miles Davis' coattails like a bridesmaid as the great jazzman played his trumpet. When he came off, he almost collapsed in Pivar's arms. "Get me out of here, Stuart," he gasped. "I feel like I'm gonna die!"

The next day, he stopped in at the Mel Davis dog-grooming salon on East Forty-ninth Street to have one of his dachshunds' claws clipped. "You look familiar to me," Davis said.

"Yeah," replied Andy, "I'm the undertaker."

In the afternoon, he went to the office of his internist, Dr. Cox, complaining of having felt sick for a month. After a thorough examination, Cox diagnosed a badly infected gallbladder in danger of becoming gangrenous, and he advised Warhol to have the gallbladder removed as soon as possible.

On Thursday, Andy caught a chill, which aggravated his condition. A second sonogram taken that day by Dr. Cox revealed the gallbladder to be severely infected, inflamed, and filled with fluid. He couldn't wait any longer.

On Friday, Andy had been scheduled to model for drawing students of Stuart Pivar at the New York Academy of Art. Reluctantly, he made arrangements to go into New York Hospital instead. It was fixed that he would have the operation on Saturday and be out by Sunday. Apart from his closest aides, no one, not even his family, was to know. "They're coming for me with handcuffs," he told Dr. Bernsohn. According to an aide, Ken Leland: "He told all of his doctors, 'Oh, I'm not going to make it.' When they tried to reassure him he said, 'Oh, no, I'm not coming out of the hospital.' " Still, he told Paige Powell not to cancel their ballet tickets for Sunday night.

Before checking into the hospital on Friday afternoon, he locked many of his valuables in the safe at his house. Ken Leland was with him: "Andy was in the back room rummaging through stuff and I was hurrying him up because the car [sent by Stuart Pivar] was waiting. A gate outside his house was broken and he said he wanted to get it fixed once the weather was warmer. He didn't let on to me that he was scared. At the hospital, we checked in with this lady named Barbara, who said, 'If you want to change your room, you can.' Andy asked if there were any big stars at the hospital, and Barbara replied, 'You're the biggest.' He explained that he didn't want any visitors or anything, so she asked what name he would like to be disguised under. Andy said, 'Oh, make it Barbara.' She giggled and said she couldn't do that, so he said, 'Just make it Bob Robert.' And she did."

According to a report later compiled for the *New York Times Magazine* by M. A. Farber and Lawrence Altman:

> After fifteen hours of preparation, Warhol's surgery was performed between 8:45 A.M. and 12:10 P.M. on Saturday, February 21, 1987. There were no complications at the time—and none were found during the autopsy or by any of the doctors who have reviewed the case. Warhol spent three hours in recovery following surgery, and at 3:45 P.M. was taken to his private room on the twelfth floor of Baker Pavilion. For comfort, precaution and on the recommendation of Dr. Cox, his regular physician, Warhol was placed in the hands of a private duty nurse, rather than the normal complement of staff nurses. He was examined during the afternoon and early evening by the senior attending physicians, who noted nothing unusual. Alert and seemingly in good spirits, Warhol watched television and, around 9:30 P.M., spoke to the housekeeper at his East Side home, a few blocks away.

Whether the private nurse, Min Chou, remained at her post throughout the night is not known. Subsequent investigations have alleged that she did not, and that she failed to record Warhol's vital signs, his urine output, and the time and dosage of painkilling drugs. New York Hospital would also face allegations of neglect in failing to obtain the patient's complete medical records; ignoring his allergy to penicillin and administering Cefoxitin, a drug that can cause similar allergic reactions; failure of the staff nurses to measure properly his fluid intake and output; and failure of hospital staff members to replace a malfunctioning suction device to permit reduction of fluids even after it was requested by a physician. The chances of dying from complications of routine gallbladder surgery are many thousands to one, but whether any of these other factors contributed to Andy Warhol's death is uncertain.

As Farber and Altman wrote:

> At 10 P.M. and at 4 A.M. on Sunday, February 22, Min Chou, the private nurse who had been selected by the hospital from a registry, took Warhol's blood pressure and found it stable. She gave a progress report to the chief surgical resident by telephone at 11 P.M., presumably while the patient slept.
>
> At 5:45 A.M., Ms. Chou noticed that Warhol had turned blue, and his pulse had weakened. Unable to waken him, she summoned the floor nurse who, in the words of a colleague, "almost had a stroke." A cardiac arrest team began resuscitation efforts but, according to hospital sources, had difficulty putting a tube in Warhol's windpipe because rigor mortis had started to set in. At 6:31 A.M. the artist was pronounced dead.

Fred Hughes was the first to be alerted. Ever prudent, he called his lawyer, Edward Hayes, a rakish former assistant district attorney (and later the model for Tom Killian, the wily lawyer in Tom Wolfe's *The Bonfire of the Vanities*). Hayes called a security agency and within hours after Warhol's death had guards stationed around the house on East Sixty-sixth Street and the Factory. The two men arrived at Andy's house in mid-morning and were let in by his maids, Nena and Aurora, both in tears.

There, the safe was opened and Hayes began to pore over its contents, while Hughes, dazed, wandered through the clutter. The phone rang at eleven: It was John Warhola calling from Pittsburgh for his customary Sunday chat with his brother. Hughes picked up the receiver and, according to John, said without warning or introduction: "John, you're calling for Andy. Andy died."

As John later recalled the conversation, he said to Hughes: "Well, we're coming up. What happened?"

Hughes answered, "Well, he died in the hospital."

John repeated, "Well, we're coming up." Hughes told him: "Don't bother coming to the house. We're putting a padlock on it."

John then called his brother Paul. As Paul remembered: "He said, 'Andy's dead,' and I says, 'Andy who?' And he says, 'Andy—you know, your brother.' Andy was already dead for five hours. They didn't notify nobody. They went right over to the house and started rooting through."

The Cable News Network broke the story of Warhol's death at noon. There was no network coverage until later in the day; in the interim, telephone messages carried the news.

The next morning, it would be on front pages around the world, accompanied by hastily assembled obituaries and assessments, the most judicious of which was John Russell's in the *New York Times,* which stated: "Posterity may well decide that his times deserved him and were lucky to have got him."

By Sunday evening, small groups had gathered throughout New York to mourn. Paul and John Warhola arrived from Pittsburgh and, despite Hughes's warning, went straight to East Sixty-sixth Street, hoping to spend the night there. Both men felt there was something suspicious going on. Paul, in fact, had the thought that Andy might have been murdered in some conspiracy. When they arrived, recalled Paul, Hughes and Hayes "were rooting through the place. Ed Hayes was in his T-shirt, sweating. I says, 'Who are you?' " Hughes remained firm: They would have to stay in a hotel. They would all meet, he said, the following morning to go over Andy's will, which they had found in the safe.

In his last book, *America,* Andy had written, "Dying is the most embarrassing thing that can ever happen to you, because someone's got to take care of all your details . . . someone's got to take care of the body, make the funeral arrangements, pick out the casket and the service and the cemetery and the clothes for you to wear and get someone to style you and put on the makeup. You'd like to help them, and most of all you'd like to do the whole thing yourself, but you're dead so you can't."

On Monday morning, it was left to Paul and John to identify their brother's body at the city morgue. Paul recalled that Dr. Elliot Gross, the chief medical examiner, seemed oddly agitated, pacing back and forth in front of his desk, as if something were wrong, but he and John were relieved to see that Andy looked peacefully asleep.

Their meeting with Hughes and Hayes took place in the law offices of Hayes's brother Stephen. (Hughes, who was rapidly taking control, would dismiss Andy's lawyers, the firm of Paul Weiss Rifkind Wharton and Garrison, and make Ed Hayes the attorney for the estate.) There they learned of Andy's legacy: He had left $250,000 to Hughes, whom he had named as his executor, directing him to give up to $250,000 to each of the Warhola brothers. The rest of the estate was to go to a "Foundation for Visual Arts," to be run by Hughes and a board consisting of him, John Warhola, and Vincent Fremont, the Factory administrator. Andy's life may have seemed largely a matter of serendipity, but he had been meticulous in planning for the aftermath of his death.

Hughes, the brothers remembered, was strictly business: If Paul and John signed a waiver promising not to contest the will, they would each receive $250,000. Paul, who believed with some accuracy that Andy's estate might be worth as much as $100 million, protested: "Just a minute. You throw all this up and want me to sign that waiver. You don't even give me the courtesy of having counsel with me. Give me a day to think about it." John felt pressured too, but was ready to sign. Paul continued to object. Finally, Paul asked, "What about the funeral?" remembering that it had been their mother's request to have Andy buried next to her in Pittsburgh. "Oh, you can have the body," replied Hughes.

Andy's body was transported to Pittsburgh the following morning, looking, Paul recalled, considerably less "good" after the autopsy. An open-coffin wake had been scheduled for Wednesday at the Thomas P. Kunsak Funeral Home, requiring a rush job of getting the body made up and dressed. To a reporter, the funeral home director boasted: "The competition is sure jealous today. It was all the talk of the funeral trade about how I landed the Warhol body."

Andy's last costume was a black suit, a colorful paisley tie, and one of his favorite platinum wigs. After considerable argument, Paul and John agreed that he should be buried in his sunglasses. To one reporter the sight of Andy lying in the white-upholstered bronze coffin, holding a small black prayer book and a red rose, was "Warhol's final discomfiting work."

Fearing a horde of gate-crashers, Paul and John posted a guard at the door of the funeral home and, the next day, at the Holy Ghost Byzantine Catholic Church for the funeral service. But it wasn't necessary. Most of the mourners were Andy's relatives and a few old friends from childhood, such as Joseph Fitzpatrick, his art teacher at Schenley High. Flowers had been sent by Leo Castelli, Mick Jagger and Jerry Hall, and the staff of *Interview,* but Hughes had taken it upon himself to announce that the Warholas wanted as few guests as possible, and not a single famous name turned up—to the disappointment of some of the mourners. Indeed, only Hughes, Brigid Polk, Paige Powell, Wilfredo Rosado, Gael Love, Vincent Fremont and his wife, and a few others from the Factory made the trip from New York.

After the mass and anthems by a male choir, the eulogy by Monsignor Peter Tay began well enough: "The whole world will remember Andy. While he said everybody would be famous for fifteen minutes, his own fame spanned three decades. . . . Andy never knocked anyone. He had a deep, loving trust in God . . ." But Tay, who had never met Warhol, could not let the deceased's more impious worldly deeds pass unnoticed: "Though it seems at times that he wandered far from his church, we do not judge him. Jesus forgave the thief on his right. He did not forgive the thief on his left. . . . It means there is always hope, but it also means nobody should take salvation too much for granted." Nervously, the Warholas exchanged glances across the pews.

A cortege of twenty cars accompanied the coffin, covered by a blanket of white roses and asparagus ferns, on the twenty-five-mile journey through the working-class Northside of Pittsburgh to Saint John the Divine Cemetery in Bethel Park. On a barren hillside overlooking U.S. Route 88, an old trolley line, and a cluster of matchbox houses, the procession stopped. A brief service was held at a small chapel near the cemetery entrance, then the mourners proceeded to the gravesite beside the remains of Andrei and Julia Warhola. Andy had once written that he wanted his tombstone either to be blank or else to be inscribed with the single word *figment.* Instead, a small, simple marble slab, bearing only his name and the dates of his birth and death, marks the spot.

The priest said a brief prayer and sprinkled holy water three times over the casket.

Paige Powell dropped a copy of *Interview* and a bottle of Esteé Lauder perfume into the grave before the casket was lowered.

Nearby, three gravediggers waited, their shovels face down on the cold ground. To a reporter one of them whispered: "This is my first famous funeral."

Epilogue

IT WILL TAKE my death for the Museum of Modern Art to recognize my work," Andy Warhol had once lamented to Henry Geldzahler. So it did. Within weeks after Warhol's death, the premier museum of twentieth-century art in the world began organizing its most ambitious recognition of an artist's work since the Picasso blockbuster of 1980.

Nearly two years later, on February 1, 1989, MOMA celebrated the opening of *Andy Warhol: A Retrospective* by throwing a party that might have exceeded even Andy's wildest dreams. There, spread over two floors, was an overwhelming array of three hundred paintings, drawings, sculptures, photographs, and films. Culled by the curator Kynaston McShine from dozens of public and private collections in nine countries, it was not just a testament to the astonishing output of Warhol and his Factory, but a replay of more than three decades of American cultural, social, and political taste and turbulence.

There, from the time of Andy's first break in the New York commercial-art world in the fifties, were the pen-and-ink drawings of ladies' shoes, still arresting for the lyrical line and loving detail invested in such frivolous objects. There, marking his crossover into the fine-art world, was an installation reminiscent of a window display he had designed for Bonwit Teller in 1961: mannequins in prim dresses posturing in front of an exploding world of painted, blown-up comic strips and newspaper ads.

With the passage of time, Warhol's early pop paintings and objects had taken on the presence of totems: The infamous painted cartons with their brand names of Brillo, Del Monte, Campbell's, and Kellogg's now seemed less banal than eerie—old household ghosts. The silk-screened canvases of Marilyn Monroe, Elizabeth Taylor, Jackie Kennedy, Elvis Presley, and others were more disturbing and moving than ever—icons burnished by the "rubbing" of so many eyes, so many fantasies.

The rarely seen series of "disasters"—car crashes, race riots, a gangster funeral—now seemed definitive reflections of a society's numbing obsession with violence. From the long period of celebrity portraits, beginning with the epic Mao series, many faces—his mother, Truman Capote, Mick Jagger, Lana Turner—appeared as cunningly colored, as sharply poignant, as a Gauguin. And the late works—the *Camouflage Self-Portrait,* the enormous pop pastiche of *The Last Supper*—gave the lie to those who had complained that Warhol had never "developed." Here was the fully mature artist, looking back and looking beyond, as summed up in his very last image, *Moonwalk (History of TV Series),* which showed the famous image of the astronaut Neal Armstrong, having just planted the American flag on the moon. In Andy's hands, the hero's face had been made to look like a television screen, across which was scrawled like a flash of lightning the initials A. W.

Here, too, elbow to elbow under a ceiling of helium-filled replicas of Andy's *Silver Pillows,* craning to see and be seen in the glare of TV lights and camera flashes, to hear and be heard against thumping music by the Velvet Underground, was perhaps the greatest family reunion the American art world had ever known. Among the thousands of celebrants were Philip Pearlstein, Leo Castelli, Henry Geldzahler, John Giorno, Billy Name, Gerard Malanga, Fred Hughes, Christopher Makos, Paul Morrissey, Emile de Antonio, Bianca Jagger, Ronnie Cutrone, John Richardson, Irving Blum; Dennis Hopper, David Bourdon, Tony Shafrazi, Roy Lichtenstein, Geraldine Stutz, Keith Haring, Brigid Polk, members of the de Menil family, Bob Colacello, Vito Giallo, Stuart Pivar, Ultra Violet,

Nathan Gluck, Vincent Fremont, and Steve Rubell, to name only a few of those present who had loved, hated, worked, and fought with Andy Warhol, and become, in the process, members of a new race: Warhol People.

And here from Pittsburgh were the Warholas—the eldest brother, Paul, retired from the scrap metal business, and John, a retired appliance parts clerk for Sears. Two of John's sons were there, too, as was Paul's son James, whom Andy had taught to stretch canvases when he was eight. Not a day had gone by since Andy's death, they said, when they hadn't thought of him, and they still could not believe that he was dead.

If you glanced around for a stunning second, he wasn't: There, off to one side, was a figure with the platinum-white wig, thick-rimmed glasses, pancake-white pallor, dark jacket, loose tie, jeans, and tentative half-open smile of Andy himself. It was Allen Midgette, the Warhol actor who had impersonated the artist on college campuses in the sixties, doing it all over again at the end of the eighties.

For Paul and John Warhola, this was the first time in all those years that they had been to a show of their brother's art. For many others, it was an event that seemed always to have been and would always be—another Warhol opening. Before the revels were over, they would pull down the silver pillows and run out into the night to release them into the New York sky.

Bibliography

BOOKS BY ANDY WARHOL

a, a novel. New York: Grove Press, 1968.

America, photos and text. New York: Harper & Row, 1985.

Andy Warhol's Exposures, photos with text by Andy Warhol and Bob Colacello. New York: Andy Warhol Books/Grosset and Dunlap, 1979.

Andy Warhol's Index Book. New York: Random House, 1967.

The Philosophy of Andy Warhol (from A to B and Back Again). New York: Harcourt Brace Jovanovich, 1975.

With Pat Hackett. *Andy Warhol's Party Book.* New York: Crown, 1988.

With Pat Hackett. *POPism: The Warhol Sixties.* New York: Harcourt Brace Jovanovich, 1980.

BOOKS ABOUT ANDY WARHOL

David Bailey. *Andy Warhol: Transcript of David Bailey's ATV Documentary.* London: A Bailey Litchfield/Mathews Miller Dunbar Co-production, 1972.

Andreas Brown. *Andy Warhol: His Early Works, 1947–1959.* New York: Gotham Book Mart, 1971.

Catalogues of The Andy Warhol Collection. 6 vols., boxed. New York: Sotheby's, 1988.

John Coplans, with contributions by Jonas Mekas and Calvin Tomkins. *Andy Warhol.* New York: New York Graphic Society, 1970.

Rainer Crone. *Andy Warhol.* Translated by John William Gabriel. London: Thames and Hudson, 1970.

Rainer Crone. *Andy Warhol: A Picture Show by the Artist.* Translated by Martin Scutt. New York: Rizzoli, 1987.

Peter Gidal. *Andy Warhol: Films and Painting.* London: Studio Vista Dutton Paperback, 1971.

Stephen Koch. *Stargazer: Andy Warhol and His Films.* New York: Praeger, 1973.

Christopher Makos. *Warhol Makos: A Personal Photographic Memoir.* London: Virgin, 1988.

Carter Ratcliff. *Andy Warhol.* New York: Modern Masters Series, Abbeville Press, 1983.

Patrick S. Smith. "Art *in Extremis:* Andy Warhol and His Art." 3 vols. Ph.D. dissertation, Northwestern University, Evanston, Illinois, 1982. (A shortened version was published in 1986 by UMI Research Press, Illinois, as *Andy Warhol's Art and Films.*)

Jean Stein. Edited with George Plimpton. *Edie: An American Biography.* New York: Knopf, 1982.

Ultra Violet. *Famous For Fifteen Minutes.* San Diego: Harcourt Brace Jovanovich, 1988.

Viva. *Superstar.* New York: G. P. Putnam's Sons, 1970.

John Wilcock. *The Autobiography and Sex Life of Andy Warhol.* New York: Other Scenes, 1971.

Source Notes

PROLOGUE

Based on:
Catalogues of The Andy Warhol Collection, 6 vols. (New York: Sotheby's, 1988).
Rita Reif, "At the Warhol Sale: A Hunt for Collectibles," *New York Times,* April 28, 1988.
Peter Watson, "Andy Warhol's Final Sale," *Observer* (London), March 6, 1988.

CHAPTER ONE

Based on interviews with John Elachko, Lillian Gracik (née Lanchester), Robert Heidie, Mina Kaveler (née Serbin), Benjamin Liu, Ann Madden (née Elachko), Catherine Metz, Justina Swindell (née Preksta), Andy Warhol, Ann Warhola, John Warhola, Margaret Warhola, and Paul Warhola.
Also based on material published in the following sources:
David Bailey, *Andy Warhol: Transcript of David Bailey's ATV Documentary* (London: A Bailey Litchfield/Mathews Miller Dunbar Co-production, 1972).
Burton Hersh, *The Mellon Family* (New York: William Morrow, 1978).
Philip Klein, *A Social Study of Pittsburgh* (1938).
Julia Markus, "Andy Warhol, Psyched by His Century," *Smithsonian Magazine* (February 1989).
H. L. Mencken, *A Mencken Chrestomathy* (New York: Knopf, 1927).
Ralph Pomeroy, "The Importance of Being Andy," *Art and Artists* (London) (February 1971).
John Richardson, "The Secret Warhol," *Vanity Fair,* 50, no. 7 (1987).
Jean Stein, ed. with George Plimpton, *Edie: An American Biography* (New York: Knopf, 1982).
Robert Tomsho, "Looking for Mr. Warhol," *Pittsburgher Magazine,* 3, no. 12 (1980).
Viva, *Superstar* (New York: G. P. Putnam's Sons, 1970).
Andy Warhol, *The Philosophy of Andy Warhol (from A to B and Back Again)* (New York: Harcourt Brace Jovanovich, 1975).
Bernard Weintraub, "Andy Warhol's Mother," *Esquire,* 64, no. 5 (November 1966).
Eva Windmuller, "A Conversation with Andy Warhol, *Stern* (West Germany), October 8, 1981.

CHAPTER TWO

Based on interviews with Avram Blumberg, Leila Davies, Perry Davis, Betty Ash Douglas, Arthur and Lois Elias, Joseph Fitzpatrick, Albert Goldman, Harold Greenberger, Dorothy Kanrich, Lee Karageorge, Leonard Kessler, George

Klauber, Robert Lepper, Mary Adeline McKibblin, Catherine Metz, Irene Passinski, Elvira Peake, Dorothy Kantor Pearlstein, Philip Pearlstein, Grace Regan, Libby Rosenberg, Gretchen Schmertz, Bill Shaffer, Walter Steding, Russell Twiggs, Edwin L. Vollmer, Ann Warhola, John Warhola, and Paul Warhola. Also:

George Anderson, " 'Hope': Child's View of War," *Pittsburgh Post Gazette,* January 22, 1988.

Gretchen Berg, "Andy Warhol: My True Story," *Los Angeles Free Press,* 6, no. 11 (1967).

John Malcolm Brinnin, *Sextet: T. S. Eliot & Truman Capote & Others* (New York: Delacorte/Seymour Lawrence, 1981).

John Costello, "Love, Sex, and War" (London: Pan Books, 1986).

Rainer Crone, trans. John William Gabriel, *Andy Warhol* (London: Thames and Hudson, 1970).

Great American Audio Corp., "The Fabulous Forties" (cassette tapes).

Ben Kartmen and Leonard Brown, *Disaster* (A Berkeley Medallion Book, 1960).

Julia Markus, "Andy Warhol: Psyched by His Century."

Sam McCool, *Sam McCool's New Pittsburghese: How to Speak Like a Pittsburgher* (Pittsburgh: New Image Press, 1982).

Patrick Smith, "Art in Extremis: Andy Warhol and His Art" (Ph.D. diss., Northwestern University, 1972).

Jean Stein, *Edie.*

Robert Tomsho, "Looking for Mr. Warhol."

Ultra Violet, *Famous for Fifteen Minutes* (San Diego: Harcourt Brace Jovanovich, 1988).

Andy Warhol, *America* (New York: Harper & Row, 1985).

Andy Warhol, *The Philosophy of Andy Warhol.*

CHAPTER THREE

Based on interviews with Francesca Boas, Leila Davies, Perry Davis, Lois Elias, Vito Giallo, Nathan Gluck, Albert Goldman, Leonard Kessler, George Klauber, Grace Regan, Ralph Ward, John Warhola, Paul Warhola, and Carl Willers. Also:

Andreas Brown, *Andy Warhol: His Early Works, 1947–1959* (New York: Gotham Bookmart, 1971).

Gerald Clarke, *Capote* (New York: Simon and Schuster, 1988).

Martin Duberman, *About Time: Exploring the Gay Past* (New York: A Seahorse Book, Gay Presses of New York, 1986).

Lawrence Grobell, *Conversations with Capote* (New York: New American Library, 1985).

Stephen Koch, "Warhol," *Motion Picture,* 11, no. 1 (1987).

Philip Pearlstein, "Andy Warhol, 1928–1987," *Art in America,* 75, no. 5 (1987).

Patrick Smith, "Art in Extremis: Andy Warhol and His Art."

Jean Stein, *Edie.*

Calvin Tomkins, *Off the Wall: Robert Rauschenberg and the Art of Our Times* (New York: Penguin, 1981).

Calvin Tomkins, "Raggedy Andy," in John Coplans, *Andy Warhol* (New York: New York Graphic Society, 1970).

Andy Warhol, *The Philosophy of Andy Warhol.*

Andy Warhol, "Sunday with Mister C: An Audio-Documentary by Andy Warhol Starring Truman Capote," *Rolling Stone,* April 12, 1973.

CHAPTER FOUR

Based on interviews with Seymour Berlin, Stephen Bruce, Vito Giallo, Nathan Gluck, Bert Greene, Leonard Kessler, George Klauber, David Mann, John Warhola, Paul Warhola, and Carl Willers. Also:

Hilton Al's review of Rainer Crone, *Andy Warhol: A Picture Show by the Artist, Village Voice,* 1987.

Ann Curran, "CMU's Other Andy," *Carnegie Mellon Magazine,* 3, no. 3 (1985).

James Fitzsimmons, *Art Digest* (July 1952).

Barbara Guest, *Art News* (June 1954).

Ingber Gallery, New York, 1988, symposium on Warhol's work in the 1950s.

Beauregard Houston-Montgomery, "Remembering Andy Warhol: An Impressionist Canvas," *Details* (May 1987).

John Richardson, "The Secret Warhol," *Vanity Fair,* 50, no. 7 (1987).

Patrick Smith, "Art in Extremis: Andy Warhol and His Art."

Calvin Tomkins, "Raggedy Andy," in John Coplans, *Andy Warhol.*

Andy Warhol, *The Philosophy of Andy Warhol.*

Andy Warhol and Pat Hackett, *POPism: The Warhol Sixties* (New York: Harcourt Brace Jovanovich, 1980).

CHAPTER FIVE

Based on interviews with Seymour Berlin, Emile de Antonio, Arthur Elias, Suzi Frankfurt, Vito Giallo, Nathan Gluck, Robert Heidie, Charles Lisanby, David Mann, Duane Michals, John Wallowitch, Ralph Ward, John Warhola, and Paul Warhola. Also:

Patricia Bosworth, *Diane Arbus* (New York: Knopf, 1984).

Rainer Crone, *Andy Warhol.*

Robert Hughes, "The Rise of Andy Warhol," *New York Review of Books,* 29, no. 2 (1982).

Ingber Gallery, New York, 1988 symposium.

Life Magazine, 42, no. 3 (1957).

Douglas T. Miller and Marion Novak, *The Fifties* (New York: Doubleday, 1975).

Philip Pearlstein, "Andy Warhol, 1928–1987."

Patrick Smith, "Art in Extremis: Andy Warhol and His Art."

Jean Stein, *Edie.*

Calvin Tomkins, "Raggedy Andy," in John Coplans, *Andy Warhol.*

Andy Warhol, *The Philosphy of Andy Warhol.*

Andy Warhol and Pat Hackett, *POPism.*

CHAPTER SIX

Based on interviews with David Bourdon, Leo Castelli, David Dalton, Emile de Antonio, John Giorno, Robert Heidie, Ray Johnson, Ivan Karp, Leonard Kessler, David Mann, Taylor Mead, and Patti Oldenburg. Also:

Emile de Antonio and Mitch Tuchman, *Painters Painting* (New York: Abbeville Press, 1984).

Laura de Coppet and Alan Jones, *The Art Dealers* (New York: Clarkson N. Potter, 1984).

Frederick Eberstadt, "Andy Warhol," *Quest Magazine* (October 1987).

Henry Geldzahler, "Andy Warhol: A Tribute," *Vogue* (UK), 144, no. 5 (1987).

Barbara Haskell, *Blam! The Explosion of Pop, Minimalism, and Performance, 1958–1964* (New York: Whitney Museum of American Art in association with W. W. Norton and Company, 1984).

John Heilpern, "The Fantasy World of Andy Warhol," *Observer (London)*, June 12, 1966.

Stephen Koch, "Warhol."

John Richardson, "The Secret Warhol."

Patrick S. Smith, "Art in Extremis: Andy Warhol and His Art."

Jean Stein, *Edie.*

Calvin Tomkins, "Raggedy Andy," in John Coplans, *Andy Warhol.*

Andy Warhol and Pat Hackett, *POPism.*

John Wilcock, *The Autobiography and Sex Life of Andy Warhol* (New York: Other Scenes, 1971).

Tom Wolfe, *The Painted Word* (New York: Farrar Straus & Giroux, 1975).

CHAPTER SEVEN

Based on interviews with Irving Blum, David Bourdon, John Coplans, David and Sarah Dalton, Emile de Antonio, Vito Giallo, John Giorno, Nathan Gluck, Bert Greene, Alan Groh, Ivan Karp, Ruth Kligman, Charles Lisanby, David Mann, Taylor Mead, Patti Oldenburg, John Wallowitch, George Warhola, James Warhola, and John Wilcock. Also:

Mario Amaya, *Pop Art . . . and After* (New York: Viking, 1965).

Gretchen Berg, "Andy Warhol: My True Story."

Ann Curran, "CMU's Other Andy."

Arthur C. Danto, "Who Was Andy Warhol?" *Artnews*, 86 (May 1987).

Francis, "Brother of the Universe," 1, no. 1 (Marvel Comics Group, 1982).

Henry Geldzahler, "Andy Warhol: A Tribute."

Henry Geldzahler, introduction to catalogue of a traveling pop art exhibition, Australia, 1986.

Winston Leyland, *Gay Sunshine Interviews* (San Francisco: Gay Sunshine Press, 1987).

Kurt Loder, "Andy Warhol, 1928–1987," *Rolling Stone*, 497 (1987).

Christopher Makos, *Warhol Makos: A Personal Photographic Memoir* (London: Virgin, 1988).

William O'Neil, *Coming Apart: An Informal History of America in the 1960s* (Chicago: Quadrangle Books, 1971).
The Editors of *Rolling Stone*, *The Sixties* (San Francisco: Straight Arrow Books, 1977).
John Rublowsky, *Pop Art* (New York: Basic Books, 1965).
Kenneth E. Silver, "Andy Warhol, 1928–1987," *Art in America*, 75, no. 5 (1987).
Jean Stein, *Edie*.
Ronald Sukenick, *Down and In* (New York: Beech Tree Books, 1987).
Gene Swenson, "What Is Pop Art?", *Art News*, 62, no. 7 (1963).
Time, "The Piece of Cake School," May 11, 1962.
Calvin Tomkins, *Off the Wall: Robert Rauschenberg and the Art of Our Times*.
Calvin Tomkins, "Raggedy Andy," in John Coplans, *Andy Warhol*.
John Wilcock, *The Autobiography and Sex Life of Andy Warhol*.
Tom Wolfe, *The Painted Word*.

CHAPTER EIGHT

Based on interviews with Heiner Bastian, David Bourdon, John Giorno, Ruth Kligman, Charles Lisanby, Gerard Malanga, and Patti Oldenburg. Also:
David Bailey, *Andy Warhol: Transcript of David Bailey's ATV Documentary*.
Gretchen Berg, "Andy Warhol: My True Story."
Emile de Antonio and Mitch Tuchman, *Painters Painting*.
Henry Geldzahler, "Andy Warhol," *Art International*, 8 (April 1964).
Bruce Glaser, "Oldenburg, Lichtenstein, Warhol: A Discussion," *Artforum*, no. 6 (February 1966).
Jeff Goldberg, interview with Robert Indiana, unpublished.
Jeff Goldberg, interview with Marisol, unpublished.
Robert Hughes, "The Rise of Andy Warhol."
Sam Hunter, *Masters of the Sixties* (New York: Marisa Del Re Gallery, 1984).
Alain Jouffroy and Ileanna Sonnabend, "Death and Disasters Catalogue" (Paris, 1964).
Gerard Malanga and Charles Giuliano, "Working with Warhol," *Art New England* (September 1988).
John Rublowsky, *Pop Art*.
Jean Stein, *Edie*.
Gene Swenson, "What Is Pop Art?"
Andy Warhol and Pat Hackett, *POPism*.

CHAPTER NINE

Based on interviews with Suzi Frankfurt, John Giorno, Nathan Gluck, Alan Groh, Robert Heidie, George Klauber, Ruth Kligman, Billy Linich, Charles Lisanby, Gerard Malanga, Taylor Mead, Sterling Morrison, Ondine, and Robert Tavel. Also:
Gretchen Berg, "Andy Warhol: My True Story."
Henry Geldzahler, "The Secret Warhol," *Vanity Fair*, 50, no. 7 (1987).

Stephen Koch, "Andy Warhol," *Art and Auction*, 1984.
Stephen Koch, *Stargazer: Andy Warhol and His Films* (New York: Praeger, 1973).
Marshall McLuhan, *The Mechanical Bride* (New York: Vanguard, 1951).
Jean Stein, *Edie.*
Gene Swenson, "What Is Pop Art?"
Ultra Violet, *Famous for Fifteen Minutes.*
Andy Warhol and Pat Hackett, *POPism.*

CHAPTER TEN

Based on interviews with Suzi Frankfurt, John Giorno, Nathan Gluck, Alan Groh, Robert Heidie, George Klauber, Ruth Kligman, Billy Linich, Charles Lisanby, Gerard Malanga, Taylor Mead, Sterling Morrison, Ondine, and Carl Willers. Also:
Mario Amaya, *Pop Art . . . and After.*
David Bailey, *Andy Warhol: Transcript of David Bailey's ATV Documentary.*
Lester Bangs, *Psychotic Reactions and Carburetor Dung* (New York: Knopf, 1987).
Gretchen Berg, "Andy Warhol: My True Story."
Rainer Crone, *Andy Warhol.*
Jeff Goldberg, interview with Robert Indiana.
John Heilpern, "The Fantasy World of Andy Warhol."
Mary Josephson, "Warhol: The Medium as Cultural Artifact," *Art in America* (May-June 1971).
Stephen Koch, "Andy Warhol."
Stephen Koch, "Warhol."
Gerard Malanga, introduction to "The Secret Diaries," *Radar Magazine* (Basel, 1986).
Jonas Mekas, "Andy Warhol Sixth Annual Filmmakers Co-op Awards," *Film Culture*, no. 33 (Summer 1964).
Jonas Mekas, "Notes on Re-seeing the Films of Andy Warhol," in John Coplans, *Andy Warhol.*
Irving Hershel Sandler, *New York Post,* December 2, 1962.
Peter Schjeldahl, *Andy Warhol* (London: Saatchi Collection Catalogue, 1985).
Patrick Smith, "Art in Extremis: Andy Warhol and His Art."
Jean Stein, *Edie.*
Andy Warhol and Pat Hackett, *POPism.*
John Wilcock, *The Autobiography and Sex Life of Andy Warhol.*
Peter York, "The Voice," *Vanity Fair* (April 1984).

CHAPTER ELEVEN

Based on interviews with Emile de Antonio, John Giorno, Gerard Malanga, Taylor Mead, Ondine, Ronald Tavel, John Wilcock, and Mary Woronov. Also:
David Bailey, *Andy Warhol: Transcript of David Bailey's ATV Documentary.*
Lester Bangs, *Psychotic Reactions and Carburetor Dung.*
Rainer Crone, *Andy Warhol.*

Otto Hahn, "Flowers Catalogue," Ileanna Sonnabend Gallery, Paris, 1964.
John Heilpern, "The Fantasy World of Andy Warhol."
Gary Indiana, "I'll Be Your Mirror," *Village Voice*, 111, no. 1 (1987).
Stephen Koch, *The Bachelor's Bride* (London: Marion Boyars, 1986).
Philip Leider, "Saint Andy: Some Notes on an Artist Who for a Large Section of a Younger Generation Can Do No Wrong," *Artforum*, 3, no. 5 (1965).
Lucy Lippard, *Pop Art* (New York: Oxford University Press, 1966).
Gerard Malanga, lecture notes, unpublished.
Gerard Malanga, "Working with Warhol," *Village Voice*, 111, no. 1 (1987).
Gerard Malanga and Charles Giuliano, "Working with Warhol."
Jonas Mekas, "Sixth Annual Filmmakers Co-op Awards."
Carter Ratcliff, *Andy Warhol* (New York: Modern Masters Series, Abbeville Press, 1983).
Robert Rosenblum, "Saint Andrew," *Newsweek*, December 7, 1964.
Patrick Smith, "Art in Extremis: Andy Warhol and His Art."
Jean Stein, *Edie*.
Andy Warhol and Pat Hackett, *POPism*.

CHAPTER TWELVE

Based on interviews with David Bourdon, Sam Greene, Robert Heidie, Gerard Malanga, Paul Morrissey, Ronald Tavel, James Warhola, and John Wilcock. Also:
John Ashbery, "Andy Warhol Causes Fuss in Paris," *International Herald Tribune*, May 18, 1965.
David Bailey, *Andy Warhol: Transcript of David Bailey's ATV Documentary*.
Marilyn Bender, *The Beautiful People* (New York: Dell, 1967).
Gretchen Berg, "Nothing To Lose," *Cahiers du Cinéma*, no. 10 (May 1967).
David Bourdon, "Andy Warhol, 1928–1987," *Art in America* (May 1987).
David Bourdon, *Village Voice*, December 3, 1964.
Grace Glueck, *New York Times*, March 1965.
John Heilpern, "The Fantasy World of Andy Warhol."
Stephen Koch, "Warhol."
Leo Lerman, "Andy and Edie," *Mademoiselle*, December 15, 1965.
Ninette Lyon, "Robert Indiana, Andy Warhol: A Second Fame: Good Food," *Vogue*, 145 (March 1965).
Gerard Malanga, letter to Stephen Sprouse, unpublished.
Gerard Malanga, Paris diary, unpublished.
Gerard Malanga and Charles Giuliano, "Working with Warhol."
Peter Manso, *Mailer* (New York: Simon and Schuster, 1985).
Jonas Mekas, "Filmography," in John Coplans, *Andy Warhol*.
The Editors of *Rolling Stone, The Sixties*.
Peter Schjeldahl, "Andy Warhol, 1928–1987," *Art in America* (May 1987).
Patrick Smith, "Art in Extremis: Andy Warhol and His Art."
Jean Stein, *Edie*.
Ultra Violet, *Famous for Fifteen Minutes*.
Andy Warhol, *a, a novel* (New York: Grove Press, 1968).

Andy Warhol, Filmmaker's Cinematheque, program notes for *Kitchen*, 1966.
Andy Warhol and Pat Hackett, *POPism*.
Neal Weaver, *After Dark*, 1969.
John Wilcock, *The Autobiography and Sex Life of Andy Warhol*.

CHAPTER THIRTEEN

Based on interviews with Ronnie Cutrone, Robert Heidie, Ivan Karp, Billy Linich, Gerard Malanga, Sterling Morrison, Paul Morrissey, Ronald Tavel, and Mary Woronov. Also:

Lester Bangs, *Psychotic Reactions and Carburetor Dung*.
Gretchen Berg, "Andy Warhol: My True Story."
Victor Bockris and Gerard Malanga, *Uptight: The Velvet Underground Story* (New York: Morrow, 1984).
Jordan Crandall, "Interview with Ultra Violet," *Splash*, 1986.
David Fricke, "Lou Reed," *Rolling Stone*, no. 152 (1987).
Bill Holdship, "Interview with Lou Reed," *Creem*, 19, no. 3 (1987).
Stephen Koch, *Stargazer*.
Kurt Loder, "Andy Warhol, 1928–1987," *Rolling Stone*, no. 497 (1987).
Gerard Malanga, "Working with Warhol."
Gerard Malanga and Charles Giuliano, "Working with Warhol."
Jonas Mekas, "Notes on Re-seeing the Movies of Andy Warhol," in John Coplans, *Andy Warhol*.
Richard Morphet, catalogue for Andy Warhol retrospective, Tate Gallery, London, 1971.
Bob Spitz, *Dylan: A Biography* (New York: McGraw-Hill, 1988).
Jean Stein, *Edie*.
Charles T. Stuckey, "Andy Warhol, 1928–1987," *Art in America* (May 1987).
Calvin Tomkins, "Raggedy Andy," in John Coplans, *Andy Warhol*.
Roy Trakin, "Interview with John Cale," *Creem*, 19, no. 3 (1987).
Viva, *Superstar*.
Andy Warhol, *a, a novel*.
Andy Warhol, *The Philosophy of Andy Warhol*.
John Wilcock, *The Autobiography and Sex Life of Andy Warhol*.

CHAPTER FOURTEEN

Based on interviews with Ronnie Cutrone, Billy Linich, Gerard Malanga, Sterling Morrison, Paul Morrissey, Ondine, Ronald Tavel, and Mary Woronov. Also:

Gretchen Berg, "Andy Warhol: My True Story."
Victor Bockris and Gerard Malanga, *Uptight: The Velvet Underground Story*.
Shirley Clarke, advertising flyer for *The Chelsea Girls*, 1966.
Bosley Crowther, "The Underground Overflows," *New York Times*, December 11, 1966.
Stephen Koch, *Stargazer*.
Robert Levinson, interview with Paul Morrissey, *Coast FM & Fine Arts*, 1969.
Gerard Malanga, "The Secret Diaries of Gerard Malanga," unpublished.

Jonas Mekas, advertising flyer for *The Chelsea Girls,* 1966.
Rex Reed, *Big Screen, Little Screen* (New York: Macmillan, 1971).
Barbara Rose, *Rauschenberg* (New York: Elizabeth Avedon Editions, Vintage, 1987).
Patrick Smith, "Art in Extremis: Andy Warhol and His Art."
Jean Stein, *Edie.*
Calvin Tomkins, *Off the Wall: Robert Rauschenberg and the Art World of Our Times.*
Ultra Violet, *Famous for Fifteen Minutes.*
Andy Warhol, "Sunday with Mr. C."
Bernard Weintraub, "Andy Warhol's Mother."
John Wilcock, *The Autobiography and Sex Life of Andy Warhol.*

CHAPTER FIFTEEN

Based on interviews with Emile de Antonio, Fred Hughes, Billy Linich, Gerard
   Malanga, Taylor Mead, Allen Midgette, Paul Morrissey, Ondine, Rex Reed,
   Geraldine Smith, Ronald Tavel, Viva, and Louis Waldon. Also:
Jean Clay, "Andy's Warhorse," *Realités,* no. 205 (December 1967).
Serge Gavronsky, *Cahiers du Cinéma,* no. 10 (May 1967).
Bill Holdship, "Interview with Lou Reed."
Susan Pile and Joel Klaperman, "Everything Happens: A Discussion at Andy
   Warhol's Factory," *Crown Essays,* 15, no. 1 (1967).
Andy Warhol and Pat Hackett, *POPism.*

CHAPTER SIXTEEN

Based on interviews with David Bourdon, Fred Hughes, Billy Linich, Gerard
   Malanga, Taylor Mead, Paul Morrissey, Terry Noel, Ondine, Ronald Tavel, Viva,
   and Louis Waldon. Also:
Steven M. L. Aronson, "Andy's Heir Apparent," *Vanity Fair,* 50, no. 7 (1987).
Tom Baker, "In an Above-Ground Society," *Cinema Magazine.*
Gretchen Berg, "Nothing to Lose," *Cahiers du Cinéma,* no. 10 (May 1967).
Ted Castle, "Occurrences: Cab Ride with Andy Warhol," *Artnews,* 66 (February
   1968).
Grace Glueck, "Warhol Unveils * of **** Film," *New York Times,* July 8, 1967.
Barbara Goldsmith, "La Dolce Viva," *New York Magazine* (April 1968).
Robert Hughes, "The Rise of Andy Warhol."
Stephen Koch, "Warhol."
Jane Kramer, *Allen Ginsberg in America* (New York: Random House, 1968).
Gerard Malanga, Rome diaries, unpublished.
Gerard Malanga, "The Secret Diaries of Gerard Malanga."
Pat Patterson, *Nico: Chelsea Girl,* liner notes, Verve, 1967.
Susan Pile and Joel Klaperman, "Everything Happens."
Rex Reed, *Big Screen, Little Screen.*
John Richardson, "The Secret Warhol."
Valerie Solanas, *SCUM Manifesto* (New York: Olympia Press, 1968).
Ultra Violet, *Famous for Fifteen Minutes.*
Viva, *Superstar.*

Viva, "The Superstar and the Heady Years," *New York Woman* (May-June 1987).
Viva, "Viva and God," *Village Voice*, 111, no. 1 (1987).
Andy Warhol, *a, a novel.*
Andy Warhol, *Andy Warhol's Index Book* (New York: Random House, 1967).
Andy Warhol, "Sunday with Mr. C."
Andy Warhol and Pat Hackett, *POPism.*
Roger Wolmuth, "Flower Power Revisited," *People Magazine*, June 22, 1987.

CHAPTER SEVENTEEN

Based on interviews with David Bourdon, Fred Hughes, Gerard Malanga, Taylor Mead, Viva, and Louis Waldon. Also:
The Federal Bureau of Investigation files on Andy Warhol, FBI Headquarters, Washington, D.C., 1969.
Gerard Malanga, "Introduction to the Secret Diaries."
Jonas Mekas, "Filmography," in John Coplans, *Andy Warhol.*
Andy Warhol and Pat Hackett, *POPism.*

CHAPTER EIGHTEEN

Based on interviews with Tom Hedley, Robert Heidie, Fred Hughes, Jed Johnson, Billy Linich, Gerard Malanga, Taylor Mead, Paul Morrissey, Ondine, Geraldine Smith, Louis Waldon, George Warhola, James Warhola, John Warhola, Margaret Warhola, and Paul Warhola. Also:
Marilyn Bender, "Valerie Solanas: A Heroine to Feminists," *New York Times*, June 14, 1968.
Jim Carroll, *Forced Entries: The Downtown Diaries, 1971–1973* (New York: Penguin Books, 1987).
Paul Carroll, "What's a Warhol?" *Playboy*, 16, no. 9 (1969).
Peter Coutros, "Off-beat Artist-Producer Used Girls as Film Props," *Daily News*, June 4, 1968.
Frank Faso, Martin McLaughlin, and Richard Henry, "Andy Warhol Wounded by Actress," *Daily News*, June 4, 1968.
Maurice Girodias, publisher's preface in Valerie Solanas, *SCUM Manifesto.*
Derek Hill, interview with Paul Morrissey, 1969.
Leticia Kent, "Andy Warhol: 'I Thought Everyone Was Kidding,' " *Village Voice*, September 12, 1968.
Stephen Koch, *Stargazer.*
Phyllis and Eberhard Kronhausen, *Erotic Art* (New York: Grove Press, 1968–1970).
Gerard Malanga, "The Secret Diaries of Gerard Malanga."
Joseph Mancini, "Andy Warhol Fights for Life," *New York Post*, June 4, 1968.
Robert Marmorstein, "A Winter Memory of Valerie Solanas," *Village Voice*, June 13, 1968.
Robert Mazzocco, "aaaaa . . . ," *New York Review of Books*, 12, no. 8 (1969).
Rex Reed, *Big Screen, Little Screen.*
Barbara Rose, "In Andy Warhol's Aluminum Foil, We All Have Been Reflected," *New York Magazine*, May 31, 1971.

Richard Shepherd, "Warhol Gravely Wounded in Studio," *New York Times,* June 4, 1968.

Howard Smith, "The Shot That Shattered the Velvet Underground," *Village Voice,* 15, no. 34 (1968).

Patrick Smith, "Art in Extremis: Andy Warhol and His Art."

Jean Stein, *Edie.*

Time, "Felled by Scum," June 14, 1968.

Viva, *Superstar.*

Andy Warhol, *a, a novel.*

Andy Warhol and Pat Hackett, *POPism.*

John Wilcock, *The Autobiography and Sex Life of Andy Warhol.*

CHAPTER NINETEEN

Based on interviews with Heiner Bastian, David Bourdon, John Coplans, Emile de Antonio, Suzi Frankfurt, Vincent Fremont, John Giorno, Catherine Guinness, Tom Hedley, Robert Heidie, Fred Hughes, Jed Johnson, Billy Linich, Gerard Malanga, Taylor Mead, Beauregard Houston-Montgomery, Daniela Morera, Paul Morrissey, Glenn O'Brien, Geraldine Smith, Viva, Louis Waldon, and John Wilcock. Also:

David Bailey, *Andy Warhol: Transcript of David Bailey's ATV Documentary.*

David Bourdon, "Plastic Man Meets Plastic Man," *New York,* 2, February 10, 1969.

Jim Carroll, *Forced Entries: The Downtown Diaries, 1971–1973.*

Paul Carroll, "What's a Warhol?"

Barbara Catoir, "The New German Collectors," *Artnews* (April 1986).

Bob Colacello, "King Andy's German Conquest," *Village Voice,* March 11, 1971.

Bob Colacello, "Working with Warhol," *Vanity Fair,* 50, no. 7 (1987).

Nicholas Coleridge, *The Fashion Conspiracy* (New York: Harper & Row, 1988).

Emile de Antonio and Mitch Tuchman, *Painters Painting.*

Federal Bureau of Investigation files on Andy Warhol.

Grace Glueck, "Or, Has Andy Warhol Spoiled Success?" *New York Times,* May 9, 1971.

John Hallowell, *After Dark,* 1969.

Fred Hughes, preface to The Andy Warhol Collection catalogues, Sotheby's.

Robert Hughes, "The Rise of Andy Warhol."

Mary Josephson, "Warhol: The Medium as Cultural Artifact."

Leticia Kent, "Andy Warhol: Movieman," *Vogue* (March 1970).

Gerard Malanga, lecture notes, unpublished.

Jonas Mekas, "Notes on Re-seeing the Movies of Andy Warhol," in John Coplans, *Andy Warhol.*

Richard Morphet, catalogue for Warhol retrospective, Tate Gallery, London, 1971.

Paul Morrissey, *Daily Telegraph* (London), 1971.

John Perrault, "Expensive Wallpaper," *Village Voice,* May 13, 1971.

John Perrault, "Andy Warhol," *Vogue,* 155 (March 1970).

"Pseuds Corner," *Private Eye,* 1971.

Dotson Rader, "Andy's Children: They Die Young," *Esquire* (March 1974).

George Rush, "Andy Warhol Inc." *Manhattan Inc.*, 29, no. 2 (1984).
John Russell Taylor, *Directors Directing: Cinema for the Seventies* (New York: Hill and Wang, 1975).
Parker Tyler, *Underground Cinema: A Critical History* (New York: Grove Press, 1969).
Calvin Tomkins, "Raggedy Andy," in John Coplans, *Andy Warhol.*
Andy Warhol and Pat Hackett, *POPism.*
Peter Watson, "Andy Warhol's Final Sale."
John Wilcock, *The Autobiography and Sex Life of Andy Warhol.*

CHAPTER TWENTY

Based on interviews with Ronnie Cutrone, Suzi Frankfurt, Vincent Fremont, Tom Hedley, Fred Hughes, Jed Johnson, Gerard Malanga, Daniela Morera, Glenn O'Brien, Geraldine Smith, Ronald Tavel, John Warhola, Margaret Warhola, and Paul Warhola. Also:
David Bailey, *Andy Warhol: Transcript of David Bailey's ATV Documentary.*
Jim Carroll, *Forced Entries: The Downtown Diaries, 1971–1973.*
Paul Carroll, "What's a Warhol?"
Giovanni Dadomo, "The Legend of the Velvet Underground," *Sounds,* 1972.
Paul Gardner, *New York Times,* 1972.
Jesse Kornbluth, "Andy: The World of Warhol," *New York,* 20, no. 10 (1987).
Dotson Rader, "Andy's Children: They Die Young."
Lou Reed, *Rock 'n' Roll Animal* (London: Babylon Books).
Barbara Rose, *Rauschenberg.*
Tony Sanchez, *Up and Down with the Rolling Stones* (New York: Morrow, 1979).
Patrick Smith, "Art in Extremis: Andy Warhol and His Art."
Jean Stein, *Edie.*
Andy Warhol, *The Philosophy of Andy Warhol.*
Andy Warhol, "Sunday with Mr. C."
Andy Warhol and Bob Colacello, *Andy Warhol's Exposures* (New York: Andy Warhol Books/Grosset and Dunlap, 1979).
Andy Warhol and Pat Hackett, *POPism.*
Peter Watson, "Andy Warhol's Final Sale."
John Wilcock, *The Autobiography and Sex Life of Andy Warhol.*
Anthony Zanetta and Henry Edwards, *Stardust: The David Bowie Story* (New York: McGraw-Hill, 1986).

CHAPTER TWENTY-ONE

Based on interviews with Ronnie Cutrone, Suzi Frankfurt, Fred Hughes, Victor Hugo, Jed Johnson, Benjamin Liu, Taylor Mead, Daniela Morera, Paul Morrissey, Geraldine Smith, Susan Sontag, Ronald Tavel, and Paul Warhola. Also:
Bob Colacello, "The Liz and Andy Show," *Vogue* (January 1974).
Bob Colacello, "OUT," *Interview,* 1974.
Linda Bird Francke, "The Warhol Tapes," *Newsweek,* April 22, 1974.
Paul Gardner, "Warhol—from Kinky Sex to Creepy Gothic," *New York Times,* July 14, 1974.

Kitty Kelley, *Elizabeth Taylor: The Last Star* (New York: Simon and Schuster, 1981).
Roman Polanski, *Roman* (New York: Morrow, 1984).
Carter Ratcliff, *Andy Warhol.*
George Rush, "Andy Warhol Inc."
Andy Warhol, interview with Anna Karina, *Interview*, 1973.
Andy Warhol, interview with Bette Midler, *Interview*, 1974.
Andy Warhol, "Sunday with Mr. C."
John Wilcock, *The Autobiography and Sex Life of Andy Warhol.*

CHAPTER TWENTY-TWO

Based on interviews with Ronnie Cutrone, Vincent Fremont, Victor Hugo, and Daniela Morera. Also:
David Bourdon, "Andy Warhol and the Society Icon," *Art in America* (January-February 1975).
Bob Colacello, "Working with Warhol," *Vanity Fair*, 50, no. 7 (1987).
Robert Hughes, "King of the Banal," *Time*, August 4, 1975.
Christopher Makos, "Warhol Makos."
George Rush, "Andy Warhol Inc."
Rupert Smith, "Acquisition and Accumulation," The Andy Warhol Collection catalogues, Sotheby's.

CHAPTER TWENTY-THREE

Based on interviews with Heiner Bastian, Vincent Fremont, and Jed Johnson. Also:
Steven M.L. Aronson, "Possession Obsession," *House and Garden*, 159, no. 12 (1987).
Tom Buckley, "Job Hunting." Taro Mother Language Convention, *New York Times*, December 30, 1974.
Bob Colacello, "Working with Warhol."
Bob Colacello, "OUT," *Interview*, 1974.
Barbara Goldsmith, "The Philosophy of Andy Warhol," *New York Times Book Review*, September 14, 1975.
Bianca Jagger and Andy Warhol, interview with Jack Ford, *Interview*, 1975.
Jed Johnson, "Inconspicuous Consumption," the Andy Warhol Collection catalogues, Sotheby's.
Jack Kroll, "Raggedy Andy," *Newsweek*, 86 (September 1975).
John Phillips, *Papa John* (New York: 1986).
John Richardson, "The Secret Warhol."
George Rush, "Andy Warhol Inc."
William Shawcross, *The Shah's Last Ride* (New York: Simon and Schuster, 1988).
Andy Warhol, "Sunday with Mr. C."
Andy Warhol and Bob Colacello, *Andy Warhol's Exposures.*

CHAPTER TWENTY-FOUR

Based on interviews with Muhammad Ali, David Bourdon, Vincent Fremont, Henry Geldzahler, Vito Giallo, Catherine Guinness, Stellan Holm, Fred Hughes,

Victor Hugo, Jed Johnson, Daniela Morera, Walter Steding, Margaret Warhola, and Andrew Wylie. Also:

David Bourdon, "Warhol Serves Up Retooled Icons à la Russe," *Village Voice,* January 24, 1977.

Sandra Brant, *Andy Warhol's Folk and Funk* (New York: The Museum of American Folk Art, 1977).

Alexander Cockburn, *Corruptions of Empire* (London: Verso, 1987).

Bob Colacello, "OUT," *Interview,* 1976.

Bob Colacello, "OUT," *Interview,* 1977.

Trevor Fairbrother, "Skulls," in Gary Garrels, ed. *The Work of Andy Warhol,* Discussions in Contemporary Culture, no. 3 in series from Dia Art Foundation, New York (Seattle: Bay Press, 1989).

Fred Hughes, preface, The Andy Warhol Collection catalogues, Sotheby's.

Gary Indiana, "I'll Be Your Mirror."

Stephen Koch, "Warhol."

Christopher Makos, *Warhol Makos.*

Patrick Smith, "Art in Extremis: Andy Warhol and His Art."

Paul Taylor, "Warhol Leaks to the Press," *Vanity Fair,* 48, no. 2, February, 1985.

Ultra Violet, *Famous for Fifteen Minutes.*

Andy Warhol and Bob Colacello, *Andy Warhol's Exposures.*

Peter Watson, "Andy Warhol's Final Sale."

James Wolcott, *Vanity Fair,* 1986.

CHAPTER TWENTY-FIVE

Based on interviews with Heiner Bastian, Dr. Andrew Bernsohn, Toni Brown, William Burroughs, Ronnie Cutrone, Raymond Foye, Suzi Frankfurt, Vincent Fremont, Vito Giallo, Albert Goldman, Catherine Guinness, Jed Johnson, Benjamin Liu, Christopher Makos, Daniela Morera, Dona Peltin, Susan Sontag, Walter Steding, and Paul Warhola. Also:

Jane Addams Allen, "Speculating," *Insight,* March 31, 1986.

Alexander Cockburn, *Corruptions of Empire* (London: Verso, 1987).

Bob Colacello, "OUT," *Interview,* 1978.

Bob Colacello, "OUT," *Interview,* 1979.

Bob Colacello, "OUT," *Interview,* 1980.

Bob Colacello, "Working with Warhol."

Vito Giallo and Steven M. L. Aronson, "Andy's Routine," The Andy Warhol Collection catalogues, Sotheby's.

Lita Hornock, "Night Flight," The Kulchur Foundation, 1982.

Fred Hughes, preface, The Andy Warhol Collection catalogues, Sotheby's.

Robert Hughes, "The Rise of Andy Warhol."

Hilton Kramer, "Whitney Shows Warhol Work," *New York Times,* November 23, 1979.

Donald Kuspit, "Andy's Feelings," *Artscribe* (Summer 1987).

Christopher Makos, *Warhol Makos.*

Maura Moynihan, "The Cover Girl and the Prosperous Years," *New York Woman* (May-June 1987).

Dona Peltin, unpublished article on working at *Interview,* 1980.

John Richardson, "The Secret Warhol."

John Richardson, "Warhol, the Collector," The Andy Warhol Collection catalogues, Sotheby's.

Peter Schjeldahl, "Warhol and Class Content," *Art in America* (May 1980).

William Shawcross, *The Shah's Last Ride.*

Patrick Smith, "Art in Extremis: Andy Warhol and His Art."

Calvin Tomkins, "The Art World." The New Yorker, May 5, 1980.

Andy Warhol, *America.*

Andy Warhol, "Liza Minnelli," *Interview,* 1979.

Peter Watson, "Andy Warhol's Final Sale."

Eva Windmuller, "A Conversation with Andy Warhol," *Stern* (West Germany), October 8, 1981.

CHAPTER TWENTY-SIX

Based on interviews with Heiner Bastian, Dr. Andrew Bernsohn, Ronnie Cutrone, Emile de Antonio, Maryann Erdos, Raymond Foye, Suzi Frankfurt, Vincent Fremont, Catherine Guinness, Stellan Holm, Victor Hugo, Benjamin Liu, Michelle Loud, Christopher Makos, Daniela Morera, George Warhola, and John Warhola. Also:

Dorothea Baumer, "Ich Mach's Halt Nur," *Süddeutsche's Zeitung,* May 7, 1980.

Jessica Berens, "In Warhol's Footsteps," *HG* (April 1988).

Roberta Bernstein, *Andy Warhol Prints* (New York: Abbeville Press, 1985).

Rainer Crone and Georgia Marsh, *Clemente* (New York: Elizabeth Avedon Editions, Vintage, 1987).

Christopher Makos, "Warhol Makos."

Cathleen McGuigan, "New Art, New Money," *New York Times Magazine,* February 10, 1985.

Achille Bonito Oliva, *Industrial Metaphysics: Warhol verso de Chirico* (Milan: Electra, 1982).

Peter Plagens, *Art in America* (March 1982).

Carter Ratcliff, *Andy Warhol.*

George Rush, "Andy Warhol Inc."

Meryle Secrest, "Leo Castelli: Dealing in Myths," *Artnews* (Summer 1982).

CHAPTER TWENTY-SEVEN

Based on interviews with Heiner Bastian, Dr. Andrew Bernsohn, Maryann Erdos, Suzi Frankfurt, Vincent Fremont, Catherine Guinness, Stellan Holm, Victor Hugo, Benjamin Liu, Christopher Makos, Daniela Morera, George Warhola, John Warhola, Paul Warhola, and Andrew Wylie. Also:

Barry Blinderman, "Andy Warhol," *Art Magazine* (October 1981).

Adam Edwards, *London Daily Mail*, 1985.

Keith Haring, interview, *New York Talk*, 1985.

Gary Indiana, "I'll Be Your Mirror."

Stephen Koch, "Warhol."

Christopher Makos, *Warhol Makos*.

Beauregard Houston-Montgomery, "Remembering Andy Warhol: An Impressionist Canvas," *Details* (May 1987).

Fiona Powell, "Interview with Andy Warhol," *The Face*, 1985.

John Richardson, "The Secret Warhol."

John Richardson, "Warhol, the Collector."

Peter Schjeldahl, *David Salle* (New York: Elizabeth Avedon Editions, Vintage, 1987).

Andy Warhol, *America*.

Andy Warhol, "Jodie Foster," *Interview*, 1982.

John Wilcock, *The Autobiography and Sex Life of Andy Warhol*.

CHAPTER TWENTY-EIGHT

Based on interviews with Dr. Andrew Bernsohn, Vincent Fremont, Vito Giallo, John Giorno, John Hanhardt, Victor Hugo, Michelle Loud, Christopher Makos, Taylor Mead, Daniela Morera, George Warhola, James Warhola, John Warhola, Margaret Warhola, and Paul Warhola. Also:

David Bourdon, "Andy Warhol, 1928–1987."

Gordon Burn, with Liz Jobey, Michael Watts, and Georgina Howell, "Andy Warhol, 1928–1987," *London Sunday Times Magazine*, March 29, 1987.

John Caldwell, *Carnegie Mellon Magazine*, 1986.

Laura de Copet and Alan Jones, *The Art Dealers*.

Polly Devlin, *The International Herald-Tribune*, July 19–20, 1986.

M. A. Farber and Lawrence K. Altman, "A Great Hospital in Crisis," *New York Times Magazine*, January 24, 1988.

Doug Feiden, "Andy's Home at Last," *New York Post*, February 27, 1987.

Doug Feiden, "Warhol Goes to the Grave in Paisley Tie and Shades," *New York Post*, February 26, 1987.

Martin Filler, "Andy Warhol: A Tribute," *Art in America* (May 1987).

Denis Hamill, "Enigma Wrapped in Style," *New York Newsday*, February 23, 1987.

Nicholas Haslam, "Andy Warhol: A Tribute," *Vogue* (UK), 144, no. 5 (1987).

Robert Katz, *Fassbinder: Love Is Colder Than Death* (New York: Random House, 1987).

Jesse Kornbluth, "Andy: The World of Warhol."

Patricia Lowry, "Warhol Was a Drug and We Were Addicted," *Pittsburgh Press*, February 27, 1987.

Beauregard Houston-Montgomery, "Remembering Andy Warhol: An Impressionist Canvas."

New York Post, February 25, 1987.

Fiona Powell, "Interview with Andy Warhol."

Carter Ratcliff, "Andy Warhol, Inflation Artist," *Artforum* (March 1985).

Pierre Restany, "Andy Warhol: Less Is More," *Galeries Magazine*, no. 18 (April-May 1987).
John Richardson, "The Secret Warhol."
John Richardson, "Warhol, the Collector."
Paul Taylor, "Andy Warhol," *Flash Art*, no. 133 (April 1987).
Andy Warhol, *America*.
Jonathan Yardley, "Andy Warhol's Artless Achievement," *New York Post*, March 4, 1987.

EPILOGUE

Based on interviews with James Warhola, John Warhola, and Paul Warhola. Also: Julia Markus, "Andy Warhol, Psyched by His Century."

Index

INDEX

INDEX

INDEX

INDEX